Cloud Computing for Data-Intensive Applications

Xiaolin Li • Judy Qiu

Editors

Cloud Computing for Data-Intensive Applications

 Springer

Editors
Xiaolin Li
University of Florida
Gainesville, FL, USA

Judy Qiu
Indiana University
Bloomington, IN, USA

ISBN 978-1-4939-5515-2   ISBN 978-1-4939-1905-5 (eBook)
DOI 10.1007/978-1-4939-1905-5
Springer New York Heidelberg Dordrecht London

Foreword

This collection of papers is the first volume to explore the rapidly evolving role of cloud computing in scientific data analytics. This topic is important because almost every field of science is now data driven. The data comes from sources ranging in scale from massive physics experiments and instruments that read our DNA to the multitude of sensors that monitor our environment. It also comes from our digitized libraries, our media streams, and our personal health monitors. The "Internet of Things" is set to go through an explosive growth, profoundly changing the way we understand the world around us. By tapping into vast amounts of data we can use analytics and machine learning to discover properties of complex systems that were not visible to us before. This is truly the age of the fourth paradigm of science where data analytics joins experiment, theory, and computational simulation as a fundamental pillar of discovery. For example, by doing genome-wide association studies of large populations we can now begin to understand the causes of many diseases. The sensors in our urban environments are beginning to help us understand how to improve the health of our cities and better plan for the future. Machine learning based on big data is also transforming our personal devices. The computer vision required to build a driverless car is now enabled by massive deep neural networks analyzing streams from millions of hours of video and other data. These same unsupervised machine learning techniques now allow us to do real-time voice-to-voice natural language translation.

Many of the primary software tools used to do the large-scale data analysis required by these applications were born in the cloud. Massive cloud data centers were created to provide the computational foundation for the online services that are now part of everyday life for billions of people. This includes Internet web search, e-mail, online commerce, social networks, geo-location and map services, photo sharing, automated natural language translation, document preparation and collaboration, media distribution, teleconferencing, and online gaming. These applications all accrue massive amounts of data, and optimizing their performance requires analysis of the data. For example, understanding how to return the best results from a web search query requires more than a simple index lookup. Sophisticated machine learning techniques are required to make the best selection of links to return to the user. It did not take long for these ideas to be applied to the full range of scientific challenges.

The cloud software stack for scalable data analysis has evolved rapidly and so too has the cloud architecture model. Early cloud data centers are being rebuilt with new technologies to better support massive data analytics. Data center networks are starting to take ideas from supercomputer systems to improve bisection bandwidth, and software defined networking is now a standard part of the designs. Some cloud providers are starting to consider GPUs in the mix of servers. Private and public clouds are now working together and clouds and supercomputers are being used in creative combinations. This volume is extremely timely. It is the first book to cover the entire spectrum of research on the topic of cloud computing and data intensive applications. The topics range from basic architecture issues to the challenges of data analysis for complex scientific applications. It is a "must read" for any student of modern computing. We are delighted that Professors Li and Qiu have undertaken this project.

Tony Hey
Dennis Gannon
Microsoft Research, Redmond, WA, USA

Contents

Part I   Systems and Applications

Scalable Deployment of a LIGO Physics Application on Public Clouds: Workflow Engine and Resource Provisioning Techniques 3
Suraj Pandey, Letizia Sammut, Rodrigo N. Calheiros, Andrew Melatos, and Rajkumar Buyya

The FutureGrid Testbed for Big Data 27
Gregor von Laszewski and Geoffrey C. Fox

Cloud Networking to Support Data Intensive Applications 61
Maurício Tsugawa, Andréa Matsunaga, and José A.B. Fortes

IaaS Cloud Benchmarking: Approaches, Challenges, and Experience 83
Alexandru Iosup, Radu Prodan, and Dick Epema

GPU-Accelerated Cloud Computing for Data-Intensive Applications 105
Baoxue Zhao, Jianlong Zhong, Bingsheng He, Qiong Luo, Wenbin Fang, and Naga K. Govindaraju

Adaptive Workload Partitioning and Allocation for Data Intensive Scientific Applications 131
Xin Yang and Xiaolin Li

DRAW: A New Data-gRouping-AWare Data Placement Scheme for Data Intensive Applications with Interest Locality 149
Jun Wang, Pengju Shang, and Jiangling Yin

Part II   Resource Management

Efficient Task-Resource Matchmaking Using Self-adaptive Combinatorial Auction 177
Han Zhao and Xiaolin Li

**Federating Advanced Cyberinfrastructures with Autonomic
Capabilities** 201
Javier Diaz-Montes, Ivan Rodero, Mengsong Zou,
and Manish Parashar

Part III   Programming Models

**Migrating Scientific Workflow Management Systems
from the Grid to the Cloud** 231
Yong Zhao, Youfu Li, Ioan Raicu, Cui Lin, Wenhong Tian,
and Ruini Xue

Executing Storm Surge Ensembles on PAAS Cloud 257
Abhirup Chakraborty, Milinda Pathirage, Isuru Suriarachchi,
Kavitha Chandrasekar, Craig Mattocks, and Beth Plale

Cross-Phase Optimization in MapReduce 277
Benjamin Heintz, Abhishek Chandra, and Jon Weissman

**Asynchronous Computation Model for Large-Scale Iterative
Computations** 303
Yanfeng Zhang, Qixin Gao, Lixin Gao, and Cuirong Wang

Part IV   Cloud Storage

**Big Data Storage and Processing on Azure Clouds:
Experiments at Scale and Lessons Learned** 331
Radu Tudoran, Alexandru Costan, Gabriel Antoniu,
and Brasche Goetz

**Storage and Data Life Cycle Management in Cloud
Environments with FRIEDA** 357
Lavanya Ramakrishnan, Devarshi Ghoshal, Valerie Hendrix,
Eugen Feller, Pradeep Mantha, and Christine Morin

Managed File Transfer as a Cloud Service 379
Brandon Ross, Engin Arslan, Bing Zhang, and Tevfik Kosar

**Supporting a Social Media Observatory with Customizable
Index Structures: Architecture and Performance** 401
Xiaoming Gao, Evan Roth, Karissa McKelvey, Clayton Davis,
Andrew Younge, Emilio Ferrara, Filippo Menczer, and Judy Qiu

Part I
Systems and Applications

Automated scalable PaaS platform makes it easier to choose resources on clouds. FutureGrid: testbed for Big Data scientific computing on cloud/grid/HPC. Evaluating available cloud network applications and capabilities. Benchmarking to improve IaaS cloud services. MapReduce applied in GPUs to handle data-heavy applications. Study of state-transition applications in parallel systems to handle large data loads and difficult algorithms; focuses on analysis of system's processor speed. Argues against random data placement in frameworks like Hadoop and MapReduce; proposes DRAW to reorganize data distribution to achieve optimal parallelism.

Scalable Deployment of a LIGO Physics Application on Public Clouds: Workflow Engine and Resource Provisioning Techniques

Suraj Pandey, Letizia Sammut, Rodrigo N. Calheiros, Andrew Melatos, and Rajkumar Buyya

Abstract Cloud computing has empowered users to provision virtually unlimited computational resources and are accessible over the Internet on demand. This makes Cloud computing a compelling technology that tackles the issues rising with the growing size and complexity of scientific applications, which are characterized by high variance in usage, large volume of data and high compute load, flash crowds, unpredictable load, and varying compute and storage requirements. In order to provide users an automated and scalable platform for hosting scientific workflow applications, while hiding the complexity of the underlying Cloud infrastructure, we present the design and implementation of a PaaS middleware solution along with resource provisioning techniques. We apply our PaaS solution to the data analysis pipeline of a physics application, a gravitational wave search, utilizing public Clouds. The system architecture, a load-balancing approach, and the system's behavior over varying loads are detailed. The performance evaluation on scalability and load-balancing characteristics of the automated PaaS middleware demonstrates the feasibility and advantages of the approach over existing monolithic approaches.

1 Introduction

Cloud computing enables users to get virtually unlimited computational resources that can be accessed on demand from anywhere at any time. The main features of Clouds such as elasticity and pay-per-use cost model enable low upfront investment

S. Pandey
IBM Research Australia, Melbourne, Australia
e-mail: suraj.pandey@au.ibm.com

L. Sammut • A. Melatos
School of Physics, The University of Melbourne, Parkville, VIC 3010, Australia
e-mail: l.sammut@student.unimelb.edu.au; amelatos@unimelb.edu.au

R.N. Calheiros (✉) • R. Buyya
Cloud Computing and Distributed Systems (CLOUDS) Laboratory, Department of Computing
and Information Systems, The University of Melbourne, Parkville, VIC 3010, Australia
e-mail: rnc@unimelb.edu.au; rbuyya@unimelb.edu.au

© Springer Science+Business Media New York 2014
X. Li, J. Qiu (eds.), *Cloud Computing for Data-Intensive Applications*,
DOI 10.1007/978-1-4939-1905-5_1

and low time to market, which in turn enables small to large software applications to use the Cloud as a hosting platform, in contrast to traditional enterprise infrastructure settings. This makes Cloud computing a compelling technology to tackle the issues rising with the growing size and complexity of scientific applications. For instance, for a typical problem size, a single physics application may scale to a few thousand processors, and multi-physics applications not only are increasing in size, but are also requiring more sophisticated workflows for their execution [1].

Most large-scale applications, such as scientific applications, are characterized by high variance in usage, mixture of data and compute load, flash crowds, unpredictable load, and varying compute and storage requirements. This makes the management of the computational infrastructures supporting such applications a complex task, even when public Infrastructure as a Service (IaaS) Cloud resources—such as virtual machines—are used as the underlying system infrastructure.

The above situation can be mitigated with the utilization of *Platform as a Service* (PaaS). PaaS Clouds offer to users a complete platform for hosting user-developed applications, while hiding the underlying infrastructure. Therefore, complex operations such as automatic scaling, load balancing, and management of virtualized environments are completely transparent to users, and happen without their direct interference.

In this article, we describe the design and implementation of a system delivering a scalable solution to scientific workflow applications, specifically focusing on the data analysis pipeline underpinning a high-profile scientific (physics) application: gravitational wave searches. The proposed solution is a PaaS middleware that uses resources from public Cloud infrastructures (IaaS) for hosting the management and application services.

Gravitational waves (GW) are ripples in the fabric of space–time that result from galactic collisions, stellar explosions, or rapid acceleration of large and extremely dense objects such as neutron stars [22]. In principle, the ripples can be detected by measuring minute changes in the separation of test masses on Earth, for example the mirrors on a long-baseline, laser, Michelson interferometer. However, the changes in separation are so small—one part in 10^{21} for the strongest predicted sources—that they have not yet been detected. A worldwide effort is currently under way to achieve the first detection, led by a new generation of interferometric antennas like the Laser Interferometer Gravitational-Wave Observatory (LIGO) and partner facilities around the world like VIRGO, GEO600, and TAMA300 [2].

Numerous search algorithms have been applied to the GW data from the above detectors, all of them computationally intensive. There are four main types of GW signal: stochastic, burst, continuous, and compact binary coalescence. Each search for a specific type of source covers a wide parameter space, with an optimal balance required between parameter space mismatch and computational resources. The search space is especially large for blind, all-sky searches where the electromagnetic counterpart of the source is unknown. In this paper, we concentrate on a search for periodic gravitational waves from Sco X-1. Sco X-1 is the brightest X-ray source in the sky. It is thought to be an accreting neutron star [22]. Theoretical analysis indicates that it may also be a strong GW candidate [4, 16, 24].

GW searches can be represented as a workflow consisting of tasks linked through data dependencies. Execution of the workflow can be parallelized in such a way that each parallel instance operates in a different multi-dimensional parameter set. Therefore, with an appropriate support from a platform, numerous scientists can simultaneously and independently use these workflows to analyse and search for GWs using their own parameter sets. As the number of concurrent workflow executions grows and shrinks, the platform can automatically increase and decrease the number of infrastructural resources deployed to support the platform, in such a way that the execution time of each individual workflow is not affected by the number of running workflows. Without support for scheduling and management of data and tasks, in the worst case, the parallel execution of these workflows will be reduced to sequential execution due to insufficient resources.

Parallel executions of workflows can lead to resource contention, as each workflow instance often requires the same set of data as input, requires a specific number of compute resources, which can be limited, and are bound by deadlines set by users. Hence, the challenges are to:

1. allocate Cloud resources to tasks, workflows, and users effectively to avoid resource contention—dynamic resource provisioning problem;
2. minimize execution time of individual workflows—task/workflow scheduling problem;
3. dynamically expand or shrink Cloud services based on varying load.

In order to tackle the above challenges, we designed a scalable PaaS middleware and built a prototype system that facilitates the search for Sco X-1. This article describes the PaaS middleware design, implementation, and performance evaluation with the support of the GW data analysis application use-case. Specifically, this paper makes the following **novel contributions**:

1. **Dynamically Provisioning of Multiple PaaS middleware Pools:** Our PaaS middleware is composed of workflow engines that manage a pool of workers in the Cloud. Instances of the workflow engine can be added and removed on demand in order to adapt to the observed demand of the system.
2. **Load Balancing and Distribution:** Our system contains a layer that distributes user requests to PaaS middleware pools and maintains load balance on each pool of workers by scaling load across recently spawned PaaS middleware, releasing resources when not in use.
3. **Cloud-Enabled LIGO Software Application (LALApps):** We describe how we used a LIGO software application and executed its operations using our propose system hosted in a public Cloud infrastructure.

The remainder of the paper is organized as follows: Sect. 2 presents closely related work in workflow systems and deployment of scientific applications in Cloud computing environments. We describe the scalable system design in Sect. 3. We then present the description of the GW data analysis pipeline in Sect. 4. Using the case-study as workload, we present performance evaluation in Sect. 5. We conclude and present future directions in "Conclusions and Future Work" section.

2 Related Work

Efforts for accelerating the execution of LIGO applications in distributed systems date back to 2002 [7]. Such a project established the workflows and data access policies used for earlier generation of LIGO experiments. After the rise of Clouds as suitable platforms for execution of scientific operations, Zhang et al. [25] developed an algorithm for execution of a LIGO workflow in a public Cloud. The application differs from ours in the method used for detecting the gravitational waves, and the algorithm is customized for the particular application. Our work proposes a two-level provisioning approach to scale either the application or the workflow execution platform. Therefore, Zhang's LIGO application and the corresponding scheduling algorithm could be integrated in our proposed system. Chen et al. [6] proposed an approach for generation of virtual machine images for the LIGO project. This virtual machine images can be used by platforms (such as the one proposed in this paper) or directly by researchers wanting to deploy their LIGO application in the Cloud.

Auto scaling of Cloud services and infrastructure results in significant cost reduction, green energy use, and sustainability. Dougherty et al. [9] proposed a model-driven configuration of Cloud auto-scaling infrastructure and applied it to an e-commerce application running on Amazon EC2 platform. Mao and Humphrey [14] used auto scaling of Cloud resources to minimize deployment costs while taking into account both user performance requirements and budget concerns.

In the context of platform support for execution of Workflow applications in Clouds, Workflow Management Systems that were originally proposed for Grids, such as Pegasus [8, 18], Askalon [20], Kepler [13], Taverna [19], and Cloudbus Workflow Engine [21] were extended to support utilization of Cloud resources. However, these systems have limited scalability regarding the total number of resources and application that can be simultaneously managed by them. Therefore, our proposed architecture groups such systems in a Platform as a Service layer and enable the deployment of multiple of such engines to increase the overall system scalability. In this sense, any of the above systems could be used in the PaaS layer of our architecture, even though in this paper we used Cloudbus Workflow Engine for this purpose.

Lu et al. [12] proposed a workflow for large-scale data analytics and visualization with emphasis in spatio-temporal climate data sets that targets public Cloud environments as the source of resources for workflow execution. However, the target scenario of such a tool is one user operating over one dataset, whereas our proposed solution targets multiple users accessing multiple data sets concurrently.

Kim et al. [11] proposed a system supporting execution of workflows in hybrid Clouds. This approach differ from our proposal in the sense that the main objective of such tool is typically keeping the utilization of local infrastructure as high as possible and keep utilization of public Clouds low, in order to reduce the extra costs related to public Clouds. Such approach has also to work in the selection of work-loads to be moved to the public Clouds and the workloads to be kept on premises. Furthermore, it scales only the number of workers, while our approach is able to scale the number of engines to support more simultaneous users and resources.

On the topic of automatic scaling of applications in Clouds, Vaquero et al. [23] presents a survey on the topic. It categorizes how scalability can be achieved on IaaS and PaaS Clouds. According to their classification for the problems, our work is classified as PaaS scaling via container replication.

Mao and Humphrey [15] proposes a solution for the problem of auto-scaling Clouds for execution of workflow applications. The approach considers a single workflow engine that is able to scale resources available for processing workflow applications. Our approach, on the other hand, considers a two-layers scaling approach where the number of workflow engines can also be scaled to further increase the total capacity of the system in managing and executing multiple simultaneous applications.

Casalicchio and Silvestri [5] explore different architectures for monitoring and scaling of applications in Clouds. The architectures explore different mixes of public Cloud provider services with local services for achieving scalability of VM applications. The proposed architectures operate at the IaaS layer, and utilize with arbitrary metrics for scalability decisions (for example, application throughput). The architectures are not aware of dependencies between tasks in workflow applications, and therefore they are not optimal for this type of application, unlike our approach.

Finally, it is worth noticing that public Cloud providers such as Amazon,[1] Microsoft,[2] RightScale,[3] and Rackspace[4] also offer solution for auto-scaling based on web services or APIs. They allow users to determine simple rules, typically based on monitored performance metrics (CPU and memory utilization, application response time), that trigger the auto-scaling process. Rules are used to determine the amount of machines to be added or removed from the system, typically proportional to the amount of resources in use (e.g., *increase number of resources by 20 % if average memory utilization is above 80 %*) or fixed (e.g., *reduce the number of resources to 5 if utilization is below 40 %*). Our approach enables more complex decisions that are determined algorithmically, and performed at two different levels (platform and application).

3 System Architecture and Design

In this section, we detail the design of the proposed PaaS middleware for execution of scientific workflows. Table 1 defines the symbols used in the rest of the article.

The system has a layered design in order to process multiple users and their workflows in a scalable manner, as depicted in Fig. 1. The bottommost layer is composed of virtualized resources, provided by public IaaS Cloud service providers,

---

[1]http://aws.amazon.com/autoscaling/.

[2]http://www.windowsazure.com/.

[3]http://www.rightscale.com/products/automation-engine.php.

[4]http://www.rackspace.com/cloud/loadbalancers/.

Table 1 Description of symbols used in the article

Symbol	Description
Q	Queue containing the list of tasks submitted to the system for execution as applications by end-users
$E_{engines}$	Set of compute resources where the workflow engine has been installed. Resources in this set compose the PaaS middleware
VM	A virtual machine deployed to support our platform
$R_{workers}$	Set of VMs that are configured to execute end-user applications
W_{pE}	Workers per Engine. This constant directs the algorithms to allocate up to the W_{pE} compute resources (workers) to each workflow engine that is running. For example if there are three engines and $W_{pE} = 5$, then each engine will have five worker VMs under its management
N_{tW}	Number of Tasks submitted to each worker. Higher values enable multiple tasks to be submitted to a worker to run in parallel
$sizeof(Array)$	This function returns the length of the array that is passed to it as a parameter
$CCE(integer)$	This is the capacity calculation algorithm. Its argument is the length of the task queue Q
$MAXCompTime$	This value signifies the maximum completion time for a task submitted by the user

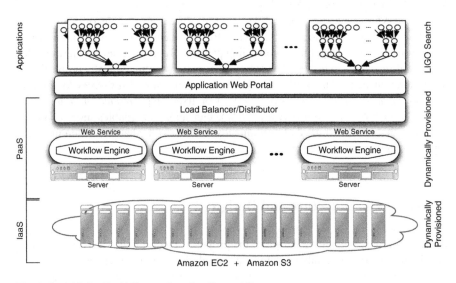

Fig. 1 Scalable PaaS middleware for scientific workflows

where the application is actually executed. In particular, for supporting LIGO data analysis we choose Amazon AWS as the public IaaS provider. The entire system is deployed on Amazon EC2, so that data transfers happen within the same Cloud provider with lower latency than when using multiple Cloud providers. Virtualized resources are managed by software components at the next level, which we name *platform services*. To implement this layer, we use our existing middleware solution—Workflow Engine [21]—for managing application workflows submitted by end-users for execution on the Cloud resources.

Because the overhead incurred to each workflow engine increases with the number of managed workflows, better scalability and response times can be obtained if multiple workflow engines are deployed and the load is balanced among them. Thus, the next layer is composed of a Load Balancer/Distributor that is responsible for enabling dynamic scaling of the platform services. The Load Balancer can dynamically create workflow engines instances, each running on a separate VM, at run-time. The provisioning of additional platform services is based on: (a) the number of waiting jobs (the difference between user requests arriving to the server and the request-level parallelism) over a period of time, and (b) average completion time of workflow applications submitted by users.

Finally, at the topmost layer, the Application Web Portal is the interface provided to end-users, who submit workflow application execution requests and monitor their progress.

Our architecture enables independent resource scaling at two different levels— the platform level composed of workflow engine instances that can manage the actual execution of tasks—and at the infrastructure level, where resources are deployed to execute the tasks. With the coordination of platform services provisioning and compute resource provisioning at the infrastructure level, the system is able to efficiently manage multiple workflows submitted by large number of users.

Figure 2 depicts the sequential interaction among different entities in order to achieve automatic scaling of Cloud resources. The interaction starts with a user sending an authentication request to access the web portal. After the authorization is granted, the user sets the parameters of the application workflow, determines the configuration files, and submits the workflow for execution. Depending on the number of tasks in the application, the load balancer calculates the number of VMs (engines) and computing machines (workers) needed and sends the invocation request to the public Cloud resource provider, as detailed in the next section. Workers are assigned to a specific workflow engine, and therefore all the tasks executed from a worker belong to jobs managed by its corresponding engine.

Once the number of required engines and workers is defined, the Load balancer submits requests for machines to Cloud resource provider, which starts the type and number of virtual machines according to the request. Once there are enough available virtual machines to start execution of tasks, the load balancer sends tasks to the workflow engine, which in turn forwards them to its associated workers for actual execution.

The worker sends the end result to its assigned workflow engine in order to direct it to store the data on the Cloud storage. The user can monitor the process of application execution through the web portal, which is able to supply statistics such as submission time, allocated resources, execution status, total execution time, and total stage-out time. Once results of workload execution is available, the user can download it directly from the Cloud storage. During the whole process, the load balancer continuously enforces distribution of applications among workflow

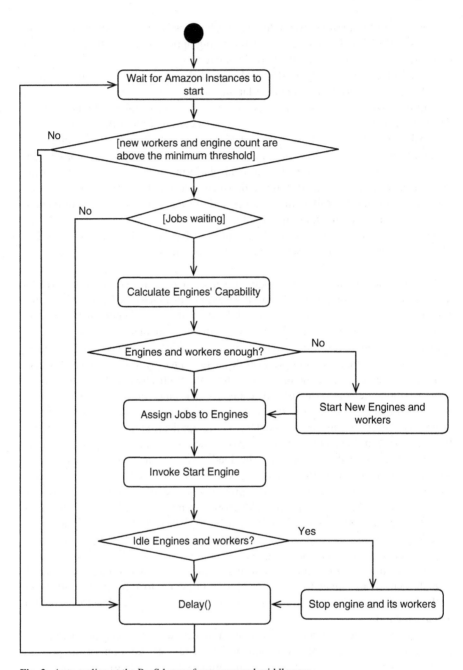

Fig. 2 Auto scaling at the PaaS layer of our proposed middleware

engines by provisioning the right amount of virtual machines (both workers and workflow engines). It does so by increasing or decreasing the number of running virtual machines based on the number of tasks to run and the capability of each VM (see Algorithms 1 and 2). Therefore, if all the submitted applications finish execution and no further application are submitted, running engines and workers are turned off automatically by the load balancer, as detailed in the next section.

Algorithm 1: PaaS load balancing algorithm

Input: W_{pE}: Application-dependent worker-per-engine rate.
while *There are incomplete Tasks in L in Q* **do**

    Update $R_{workers}$;
    Apply the CCE Algorithm to divide newly added instances between $E_{engines}$ and $R_{workers}$;
    Associate up to W_{pE} workers in $\{R_{workers}\}$ to each engine $e_i \in E_{engines}$;
    if (($|R_{workers}| \geq 0$) *OR all waiting compute resources available) AND* ($|Q| > 0$) **then**
        Number of tasks remaining to be submitted for execution
        $nPending = CCE(sizeof(Q))$;

    if $nPending > 0$ **then**
        Workers to run $wr = nPending/N_{tw}$;
        $wPending = wr$;
        foreach *Engine* $e_i \in E_{engines}$ **do**
            Free slots for engine e_i : $es = W_{pE} - (current\_number\_of\_workers\_in\_e_i)$;
            $wPending = wPending - es$;
            if $wPending > 0$ **then**
                Engines to run $er = \lfloor wPending/W_{pE} \rfloor$;

            Provision er engines in the Cloud;
            Provision wr workers in the Cloud;

    foreach *Engine* $e_i \in E_{engines}$ **do**
        repeat
            Assign tasks in Q to e_i;
        until *current_engine reaches it maximum load*;
        Start execution of tasks assigned to engine e_i;

3.1 Load Balancing

Load balancing in our proposed architecture is managed by the *Load Balancer/ Distributor* component. This component acts both at task level, in order to balance the load of workers, and also at the middleware level, by controlling the number of running Workload Engine instances and balancing the number of jobs submitted to each engine. The general operation of the Load balancer is detailed in Algorithm 1.

When jobs are submitted to the system, their corresponding tasks are queued at the Load Balancer (LB) in a queue Q. The LB groups the running resources in two sets: workflow engines $E_{engines}$ and computing workers $R_{workers}$. Application-dependent, user-defined W_{pE} workers are assigned to each engine running in the system. If new virtual machines were started since the last execution of the algorithm, each new VM is assigned to an already running workflow engine in a round-robin basis.

After all the provisioned VMs are ready to accept requests, the Load balancer checks for jobs waiting. Definition of number of engines to be added to the platform layer and the number of workers to be added to these engines is based on several factors. One such factor is the estimated capacity of available resources to handle extra tasks, which is determined using the method presented in Algorithm 2. The Load balancer computes the average tasks completion time observed in a configurable timespan and uses this value to estimate resource availability for the next time span. The availability estimation and number of waiting tasks are then compared in order to determine whether existing engines are enough to handle all the tasks or not.

Algorithm 2: CCE: engine capacity/load calculating algorithm

Set the capability of each free worker to N_{tW};
Set the threshold of completion time of a single task to *MAXCompTime*;
foreach $e_i \in E_{engines}$ **do**
  Get average task completion time ct_{e_i} of e_i during the last n minutes;
  Compute the availability a_i of e_i,
  $a_i = (ct_{ei} - MAXCompTime)/MAXCompTime$;
  Compute the capability c_i of e_i, $c_i = a_i \times$(number of workers of e_i)$\times$ (max tasks per worker);

Refresh compute resource status;
if *New workers are ready* **then**
  Increase the capability of its engine by N_{tW};

return *list of unassigned tasks*;

If the algorithm determines that available resources are not enough, the number of extra workers and engines is computed and the corresponding number of resources is started in the public Cloud provider. Each new engine, once ready, receives waiting tasks belonging to the same job. The assignment step is repeated until each engine reaches its maximum load or until no more waiting jobs exist. The engines then start applications that have been assigned for execution, and availability of resources is recomputed. The load balancing process is repeated until all tasks are finalized (either completed or canceled after a maximum number of failures).

The algorithm initially sets the capability of each free worker to N_{tW}, which is the maximum number of tasks that can be allocated to a worker while ensuring that the tasks can be completed in a reasonable time. The threshold of completion time of a single task is set *MAXCompTime*, which is the default threshold for determination if the engine is overloaded. If it is overloaded, it stops having tasks assigned to it. Afterwards, for each engine of $E_{engines}$, the algorithm computes the average

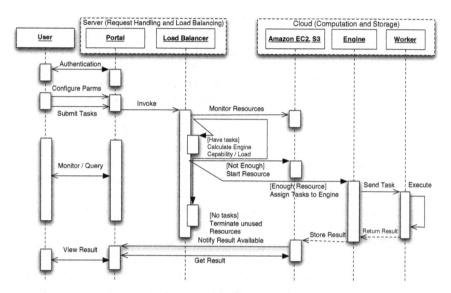

Fig. 3 Sequence diagram showing the interaction between entities involved in scaling PaaS services

completion time observed in the last time interval, so the estimated availability and capability can be computed. Based on such values, waiting tasks are assigned to running engines up to the maximum calculated capacity of each engine. Remaining tasks are taken into account when deciding to extend the number of engines (Fig. 3).

4 LIGO Data Analysis and the Search for Gravitational Waves

The system described in the previous sections was implemented and used in an application scenario: a data analysis pipeline in a gravitational wave search. The Laser Interferometer Gravitational Wave Observatory (LIGO) is one of the world's largest physics projects [2]. It will inaugurate a new era in astronomy by detecting Einstein's elusive gravitational waves, vibrations in space–time emitted by various cosmic sources. LIGO is currently the most sensitive element of an international detector network including facilities like Virgo, spaced widely around the globe to take advantage of the dramatically improved angular resolution afforded by intercontinental baselines. Sophisticated computing is the backbone of LIGO: the sheer scale of the data flows and the difficulty of detecting minuscule signals make gravitational wave searches one of the great computing challenges of our time.

To illustrate the application scenario and its requirements, we present a search for periodic GW signals from neutron starts in binary orbits [10, 17, 22]. Of this class of source, low mass X-ray binaries (LMXBs) are prime candidates due to numerous accurate observations across the electromagnetic spectrum [22, 24]. Sco X-1, the brightest X-ray source in the sky, located in the constellation Scorpius, is likely to be the LMXB that emits GW most strongly [24]. It is targeted for the development of the search application investigated in this study.

In working towards the detection of GWs, the LIGO Data Analysis Software Working Group has built several analysis tools. The sideband search is part of the LIGO Algorithm Library (LAL).[5] We use tools in LAL and its application suite (LALapps) to generate and analyze synthetic test data. Using the LAL tools we create LIGO-like data with an injected signal and synthetic noise and run the sideband search to retrieve the injected signal. The LAL tools ensure that the synthetic data resembles the data generated by actual detectors. Real data is available, but remains proprietary for now; its analysis lies outside the scope of this paper.

The sideband search has two stages. The first stage is a matched filter known as the $\mathscr{F}$-statistic [10]. It requires knowledge of the source sky position and searches over the unknown source frequency, by comparing against a signal template via a maximum likelihood approach. It is computationally intensive. If the source is in a binary system, the $\mathscr{F}$-statistic power is smeared out over many frequency bins (sidebands), spaced by integer multiples of the orbital frequency, i.e., a frequency comb. Hence, the second stage of the sideband search involves summing up semi-coherently the output of the $\mathscr{F}$-statistic at the frequency of each sideband in the comb. This requires knowledge of the orbital period and semi-major axis but is not computationally expensive. It produces a result called $\mathscr{C}$-statistic. The frequency parameter space can be split to allow parallel distribution. However the $\mathscr{F}$-statistic and $\mathscr{C}$-statistic steps must be performed sequentially. A search pipeline for this procedure is shown in Fig. 4. Coherent follow-up (Step 3) proceeds in the event of a positive provisional detection at the end of Step 2 and may leverage other signal processing algorithms, whose details lie outside the scope of this paper.

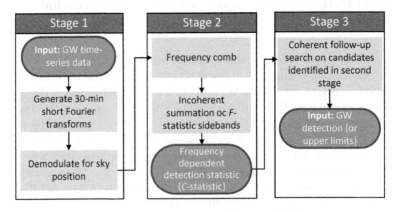

Fig. 4 The frequency comb search algorithm for periodic sources in binary systems

[5]http://www.lsc-group.phys.uwm.edu/daswg/.

Sample plots of $\mathscr{F}$- and $\mathscr{C}$-statistic output obtained from a simulated Sco X-1 search are presented in Fig. 5. The signal is injected at 505 Hz and is clearly recovered by the $\mathscr{C}$-statistic in Fig. 5d from the two-horned frequency comb structure in the $\mathscr{F}$-statistic output in Fig. 5b. Figure 5a, c shows null results from the same experiment but in a region of frequency space away from the injected frequency of the signal, where the data should contain just noise. Only a few Hz (out of a total search band of 1 kHz) are plotted for clarity.

A simple workflow for this procedure is depicted in Fig. 6. The various parameters that form the input are represented at the top of the figure. For each frequency range, one workflow task (circles in the figure) is created. For each $\mathscr{F}$-statistic computing task, a comb search is performed. Once the comb search is complete, the mean value is calculated and submitted to the last task, which provides the visualization in the form of a plot. The activity described above can be triggered multiple times by a user simultaneously considering multiple GW sources.

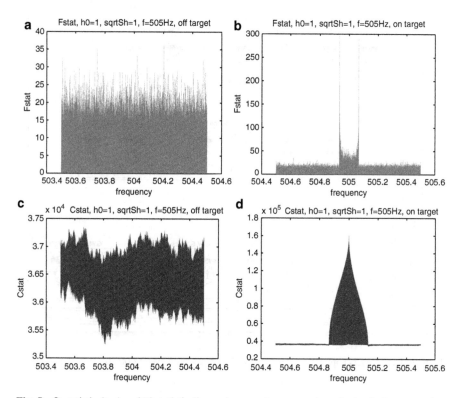

Fig. 5 $\mathscr{F}$-statistic (*top*) and $\mathscr{C}$-statistic (*bottom*) versus frequency plots obtained after processing the workflow in Fig. 4, demonstrating the noise (left) and signal (*right*) cases. The $\mathscr{F}$-statistic (**a** and **b**) calculation is the first stage of the CombSearch workflow, and also the input to the second stage, $\mathscr{C}$-statistic (**c** and **d**) calculation (Color figure online)

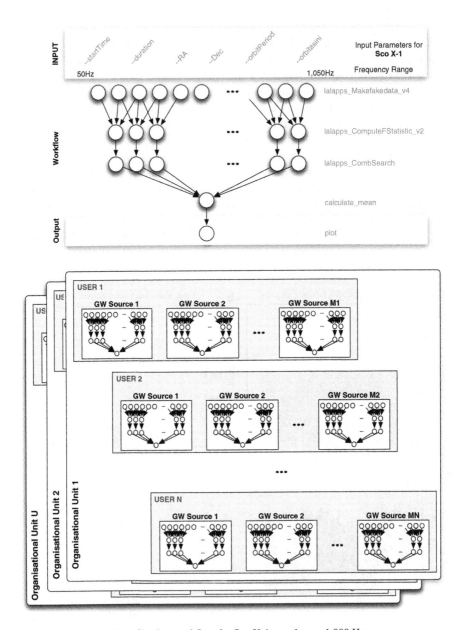

Fig. 6 A data analysis application workflow for Sco X-1 search over 1,000 Hz

The figure also depicts the fact that multiple Organizational Units (for example, research labs belonging to different universities) can have various users requesting execution of such workflow at the same time.

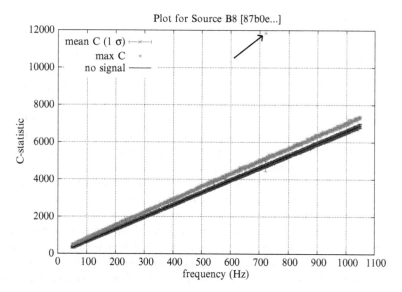

Fig. 7 $\mathscr{C}$-statistic output versus frequency after processing the workflow in Fig. 6. The *cross with error bars* represents the mean $\mathscr{C}$-statistic $+/-1$ standard deviation for each Hz band. The maximum $\mathscr{C}$-statistic from each band is indicated with *stars*. The "no signal" *black curve* refers to the theoretically expected value of the $\mathscr{C}$-statistic in the case of pure noise. The *black arrow* indicates the outlier from the $\mathscr{C}$-statistic results in the Hz band containing the signal, which was injected at 721.27 Hz (Color figure online)

As an example, a search for Sco X-1 over a 1,000 Hz band can be divided into 10^3 jobs of 1 Hz each. The result of each job is a list of $\mathscr{C}$-statistic values for every frequency bin in the 1 Hz band. The number of frequency bins is determined by the frequency resolution of the $\mathscr{F}$-statistic, $(2T)^{-1}$, which is a function of the observation time T. In our example, for $T = 10$ days, each 1 Hz band contains $\sim 10^6$ $\mathscr{C}$-statistic values.

To test for a detection, we calculate the $\mathscr{C}$-statistic for each bin in a 1 Hz band. For each band, the mean, standard deviation, minimum, and maximum values are collected and used for plotting the output. Figure 7 shows the output from a simulated search for a signal injected at 721.27 Hz with strength $h_0 = 1.6 \times 10^{-23}$ and noise $\sqrt{S_h} = 6 \times 10^{-23}$ across the 50–1,050 Hz band. Mean $\mathscr{C}$-statistic values are shown as crosses and the solid black line indicates the expected signal-free result. The plot also shows the maximum $\mathscr{C}$-statistic value in each band (stars). Since the injected signal is narrow band, it only appears in ≤ 10 bins (out of 10^6 per Hz), so the maximum $\mathscr{C}$ is a better diagnostic than the mean. The maximum $\mathscr{C}$-statistic values shows a clear outlier in the region of the injected signal around 721 Hz, highlighted by the black arrow.

4.1   Application Requirements

Data Requirements The size and quantity of data produced by the workflow depicted in Fig. 6 are substantial. In our test example, which is deliberately chosen to be small, if 10 days of synthetic data is generated by LAL, the workflow must handle 480 files of size 142 KB each, each file is a 1,800-second Short-time Fourier Transform (SFT). The total volume of data generated depends on the search duration chosen by LIGO scientists. The *ComputeFStatistic* and *CombSearch* scripts each produce 77 MB of data after processing the synthetic data. Depending on the input parameters, the result obtained after plotting the points (106 points in a single file; points are FStat-frequency and CStat-frequency, as depicted in Fig. 5) may need further processing to produce an image file (e.g. png, eps, etc.) for visualization.

It is vital to emphasize that these data volumes are small because we restrict ourselves to a small test problem in this paper. In general, full LIGO searches involve petabytes of data. The LIGO detectors sample the gravitational-wave signal channel at 16 kHz continuously for several years and generate another $\sim 10^4$ environmental channels sampled at similar rates. A typical compact binary coalescence search must process all the environmental channels, as must the pre-processing scripts that generate the SFTs for Sco X-1-like searches. The LIGO data storage requirements are determined by the rate at which data is produced by the LIGO interferometers. Each advanced LIGO interferometer is expected to produce a total data rate of $\sim$10 MB/s. This corresponds to an annual data volume of $\sim$315 TB or $\sim$200 TB with best current compression. The Advanced LIGO computing plan calls for each interferometer to maintain an archive of its own raw data as well as copies of the raw data generated by the other two interferometers. Additionally, a separate redundant archive of the raw data is to be maintained at each Tier 1 data center [2, 3].

Computational Requirements The processing time taken by *ComputeFStatistic* and *CombSearch* is around 9 min on an Intel dual core 2 GHz CPU with 7 GB memory when executed for a single source across the 10-day stretch of data with a band of 1 Hz.

Multiple GW Sources and Multi-User Environment As noted in the introduction, GWs can be detected from multiple sources. Users may elect to search for multiple sources or single sources across different sections of the data. Each source has different input parameters even though the underlying workflow is the same. This scenario is depicted in Fig. 6 as GW Source 1–GW Source N. In a LIGO organizational unit, it is expected that many users conduct searches simultaneously on different sources. In an organizational unit, e.g., a university research group, there are many users conducting different search procedures on the same and/or different GW sources. These users are depicted as User 1–User N in Fig. 6.

Execution Time in Clouds In order to evaluate the expected execution time of the application in public Clouds, we executed the search procedure on Amazon EC2, an IaaS service enabling users to buy virtual machines (instances) with specific characteristics in terms of CPU, memory, and storage (instance types). We repeated the experiment with different instance types (Small, Large, and Extra Large). The synthetic input data was generated using *lalapps_Makefakedata_v4*. The execution times of the applications and their input/output file sizes are reported in Table 2. The values listed in Table 2 show that the application's runtime is CPU-intensive, and therefore dependent on the machine processing capacity and directly affected by the computing power of the resource in use. Furthermore, the size of data produced will help us in identifying techniques to manage the transfer and storage of such large data sets.

Table 2 Execution characteristics on Amazon AWS

Task names	Execution time (s)			Input size (KB)	Output size
	Small	Large	Extra large		
Generate data	37	17	12	–	138 kB
Compute F-statistic	2,611	1202	883	138 KB	480 MB
Comb search	184	85	N/A	480 KB	76 MB
Plot results	32	15	N/A	138 KB	100 KB

5   Performance Evaluation

In this section, we present the experiments conducted for evaluating the performance of the system design and the load balancing algorithms. We divide the experiments into two groups, namely *Platform scalability* and *Dynamic provisioning and instantiation of compute resources*.

The PaaS system and the workflow application was demonstrated at the Fourth IEEE International Scalable Computing Challenge (SCALE 2011), in California, USA, during May 23–26, 2011. The experimental results presented in this section are a result of the data collected from the executions during and after the challenge.

5.1   Platform Scalability

As discussed earlier, the PaaS middleware (the Workflow Engine) has limitations on the number of workers and concurrent workflow applications it can manage. In an environment such as that of the LIGO project, where it is expected that multiple users from multiple organizations will be simultaneously performing GW searches, a single engine can become a bottleneck for the scalability of the solution. To tackle such a limitation, our proposed system is able to dynamically scale the PaaS layer and also the worker pools by deploying multiple Engines when the demand is high.

In order to evaluate the dynamic scaling of PaaS services work, a first series of experiments was conducted. The experiments consist in a series of execution of the application described in the previous section with a fixed number of compute sources and different combination of engines and workers numbers. The application conducts the search for GW signals between the frequencies of 50 and 1,050 Hz, performing both the full-range (1,000 Hz) and proximity (within 200 Hz intervals) searches.

The maximum number of tasks executed was 40. Moreover, in order to enable us to acquire a better understanding of the practical environment, we use different sources for each experiment. Experiments were performed with a maximum of one, two, and four engines. For each number of engines, experiments were executed with 4, 8 and 16 workers per engine.

Figures 8, 9, and 10 show respectively results when the system was allowed to scale up to one, two, and four engines. The topmost plot on each figures shows the execution time of individual tasks, while the bottom plots show start and finish time of each task with different scaling levels related to number of workers.

Figure 8 shows that, when a single workflow engine is available, execution time of tasks when only four workers are deployed is smaller than when 16 workers are deployed. Also, there are bigger variation in the execution time when 16 workers are in use. This demonstrates the limitation of a single workflow engine in managing too many concurrent workers, caused by overheads related to the management of

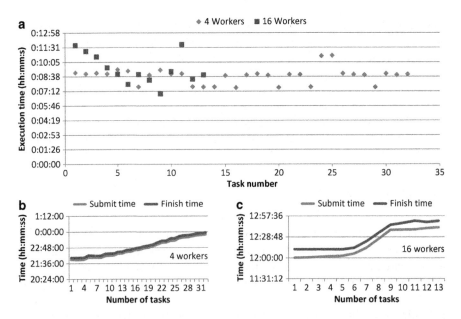

Fig. 8 Performance of a single workflow engine. (**a**) Execution time of tasks. (**b** and **c**) Submission and finish time of tasks for 4 and 16 workers, respectively

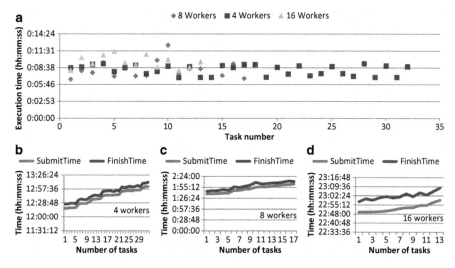

Fig. 9 Performance of two concurrent workflow engines. (**a**) Execution time of tasks. (**b–d**) Submission and finish time of tasks for 4, 8, and 16 workers, respectively

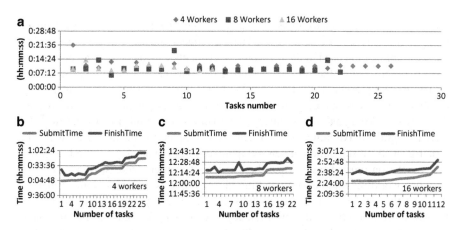

Fig. 10 Performance of four concurrent workflow engines. (**a**) Execution time of tasks. (**b–d**) Submission and finish time of tasks for 4, 8, and 16 workers, respectively

multiple workers. for the scenario with one workflow engine, utilization of only four workers makes execution time of tasks more homogeneous. The same trend is observed with two and four simultaneous workflow engines, as shown in Figs. 9 and 10, respectively. When the ratio of workers per engine is low, increase in the number of concurrent engines reduces tasks runtime.

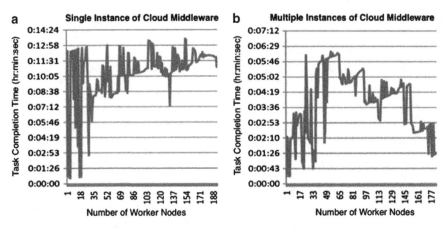

Fig. 11 (**a**) A single workflow engine handles all the user requests. (**b**) Multiple workflow engines are "dynamically" provisioned based on user requests, thus forming resource pools

5.2 Dynamic Provisioning of Workers

The next set of experiments aimed at evaluating the performance of the mechanism for dynamic provisioning of workers. The experiment consisted in the execution of the same application used in the previous experiments with an increasing number of tasks in order to stress the system, triggering the dynamic provisioning process.

The graphs presented in Fig. 11 shows tasks completion time as a function of number of resources and the number of workflow engines running. Due to overheads cause by monitoring and management of workers, as the number of workflow tasks increases until a maximum value of 40, the task completion time increases, which in turn triggers the instantiation of new compute resources (workers). Figure 11a shows the completion time of tasks when the number of workers increases linearly, with only one workflow middleware handling all the requests. It can be noticed that, in this case, the completion time steeply falls when more compute resources are added. However, we also observed that efficiency is constantly decreasing. For instance, the completion time when there are 170 workers is around 11 min, as compared to around 5 min when there are 35 resources. Although the ratio of tasks to workers is the same, a single PaaS middleware introduces higher overheads for a large number of tasks and workers, which affects the completion time. The same trend is not observed when multiple workflow engines are deployed.

In contrast, in Fig. 11b, we can observe that the completion time decreases for the same task to worker ratio as in Fig. 11a. As the completion time starts to climb, we instantiate a new workflow engine, which has an immediate impact on the completion times of new tasks. This effect is visible as a ladder-like curve in Fig. 11b. When 170 workers are instantiated, the completion time is around 2 min 20 s, nearly five times less than in Fig. 11a. Multiple workflow engines (PaaS middleware) divide the overheads of scheduling and execution.

Conclusions and Future Work

Cloud computing is a promising technology for transparently managing the challenges brought by large-scale research applications that are characterized by large volumes of data, computationally demanding applications, and execution concurrency. However, such scientific applications demand specialized platform tools capable of coordinating the different stages of execution of tasks while optimizing user-defined deadlines and Cloud usage cost. Because platforms for scientific applications supporting such features are not readily available, we designed and implemented an automated PaaS middleware that uses public IaaS providers to host and support scalable execution of scientific application workflows.

The proposed middleware is able to independently manage and scale the platform layer composed of workflow engines and the infrastructure layer composed of worker units able to execute application tasks. The scalable PaaS middleware architecture was described, algorithms for load balance and scaling were presented, and an application case study in the area of particle physics was presented. The application is a search for gravitational waves from the LIGO project, and workflows of such project were executed in a prototype of the discussed architecture in order to validate our approach and enable us to evaluate the systems performance. Results show that our goals of independent and automated scaling of different layers is achievable and enable reduction in execution time of applications even with variable pattern and size of user requests.

As future work, we intend to evaluate the impact of different types of applications in the performance of our proposed architecture. We also plan to enhance the load balance algorithm and extend them to support execution of workflows in multi-cloud scenarios, where resources from different Cloud providers, both public and private, are used at the same time in a federated environment.

Acknowledgements This project is partially supported by project grants from the University of Melbourne (Sustainable Research Excellence Implementation Fund and Melbourne School of Engineering) and the Australian Research Council (ARC). We thank Amazon for providing access to their Cloud infrastructure, the Australian and international LIGO communities for their guidance and support, and Dong Leng for his contribution towards extending the Workflow Engine for the LIGO experiment.

References

1. Large scale computing and storage requirements for basic energy sciences research. Workshop Report LBNL-4809E, Lawrence Berkeley National Laboratory, USA, Jun. 2011.
2. B. P. Abbott et al. LIGO: the laser interferometer gravitational-wave observatory. *Reports on Progress in Physics*, 72(7):076901, Jul. 2009.

3. Advanced LIGO Team.   Advanced ligo reference design.   Technical Report LIGO M060056-08-M, LIGO Laboratory, USA, May 2007.
4. Lars Bildsten. Gravitational radiation and rotation of accreting neutron stars. *The Astrophysical Journal Letters*, 501(1):L89–L93, Jul. 1998.
5. E. Casalicchio and L. Silvestri.   Architectures for autonomic service management in cloud-based systems.   In *Proceedings of the 2011 IEEE Symposium on Computers and Communications (ISCC'11)*, 2011.
6. Wei Chen, Junwei Cao, and Ziyang Li. Customized virtual machines for software provisioning in scientific clouds. In *Proceedings of the 2nd International Conference on Networking and Distributed Computing (ICNDC'11)*, 2011.
7. Ewa Deelman et al. GriPhyN and LIGO, building a virtual data grid for gravitational wave scientists. In *Proceedings of the 11th IEEE International Symposium on High Performance Distributed Computing (HPDC'02)*, 2002.
8. Ewa Deelman, Gurmeet Singh, Mei-Hui Su, James Blythe, Yolanda Gil, Carl Kesselman, Gaurang Mehta, Karan Vahi, G. Bruce Berriman, John Good, Anastasia Laity, Joseph C. Jacob, and Daniel S. Katz. Pegasus: A framework for mapping complex scientific workflows onto distributed systems. *Scientific Programming*, 13(3):219–237, Jul. 2005.
9. B. Dougherty, J. White, and D. C. Schmidt.   Model-driven auto-scaling of green cloud computing infrastructure. *Future Generation Computer Systems*, 28(2):371–378, Feb. 2012.
10. Piotr Jaranowski, Andrzej Królak, and Bernard F. Schutz. Data analysis of gravitational-wave signals from spinning neutron stars: The signal and its detection. *Physics Review D*, 58(6), Aug. 1998.
11. Hyunjoo Kim, Yaakoub el Khamra, Ivan Rodero, Shantenu Jha, and Manish Parashar. Autonomic management of application workflows on hybrid computing infrastructure. *Scientific Programming*, 19(2–3):75–89, Jun. 2011.
12. Sifei Lu, Reuben Mingguang Li, William Chandra Tjhi, Long Wang, Xiaorong Li, Terence Hung, and Di Ma. A framework for cloud-based large-scale data analytics and visualization: Case study on multiscale climate data. In *Proceedings of the 3rd International Conference on Cloud Computing Technology and Science (CloudCom'11)*, 2011.
13. Bertram Ludäscher, Ilkay Altintas, Chad Berkley, Dan Higgins, Efrat Jaeger, Matthew Jones, Edward A. Lee, Jing Tao, and Yang Zhao. Scientific workflow management and the Kepler system. *Concurrency and Computation: Practice and Experience*, 18(10):1039–1065, Aug. 2006.
14. M. Mao and M. Humphrey. Auto-scaling to minimize cost and meet application deadlines in cloud workflows. In *Proceedings of the 2011 International Conference for High Performance Computing, Networking, Storage and Analysis (SC'11)*, 2011.
15. Ming Mao and Marty Humphrey.   Auto-scaling to minimize cost and meet application deadlines in cloud workflows. In *Proceedings of the 2011 International Conference for High Performance Computing, Networking, Storage and Analysis (SC'11)*, 2011.
16. A. Melatos and D. J. B. Payne. Gravitational radiation from an accreting millisecond pulsar with a magnetically confined mountain. *The Astrophysical Journal*, 623(2):1044–1050, Apr. 2005.
17. C. Messenger and G. Woan. A fast search strategy for gravitational waves from low-mass x-ray binaries. *Classical and Quantum Gravity*, 24(19):S469–S480, 2007.
18. Ashish Nagavaram, Gagan Agrawal, Michael A. Freitas, and Kelly H. Telu. A cloud-based dynamic workflow for mass spectrometry data analysis. In *Proceedings of the 7th IEEE International Conference on eScience (eScience'11)*, 2011.
19. Tom Oinn, Matthew Addis, Justin Ferris, Darren Marvin, Martin Senger, Mark Greenwood, Tim Carver, Kevin Glover, Matthew R. Pocock, Anil Wipat, and Peter Li. Taverna: a tool for the composition and enactment of bioinformatics workflows. *Bioinformatics*, 20(17):3045–3054, Nov. 2004.
20. Simon Ostermann, Radu Prodan, and Thomas Fahringer. Extending grids with cloud resource management for scientific computing. In *Proceedings of the 10th IEEE/ACM International Conference on Grid Computing (GRID'09)*, 2009.

21. S. Pandey, D. Karunamoorthy, and R. Buyya. Workflow engine for clouds. In R. Buyya, J. Broberg, and A.Goscinski, editors, *Cloud Computing: Principles and Paradigms*, chapter 12, pages 321–344. Wiley, 2011.
22. Stuart L. Shapiro and Saul A. Teukolsky. *Black holes, white dwarfs, and neutron stars: The physics of compact objects*. Wiley-Interscience, New York, USA, 1983.
23. Luis M. Vaquero, Luis Rodero-Merino, and Rajkumar Buyya. Dynamically scaling applications in the cloud. *SIGCOMM Computer Communication Review*, 41(1):45–52, Jan. 2011.
24. Anna L. Watts, Badri Krishnan, Lars Bildsten, and Bernard F. Schutz. Detecting gravitational wave emission from the known accreting neutron stars. *Monthly Notices of the Royal Astronomical Society*, 389(2):839–868, 2008.
25. Fan Zhang, Junwei Cao, Kai Hwang, and Cheng Wu. Ordinal optimized scheduling of scientific workflows in elastic compute clouds. In *Proceedings of the 3rd IEEE International Conference on Cloud Computing Technology and Science (CloudCom'11)*, 2011.

The FutureGrid Testbed for Big Data

Gregor von Laszewski and Geoffrey C. Fox

Abstract In this chapter introduce you to FutureGrid, which provides a testbed to conduct research for Cloud, Grid, and High Performance Computing. Although FutureGrid has only a modest number of compute cores (about 4,500 regular cores and 14,000 GPU cores) it provides an ideal playground to test out various frameworks that may be useful for users to consider as part of their big data analysis pipelines. We focus here on the use of FutureGrid for big data related testbed research. The chapter is structured as follows. First we provide the reader with an introduction to FutureGrid hardware (Sect. 2). Next we focus on a selected number of services and tools that have been proven to be useful to conduct big data research on FutureGrid (Sect. 3). We contrast frameworks such as MPI, virtual large memory systems, Infrastructure as a Service and map/reduce frameworks. Next we present reasoning by analyzing requests to use certain technologies and identify trends within the user community to direct effort in FutureGrid (Sect. 4). The next section reports on our experience with the integration of our software and systems teams via DevOps (Sect. 5). Next we summarize Cloudmesh, which is a logical continuation of the FutureGrid architecture. It provides abilities to federate cloud services and to conduct cloudshifting; that is to assign servers on-demand to HPC and Cloud services (Sect. 6). We conclude the chapter with a brief summary (Sect. 6).

1 Introduction

FutureGrid [11, 27] is a project led by Indiana University (IU) and funded by the National Science Foundation (NSF) to develop a high performance grid test bed that will allow scientists to collaboratively develop and test innovative approaches to parallel, grid, and cloud computing. FutureGrid provides the infrastructure to researchers that allows them to perform their own computational experiments using distributed systems. The goal is to make it easier for scientists to conduct such experiments in a transparent manner. FutureGrid users will be able to deploy their own hardware and software configurations on a public/private cloud, and run

G. von Laszewski (✉) • G.C. Fox
Indiana University, Bloomington, IN, USA
e-mail: laszewski@gmail.com; gcf@indiana.edu

© Springer Science+Business Media New York 2014
X. Li, J. Qiu (eds.), *Cloud Computing for Data-Intensive Applications*,
DOI 10.1007/978-1-4939-1905-5_2

their experiments. They will be able to save their configurations and execute their experiments using the provided tools. The FutureGrid test bed is composed of a high speed network connecting distributed clusters of high performance computers. FutureGrid employs virtualization technology that will allow the test bed to support a wide range of operating systems.

2 Overview of FutureGrid

2.1 Hardware Overview

FutureGrid contains a number of clusters of different types and size that are interconnected with up to a 10 GB Ethernet among its sites. The sites include Indiana University, University of Chicago, San Diego Supercomputing Center, Texas Advanced Computing Center, and University of Florida.

2.1.1 Overview of the Clusters

Table 1 provides a high level overview of the clusters currently available in FutureGrid. The biggest cluster is located at IU. It is called India and contains 128 servers with 1,024 cores. In total, we currently have 481 compute servers with 1,126 CPUs and 4,496 Cores. In addition, we have 448 GPU cores. The total RAM is about 21.5 TB. Secondary storage is about 1 PB. A more detailed table is provided in Table 2. We found that India is one of the most popular resources on FutureGrid.

Table 1 FutureGrid compute resources

Name	System type	Nodes	CPUS	Cores	TFLOPS	RAM (GB)	Storage (TB)	Site
India	IBM iDataplex	128	256	1,024	11	3,072	335	IU
Hotel	IBM iDataplex	84	168	672	7	2,016	120	UC
Sierra	IBM iDataplex	84	168	672	7	2,688	96	SDSC
Foxtrot	IBM iDataplex	32	64	256	3	768	0	UF
Alamo	Dell Poweredge	96	192	768	8	1,152	30	TACC
Xray	Cray XT5m	1	166	664	6	1,328	5.4	IU
Bravo	HP Proliant	16	32	128	1.7	3,072	128	IU
Delta	SuperMicro GPU Cluster	16	32	192		1,333	144	IU
Lima	Aeon Eclipse64	8	16	128	1.3	512	3.8	SDSC
Echo	SuperMicro ScaleMP Cluster	16	32	192	2	6,144	192	IU
		481	1, 126	[1]4696	47	22,085	1,054.2	

[1] GPU cores on machines not included

Table 2 FutureGrid cluster details

Name	Echo	Alamo	Bravo	Delta	Foxtrot	Hotel	India	Lima	Sierra	Xray
Organization	IU	TACC	IU	IU	UF	UC	IU	SDSC	SDSC	IU
Machine type	Cluster SclaeMP	Cluster	Cluster	Cluster	Cluster	Cluster	Cluster	Cluster	Cluster	Cluster
System type	SuperMicro	Dell PowerEdge M610 Blade	HP Proliant		IBM iDataPlex dx 360 M2	IBM iDataPlex dx 360 M2	IBM iDataPlex dx 360 M2	Aeon EclipseA64	IBM iDataPlex dx 340	Cray XT5m
CPU type	Xeon E5-2640	Xeon X5550	Xeon E5620	Xeon 5660	Xeon X5520	Xeon X5550	Xeon X5550	Opteron 6212	Xeon L5420	Opteron 2378
CPU speed	2.50 GHz	2.66 GHz	2.40 GHz	2.80 GHz	2.26 GHz	2.66 GHz	2.66 GHz	1.4 GHz	2.5 GHz	2.4 GHz
CPUs		192	32	32	64	168	256	16	168	168
Servers	12	96	16	16	32	84	128	8	84	1
RAM		12 GB DDR3 1333 MHz	192 GB DDR3 1333 MHz	192 GB DDR3 1,333 MHz	24 GB DDR3 1,333 MHz	24 GB DDR3 1,333 MHz	24 GB DDR3 1,333 MHz	64 GB DDR3	32 GB DDR2-667	8 GB DDR2-800
Total RAM		1,152 GB	3,072 GB	3,072 GB	768 GB	2,016 GB	3,072 GB	64 GB DDR3	2,688 GB	1,344 GB
Number of cores	144	768	128		256	672	1,024	128	672	672
Tflops	2.8	8	1.7		3	7	11		7	6
Disk size (TB)		48		15	20	120	335		72	335
Hard drives		500 GB 7.2 K RPM SAS	6x 2 TB 7.2 K RPM SATA	92 GB 7.2 K RPM SAS2	500 GB 7,200 RPM SATA	1 TB 7,200 RPM SATA	3,000 GB 7,200 RPM SATA	1 TB 7,200 RPM, 480 GB SSD	160 GB 7,200 RPM SATA Drive	6 TB Lustre
Shared storage		NFS	NFS	NFS	NFS	GPFS	NFS	ZFS	ZFS 82.2 TB	NFS
Interconnect		Mellanox 4x QDR IB	Mellanox 4x DDR IB			Mellanox 4x DDR IB	Mellanox 4x DDR IB	10 GbE Mellanox ConnectX	Mellanox 4x DDR IB	Cray SeaStar

IB = InfiniBand, Xenon = INtel Xenon, Opteron = AMD Opteron

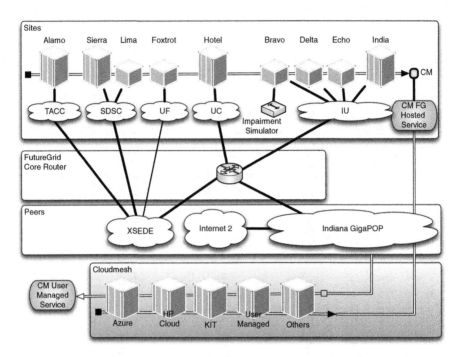

Fig. 1 High level network diagram and conceptual integration of Cloudmesh resources

2.1.2 Overview of Networking

The significant number of distinct systems within FutureGrid provides a hetero-geneous distributed architecture. They are connected by high-bandwidth network links supporting distributed system research [11]. The FutureGrid network used to have a dedicated network between sites [11]. However, the network infrastructure has recently changed due to modifications related to the major network operator the National Lambda Rail. Due to these changes the operation of the network between the sites has switched from the National Lambda Rail to XSEDE and are no longer exclusive. However, this is so far no major handicap for the projects conducted on FutureGrid based on our project portfolio. The current high level network diagram is depicted in Fig. 1. Hence, the core resources to FutureGrid at SDSC, IU, TACC, and UF are now all connected via the XSEDE network and integrated via the FG core router in Chicago. Within the IU network additional clusters are integrated and are described in more detail in Sect. 2.1.1.

A Spirent H10 XGEM Network Impairment emulator [14] can be collocated with resources at Indiana University, to enable experiments to include network latency, jitter, loss, and errors to network traffic.

In addition we have added several components that are related to a special software service called Cloudmesh, which we explain in more detail in Sect. 6.

Table 3 Storage resources of
FutureGrid

System type	Capacity (TB)	File system	Site
Xanadu 360	180	NFS	IU
DDN 6620	120	GPFS	UC
Sunfire x4170	96	ZFS	SDSC
Dell MD3000	30	NFS	TACC
IBM dx360 M3	24	NFS	UF

2.1.3 Overview of Storage

FutureGrid does not provide capacity for long-term storage or long-term experiments. FutureGrid has a limited amount of storage space and users are requested to remove their storage after use. However, users with special needs may be accommodated by special storage setups. The list of storage services is shown in Table 3.

3   Services and Tools for Big Data

FutureGrid offers a very rich environment to its users. We can categorize them in a stacked service architecture as depicted in Fig. 2. We distinguish the following categories: Cloud PaaS, IaaS, GridaaS, HPCaaS, TestbedaaS, which we will explain in more detail in the next sections. The services in these categories are integrated in our general FutureGrid high-level architecture depicted in Fig. 3. More details about the architecture can be found in [11, 27]. Within this paper we will focus on describing services that have been explicitly used for big data research in FutureGrid.

3.1   Testbed as a Service (TestbedaaS)

It is a well-accepted paradigm that today a lot of research is carried out by interdisciplinary scientific teams. Thus, FutureGrid provides an advanced framework to manage user and project affiliation and propagates this information to a variety of subsystems constituting the FG service infrastructure. This includes operational services (not explicitly mentioned in Fig. 2) to deal with authentication, authorization and accounting. In particular, we have developed a unique metric framework that allows us to create usage reports from our entire Infrastructure as a Service (IaaS) frameworks. Repeatable experiments can be created with a number of tools including Pegasus, Precip and Cloudmesh. VMs can be managed on high

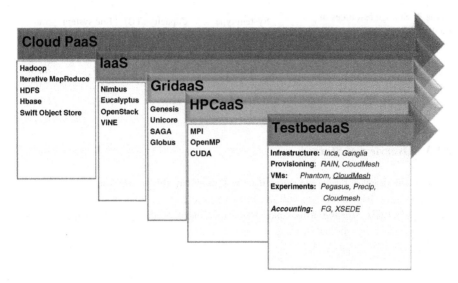

Fig. 2 FutureGrid high-level user services

level either via Cloudmesh (see Sect. 6). Provisioning of services and images can be conducted by RAIN [9, 10]. Infrastructure monitoring is enabled via Nagios [7], Ganglia [17], and Inca [22] and our own cloud metric system [29].

3.2 Traditional High Performance Computing as a Service (HPCaaS)

Within the traditional High Performance Computing (HPC) services FG offers a traditional MPI/batch queuing system and a virtual large memory system that are beneficial for big data calculations.

3.2.1 MPI and Batch Queues

The traditional HPC environment provided by queuing systems and Message Passing Interface (MPI) programs creates a suitable infrastructure not only for simulations, but also for the analysis of large data. However, considerable amount of work has to be conducted to optimize the available infrastructure to deal with distributed domain decompositions. Optimized use via traditional HPC has been successfully demonstrated for many biological applications. Additionally, the existence of a queuing system can provide some advantages when the available resources are over utilized while sharing the resources with other users. This has

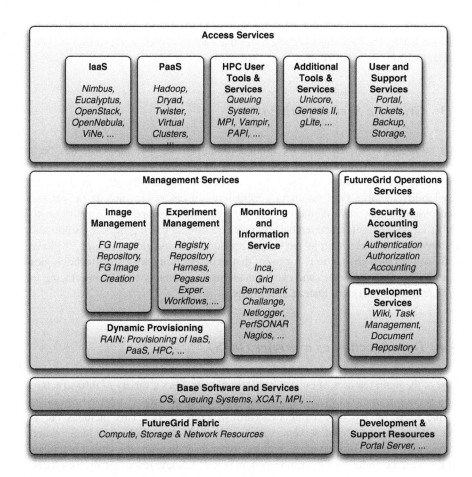

Fig. 3 FutureGrid high-level architecture

been especially useful in FutureGrid to support educational activities for classes with many users that, for example, want to test map reduce activities controlled by a queuing system as described in Sect. 3.5.1.

3.2.2 Virtual Large-Memory System

One of the demands often posed in big data analysis it to place the data as much as possible into memory to speed up calculations and in some cases to fit the entire dataset into memory. However, this analysis may come at a cost as, for example, the use of HPC computing via MPI adds additional programming complexity within a cluster. Therefore, it is desirable to virtualize the memory from multiple servers in a cluster to provide one big memory system that can be easily accessed by the underlying software. One such implementation, vSMP by ScaleMP [11, 21]. vSMP is installed on the FutureGrid echo cluster that has 16 servers and can access up to 3 TB in shared virtual memory.

3.3   Grid as a Service (GridaaS)

Not surprisingly the demand for computational Grids on FutureGrid has been relatively small. While we saw few requests for Globus we decided to focus on the installation of more popular systems. The low use can be explained by the availability of large Grid production infrastructure elsewhere such as in XSEDE and based on the move of the community away from complex Grid solutions to either cloud computing or even back to more traditional batch processing solutions. Furthermore, toolkits such as the CoG Kit also known as jglobus [24, 26, 28] have provided enough abstractions for users that experimenting with such technologies has become less prominent and can be made on the client side while interfacing to production Grid services instead of testbeds.

3.4   Infrastructure as a Service (IaaS)

One of the main features of FutureGrid is to offer its users a variety of infrastructure as a service frameworks [25, 31]. These frameworks provide virtualized resources to the users on top of existing cyberinfrastructure fabric. This includes but is not limited to virtualized servers, storage, network, disk, and other IaaS related services. In FutureGrid the most common hypervisor that runs the virtual machines as guest on the underlying operating system is KVM. Some resources also run XEN, however most recently the demand for KVM has increased and some services will be switched from XEN to KVM. Through the ability to provide large numbers of virtual machines to the users, the access mode to utilize resources, in contrast to traditional HPC, has been changed from a reservation-based service to an on-demand service. This comes with the benefit that if enough resources are available they will be immediately allocated to the user. However, if not enough resources can be offered, the system will define the request and return with an error. Based on our experience with FutureGrid over the last couple of years, it is advantageous to offer a mixed operation model. This includes a standard production cloud that operates on-demand, but also a set of cloud instances that can be reserved for a particular project. We have conducted this for several projects in FutureGrid, including those that required dedicated access to resources as part of big data research such as classes [18, 19] or research projects with extremely large virtual machines [20].

The IaaS services that are offered in FutureGrid contain the following:

OpenStack   has become most recently, next to HPC, the most requested service
   in FutureGrid based on newly started projects. OpenStack is an open source

cloud infrastructure as a service framework to deliver public and private clouds. It contains a number of components that together build a powerful and flexible set to create a cloud service offering. Services include a compute service, and object storage, an image service, a monitoring service, and an orchestration service. OpenStack has received considerable momentum due to its openness and the support of companies. Within FutureGrid OpenStack clouds are currently deployed on India, Sierra, Hotel, and Alamo, while currently India provides the most up to date services.

Nimbus   is an open source service package allowing users to run virtual machines on FutureGrid hardware. Just as in OpenStack users can upload their own virtual machine images or customize existing ones. Nimbus, next to Eucalyptus is one of the earlier frameworks that make managing virtual machines possible. Nimbus provides a basic set of cloud services including services to orchestrate the deployment of virtual machines. However, Eucalyptus and OpenStack now also provide such services.

Nimbus provides a selected subset of AWS protocols such as EC2. Accounting of Nimbus VMs does not currently provide features for project management. Such group-based and role based user management is essential for proper administrative resource and project management and is provided by other IaaS frameworks. In Nimbus it is only conducted on a user-by-user basis. This has significant implications on user management as in large-scale deployments project management features are highly desired but are not offered in Nimbus. Although, single users may not be interested in this feature, it is essential to provide proper project management of groups of users.

Eucalyptus   is an open source software IaaS framework for cloud computing. Eucalyptus provides an Amazon Web Services (AWS) compliant EC2-based web service interface to its users enabling the easy integration between a local cloud managed with Eucalyptus and AWS. However, as other IaaS frameworks such as OpenStack also provide EC2 interfaces for many application users OpenStack has become a viable alternative.

Which of the IaaS frameworks to choose is a question that is not that easy to answer. Many of our projects evaluate several of them in order to choose the one best suited for their use case. At other times users chose a framework that they had previously successfully used. Over time the quality of the IaaS framework has significantly changed. Within the last year OpenStack has become the most popular platform on FutureGrid.

3.5   Cloud Platform as a Service (PaaS)

3.5.1   Map Reduce

Map reduce models have been familiar to the programming and distributed computing community for a long time and have been historically associated with the functional programming's map and reduce. However the map and reduce framework introduced recently [8] distinguishes itself from such efforts while applying it repeatedly, with fault tolerance on a very large distributed data set [4].

Instead of bringing the data to the computer in map reduce application we often use the concept of bringing the computing to the data. This makes a lot of sense when we assume that a large number of data is distributed over many servers and repeated search queries are cast to find results across them (as in the case of Google motivating map/reduce).

In general, we can define a *map* step that takes the input problem and divides it into smaller sub-problems distributing it among worker nodes. The map function is then executed on the data distributed on the various servers. The *reduce* step collects the answers of the subproblem and combines them in some fashion (Fig. 4).

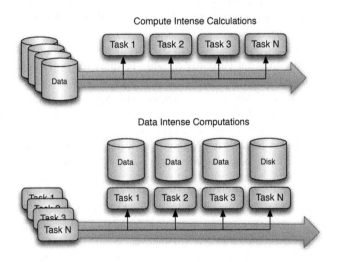

Fig. 4 Bring the data to the computation vs. bring the computation to the data

Hadoop

Hadoop [1] is an Apache project delivering an opensource software that uses the map/reduce framework in a distributed environment while focusing on scalability and reliability. Its design includes the Hadoop File System (HDFS) which provides an easy-to-use file system to distribute the data among the servers on which the calculations will be executed. Hadoop is designed to deal with faults through redundancy which is an important feature when conducting data analysis on very large distributed databases [1]. Hadoop is written in Java and provides the essential map reduce functionality and allows the system to be configured for existing hardware.

myHadoop

MyHadoop [15, 16], which is installed on many of the compute clusters in Future-Grid, enables users to launch Hadoop clusters via traditional high-performance compute clusters. For this, it utilizes the underlying batch scheduling system.

The reasons for managing Hadoop jobs via a batch system are manifold. First, the available infrastructure is resource constrained, and utilization of disks and compute resources must be specially accounted for to allow shared usage by many users. This naturally happens in the educational research community quite frequently. Second, to efficiently utilize the compute and data infrastructure researchers may not run Hadoop or MPI jobs continuously. At times they may need a Hadoop environment. At other times they may prefer a traditional message passing environment while at the same time being under resource constraints.

The idea of myHadoop is to submit a job to the queuing system that sets up a Hadoop cluster for the length of the reservation and the researcher can then use it to conduct experiments either via predefined jobs or in interactive mode. This is achieved by first identifying a number of resources via the scheduler, followed by the deployment of the Hadoop software across the identified servers. The user will then be presented with information on how to access this newly provisioned Hadoop cluster. MyHadoop, in its new version [16] is supported for Oracle Grid Engine (formerly known as Sun Grid Engine), PBS, and SLURM.

Once Hadoop has been initialized, it can be accessed through regular job scripts as shown in Fig. 5. This example script uses eight nodes. It is important to set the processor per node to 1 to assure the various Hadoop daemons are scheduled on different servers. The rest of the script is not depicted as it contains the actual details on setting up Hadoop via the script and is beyond the scope of this chapter. The user should replace the text in < ... > to customize the job. As Hadoop is a user level program, it is also possible to run a usermodified version of Hadoop which helps in adding new features or trying out newer versions of Hadoop than the default version that is installed for my Hadoop. The FutureGrid manual provides more details on how to practically use myHadoop on FutureGrid [13].

```
#!/bin/bash
#PBS -q <queue_name>
#PBS -N <job_name>
#PBS -l nodes=8:ppn=1
#PBS -o <output file>
#PBS -e <error_file>
#PBS -A <allocation>
#PBS -V
#PBS -M <user email>
#PBS -m abe

...further details omitted
```

Fig. 5 PBS script to start hadoop

Twister

Twister [6] is an extension to MapReduce to allow more easily the introduction of iterative map reduce processes. In addition twister has introduced a number of concepts including distinction between static and variable data, long running tasks, publish/subscriber based communication, and various other enhancements. Twister is developed at Indiana University, and is used as part of classes on distributed systems and other educational activities; hence, it reaches popularity within FutureGrid.

Virtual Clusters

In addition to the map/reduce platforms offered on FutureGrid, it is also possible to deploy virtual clusters. One of the earliest such frameworks has been showcased by von Laszewski [30] while deploying a SLURM cluster. Such a cluster can then be used as a teaching tool or provides additional mechanisms to custom create queues and reservations. However, the most advanced feature of FutureGrid will be via Cloudmesh, which will allow the deployment of clusters not only in virtual machines, but on baremetal.

4 FutureGrid Usage

When offering services such as FutureGrid to the community, we have to analyze and predict which services may be useful for the users. We have therefore established a number of activities that monitor external and internal data. Externally, we look, for example, at information provided by Gartners technology hype curve [2] or Google trend information as shown in Fig. 6. From Google Trend data we observe that the popularity of Grid computing has been very low in the recent years and much attention has shifted to cloud computing. Therefore we removed this information from the figure and focus exemplary on cloud related terms such as *Cloud Computing*, *Big Data*, *OpenStack*, and *VMWare*. From this information we see that all but VMWare are rising, with Cloud Computing dominating the Google trends in comparison to the others. This trend is important as it shows a shift in the cloud computing community buzz away from a traditional commercial market leader in virtualization technology. We believe that is correlated with a large number of vendors offering alternative products and services while at the same time the novelty from VMWare is reduced.

To give an informal overview of the more than 300 projects conducted on FutureGrid, we have taken their titles and displayed them in a word cloud (see Fig. 7). Additionally, we have taken keywords that are provided by the project leads and also displayed them in a word cloud (see Fig. 8). Although the images do not give quantitative perspective about the project it helps to identify some rough idea

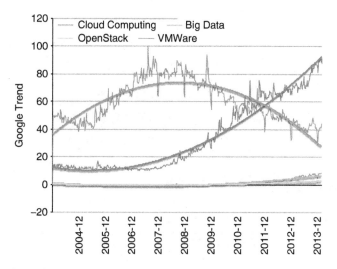

Fig. 6 Google trends

about the activities that are ongoing in FutureGrid. As expected the terms cloud computing and terms such as mapreduce, OpenStack, Nimbus, and Eucalyptus appear quite frequently. It is, therefore, worthwhile to analyze this data in a more quantitative form.

FutureGrid supports a rich set of projects, of which many are principally related directly or indirectly to big data systems. In Table 4 we list the areas of research and the number of projects conducted in these areas over a time period identified between November 2011 and December 2013. One of the focal observations is that the majority of projects are related to computer science research which can be found in the table in more detail. Domain Science and Education related projects take on a large portion.

As part of our project management in FutureGrid, we have designed a simple project application procedure that includes prior to a project being granted access, gathers information about which technologies are anticipated to be used within the project. The list of technologies is fairly extensive and includes Grid, HPC, and Cloud computing systems, services, and software. However, for this paper we will focus primarily on technologies that are dominantly requested and depicted in Fig. 9. Clearly we can identify the trend that shows the increased popularity of OpenStack within the services offered on FutureGrid. Nimbus and Eucalyptus are on a significant downward trend. ObenNebula was also at one point more requested than either Nimbus or Eucalyptus, but due to limited manpower an official version of OpenNebula was not made available on FutureGrid. As we have not offered it and pointed it out on our Web page, requests for OpenNebula have vanished. However, we have internally used OpenNebula for projects such as our Cloudmesh rain framework. All other sixteen technologies are relatively equally distributed over

Fig. 7 Project title word cloud

Fig. 8 Project keyword word cloud

the monitoring period. The lesson that we took form this is that FutureGrid has put recently more emphasis in offering OpenStack services.

From the overall project information we have also analyzed the frequency of the number of project members within the project and show it in Fig. 10. Here we depict on the abscissa, classes of projects with varying members. Assume we look at the abscissa at the value of 10. This means that these are all projects that have project

Table 4 FutureGrid supports a rich set of projects, of which many are importantly related directly or indirectly to big data systems

Discipline	Count
Domain science	44
Education[a]	42
Technology evaluation	19
Core virtualization	17
Programming models	12
Cyberinfrastructure	11
Security and privacy	10
Data systems	10
Resource management	9
Distributed clouds and systems	8
Artificial intelligence	7
Cyber-physical CPS and mobile systems	5
Fault-tolerance	5
Data analytics/machine learning	5
Networking	3
Network/web science	3
Interoperability	3
Storage	2
Streaming data	2
P2P	2
Software engineering	2

[a] 90 % of which on computer science

members between 10 and its previous category, in this case 5. Hence, it will be all projects greater than 5 and smaller or equal to 10. With this classification we see that the dominant unique number of members within all projects is either one, two or three members. Then we have another class between four and ten members, and the rest with more than ten members. One of the projects had 186 registered members overall for an education class as part of a summer school. Looking at the distribution of the members and associating them with research and education projects, we find all projects with larger numbers of projects to be education projects.

When we look in more detail into the map/reduce related technology requests over the entire period FutureGrid has been active, we identified the distributions as depicted in Fig. 13. We can see that the requests for IaaS together with map/reduce technology requests dominate. HPC requests are much fewer. The reason why the other category in Fig. 13 is that high is because we have a significant number of other choices, each with a very low total count. Also, we would like to remind the reader that users can chose multiple categories for their projects. Within the category of map/reduce, users had the choice of Hadoop, Map/Reduce, or Twister as a technology. The breakdown of these choices is shown in the right part of Fig. 13 dominated by the choice for Map/Reduce and Hadoop representing 85 % of all choices.

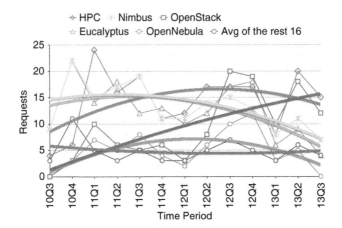

Fig. 9 Requested technologies by project

Next we have analyzed all projects that requested either mapreduce, hadoop, twister, MPI and ScaleMP (147 of all 374 active projects, which is 39 % of all projects) and categorized them by discipline as shown in Fig. 11. In contrast to XSEDE, which provides a production HPC system to the scientific community, the usage of FutureGrid for map reduce frameworks is dominated with 50 % by computer science related projects followed by education with 19 %.

Looking further into this data, we present in Fig. 12 the number of projects in a particular category as well as the Fraction of technologies within a discipline. As we are focusing in this paper on the impact on big data, we have looked in particular at requests for mapreduce, Hadoop, and twister, while also looking at requests for MPI and ScaleMP. It is interesting to note that the perceptual distribution of the technologies among these projects is about constant, if we exclude technology evaluations and interoperability. As MPI is more popular with domain sciences, we find a slight increase in projects requesting MPI (Fig. 13). However, with the life sciences we see the opposite as map/reduce and associated technologies are more popular here. MPI and ScaleMP are not much requested as part of technology evaluations and interoperability experimentation as they either project a very stable framework and do not require evaluation, or the question of interoperability is not of concern for most of the projects.

5 System Management

The goal of FutureGrid is to offer a variety of services as part of its testbed features, thereby going beyond services that are normally offered by data and supercomputing centers for research. This provides a number of challenges that need to be overcome

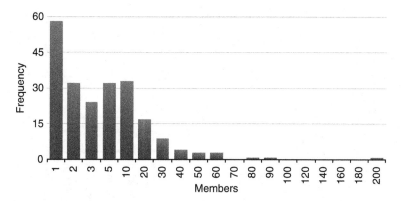

Fig. 10 Project frequency

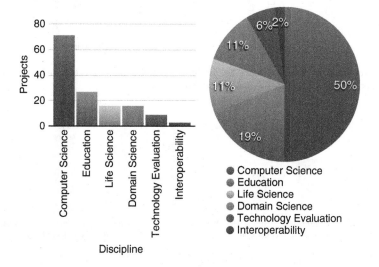

Fig. 11 Distributon of project disciplines

in order to efficiently manage the system and provide services that have never been
offered to users as they exist on FutureGrid.

5.1 Integration of Systems and Development Team

FutureGrid started initially with a model where the systems team and the software
team were separated. An unnecessary wall between teams was erected that resulted
in multiple challenges:

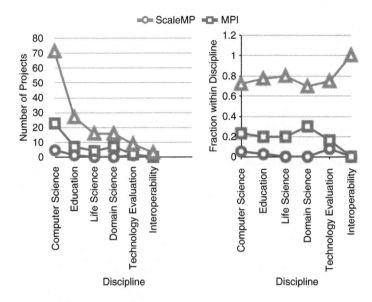

Fig. 12 Requests by of technologies by discipline within a project. (*Triangle*) Map reduce, Hadoop, or Twister, (*square*) MPI, (*circle*) ScaleMP

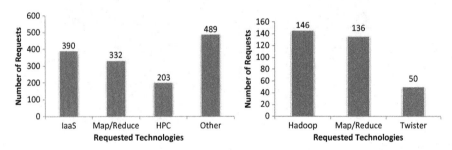

Fig. 13 Map reduce related technology requests

1. The system setup and management were completely separated from the software development team focusing mostly on the deployment of existing technologies. However the technologies deployed were themselves under heavy development and required intercorrelations between developers and system teams.
2. The deployed system was complex, but its deployment was documented to a limited extent, which resulted in developers having insufficient information to utilize the system properly or to know what had been deployed.
3. Lack of trust by the systems team did not allow the software team to have a valid development environment as proper privileges were not issued to the developers. As the development team needed to use privileged system services, the development could not be carried out.

4. The software developed needed a testbed within the testbed that was not necessarily reflecting the actual system setup.

Together, these issues made it extremely difficult, if not impossible, to further any development in regards to the design of a testbed infrastructure as proposed by our original ambitious goals.

To overcome these difficulties it was decided early on in the project that the systems team must be integrated in some fashion into the software team and become part of the development process. This integration is not an isolated instance within FutureGrid, but is also executed in many modern data centers and is now recognized with its own term called *DevOps*.

5.2   DevOps

DevOps is not just a buzzword from industry and research communities. It provides value added processes to the deployment and development cycles that are part of modern data centers. It can today be understood as a software development method that stresses collaboration and integration between software developers and information technology professionals such as system administrators.

While using an infrastructure such as clouds we recognized early on that the lifetime of a particular IaaS framework is about 3–6 months before a new version is installed. This is a significant difference to a traditional High Performance Computing Center that is comprised of many software tools experiencing much longer life spans. This is not only based on security patches but significant changes, for example, in the evolving security infrastructure and user services, as well as, the deployment of new services that become available in rapid procession.

This rapid change of the complex infrastructure requires rethinking how systems in general are managed and how they can be made available to the development teams. While previously it may have been enough to install updates on the machines, DevOps frameworks provide the developer and system administrators a way to create and share environments that are used in production and development while at the same time increasing quality assurance by leveraging each other's experiences (see Fig. 14).

5.2.1   DevOps Cycle

While combining the steps executed by the development and operational team from planning to coding, building and testing, to the release, deployment and operation and monitoring (see Fig. 15), each of the phases provides a direct feedback between the DevOps team members, thus shortening the entire development phase. It also allows testing out new services and technologies in a rapid progression. Hence, it is possible to roll out new developments into production much faster. This leads to a much more rapidly integrated cycle than would not be possible without the correlation between development and operation.

Fig. 14 DevOps intersection

Fig. 15 DevOps cycle

5.2.2 DevOps Supporting Tools

A number of tools are available that make the introduction of DevOps strategies more efficient. The first is the need for an simplified communication pathway to manage tasks not only between developers but also between users. Thus the ideal system would provide a complete integration of a project management system that allows managing tasks for both developers and operators, but also to easily integrate tickets and transform them into tasks. In XSEDE and other supercomputing centers a system called RT [5] is typically used for user ticket management. Other systems such as jira, mantis, and basecamp are often used to manage the software and systems related tasks. Unfortunately, personal or organizational constraints often prevent the integration of the two systems and additional overhead is needed to move user tickets into tasks and the development cycle. Within FutureGrid, as part of our opensource development, we experimented extensively with jira as systems and ticketing system [3] revealing that newest development in such areas motivated by DevOps teams led to tools that support the overall cycle including user ticket management in a single system (see Fig. 16). However, the integration of FutureGrid within the overall much larger XSEDE effort made it not possible to switch from RT to jira for user ticket management. To stress this user integration we term this framework *UseDevOps*. Tools to integrate Development and Operation deployment include puppet, chef, ansible, cfengine and bcfg2. While FutureGrid started out with bcfg2 we have since switched to other tools due to their prevalence within the community. Chef, puppet, and ansible have significant amount of traction. Due to expertise within our group we currently explore chef and ansible.

Fig. 16 User Support integrated into DevOps leads to UseDevOps

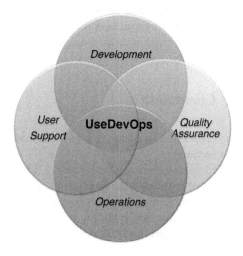

5.3 *Support for Education*

To support the many educational and research projects on FutureGrid, we have provided, through a portal, a significant amount of material on how to use the discussed services. In addition, we realized that not every educational project has users with advanced computer experience, therefore we provide for such projects a streamlined user interface rather than having the users fight with complex command line syntax and parameters. For example, we provided for a recent MOOC on big data taught with resources on FutureGrid the basic functionality not only to start VMs as part of the IaaS framework, but also to deploy sophisticated images that contain preinstalled software and allow services to be hosted by the users such as iPython, R and much more. This was implemented on top of OpenStack while utilizing the newest OpenStack services such as Heat. The management of the VMs and starting of the iPython server was controlled by a python application that provides the user with a menu system. Thus, the management of them became literally as easy as pressing 1, 2, 3, ... in the menu. For other classes, we have also provided completely separate OpenStack deployments as the teachers were afraid that students would not have enough resources due to the shared environment. However, we learned from this that the teachers overestimated the actual utilization of the project and many resources were not used. Based on this analysis we now have a model to justify the creation of more relaxed access policies and can justify that even classes should be utilizing the public region that are provided by FutureGrid. If resource contention would become an issue, we could set aside a special region for a limited amount of time. Reconfiguration needs have also arisen where one day a class may want to explore traditional MPI, while the next they want to experiment with Hadoop. Furthermore, we identified that several users wanted to combine various cloud IaaS platforms in order to avoid resource over-provisioning or were interested in combining all resources.

6 Cloudmesh

At [12] we find an extensive set of information about Cloudmesh that is cited within this section.

From the experience with FutureGrid we identified the need for a more tightly integrated software infrastructure addressing the need to deliver a software-defined system encompassing virtualized and baremetal infrastructure, networks, application, systems and platform software with a unifying goal of providing Cloud Testbeds as a Service (CTaaS). This system is termed Cloudmesh to symbolize

(a) The creation of a tightly integrated mesh of services targeting multiple IaaS frameworks.
(b) The ability to federate a number of resources from academia and industry. This includes existing FutureGrid infrastructure, Amazon Web Services, Azure, HP Cloud, Karlsruhe, using not only one IaaS framework, but many.
(c) The creation of an environment in which it becomes more easy to experiment with platforms and software services while assisting to deploy them effortlessly.

In addition to virtual resources, FutureGrid exposes baremetal provisioning to users, but also a subset of HPC monitoring infrastructure tools. Services will be available through command line, API, and Web interfaces.

6.1 Functionality

Due to its integrated services Cloudmesh provides the ability to be an onramp for other clouds. It also provides information services to various system level sensors to give access to sensor and utilization data. They internally can be used to optimize the system usage. The provisioning experience from FutureGrid has taught us that we need to provide the creation of new clouds, the repartitioning of resources between services (cloud shifting), and the integration of external cloud resources in case of over provisioning (cloud bursting). As we deal with many IaaS we need an abstraction layer on top of the IaaS framework. Experiment management is conducted with workflows controlled in shells [23], Python/iPython, as well as systems such as OpenStack's Heat, Accounting is supported through additional services such as user management and charge rate management. Not all features are yet implemented. Figure 17 shows the main functionality that we target at this time to implement.

6.2   Architecture

The three layers of the Cloudmesh architecture include a Cloudmesh Management Framework for monitoring and operations, user and project management, experiment planning and deployment of services needed by an experiment, provisioning and execution environments to be deployed on resources to (or interfaced with) enable experiment management, and resources (Fig. 18).

6.2.1   System Monitoring and Operations

The management framework contains services to facilitate FutureGrid day-to-day operation, including federated or selective monitoring of the infrastructure. Cloudmesh leverages FutureGrid for the operational services and allows administrators to view ongoing system status and experiments, as well as interact with users through ticket systems and messaging queues to inform subscribed users on the status of the system.

The Cloudmesh management framework offers services that simplify integration of resources in the FutureGrid nucleus or through federation. This includes, for user management, access to predefined setup templates for services in enabling resource and service provisioning as well as experiment execution. To integrate IaaS frameworks Cloudmesh offers two distinct services:

(a) a federated IaaS frameworks hosted on FutureGrid, (b) the availability of a service that is hosted on FutureGrid, allowing the integration of IaaS frameworks through user credentials either registered by the users or automatically obtained from our distributed user directory.

For (b) several toolkits exist to create user-based federations, including our own abstraction level which supports interoperability via libcloud, but more importantly it supports directly the native OpenStack protocol and overcomes limitations of the EC2 protocol and the libcloud compatibility layer. Plugins that we currently develop will enable access to clouds via firewall penetration, abstraction layers for clouds with few public IP addresses and integration with new services such

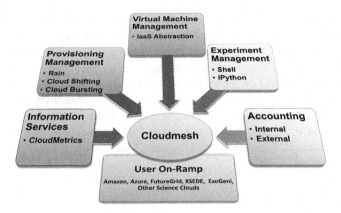

Fig. 17 CM functionality

as OpenStack Heat. We successfully federated resources from Azure, AWS, the HP cloud, Karlsruhe Institute of Technology Cloud, and four FutureGrid clouds using various versions of OpenStack and Eucalyptus. The same will be done for OpenCirrus resources at GT and CMU through firewalls or proxy servers.

Additional management flexibility will be introduced through automatic cloud bursting and shifting services. While cloud bursting will locate empty resources in other clouds, cloud shifting will identify unused services and resources, shut them down and provision them with services that are requested by the users. We have demonstrated this concept in 2012 moving resources for more than 100 users to services that were needed based on class schedules. A reservation system will be used to allow for reserved creation of such environments, along with improvements of automation of cloud shifting.

6.2.2   User and Project Services

FutureGrid user and project services simplify the application processes needed to obtain user accounts and projects. We have demonstrated in FutureGrid the ability to create accounts in a very short time, including vetting projects and users allowing fast turn-around times for the majority of FutureGrid projects with an initial startup allocation. Cloudmesh re-uses this infrastructure and also allows users to manage proxy accounts to federate to other IaaS services to provide an easy interface to integrate them.

6.2.3   Accounting and App Store

To lower the barrier of entry, Cloudmesh will be providing a shopping cart which will allow checking out of predefined repeatable experiment templates. A cost is

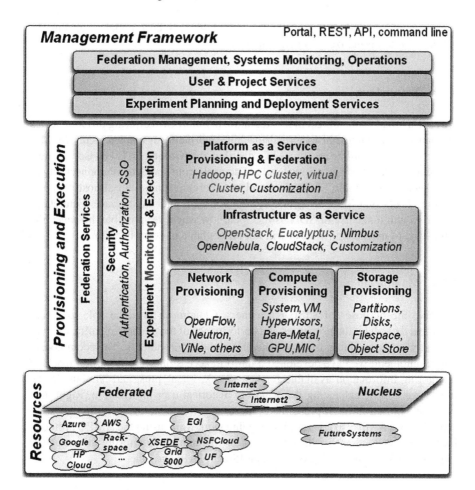

Fig. 18 CM architecture

associated with an experiment making it possible to engage in careful planning and to save time by reusing previous experiments. Additionally, the Cloudmesh App Store may function as a clearing-house of images, image templates, services offered and provisioning templates. Users may package complex deployment descriptions in an easy parameter/form-based interface and other users may be able to replicate the specified setup.

Due to our advanced Cloudmesh Metrics framework, we are in the position to further develop an integrated accounting framework allowing a usage cost model for users and management to identify the real impact of an experiment on resources. This will be useful to avoid over-provisioning and inefficient resource usage. The cost model will be based not only on number of core hours used, but also the capabilities of the resource, the time, and special support it takes to set up the experiment. We will expand upon the metrics framework of FutureGrid that allows measuring of VM and HPC usage and associate this with cost models. Benchmarks will be used to normalize the charge models.

6.2.4   Networking

We have a broad vision of resource integration in FutureGrid offering different levels of control from baremetal to virtual machine and platform management. We also offer the ability to utilize resources in a distributed environment. Likewise, we must utilize networks offering various levels of control, from standard IP connectivity to completely configurable SDNs, as novel cloud architectures will almost certainly leverage NaaS and SDN alongside system software and middleware. FutureGrid resources will make use of SDN using OpenFlow whenever possible, however, the same level of networking control will not be available in every location.

6.2.5   Monitoring

To serve the purposes of CISE researchers, Cloudmesh must be able to access empirical data about the properties and performance of the underlying infrastructure beyond what is available from commercial cloud environments. To accommodate this requirement, we have developed a uniform access interface to virtual machine monitoring information available for OpenStack, Eucalyptus, and Nimbus. In the future, we will be enhancing the access to historical user information. Right now they are exposed through predefined reports that we create on a regular basis. To achieve this we will also leverage the ongoing work while using the AMPQ protocol. Furthermore, Cloudmesh will provide access to common monitoring infrastructure as provided by Ganglia, Nagios, Inca, perfSonar, PAPI and others.

6.3   Cloud Shifting

We have already demonstrated via the RAIN tool in Cloudmesh that it is possible to easily shift resources between services. We are currently expanding upon this idea and developing more easy to use user interfaces that assist administrators and users through role and project based authentication to move resources from one service to another (see Fig. 19).

6.4   Graphical User Interface

Despite the fact that Cloudmesh was originally a quite sophisticated command shell and command line tool, we have recently spent more time in exposing this

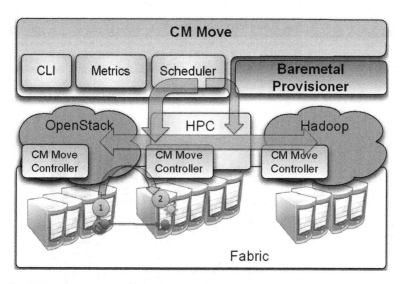

Fig. 19 Shifting resources makes it possible to offer flexibility in the service distribution in case of over or underprovisioning

functionality through a convenient Web interface (Fig. 20). Some more popular views in this interface are depicted in Fig. 21 hinting at how easy it is with a single button to create multiple VMs across a variety of IaaS. This not only includes resources at IU but also at external locations, making it more practical for users.

Hence, this easy management provides a more sophisticated experience for the user while associating one-click deployments. These deployments include the ability to instantiate virtual clusters, Hadoop environments, and other more elaborate setups. We provide an early prototype screenshot in Fig. 22.

6.5   Command Shell and Command Line Interface

Cloudmesh contains the ability to access much of its functionality through a commandline interface. This is enabled through a command shell that can function both as regular Linux command as well as command shell. The command shell can be invoked with cm on the regular Linux shell, or by specifying a number of parameters to call it without starting the interactive shell. The commands accessible to the users allow the management of virtual machines, and bare metal provisioning. To find out the detailed option of each command one can invoke a help command. An important property of this shell is that it can be easily extended and plugins can be distributed not only in a system wide plugin directory, but also in one provided by the user. This makes it possible to customize the shell commands available

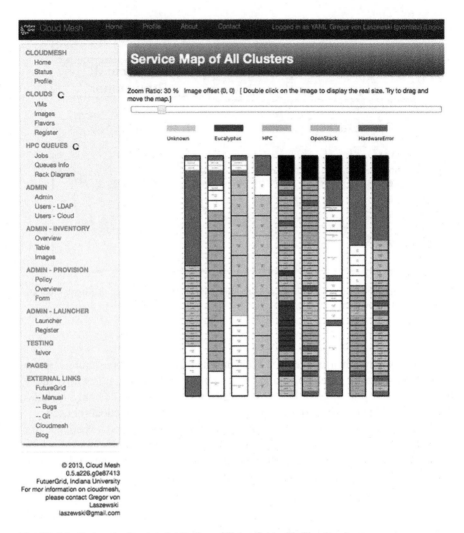

Fig. 20 Monitoring the Service distribution of FutureGrid with Cloudmesh

based on user needs by either removing unnecessary commands or introducing new ones. For example it would be possibly for users only interested in virtual machine management to remove the commands related to baremetal provisioning. Figure 23 shows the startup of the command shell and the invocation of the help command to list the available commands for this user. Please note that all commands are yet implemented. We have categorized some of the commands as cloud commands listed in a special section in the help. Figure 24 shows the use of the first command in that list called cloud that lists the available clouds for the user. Important to note is that Cloudmesh can be set up as a server so that the GUI and the command shell share variables that are managed in a jointly used database. Thus, it is possible to

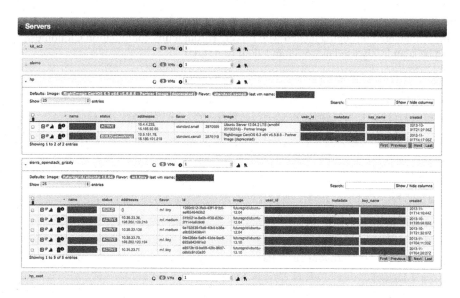

Fig. 21 Screenshot demonstrating how easy it is to manage multiple VMs across various clouds

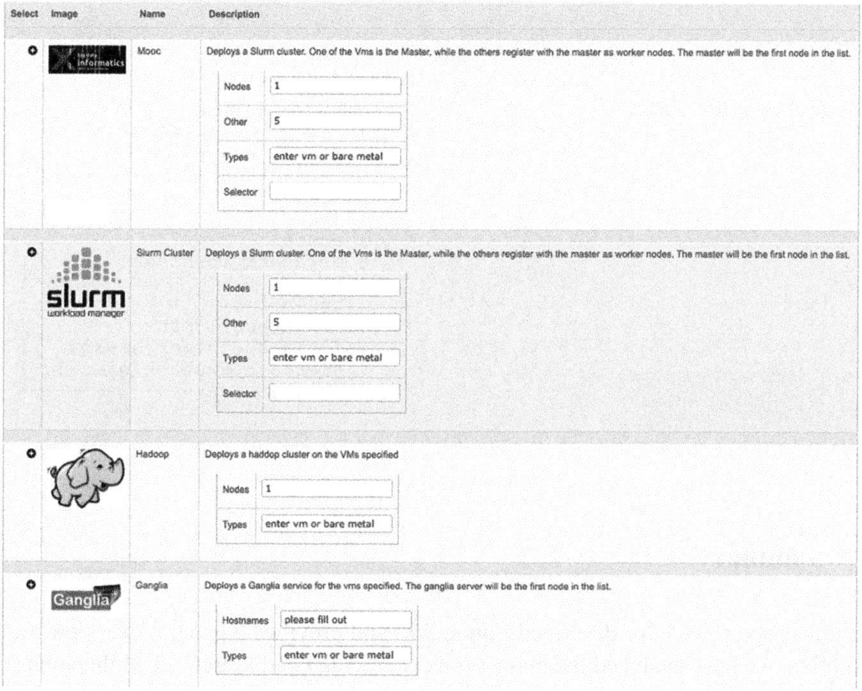

Fig. 22 One click deployment of platforms and sophisticated services that could even spawn multiple resources

register new clouds with the command shell, and have them show up also in the GUI that is managed through a hosted web server. Through this combination Cloudmesh can be seamlessly used as command shell or as GUI.

```
  /___| |  _   _  _  _    _ |  |_  _  _  _  _ |  |___
 |  ___| | / \ \| | | |_ / \| | | | |  _/\ \ | | | |
 | |___| |( O )| |_| |  _| \ \_| | | | |_/\ \ | | | |
 \_____|_|\___/ \__,_|\___|_| |_|_| |_|\___|_||__/_| |_|
========================================================
                    Cloudmesh Shell

cm> help

Documented commands (type help <topic>):
==========================================
EOF      defaults  graphviz   keys   metric   py        script  var
banner   dot2      help       label  open     q         storm   verbose
clear    edit      info       list   pause    quit      timer   version
cloud    exec      init       login  plugins  rain      use     vm
count    exp       inventory  man    project  register  user

Cloud Commands
==============
cloud     exp   inventory  list    rain      storm  vm    project
defaults  init  label      metric  register  user   keys
```

Fig. 23 The cloudmesh shell

Fig. 24 Listing the clouds

```
cm> cloud list
+--------------------------+
| Clouds                   |
+--------------------------+
| alamo                    |
| aws                      |
| azure                    |
| devstack_icehouse        |
| hp                       |
| hp_east                  |
| india_eucalyptus         |
| india_openstack_havana   |
| sierra_openstack_grizzly |
+--------------------------+
```

7 Summary

In this chapter, we have described FutureGrid and provided a general overview. In addition, we have analyzed the many projects executed on FutureGrid while paying attention on those requesting and using technologies relevant for big data analysis. Based on the discussion, it is clear that systems such as FutureGrid is extremely complex but provides to its users the benefit to offer multiple services within the same infrastructure. This includes bare metal provisioning. Thus, performance experiments can not only be conducted on virtual machines, but on a variety of IaaS and PaaS environments. Moreover, these experiments can directly be compared to bare metal provisioned services. Hence, users can evaluate what impact such technologies have on their codes. Comparisons of different programming frameworks can be achieved and future activities in regards to efficiency and usability can be deducted. The lessons learned from FutureGrid are motivating a toolkit, Cloudmesh, that currently allows managing virtual machines on a variety of infrastructure as service frameworks. The easy deployment of sophisticated setups with one-click has been validated as part of an infrastructure designed for a MOOC. Furthermore the novel concept of shifting resources [29] between services to support services that need more resources is a significant contribution by Cloudmesh. Image management and creation under security restrictions [10] is furthermore an important aspect. We will continue to develop the Cloudmesh environment and make it available to our users.

Acknowledgements Some of the text published in this chapter is available form the FutureGrid portal. The FutureGrid project is funded by the National Science Foundation (NSF) and is led by Indiana University with University of Chicago, University of Florida, San Diego Supercomputing Center, Texas Advanced Computing Center, University of Virginia, University of Tennessee, University of Southern California, Dresden, Purdue University, and Grid 5000 as partner sites. This material is based upon work supported in part by the National Science Foundation under Grant No. 0910812 [11]. If you use FutureGrid and produce a paper or presentation, we ask you to include the references [11, 27] as well as this chapter. We like to thank Fugang Wang for the development of the framework that allowed us to produce the statistical data and Hyungro Lee for assisting in the creation of the data tables that lead to the creation of Figs. 11 and 12. Furthermore we like to thank Barbara O'Leary for proofreading this paper.

References

1. "Apache Hadoop Project." [Online]. Available: http://hadoop.apache.org
2. "Gartner's 2013 hype cycle for emerging technologies maps out evolving relationship between humans and machines," Press Release. [Online]. Available: http://www.gartner.com/newsroom/id/2575515
3. "Jira ticket system," Web Page. [Online]. Available: https://confluence.atlassian.com/display/JIRAKB/Using+JIRA+for+Helpdesk+or+Support
4. "Map reduce," Wikepedia. [Online]. Available: http://en.wikipedia.org/wiki/MapReduce
5. "Rt: Request tracker," Web Page. [Online]. Available: http://www.bestpractical.com/rt/
6. "Twister: Iterative mapreduce," Web Page. [Online]. Available: http://www.iterativemapreduce.org
7. W. Barth, *Nagios. System and Network Monitoring*, u.s. ed ed. No Starch Press, 2006. [Online]. Available: http://www.amazon.de/gp/redirect.html%3FASIN=1593270704%26tag=ws%26lcode=xm2%26cID=2025%26ccmID=165953%26location=/o/ASIN/1593270704%253FSubscriptionId=13CT5CVB80YFWJEPWS02
8. J. Dean and S. Ghemawat, "Mapreduce: Simplified data processing on large clusters," *Commun. ACM*, vol. 51, no. 1, pp. 107–113, Jan. 2008. [Online]. Available: http://doi.acm.org/10.1145/1327452.1327492

9. J. Diaz, G. von Laszewski, F. Wang, and G. C. Fox, "Abstract Image Management and Universal Image Registration for Cloud and HPC Infrastructures," in *IEEE Cloud 2012*, Honolulu, Jun. 2012. [Online]. Available: http://cyberaide.googlecode.com/svn/trunk/papers/12-cloud12-imagemanagement/vonLaszewski-12-IEEECloud2012.pdf

10. J. Diaz, G. von Laszewski, F. Wang, A. J. Younge, and G. C. Fox, "FutureGrid Image Repository: A Generic Catalog and Storage System for Heterogeneous Virtual Machine Images," in *Third IEEE International Conference on Coud Computing Technology and Science (CloudCom2011)*, Athens, Greece, 12/2011 2011, paper, pp. 560–564. [Online]. Available: http://cyberaide.googlecode.com/svn/trunk/papers/11-cloudcom11-imagerepo/vonLaszewski-draft-11-imagerepo.pdf

11. G. C. Fox, G. von Laszewski, J. Diaz, K. Keahey, J. Fortes, R. Figueiredo, S. Smallen, W. Smith, and A. Grimshaw, *Contemporary HPC Architectures*, draft ed., 2012, ch. FutureGrid - a reconfigurable testbed for Cloud, HPC and Grid Computing. [Online]. Available: http://cyberaide.googlecode.com/svn/trunk/papers/pdf/vonLaszewski-12-fg-bookchapter.pdf

12. Gregor, "Cloudmesh on Github," Web Page. [Online]. Available: http://cloudmesh.github.io/cloudmesh/

13. S. Krishnan and G. von Laszewski, "Using hadoop on futuregrid," Web Page, Manual, 2013. [Online]. Available: http://futuregrid.github.io/manual/hadoop.html

14. "The Network Impairments device is Spirent XGEM," 2012. [Online]. Available: http://www.spirent.com/Solutions-Directory/ImpairmentsGEM.aspx?oldtab=0&oldpg0=2

15. S. Krishnan, M. Tatineni, and C. Baru, "myHadoop - Hadoop-on-Demand on Traditional HPC Resources," Tech. Rep., 2011. [Online]. Available: http://www.sdsc.edu/~allans/MyHadoop.pdf

16. G. K. Lockwood, "myhadoop 2." [Online]. Available: https://github.com/glennklockwood/myhadoop

17. M. L. Massie, B. N. Chun, and D. E. Culler, "The Ganglia Distributed Monitoring System: Design, Implementation, and Experience," in *Journal of Parallel Computing*, April 2004.

18. J. Qiu, "Course: Fall 2013 P434 Distributed Systems Undergraduate Course." [Online]. Available: https://portal.futuregrid.org/projects/368

19. ——, "Spring 2014 CSCI-B649 Cloud Computing MOOC for residential and online students." [Online]. Available: https://portal.futuregrid.org/projects/405

20. L. Ramakrishnan, "FRIEDA: Flexible Robust Intelligent Elastic Data Management." [Online]. Available: https://portal.futuregrid.org/projects/298

21. "ScaleMP," 2012. [Online]. Available: http://www.scalemp.com/

22. S. Smallen, K. Ericson, J. Hayes, and C. Olschanowsky, "User-level grid monitoring with inca 2," in *Proceedings of the 2007 workshop on Grid monitoring*, ser. GMW '07. New York, NY, USA: ACM, 2007, pp. 29–38. [Online]. Available: http://doi.acm.org/10.1145/1272680.1272687

23. G. von Laszewski, "Cmd3," Github Documentation and Code. [Online]. Available: http://cloudmesh.futuregrid.org/cmd3/

24. ——, "Workflow Concepts of the Java CoG Kit," *Journal of Grid Computing*, vol. 3, pp. 239–258, Jan. 2005. [Online]. Available: http://cyberaide.googlecode.com/svn/trunk/papers/anl/vonLaszewski-workflow-taylor-anl.pdf

25. G. von Laszewski, J. Diaz, F. Wang, and G. C. Fox, "Comparison of Multiple Cloud Frameworks," in *IEEE Cloud 2012*, Honolulu, HI, Jun. 2012. [Online]. Available: http://cyberaide.googlecode.com/svn/trunk/papers/12-cloud12-cloudcompare/laszewski-IEEECloud2012_id-4803.pdf

26. G. von Laszewski, I. Foster, J. Gawor, and P. Lane, "A Java Commodity Grid Kit," *Concurrency and Computation: Practice and Experience*, vol. 13, no. 8–9, pp. 645–662, 2001. [Online]. Available: http://cyberaide.googlecode.com/svn/trunk/papers/anl/vonLaszewski-cog-cpe-final.pdf

27. G. von Laszewski, G. C. Fox, F. Wang, A. J. Younge, Kulshrestha, G. G. Pike, W. Smith, J. Voeckler, R. J. Figueiredo, J. Fortes, K. Keahey, and E. Deelman, "Design of the FutureGrid Experiment Management Framework," in *Proceedings of Gateway Computing Environments 2010 (GCE2010) at SC10*. New Orleans, LA: IEEE, Nov. 2010. [Online]. Available: http://cyberaide.googlecode.com/svn/trunk/papers/10-FG-exp-GCE10/vonLaszewski-10-FG-exp-GCE10.pdf

28. G. von Laszewski, M. Hategan, and D. Kodeboyina, *Workflows for E-science: Scientific Workflows for Grids*. Secaucus, NJ, USA: Springer-Verlag New York, Inc., 2007, ch. Grid Workflow with the Java CoG Kit. [Online]. Available: http://cyberaide.googlecode.com/svn/trunk/papers/anl/vonLaszewski-workflow-book.pdf

29. G. von Laszewski, H. Lee, J. Diaz, F. Wang, K. Tanaka, S. Karavinkoppa, G. C. Fox, and T. Furlani, "Design of an Accounting and Metric-based Cloud-shifting and Cloud-seeding Framework for Federated Clouds and Bare-metal Environments," in *Proceedings of the 2012 Workshop on Cloud Services, Federation, and the 8th Open Cirrus Summit*, ser. FederatedClouds '12. New York, NY, USA: ACM, 2012, pp. 25–32.

30. G. von Laszewski and X. Yang, "Virtual cluster with slurm," Github repository. [Online]. Available: https://github.com/cloudmesh/cluster

31. A. J. Younge, R. Henschel, J. T. Brown, G. von Laszewski, J. Qiu, and G. C. Fox, "Analysis of Virtualization Technologies for High Performance Computing Environments," in *Proceedings of the 4th International Conference on Cloud Computing (CLOUD 2011)*. Washington, DC: IEEE, July 2011, pp. 9–16. [Online]. Available: http://cyberaide.googlecode.com/svn/trunk/papers/10-fg-hypervisor/10-fg-hypervisor.pdf

Cloud Networking to Support Data Intensive Applications

Maurício Tsugawa, Andréa Matsunaga, and José A.B. Fortes

Abstract Cloud computing requires a complex networking subsystem in order to offer on-demand access to a pool of computing resources. Communication among resources (physical or virtual servers, storage, network, instruments, services, and applications) needs to be dynamically adapted to constantly changing cloud environments. This chapter looks into the available network infrastructure and technologies, the use of public and private networks in clouds, methods to simplify management of those networks to support data intensive applications, and employment of such methods in practical use cases.

1 Introduction

In cloud environments where requirements change constantly, a complex networking subsystem needs to be managed to satisfy requests from multiple users. From a cloud provider's perspective, a large pool of shared resources needs to be interconnected and appropriately partitioned so that activities among different users are sufficiently isolated. From a users' perspective, the appropriate set of resources and services, potentially across multiple providers and geographical locations, needs to be interconnected while balancing functionality, performance, and cost. A large number of networking technologies and techniques are applied in cloud computing to (a) interconnect resources within a datacenter, (b) enable scalable and shared storage, (c) isolate the resources allocated for different users, (d) allow users to scale-out (expand local capacity using cloud resources), and (e) establish multi-cloud systems. This chapter discusses fundamental networking technologies and application case studies for efficient intra-cloud networking and scale-out of virtual clusters across multiple providers as needed to support data intensive applications in multi-cloud environments.

M. Tsugawa (✉) • A. Matsunaga • J.A.B. Fortes
Advanced Computing and Information Systems Laboratory, Department of Electrical and Computer Engineering, University of Florida, LAR 339, Gainesville, FL 32611-6200, USA
e-mail: tsugawa@acis.ufl.edu; ammatsun@acis.ufl.edu; fortes@acis.ufl.edu

© Springer Science+Business Media New York 2014   61
X. Li, J. Qiu (eds.), *Cloud Computing for Data-Intensive Applications*,
DOI 10.1007/978-1-4939-1905-5_3

2   Building Blocks and Technologies for Cloud Networking

We start by reviewing network infrastructure building blocks and technologies that are frequently found in cloud environments.

2.1   Datacenter Networking

Gigabit Ethernet (GbE) [1] and 10-Gigabit Ethernet (10 GbE) [2] technologies are most commonly deployed in datacenters to connect servers, offering transmission rates of 1 and 10 Gbps respectively. As of 2014, higher rate technologies (i.e., 40 and 100 GbE) are typically used in aggregation links and inter-switch communication due to their high per-port cost. Ethernet is also popular in Infrastructure-as-a-Service (IaaS) environments, since many Ethernet devices such as network interface cards (NICs) are emulated in software by virtual machine monitors (VMMs) to offer connectivity to virtual machines (VMs).

A popular low-latency and high-throughput technology for high-performance computing is InfiniBand [3]. Infiniband can increase the performance of distributed applications by offering low latency communication (on the order of microseconds) and remote direct memory access (RDMA) capability. InfiniBand adoption in cloud environments is lower compared to Ethernet due to (1) higher cost, (2) increased difficulty in writing applications due to lack of "sockets" APIs—when IP over InfiniBand is used, performance advantage of InfiniBand is lost with overheads, and (3) limited virtualization support—VMMs are currently unable to efficiently manage the sharing of InfiniBand devices among multiple VMs.

2.2   Storage Area Network (SAN)

Storage Area Networks typically consist of a large number of storage devices (servers and disks) offering shared storage among multiple computers. A SAN provides network access to data at disk-block level so that storage partitions appear as directly attached storage devices to operating systems. Fibre Channel (FC) [4] is the most common SAN technology currently deployed in data centers. However, in order to reduce datacenter operation cost, the use of LAN technologies for storage networking is also popular. To do so, many protocols that map storage operations into regular network messages were developed, such as the Internet Small Computer System Interface (iSCSI) [5] (SCSI commands over IP networks), Fibre Channel over Ethernet (FCoE) [6] (FC frames over Ethernet), and iSCSI extensions for RDMA (iSER) [7] (iSCSI over InfiniBand).

2.3 Network Protocol Stack

The design and implementation of computer network systems can be related to the Open Systems Interconnection (OSI) conceptual model [8]. While not all seven layers can be clearly identified in all embodiments, many technologies refer to lower layers when explaining how they work. For example, layer-2 (L2) network refers to a broadcast domain—all nodes within the domain can reach each other through broadcasts, and to communicate with nodes outside the domain, layer-3 (L3) or routing services are needed (Fig. 1 shows the most used OSI layers).

When a network message flows through a protocol stack, control information is added in each layer of the stack, resulting in a final message that consists of multiple envelopes. This process, known as encapsulation, is also used for protocol matching (e.g., iSCSI, and FCoE) and network link virtualization (e.g., IP in IP tunneling [9], and Generic Routing Encapsulation [10]).

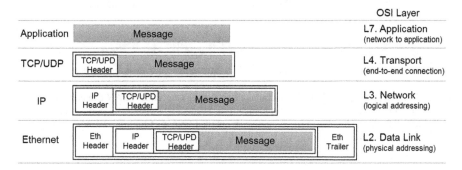

Fig. 1 TCP/IP over Ethernet stack encapsulation

2.4 Local Area Network Partitioning

Ethernet LANs are, by concept, broadcast networks—i.e., every node connected to an Ethernet LAN receives all transmitted network frames. The broadcast model was broken when Ethernet switches were introduced. Switches avoid broadcasts of every frame by learning about the devices connected in each switch port via their Media Access Control (MAC) address identifications. Switches inspect the Ethernet headers of transmitted frames, and based on the destination MAC address, decide to which port(s) a frame should be forwarded. Broadcasts are still used during learning process. The information about devices connected in each port of a switch expires periodically in order to accommodate changes in the network (e.g., a device being connected or being removed). To allow the coexistence of multiple broadcast domains, a capability of restricting broadcast traffic to a group of ports was developed, enabling what is known as Virtual Local Area Network (VLAN) [11]. A VLAN is essentially an Ethernet broadcast domain restricted to a group of switch ports. To support VLANs, the original Ethernet frame was extended to include a 4-byte VLAN tag. A switch port can be configured in access mode (connected to a single specific VLAN), or trunk mode (carries traffic of multiple VLANs). Switches guarantee that VLANs are isolated from each other, and many cloud systems use VLANs to offer isolation among VMs that belong to different tenants (Fig. 2).

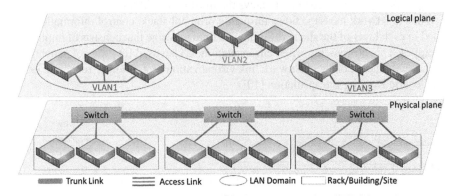

Fig. 2 VLAN-aware network. Only machines that belong to the same VLAN can communicate. VLAN tags are inserted and removed automatically, as needed, by switches for ports configured in access mode. Ports configured in trunk mode carry tagged frames of multiple VLANs allowing a VLAN to span multiple switches

2.5 Virtual Private Network (VPN)

VPN [12] is a technology used to securely connect remote network sites (site-to-site or LAN-to-LAN configuration) or a machine to a network site (user-to-LAN configuration) using a public and shared network (e.g., the Internet) as transport. VPN technology has been developed with the goal of connecting private networks without the need for expensive dedicated connections. VPN is commonly used for inter-cloud communication—i.e., establish connectivity among resources in different clouds and tenant's on-premise private networks.

The basic concepts behind the VPN technology are encapsulation, tunneling, and encryption. VPN works at the IP layer and packets that need to cross LAN boundaries are routed by VPN gateways or firewalls through encrypted tunnels. In the case of a machine accessing a remote LAN, the VPN client software running on the machine opens an encrypted tunnel to the target network VPN gateway. In site-to-site operation, VPN gateways establish the necessary tunnels and transparently handle VPN traffic for participating machines (Fig. 3).

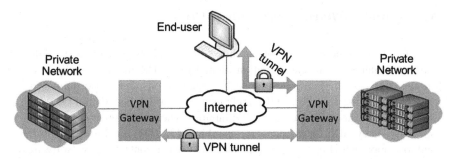

Fig. 3 Site-to-site VPN and user-to-LAN VPN. In site-to-site configuration, VPN firewalls establish an encrypted tunnel where packets between machines in different private networks will flow. In user-to-LAN VPN, a machine establishes an encrypted tunnel to VPN firewall to gain access to a private network

2.6 Virtual Networks and Overlay Networks

Virtual networking systems expose services that are compatible with known physical networks, typically at layers 2 and 3 of the protocol stack. For example, VLAN exposes L2 broadcast domains, while VPN extends private networks through L3 encrypted links. An overlay network is a computer network that runs independently on top of and supported by another network. Overlay networks use services of the infrastructure they depend on, but can expose different interfaces and services. Peer-to-peer (P2P) networks that run on top of IP networks are good examples of overlays. Many virtual networking technologies are also overlays since they depend on networking services offered by the Internet.

The application of virtual and overlay networking on clouds has been a frequent topic of research and development. Representative systems developed in the context of grid and cloud computing include VNET/P [13], VIOLIN [14], SoftUDC VNET [15], ViNe [16,17], IPOP [18], and OCALA [19]. Overlay networks can also address challenges of VM migration across wide-area networks, as described in [20–25].

2.7 High-Performance Backbones

Good inter-cloud communication is essential to run data intensive applications using multiple resource providers. As of 2014, the state-of-the-art in backbone transmission rate is 100 Gbps. In the USA, 100 Gbps infrastructures are being built by initiatives such as the Internet2 Innovation Platform [26], and the Energy Sciences Network (ESnet) [27].

On top of these backbones, advanced networking and testbed deployment research are being carried out by projects such as Global Environment for Network Innovations (GENI) [28], and FutureGrid [29].

2.8   Software-Defined Networking (SDN)

SDN refers to the emerging network architecture that allows flexible and vendor-independent management and operation of networks. The needed standards and open specifications are being developed by organizations and consortiums (e.g., Internet Engineering Task Force [30], and Open Networking Foundation [31]) with participation of industry and research communities. The most popular specification, adopted by many SDN developers, is OpenFlow [32, 33]. As illustrated by the OpenFlow approach (Fig. 4), the basic idea is to let a control entity (software), which is physically separated from the data plane, to define how the data flows. In other words, it defines how network messages/packets are forwarded and routed, instead of instructing and configuring multiple independent controllers (integrated and running in each individual network component—e.g., switch, router, firewall, and intrusion detection system) as in traditional networks.

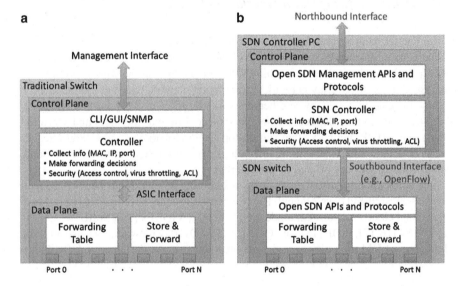

Fig. 4 Control and data plane separation in SDN (B) when compared to a traditional all-in-one switch (A)—control is performed external to the store-and-forward hardware as opposed to an integrated solution in traditional switches. Both control and data planes export programming APIs (northbound and southbound, respectively), which are being standardized

This clean and flexible architecture offered by SDN is extremely appealing for managing networks in a cloud environment. For example, VLAN technology, used in many cloud systems to keep multiple tenants isolated from each other, requires reconfiguration of network components every time a VM is instantiated or shutdown. Manual configuration by network administrators interacting with every affected switch is impractical in a very dynamic cloud environment. Automation is challenging, since it requires understanding of command-line/web interfaces exposed by vendors. Writing programs/scripts to interact with such interfaces is a complex and error prone process, especially because interfaces are different for each vendor and can change after a firmware upgrade. An open and standardized Northbound interface, as illustrated in Fig. 5, will significantly simplify the integration of network functions in cloud middleware: (1) the cloud middleware consults its database to check which VMs (VM1, VM2, and VM3) belong to a particular tenant (Tenant_A), and where those VMs are running (physical host and/or SDN switch that each VM is connected); (2) the cloud middleware invokes a SDN Northbound API to create a VLAN (VLAN_A) and connect the tenant's VM on the new VLAN; and (3) the SDN controller computes the necessary Southbound instructions and contacts the affected SDN switches. Moreover, using SDN mechanisms it would be possible to implement VLAN-like functionality without the 4096 VLAN ID limit of IEEE 802.1Q standard. For example, isolation can be enabled by allowing communication only among MAC addresses of a particular tenant (the SDN controller would compute rules based on MAC addresses).

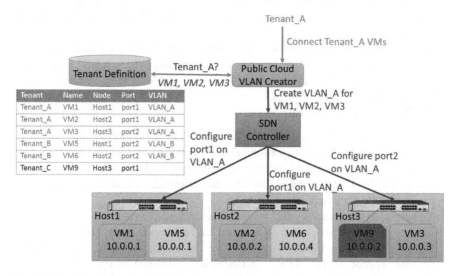

Fig. 5 Example of how cloud middleware uses SDN interfaces to control the network. The figure illustrates that VLAN management can be achieved by simply invoking a Northbound API exposed by a SDN controller. Southbound instructions to achieve the desired functionality are computed and transmitted by the SDN controller

3 Intra-Cloud Networking

Cloud networking, or Network-as-a-Service (NaaS), refers to the delivery of networking functions—e.g., connectivity, security, and management—as a service through the use of cloud resources. This section describes how networking technologies introduced previously are used in cloud management systems and/or cloud middleware to deliver NaaS.

3.1 Commercial IaaS Clouds

The Amazon Elastic Compute Cloud (EC2) [34] pioneered the commercial offering of public cloud services. EC2 IaaS offers scalable pay-as-you-go compute capacity through Amazon Web-Service (AWS) APIs. Details of EC2 internals are not publicly available, so most of technical details published in the literature have been inferred through experiments run by users and researchers and may or may not accurately reflect the actual EC2 practices.

EC2 uses the Xen hypervisor to host VMs that are connected through routed Xen network setup, i.e., the first hop of VMs is the domain zero (Dom0) they are connected to. Through address translations and filtering (L2 and L3), EC2 tries to prevent some network attacks that can be initiated within VMs (e.g., ARP poisoning, and IP spoofing).

EC2 instances are connected via Gigabit Ethernet as experiments in [35] and [36] suggest. The throughput, as reported in [36], between the two EC2 regions in the US is below 300 Mbps. Intra-cloud 10 GbE is available for large instances (e.g., "Cluster Compute 8 Extra Large").

EC2 offers the following networking services:

- Elastic IP: as EC2 instances are assigned private IP addresses that are not routed through the Internet, a mechanism is needed to map public IP addresses to instances that should be visible on the Internet. An elastic IP is a static and public IPv4 address leased by EC2 to a particular cloud user that can be programmatically mapped to an instance.
- Security Groups: groups of EC2 instances (an instance can belong to one or more security groups) to which users can assign firewall rules to control ingress traffic.
- Virtual Private Cloud (VPC): enables users to launch instances in an isolated (private) section of EC2 cloud. Instances are connected in a user-defined IP address range, and can be extended to user's local networks through direct connections using private lines, hardware VPN devices, and software VPN [37,38]. On VPC (EC2) end, Amazon Virtual Private Gateways with two distinct VPN endpoints is used, enabling users to implement redundant VPN tunnels.

Microsoft Windows Azure [39] IaaS offers similar networking services. VMs are assigned private IP addresses, which are mapped to publicly addressable end points through network address and port translations. Azure Virtual Network offers mechanisms for users to have isolated partitions of Azure cloud using preferred private IP ranges, and cross-premise connectivity through hardware and software VPN.

3.2 Open Source IaaS Clouds

Many IaaS cloud software and products were developed, targeting research, private, and public cloud deployments. Two of the most successful software stacks for IaaS cloud management, considering project sizes and deployments, are OpenStack [40] and CloudStack [41]. Both projects expose advanced networking features, services, and interfaces, as discussed in the next subsections.

3.2.1 OpenStack Cloud Software

OpenStack is a project backed by a large community of developers and supported by over 150 companies. The OpenStack architecture is modular, having components with specific functions, each of which is identified by code names (in parenthesis): compute (Nova), object storage (Swift), block storage (Cinder), VM image service (Glance), dashboard (Horizon), identity service (Keystone), and networking (Neutron).

OpenStack Neutron (formerly code-named Quantum) exposes networking services and APIs to define network connectivity among devices from other OpenStack components (e.g., compute). Through Neutron APIs, cloud administrators or tenants can define networks as shown in Fig. 6, which illustrates an advanced scenario—note that a simple flat shared network that is visible to all tenants can be easily defined. Each tenant can have one or more private isolated networks that can also be uplinked to routers. Routers enable communication across private networks and to the external network. The "floating IP" (similar to EC2 elastic IP) functionality is also implemented by routers.

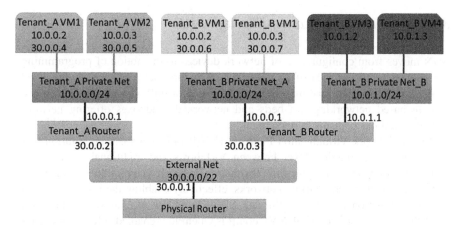

Fig. 6 Example of networking using OpenStack Neutron [43]. In this example, Tenant A has a single private network, while Tenant B operates two independent private networks

Neutron is also architected in a modular fashion, allowing different implementations of networking APIs using the concept of plugins: pluggable back-ends can use a variety of technologies to deliver services defined by the APIs. Notable Neutron plugins include support for basic Linux mechanisms (bridges, VLAN, and Netfilter), OpenFlow (Open vSwitch, NEC OpenFlow), and Cisco physical switches. Plugins for advanced services and APIs are currently under development to enable VPN-aaS, load balancing-aaS, firewall-aaS, intrusion detection system-aaS, etc.

3.2.2   Apache CloudStack Project

CloudStack is a project currently backed by the Apache Software Foundation [42] developers. CloudStack is architected in a nested infrastructure organization, where a set of hosts forms a cluster; one or more clusters connected through a L2 switch in a rack define a pod; a collection of pods in a datacenter becomes a zone; and one or more zones define a region (Fig. 7).

CloudStack allocates and dynamically garbage collects VLANs to manage cloud networks in response to requests through the administration web interface. VLANs can be private or shared (i.e., visible to all users), with isolation within shared VLANs achieved using security groups.

Supported networking services include remote access VPN, firewall, load balancing, elastic IP, virtual private cloud, and network address translations. To implement these services, the CloudStack front-end needs to configure the so called network service providers, which can be a virtual router (a CloudStack system VM, launched and controlled by the CloudStack front-end), or a hardware device (e.g., Cisco or Juniper device). Support for SDN providers are also under development.

3.3   Network Virtualization Through SDN

SDN moves from configuration of network devices to the notion of programming the network, and the idea of a "network" instruction set can be conceptualized (Fig. 8). SDN is a step forward to realize the vision of fully virtualized datacenters, campus-based networking test beds and networked sandboxes offering network virtualization mechanisms to implement NaaS.

Nicira Network Virtualization Platform (NVP) [45] is a software solution that can create an abstraction layer between VM hosts and traditional networks in cloud environments. Through this abstraction layer, it is possible to manage a large number of isolated virtual networks, effectively enabling the implementation of NaaS (isolation is achieved through SDN/OpenFlow mechanisms rather than VLANs). As depicted in Fig. 9, NVP controls OpenFlow-enabled software switches (Open vSwitch) that are available in modern hypervisors (VMware ESX, XenServer, KVM, and Hyper-V), and Open vSwitches deployed in physical or virtual machines

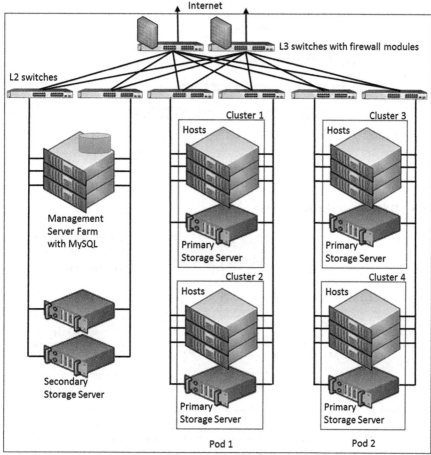

Fig. 7 CloudStack nested infrastructure organization [44]

to work as a gateway to legacy VLAN-based networks. Open vSwitches receive commands from NVP controller cluster, which exposes APIs to users and cloud middleware to program the virtual networks.

4 Inter-Cloud Networking

Section 3 covers systems and tools to manage cloud networking from a single site, with focus on isolation among tenants, and integration of cloud with user's own resources through VPN tunnels. This section introduces representative tools/projects that support networking of cloud resources across multiple providers, cloud systems, and geographical locations.

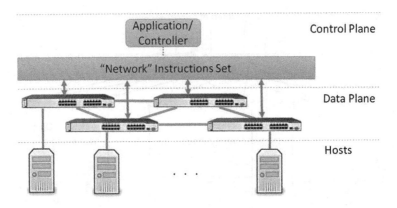

Fig. 8 SDN with a stand-alone controller

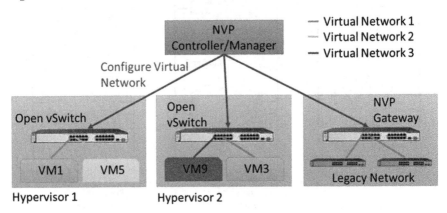

Fig. 9 Nicira Network Virtualization Platform. The NVP controller interacts with SDN-enabled switches to program the network operation

4.1 CohesiveFT VNS-Cubed

VNS-cubed (VNS3) is a commercial VPN-based overlay networking product that can be programmatically managed by end users to establish communication among resources on public clouds, private clouds, and datacenters. A software-defined network is formed by deploying VNS3 managers on locations of interest (public and private clouds), which establish the necessary tunnels to deploy a secure overlay network. Access to the overlay network from external devices can be enabled by establishing IPsec tunnels to an available VNS3 manager Fig. 10. The technology is provider, vendor, application, and operating system neutral, allowing users to federate on-premise and cloud resources with network configuration and management using VNS3 web interfaces.

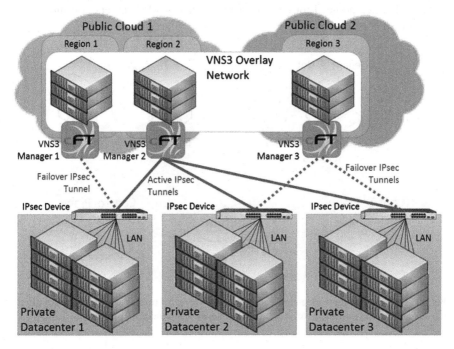

Fig. 10 CohesiveFT VNS3 overview [46] shows VNS3 managers connecting private data centers and different public cloud technologies

4.2 Pertino Cloud Network Engine

Pertino cloud network engine [47] aims to connect users to IT resources independently of the location where they are connected to the Internet. Pertino has built an overlay network on top of the global cloud infrastructure, and the use of network virtualization techniques and programmability of SDNs are translated into an easy-to-use system. The user and network management is inspired in social networks (e.g., Facebook): Pertino users need to create and register devices to a network, and send invitations to other users that are authorized to access the network.

Devices need to have the cloud network engine software installed and running in order to access Pertino networks. As illustrated in Fig. 11 the cloud network engine establishes encrypted tunnels to Pertino servers (closest to the device's Internet connection point) deployed on the cloud. The Pertino data plane is responsible for routing packets, while the Pertino control plane dictates how devices are connected according to users' requests, making the system a cloud-based software-defined network across a WAN. Pertino enables users to create a network of devices (physical or virtual) using a web-based graphical interface, requiring only Internet connectivity, i.e., no need for network devices such as VPN servers or difficult-to-configure VPN software.

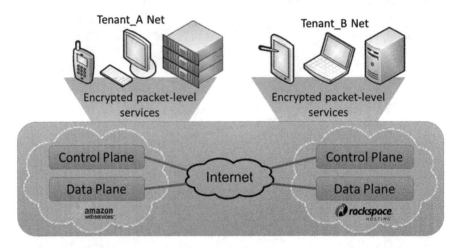

Fig. 11 Pertino cloud network engine conceptual view [47]. An overlay network is deployed on top of a multi-cloud infrastructure, enabling location-aware and social network-inspired SDN

4.3   ViNe Overlay Network Infrastructure

ViNe [16] is a virtual network approach that offers end-to-end connectivity among nodes, even if they are in private networks or guarded by firewalls (firewall traversal is performed transparently to users, applications, and devices). ViNe has been architected to support multiple mutually isolated virtual networks, which can be dynamically configured and managed, thus offering a well-defined security level to users. In terms of construction, ViNe is based on user-level network routing, which creates overlay networks using the Internet infrastructure. A machine running ViNe software becomes a ViNe router (VR), working as a gateway to overlay networks for the machines connected to the same LAN segment. When necessary (e.g., due to network limitations imposed by cloud providers [17]), ViNe can be deployed on all nodes to establish the communication (Fig. 12).

ViNe is flexible in terms of configuration and management, which can be dynamically changed by modifying the VRs operating parameters. VR operating parameters are dynamically changed by a ViNe Management Server, in response to requests by end users or cloud middleware (Fig. 13).

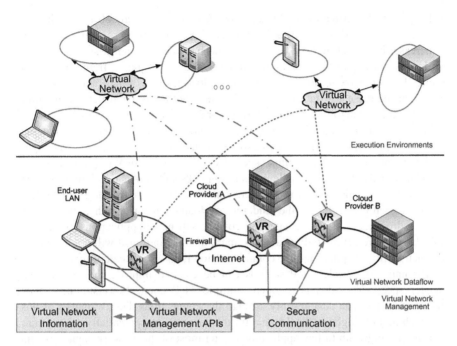

Fig. 12 Virtual Network (ViNe) architecture. Multiple independent virtual networks are overlaid on top of the Internet. ViNe routers (VRs) control virtual network traffic. Management of VNs is accomplished by dynamically reconfiguring VRs

Fig. 13 ViNe Management Architecture. The necessary VR configuration operations are controlled by a ViNe Management Server, in response to requests from users and administrators (or middleware action on behalf of users and administrators)

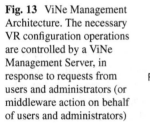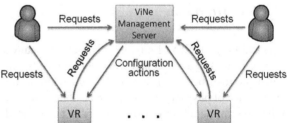

5   Case Studies

5.1   Optimizing Intra- and Inter-Cloud Data Transfer

Intra-cloud data transfer performance depends on how well physical resources are configured and allocated for users in cloud infrastructures. In large datacenters, networks are typically organized as a fat tree of switches, with uplinks often becoming bottlenecks. Keeping highly communicating VMs within a single switch (or rack) is essential to deliver high quality intra-cloud network services. However, network traffic is hard to predict making resource allocation for cloud middleware a challenging task. Virtual Layer 2 (VL2) [48] proposed by Microsoft Research after studying the network traffic of a 1,500-node datacenter, is a promising approach to increase the overall network utilization and balance the load of switch uplinks. While still not popular in cloud environments, the use of jumbo frames (Ethernet frames that can carry up to 9,000 bytes of payload instead of the traditional 1,500 bytes) can increase the data transfer throughput with additional benefit of lower CPU utilization due to fewer CPU interrupts and fragmentation processing.

In the case of inter-cloud data transfer, users need to keep in mind that achieving good TCP performance (most applications do use TCP as transport) over high-latency connections is challenging, especially as bandwidth of WAN links improve to higher speeds. The main challenge is to tune OS and application buffers so that TCP window is appropriate for the latency and available bandwidth. If the buffers are too large, it is possible for the sender to overload the receiver. When the receiver starts to drop packets, TCP congestion control will make applications experience poor data transfer. If the buffers are too small, the data in transit will not be able to completely "fill the pipe" and the communication link will be underutilized.

Alternatively, parallel TCP streams can be used to improve the overall data transfer speed. The idea is to open multiple TCP connections simultaneously and transmit the data concurrently through the connections. Disadvantages of this approach include higher CPU demand for the data transfer, potentially cause unfair sharing of bandwidth (a few applications using most of the network capacity), and potentially cause unnecessary congestion (too many TCP streams).

5.2   VM Migration

Inter- and Intra-cloud VM migration is useful in many scenarios. For example, network utilization of a datacenter can be optimized by migrating VMs within a cloud so that the distribution of network switches uplink utilization becomes balanced; maintenance of physical resources can be done without disrupting workload of users by first migrating all VMs from servers to be serviced elsewhere; make VMs use WAN links with higher available bandwidth by migrating VMs across clouds; and maintaining availability of services by migrating VMs when impending disasters are detected.

VM migration itself is a data intensive activity as the memory state (constantly increasing) and potentially the storage state needs to be transferred through the network. Since VM migration mechanisms were originally designed and implemented for LAN environments, a good intra-cloud network configuration (as described in the previous section) is important to achieve good VM migration performance within a datacenter.

For inter-cloud migration, the ability for the VMs to keep their network configurations intact (e.g., no changes in their IP addresses) is desirable. However, many challenges need to be addressed when VMs migrate over distinct IP subnets. Research has been conducted on addressing these challenges, for example in [20–25]. The use of overlay networks is an attractive solution: if an L2 overlay is established across multiple clouds, VMs can move without network reconfiguration within the L2 overlay; or alternatively, on L3 overlays, overlay routes can be automatically adjusted according to the movement of VMs.

Table 1 summarizes the results obtained when live-migrating VMs of 512 MB in size from Japan to East US (through regular Internet connection), and West US to East US (using the Internet 2—while the backbone has a 10 Gbps capacity, hosts were limited to their local 1 Gbps connections). Experiments migrating concurrently a different number of VMs using the Linux Kernel-based Virtual Machine (KVM) hypervisor were conducted.

Table 1 Number of VMs migrated per hour when migrating concurrently multiple VMs with 512 MB of guest memory

Concurrently migrated VMs	Japan to East US	East US to West US
1	74 VMs/h	194 VMs/h
2	147 VMs/h	378 VMs/h
4	212 VMs/h	612 VMs/h
6	220 VMs/h	654 VMs/h

As the live-migration mechanism utilizes a single TCP connection, the results indicate that the use of parallel TCP streams (indirectly achieved by starting multiple migrations concurrently) is beneficial when moving a large number of VMs. Moreover, the optimal number of concurrent streams is dependent of network conditions. The design, implementation, and evaluation of a feedback-based controller that monitors network conditions and controls the number of VMs to be migrated concurrently can be found in [49].

5.3 Scientific Applications on the Cloud

Scientific applications, in physics, chemistry, biology, astronomy, engineering, and bioinformatics, tend to be mainly computationally or memory intensive, even when making use of large volumes of data. Thus, it has become appealing to use a combination of public and private clouds to quickly setup and run a one-time experiment in a single or multiple clouds without upfront costs in acquiring hardware or to scale-out from a private cloud to other private or public clouds.

To take advantage of the large number of resources available in clouds, scientific applications are parallelized with the use of a supporting communication framework (e.g., Message Passing Interface or MPI, MapReduce, and Grid middleware) that requires all-to-all communication among resources. Technologies presented in the previous sections (e.g., VPN, VLAN, and overlay networks) have been successfully used to connect resources as needed by the applications. When applications are parallelized in a manner that they also become network-intensive, another factor to be considered is the performance of such connections. When comparing clouds to high-performance computing (HPC), in regards to networking infrastructure, two main sources of overhead in cloud systems are the increase of network latency due to the use of virtualization and the increased likelihood that VMs are not always co-located. For example, benchmarks from [50, 51] see increase in network latency from 2 to 60 μs when comparing physical Infiniband with Amazon EC2. Bandwidth measurements reflect the 32 and 10 Gbps capacity. In these studies, network-intensive applications did not scale in the cloud compared to dedicated HPC infrastructures, whereas non-network-intensive applications on EC2 scaled close to the HPC counterpart.

The MapReduce paradigm is one that is proving to be effective in cloud systems by forcing programmers to create idempotent tasks that can be re-executed upon failure and without inter-dependency. Success stories include the CERN ATLAS experiment running Monte Carlo simulations on Google Compute Engine cloud [52], and CloudBLAST [53, 54] experiments running bioinformatics application on FutureGrid and Grid5000 clouds [55]. ATLAS achieved good scalability with 500 workers while making use of PROOF to manage the cluster in a MapReduce fashion, and XRootD to provide access to data in a federated and scalable manner, when the transfer rate over the internet from Tier-2 to Tier-3 is 57 Mbps. CloudBLAST simplified and automated the process of creating a virtual network across all resources by combining the Nimbus contextualization service in IaaS clouds to create ViNe overlay networks and form a Hadoop MapReduce Infrastructure [56]. Good scalability was achieved even across wide-area networks (North America and Europe) as the BLAST [57] bioinformatics application essentially made use of network to distribute the input data as tasks were executed, to transfer keep-alive messages, and to collect the output. In fact, while BLAST efficiently uses cache to deal with the random access to the local genetic database, its output can often be larger than the inputs, requiring its transfer to the user, in case the next step of the pipeline is not also executed on the cloud.

Summary/Conclusions

Networking is a core component of cloud computing that is underdeveloped compared to compute and storage, but has received much attention in recent years. With a Software-Defined Networking approach, many new networking services are being developed and made available on clouds. Still, additional research and development is needed to efficiently support data intensive applications.

According to [58] the global Internet connection speed is 2.9 Mbps, and US users experience, on average, 7.4 Mbps of Internet connection speed. Even with the best Internet connectivity (14 Mbps, on average, in South Korea), it takes over 150 h to transfer 1 TB of data. This means days of

(continued)

waiting time when applications and data need to be transferred to cloud resources before processing, While it is possible to eliminate this waiting time using inter-cloud networking and scale-out mechanisms (i.e., directly attach storage resources of users to clouds), higher bandwidth in the core Internet is essential to better support data intensive applications. Forty and 100 GbE are promising technologies that are currently only available in research networks. For data intensive applications high speed intra-cloud communication is also important, but only available in special and expensive setups (e.g., 10 GbE on Amazon EC2 HPC instances).

Data transfer out of commercial clouds currently cost about $0.10/GB, so applications generating large amounts of data can contribute substantially to the total cost of running applications on the cloud.

Not all data intensive applications are suited for cloud environments. More specifically, those with (1) embarrassingly parallel profile, (2) low I/O data rate, and (3) small output data size, can be efficiently (both in terms of performance and financial cost) executed in cloud environments.

Acknowledgements This work is supported in part by National Science Foundation (NSF) grants No. 0910812, 1234983, 1240171, and the AT&T Foundation. Any opinions, findings and conclusions or recommendations expressed in this material are those of the authors and do not necessarily reflect the views of the NSF, and AT&T Foundation.

References

1. IEEE, "IEEE Std 802.3, 1998 Edition", 1998
2. IEEE, "IEEE Std 802.3, 2005 Edition", 2005
3. InfiniBand Trade Association, [Online], Available: http://www.infinibandta.org
4. Fibre Channel Industry Association, [Online], Available: http://www.fibrechannel.org
5. J. Satran, K. Meth, C. Sapuntzakis, M. Chadalapaka, and E. Zeidner. "Internet Small Computer Systems Interface (iSCSI)", RFC3720, April 2004
6. ANSI, "Information Technology - Fibre Channel - Backbone - 5 (FC-BB-5)", May 2010
7. M. Chadalapaka, H. Shah, U. Elzur, P. Thaler, and M. Ko, "A study of iSCSI extensions for RDMA (iSER)", In Proceedings of the ACM SIGCOMM workshop on Network-I/O convergence: experience, lessons, implications (NICELI '03). ACM, New York, NY, USA, pp. 209–219, 2003
8. J. D. Day and H. Zimmermann. The OSI reference model. Proceedings of the IEEE, 71(12):1334–1340, December 1983
9. W. Simpson, "IP in IP Tunneling," IETF RFC 1853, Oct. 1995
10. D. Farinacci, T. Li, S. Hanks et al., "Generic Routing Encapsulation (GRE)," IETF RFC 2784, Mar. 2000
11. IEEE, "IEEE Std 802.1Q-2005", 2006
12. B. Gleeson, A. Lin, J. Heinanen et al., "A Framework for IP Based Virtual Private Networks," IETF RFC 2764, Feb. 2000

13. L. Xia, Z. Cui, J. R. Lange, Y. Tang, P. A. Dinda, and P. G. Bridges., "VNET/P: bridging the cloud and high performance computing through fast overlay networking", In Proceedings of the 21st international symposium on High-Performance Parallel and Distributed Computing (HPDC '12), ACM, New York, NY, USA, pp. 259–270, 2012

14. P. Ruth, X. Jiang, D. Xu et al., "Virtual distributed environments in a shared infrastructure," IEEE Computer, vol. 38, no. 5, pp. 63–69, 2005

15. M. Kallahalla, M. Uysal, R. Swaminathan, D. E. Lowell, M. Wray, T. Christian, N. Edwards, C. I. Dalton, F. Gittler, "SoftUDC: A Software-Based Data Center for Utility Computing", Computer, v. 37 n. 11, p. 38–46, November 2004

16. M. Tsugawa and J. A. B. Fortes, "A virtual network (ViNe) architecture for grid computing", Proceedings of the 20th international conference on Parallel and distributed processing, p. 148–148, April 25–29, 2006, Rhodes Island, Greece

17. M. Tsugawa, A. Matsunaga, and J. A. B. Fortes, "User-level virtual network support for sky computing", In Procs. 5th IEEE e-Science, pages 72–79, 2009

18. A. Ganguly, A. Agrawal, P. O. Boykin, and R. Figueiredo, "IP over P2P: enabling self-configuring virtual IP networks for grid computing", Proceedings of the 20th international conference on Parallel and distributed processing, p. 49–49, April 25–29, 2006, Rhodes Island, Greece

19. D. Joseph, J. Kannan, A. Kubota, K. Lakshminarayanan, I. Stoica, and K. Wehrle, "OCALA: an architecture for supporting legacy applications over overlays", Proceedings of the 3rd conference on Networked Systems Design & Implementation, p. 20–20, May 08–10, 2006, San Jose, CA

20. H. Fang, T. V. Lakshman, M. Sarit et al., "Enhancing dynamic cloud-based services using network virtualization," SIGCOMM Compute. Commun. Rev., vol. 40, no. 1, pp. 67–74, 2010

21. E. Silvera, G. Sharaby, D. Lorenz et al., "IP mobility to support live migration of virtual machines across subnets," in Proc SYSTOR 2009: The Israeli Experimental Systems Conference, Haifa, Israel, 2009

22. H. Watanabe, T. Ohigashi, T. Kondo et al., "A Performance Improvement Method for the Global Live Migration of Virtual Machine with IP Mobility," in Proc. 5th Int. Conf. on Mobile Computing and Ubiquitous Networking, Seattle, 2010, pp. 194–199

23. Q. Li, J. Huai, J. Li et al., "HyperMIP: Hypervisor Controlled Mobile IP for Virtual Machine Live Migration across Networks," in Proc. 11th IEEE High Assurance Systems Engineering Symp., 2008, pp. 80–88

24. V. Manetti, R. Canonico, G. Ventre et al., "System-Level Virtualization and Mobile IP to Support Service Mobility," in Proc. Int. Conf. on Parallel Processing Workshops, 2009, pp. 243–248

25. M. Tsugawa, P. Riteau, A. Matsunaga, and J. Fortes, "User-level virtual networking mechanisms to support virtual machine migration over multiple clouds," In IEEE Intl Workshop on Management of Emerging Networks and Services, Miami, Florida, 2010, pp. 588–592

26. Internet2 Network, [Online], Available: http://www.internet2.edu/network

27. Energy Sciences Network, [Online], Available: http://www.es.net

28. geni - Exploring Networks of the Future, [Online], Available: http://www.geni.net

29. FutureGrid Project, [Online], Available: http://www.futuregrid.org

30. Internet Engineering Task Force, [Online], Available: http://www.ietf.org

31. Open Networking Foundation, [Online], Available: http://www.opennetworking.org

32. N. McKewon, T. Anderson, H. Balakrishnan, et al., "OpenFlow: Enabling Innovation in Campus Networks," White Paper, March 2008

33. OpenFlow, [Online], Available: http://www.openflow.org

34. Amazon Elastic Compute Cloud, [Online], Available: http://aws.amazon.com/ec2

35. G. Wang and T. S. E. Ng, "The Impact of Virtualization on Network Performance of Amazon EC2 Data Center", in Proceedings of IEEE INFOCOM 2010, San Diego, CA, March 2010

36. Serhiy Topchiy, "Testing Amazon EC2 Network Speed", [Online], Available: http://epamcloud. blogspot.com/2013/03/testing-amazon-ec2-network-speed.html

37. Steve Morad, "Amazon Virtual Private Cloud Connectivity Options", White Paper, October 2012
38. Amazon AWS, "Extend Your IT Infrastructure with Amazon Virtual Private Cloud", White Paper, January 2010
39. Windows Azure, [Online], Available: http://www.windowsazure.com
40. OpenStack Cloud Software, [Online], Available: http://www.openstack.org
41. Apache CloudStack, [Online], Available: http://www.cloudstack.apache.org
42. Apache Software Foundation, [Online], Available: http://apache.org
43. OpenStack Foundation, "OpenStack Networking Administration Guide", 2013
44. Apache CloudStack, "CloudStack Administrator's Guide", 2013
45. Nicira, "It's Time to Virtualize the Network - Network Virtualization for Cloud Data Centers", White Paper, 2012
46. CohesiveFT, "Cloud Security Best Practices. Part I: Using VNS3 Overlay Network with Private, Public, and Hybrid Clouds", Technical White Paper, 2013
47. Timothy P. Morgan, "Pertino uncloaks, fires 'cloud network engine' at Cisco", The Register, February 2013
48. A. Greenberg, J. R. Hamilton, N. Jain, S. Kandula, C. Kim, P. Lahiri, D. A. Maltz, P. Patel, and S. Sengupta, "VL2: a scalable and flexible data center network", In Proceedings of the ACM SIGCOMM 2009 conference on Data communication (SIGCOMM '09). ACM, New York, NY, USA, pp. 51–62, 2009
49. T. S. Kang, M. Tsugawa, T. Hirofuchi, J. Fortes, "Reducing the Migration Times of Multiple VMs on WANs using a Feedback Controller", The 18th IEEE Workshop on Dependable Parallel, Distributed and Network-Centric Systems, 2013
50. E. Walker, "Benchmarking Amazon EC2 for high-performance scientific computing", Usenix Login, 2008, v. 33(5), pp. 18–23
51. P. Mehrotra, J. Djomehri, S. Heistand, R. Hood, H. Jin, A. Lazanoff, S. Saini, and R. Biswas, "Performance evaluation of Amazon Elastic Compute Cloud for NASA high-performance computing applications," Concurrency Computat.: Pract. Exper.. 2013. doi: 10.1002/cpe.3029
52. S. Panitkin, and A. Hanushevsky, "ATLAS Experiment and GCE", Google IO Conference, May 15–17, 2013. http://www.youtube.com/watch?v=LRkLQw5rLy8
53. A. Matsunaga, M. Tsugawa, and J. Fortes, "CloudBLAST: Combining MapReduce and Virtualization on Distributed Resources for Bioinformatics Applications", IEEE eScience 2008, pp. 229, 222, 2008
54. K. Keahey, M. Tsugawa, A. Matsunaga, J.A.B. Fortes, "Sky Computing." Internet Computing, IEEE, vol. 13, no. 5, p. 43–51, Sept.-Oct. 2009
55. A. Matsunaga, P. Riteau, M. Tsugawa, J.A.B. Fortes, "Crosscloud Computing," Advances in Parallel Computing, High Performance Computing: From Grids and Clouds to Exascale, volume 20, 2011, pp. 109–123
56. Apache Hadoop project. http://hadoop.apache.org
57. S.F. Altschul, W. Gish, W. Miller, E.W. Myers, and D.J. Lipman., "Basic Local Alignment Search Tool", Journal of Molecular Biology, 1990, v. 215(3), pp. 403–410
58. Akamai, "The State of Internet Report", Fourth Quarter, 2012

IaaS Cloud Benchmarking: Approaches, Challenges, and Experience

Alexandru Iosup, Radu Prodan, and Dick Epema

Abstract Infrastructure-as-a-Service (IaaS) cloud computing is an emerging commercial infrastructure paradigm under which clients (users) can lease resources when and for how long needed, under a cost model that reflects the actual usage of resources by the client. For IaaS clouds to become mainstream technology and for current cost models to become more clientfriendly, benchmarking and comparing the non-functional system properties of various IaaS clouds is important, especially for the cloud users. In this article we focus on the IaaS cloud-specific elements of benchmarking, from a user's perspective. We propose a generic approach for IaaS cloud benchmarking, discuss numerous challenges in developing this approach, and summarize our experience towards benchmarking IaaS clouds. We argue for an experimental approach that requires, among others, new techniques for experiment compression, new benchmarking methods that go beyond blackbox and isolated-user testing, new benchmark designs that are domain-specific, and new metrics for elasticity and variability.

1 Introduction

Infrastructure-as-a-Service (IaaS) clouds are becoming a rich and active branch of commercial ICT services. Users of IaaS clouds can provision "processing, storage, networks, and other fundamental resources" [51] on-demand, that is, when needed, for as long as needed, and paying only for what is actually consumed. For the past five years, commercial IaaS clouds such as Amazon's EC2 have gained an increasing user base, from small and medium businesses [3] to scientific HPC users [14, 43]. However, the increased adoption of clouds and perhaps even the pricing models depend on the ability of (prospective) cloud users to benchmark and compare

A. Iosup (✉) • D. Epema
Delft University of Technology, EEMCS-Room HB07.050,
Mekelweg 4, 2628 CD Delft, The Netherlands
e-mail: A.Iosup@tudelft.nl; D.H.J.Epema@tudelft.nl

R. Prodan
Parallel and Distributed Systems, University of Innsbruck, Innsbruck, Austria
e-mail: Radu@dps.uibk.ac.at

© Springer Science+Business Media New York 2014   83
X. Li, J. Qiu (eds.), *Cloud Computing for Data-Intensive Applications*,
DOI 10.1007/978-1-4939-1905-5_4

commercial cloud services. In this chapter, we investigate the IaaS cloud-specific elements of benchmarking from the user perspective.

An important characteristic of IaaS clouds is good performance, which needs to be ensured on-demand and sustained when needed over a long period of time. However, as we have witnessed happening with several other new technologies while still in their infancy, notably with grid computing in the 1990s, it is likely that IaaS clouds will also undergo a period of changing performance management practices. In particular, we foresee that the branch of performance management that focuses on measuring the performance will evolve from traditional practices to meet the requirements of cloud operators and customers.

Benchmarking is a traditional approach to verify that the performance of a system meets the requirements. When benchmarking results are published, for example through mixed consumer-provider organizations such as SPEC and TPC, the consumers can easily compare products and put pressure on the providers to use best-practices and perhaps lower costs. Currently, the use of clouds is fragmented across many different application areas, including hosting applications, media, games, and web sites, E-commerce, On-Demand Workforce and CRM, high-performance computing, search, and raw resources for various usage. Each application area has its own (de facto) performance standards that have to be met by commercial clouds, and some have even developed benchmarks (e.g., BioBench [1] for Bioinformatics and RUBiS [63] for online business).

For IaaS clouds, we conjecture that the probable characteristics of current and near-future workloads can be derived from three major trends emerging from the last decade of grid and large-scale computing. First, individual jobs are now predominantly split into smaller compute or data-intensive tasks (many tasks [58]); there are almost no tightly coupled parallel jobs. Second, the duration of individual tasks is diminishing with every year; few tasks are still running for longer than 1 h and a majority require only a few minutes to complete. Third, compute-intensive jobs are split either into bags-of-tasks (BoTs) or DAG-based workflows, but data-intensive jobs may use a variety of programming models, from MapReduce to general dataflow.

Cloud benchmarking is not a straightforward application of older benchmarking techniques. In the past, there have been several large-scale computing environments that have similarities with clouds. Already decades ago, institutes such as CERN and the IBM T.J. Watson Research Center had large numbers of mainframes (using virtualization through the Virtual Machine operating system!) that also used multi-tenancy across their departments. Similarly, some vendors had large-scale installations for paid use by customers through Remote Job Entry facilities. In these environments, benchmarking and capacity planning were performed in close collaboration between owners and customers. An important difference, and advantage, for customers wishing to benchmark their prospective computing environments is that they can simply use access by credit card to deploy and benchmark their applications in the cloud: clouds do not only offer elasticity on demand, they also offer (resources for) capacity planning and benchmarking on demand. The new challenge is that customers will have to gain, through benchmarking, sufficient trust in the performance, the elasticity, the stability, and the resilience of clouds, to rely on them for the operation of their businesses. As a matter of fact, cloud customers may want to benchmark both when migrating to the cloud, and, after migration, to assess continuously the operation of their applications in the cloud. Thus, of great importance is the ability of cloud benchmarks to allow users to gain trust without requiring long setups and costly operation.

We discuss in this chapter a focused, community-based approach to IaaS cloud benchmarking in which the main challenges are jointly identified, and best-practice and experiences can be easily shared. Although we have seen in the past few years numerous approaches to benchmarking and performance evaluation of various systems, there is no unified view of the main challenges facing researchers and practitioners in the field of benchmarking. This chapter aims at providing this unified view and should thus be useful in system procurement and performance management. From traditional benchmarking, the unified view borrows from earlier efforts on benchmarking middleware [8,9], on benchmarking databases [24], on the performance evaluation of grid and parallel-system schedulers [10, 15, 20, 35], and on benchmarking systems in general [2, 44].

The unified view includes a generic architecture for IaaS cloud benchmarking. We have designed the architecture so that it can be familiar to existing practitioners, yet provide new, cloud-specific functionality. For example, current IaaS cloud operators lease to their customers resources, but leave the selection of resource types and the selection of the lease/release moments as a customer task; because such selection can impact significantly the performance of the system built to use the leased resources, the generic benchmarking architecture must include policies for provisioning and allocation of resources.

In additional to traditional benchmarking elements and the generic architecture, the unified view introduced in this chapter focuses on ten important methodological, system-, workload-, and metrics-related issues. For example, how should cloud-bursting systems, that is, systems that lease resources to complement the customer's own resources, be benchmarked? What could be realistic models for the workloads of IaaS clouds? For IaaS clouds that share resources between multiple customers, how to benchmark their ability to isolate user-environments and thus to prevent performance variability [39]? etc.

This chapter has evolved from a number of regular articles [19, 26, 27] and a series invited talks given by the authors between 2012 and 2014, including talks at MTAGS 2012 [41], HotTopiCS 2013 [32], etc.[1] This work has also benefited from valuable discussion in the SPEC Research Group's Cloud Working Group (see also Sect. 5.1).

---

[1]In inverse chronological order: Lecture at the Linked Data Benchmark Council's Fourth TUC Meeting 2014, Amsterdam, May 2014. Lecture at Intel, Haifa, Israel, June 2013. Lecture at IBM Research Labs, Haifa, Israel, May 2013. Lecture at IBM T.J. Watson, Yorktown Heights, NY, USA, May 2013. Lecture at Technion, Haifa, Israel, May 2013.

The remainder of this chapter is structured as follows. In Sect. 2, we present a primer on benchmarking computer systems. Then, we introduce a generic approach for IaaS cloud benchmarking, in Sect. 3. In Sect. 4, we discuss numerous challenges in developing our and other approaches for cloud benchmarking, with focus on methodological, system-, workload-, and metrics-related issues. We summarize our experience towards benchmarking IaaS clouds in Sect. 5. Our summary focuses on the initiatives of the SPEC Research Group and its Cloud Working Group, of which the authors are members, and our own experience with building models and tools that can become useful building blocks for IaaS cloud benchmarking. Last, we conclude in "Conclusion" section.

2   A Primer on Benchmarking Computer Systems

We review in this section the main reasons for benchmarking and the main elements of the typical benchmarking process, which are basically unchanged since the early 1990s. For more detail, we refer to canonical texts on benchmarking [24] and performance evaluation [44] of computer systems.

2.1   Why Benchmarking?

Benchmarking computer systems is the process of evaluating their performance and other non-functional characteristics with the purpose of comparing them with other systems or with industry-agreed standards. Traditionally, the main use of benchmarking has been to facilitate the informed procurement of computer systems through the publication of verifiable results by system vendors and third-parties. However, benchmarking has grown as a support process for several other situations, which we review in the following.

Use in System Design, Tuning, and Operation Benchmarking has been shown to increase pressure on vendors to design better systems, as has been for example the experience of the TPC-D benchmark [24, Ch. 3, Sec. IV]. For this benchmark, insisting on the use of SQL has driven the wide acceptance of the ANSI SQL-92; furthermore, the complexity of a majority of the queries has lead to numerous improvements in the design of aggregate functions and support for them. This benchmark also led to a wide adoption of the geometric mean for aggregating normalized results [2]. The tuning of the DAS multi-cluster system has benefited from the benchmarking activity of some of the authors of this chapter, developed in the mid-2000s [33]; then, our distributed computing benchmarks exposed various (fixable) problems of the in-operation system.

Use in Training One of the important impediments in the adoption of a new technology is the lack of expertise of potential users. Market shortages of qualified personnel in computer science are a major cause of concern for the European Union and the US. Benchmarks, through their open-source nature and representation of industry-accepted standards, can represent best-practices and thus be valuable training material.

On Alternatives to Benchmarking Several alternative methods have been used for the purposes described earlier in this section, among them empirical performance evaluation, simulation, and even mathematical analysis. We view benchmarking as an empirical evaluation of performance that follows a set of accepted procedures and best-practices. Thus, the use of empirical performance evaluation is valuable, but perhaps without the representativeness of a (de facto) standard benchmark. We see a role for (statistical) simulation [17, 22, 55] and mathematical analysis when the behavior of the system is well-understood and for long-running evaluations that would be impractical otherwise. However, simulating new technology, such as cloud computing, requires careful (and time-consuming) validation of assumptions and models.

2.2 Elements of Benchmarking

Inspired by canonical texts [24, 44], we review here the main elements of a benchmarking process. The main requirements of a benchmark—relevance, portability, scalability, and simplicity—have been discussed extensively in related literature, for example in [24, Ch. 1].

The *System Under Test (SUT)* is the system that is being evaluated. A *white box* system exposes its full operation, whereas a *black box* system does not expose operational details and is evaluated only through its outputs.

The *workload* is the operational load to which the SUT is subjected. Starting from the empirical observation that "20 % of the code consumes 80 % of the resources", simple *microbenchmarks* (*kernel benchmarks* [24, Ch. 9]) are simplified or reduced-size codes designed to stress potential system bottlenecks. Using the methodology of Saavedra et al. [59] and later refinements such as Sharkawi et al. [61], the results of microbenchmarks can be combined with application profiles to provide credible performance predictions for any platform. *Synthetic* and even *real-world (complex) applications* are also used for benchmarking purposes, as a response to system improvements that make microbenchmarks run fast but do not affect the performance of much larger codes. For distributed and large-scale systems such as IaaS clouds, *simple workloads* comprised of a single application and a (realistic) job arrival process represent better the typical system load and have been used for benchmarking [33]. *Complex workloads*, that is, the combined simple workloads of multiple users, possibly with different applications and job characteristics, have started to be used in the evaluation of distributed systems [33, 65]; we see an important role for them in benchmarking.

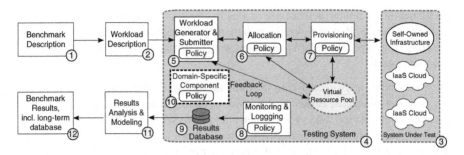

Fig. 1 Overview of our generic architecture for IaaS cloud benchmarking

The *Benchmarking Process* consists of the set of rules, prior knowledge (invariants), and procedures used to subject the SUT to the benchmark workload, and to collect and report the results.

3   A Generic Architecture for IaaS Cloud Benchmarking

We propose in this section a generic architecture for IaaS cloud benchmarking. Our architecture focuses on conducting benchmarks as sets of (real-world) experiments that lead to results with high statistical confidence, on considering and evaluating IaaS clouds as evolving black-box systems, on employing complex workloads that represent multi-tenancy scenarios, on domain-specific scenarios, and on a combination of traditional and cloud-specific metrics.

We introduce in Sect. 4 the main challenges that need to be addressed for our architecture to be realizable. In Sect. 5.2, we discuss a partial implementation of this architecture that has already achieved good results in practice [65].

3.1   Overview

Our main design principle is to adapt the proven designs for benchmarking to IaaS clouds at scale. Thus, we design an architecture that builds on our GrenchMark framework for grid benchmarking [33], as presented in Fig. 1.

The *Benchmarking Process* consists of the set of rules, prior knowledge (invariants), and procedures used to subject the SUT to the benchmark workload, and to collect and report the results. In our architecture, the process begins with the user (e.g., a prospective IaaS cloud user) defining the benchmark configuration, that is, the complex workloads that define the user's preferred scenario (component 1 in Fig. 1). The scenario may focus on processing as much of the workload as possible during a fixed test period or on processing a fixed-size workload as quickly or cheaply as possible. The benchmarking system converts (component 2) the scenario into a set of workload descriptions, one per (repeated) execution. The workload may be defined before the benchmarking process, or change (in particular, increase) during the benchmarking process. To increase the statistical confidence in obtained results, subjecting the SUT to a workload may be *repeated* or the workload may be *long-running*.

After the preparation of the workload, the SUT (component 3 in Fig. 1) is subjected to the workload through the job and resource management services provided by the testing system (component 4, which includes components 5–10). In our benchmarking architecture, the SUT can be comprised of one or several self-owned infrastructures, and public and private IaaS clouds. The SUT provides resources for the execution of the workload; these resources are grouped into a *Virtual Resource Pool*. The results produced during the operation of the system may be used to provide a *feedback loop* from the Virtual Resource Pool back into the Workload Generator and Submitter (component 5); thus, our architecture can implement open and closed feedback loops [60].

As a last important sequence of process steps, per-experiment results are combined into higher-level aggregates, first aggregates per workload execution (component 11 in Fig. 1), then aggregates per benchmark (component 12). The reporting of metrics should try to avoid the common pitfalls of performance evaluation; see for example [2, 23]. For large-scale distributed systems, it is particularly important to report not only the basic statistics, but also some of the outliers, and full distributions or at least the higher percentiles of the distribution (95-th, 99-th, etc.). We also envision the creation of a general database of results collected by the entire community and shared freely. The organization and operation of such a database is within the scope of future work.

3.2 Distinguishing Design Features

We present in the remainder of this section several of the distinguishing features of this architecture.

In comparison with traditional grid environments, commercial IaaS clouds do not provide services for managing the incoming stream of requests (components 5, 6, and 8 in Fig. 1) or the resources leased from the cloud (components 7 and 8). Our architecture supports various policies for provisioning and allocation of resources (components 6 and 7, respectively). In contrast to GrenchMark, our generic cloud-benchmarking architecture also includes support for evolving black-box systems (components 9, 11, and 12), complex workloads and multi-tenancy scenarios (components 1, 2, and 5), domain-specific components (component 10), etc.

Experiments conducted on large-scale infrastructure should be designed to minimize the time spent effectively using resources. The interplay between components 1, 2, and 5 in Fig. 1 can play a non-trivial role in resolving this challenge, through automatic selection and refinement of complex test workloads that balance the trade-off between accuracy of results and benchmark cost; the main element in a dynamic tuning of this trade-off is the policy present in component 5. The same interplay enables multi-tenancy benchmarks.

Several of the possible SUTs expose complete or partial operational information, acting as white or partially white boxes. Our architecture allows exploiting this information, combining results from black-box and white-box testing. Moreover, the presence of the increasingly higher-level aggregations (components 11 and 12 in Fig. 1) permits both the long-term evaluation of the system, and the combination of short-term and long-term results. The policy for monitoring and logging in component 8 allows the user to customize what information is processed and stored in the results database. We conclude that our architecture goes far beyond simple black-box testing.

Supports domain-specific benchmarks is twofold in our architecture. First, components 5–7 support complex workloads and feedback loops, and policy-based resource and job management. Second, we include in our architecture a domain-specific component (component 10) that can be useful in supporting cloud programming models such as the compute-intensive workflows and bags-of-tasks, and the data-intensive MapReduce and Pregel. The policy element in component 10 allows this component to play a dynamic, intelligent role in the benchmarking process.

4   Open Challenges in IaaS Cloud Benchmarking

We introduce in this section an open list of surmountable challenges in IaaS cloud benchmarking.

4.1   Methodological

Challenge 1. Experiment compression.

Long setup times, for example of over a day, and/or long periods of continuous evaluation, for example of more than a day per result, reduce the usefulness of a benchmark for the general user. This is a general problem with any experimental approach, but for IaaS clouds it has the added disadvantage of greatly and visibly increasing the cost of benchmarking. We argue that research is needed to reduce the setup and operational time of benchmarks for IaaS clouds. This can be achieved through reduced input and application sets, a clever setup of the experiments, and sharing of results across the community. We also envision the use of combined experimental approaches, in which real-world experiments are combined with emulation [64, 66] or simulation. Our vision for experiment compression represents an extension of the concept of statistical simulation [17, 22, 55], which has been used for computer architecture studies, to real-world experimentation.

Reduced benchmark input and application sets can be obtained by refining input workloads from real complex workloads, using theoretically sound methods (e.g., statistical models and goodness-of-fit tests). Such reduced benchmark inputs will contrast with traditional synthetic benchmarks, which incorporate many human-friendly parameter values (e.g., "10 % queries of type A, 90 % queries of type B") and thus may lack theoretical guarantees for representativeness.

> **Challenge 2. Beyond black-box testing through testing short-term dynamics and long-term evolution.**

Similarly to multi-cluster grids, which frequently added clusters or individual nodes to the distributed infrastructure, clouds are continuously extended and tuned by their operators. Moreover, commercial clouds such as Amazon EC2 add frequently new functionality to their systems. Thus, the benchmarking results obtained at any given time may be unrepresentative for the future behavior of the system. We argue that IaaS clouds should not be benchmarked only using traditional black-box and even white-box testing, for which the system under test does not change in size and functionality, but also through new benchmarking methods that evaluate the impact of short-term dynamics and long-term evolution. Specifically, short-term dynamics characterize system changes occurring over short periods (at most hours), and long-term evolution characterizes system changes occurring over long periods (months, years).

A straightforward approach to benchmark both short-term dynamics and long-term evolution is to measure the system under test periodically, with judiciously chosen frequencies [40]. However, this approach increases the pressure of the so-far unresolved Challenge 1.

> **Challenge 3. Impact of middleware.**

IaaS clouds are built on several layers of middleware, from the guest operating system of the VM to the data-center resource manager. Each of these layers adds new complexity to testing and possibly also visible or invisible performance bottlenecks. One of the key issues in benchmarking IaaS clouds is to measure the performance of each layer of the middleware in isolation. We argue that a solution for this problem may not be possible under the current assumption of black-box testing, and propose instead to focus on a new methodology that accounts for imprecision in the isolation of root causes of performance.

We believe that good steps towards understanding the performance of various middleware layers can be and have already been taken [8], for example in assessing the impact of virtualization, but that more work is needed to reconcile the results (the situation presented in Challenge 2, where IaaS clouds change over time, may be a source of conflicting experimental results). We have surveyed in our previous work [39, 40] over ten performance studies that use common benchmarks to assess the virtualization overhead on computation (5–15 %), I/O (10–30 %), and HPC kernels (results vary). We have shown in a recent study of four commercial IaaS clouds [39] that virtualized resources obtained from public clouds can have a much lower performance than the theoretical peak, possibly because of the performance of the middleware layer.

4.2 System Properties

Challenge 4. Reliability, availability, and related system properties.

One of the factors affecting the behavior of large-scale systems is the presence of failures, which are likely inevitable at scale. We have found endemic presence of failures in many popular large-scale systems, from grids [36] to DNS and other distributed services [47]. Benchmarking reliability and related systems properties is difficult, not in the least because of Challenge 2.

Challenge 5. Massive scale, multi-site benchmarking.

One of the main product features of IaaS clouds is the promise of seemingly infinite capacity. We argue that benchmarking this promise is difficult, very time-consuming, and very costly. We have seen in our previous work that testing tools can be built to test infrastructures of thousands of cores [33], but performance evaluation tools that work at much larger scale in heterogeneous IaaS clouds have yet to be proven in practice. An important challenge here may be the ability to generate massive-scale workloads.

We have already had experience with companies building *hybrid clouds* [51] out of their own infrastructure and resources leased from IaaS clouds (this process is also referred to as *cloud-bursting*, for example by NIST and Microsoft). Other cloud deployment models require the use of multiple sites, because the application functionality requires it [12], to improve load balancing or performance [62], to fulfill reliability targets, to avoid vendor lock-in [5], etc. We and others [53] expect multi-site cloud use to increase, as more companies, with or without existing computational capacity, try out or even decide to use cloud services. We also expect multi-site cloud use to reuse mechanisms of traditional co-allocation, that is, simultaneous allocation of resources across several organizational components with (wide) geographical spread. We argue that benchmarking across multiple sites raises additional challenges, not in the least the combined availability for testing and scalability of the infrastructure, and the increased cost.

> Challenge 6. Performance isolation.

The negative effects of the interaction between running jobs in a complex workload have been observed in distributed environments since at least the mid-1990s [6]. Following early work [30, 49], we argue that quantifying the level of isolation provided by an IaaS cloud is a new and important challenge.

Moreover, as IaaS clouds become more international, their ability to isolate performance may suffer most during periods of peak activity [30]. Thus, studying the time patterns of performance interference, and their impact on the targets of performance isolation, is worthwhile.

4.3 Workload

> Challenge 7. Realistic yet tunable models of workloads and of system performance.

Statistical workload modeling is the general technique of producing synthetic models from workload traces collected from real-world systems that are statistically similar to the real-world traces, yet may be sufficiently easy to tune for a community of non-expert users. We argue that building such statistical models raises important challenges, from data collection to trace processing, from finding good models to testing the validity of the models. We also see as an open challenge the derivation of statistical performance models, perhaps through linear regression, from already existing measurements.

We envision that IaaS clouds will also be built for specific, even niche application domains, charging premium rates for the expertise required to run specific classes of applications. This is similar to the appearance of domain-specific grids, such as BioGrid, in the early 2000s; and of domain-specific database-related technology, such as transaction-processing and data warehousing solutions, in the early 1990s [24, Ch.1]. We argue that IaaS cloud benchmarking should begin with domain-specific benchmarks, before transiting to general benchmarks.

Besides regular user workloads, most commercial IaaS clouds offer value-adding features such as backup, upgrade, (live) migration, load-balancing, scheduling and message queues, publish/subscribe-based communication services, etc. These value-adding features generate additional, cloud-internal workloads.

Toward building domain-specific benchmarks, we argue for building statistical models of domain-specific or at least programming model-specific workloads. We have conducted in the past extensive research in grid workloads [34], with results in modeling BoTs [38], and in characterizing scientific and engineering workflows [34]. Several studies [11, 21, 46, 68, 69], including our own study of four large MapReduce clusters [13], have focused on characterizing workloads of MapReduce, which is one of the most popular programming models for data processing in the loud. Open challenges in this context are the formulation of realistic models for workflows, MapReduce, and other programming models for data processing. We also find that the many-task programming model [58] is worthwhile for investigation in this context. We also refer to a recent survey of challenges associated with large-scale log analysis [54].

Challenge 8. Benchmarking performance isolation under different multi-tenancy models.

Unlike traditional system benchmarking, where interference of different elements that affect performance—multiple users competing for resources, stressing multiple system resources at the same time—is generally avoided, the expected cloud workload is complex. We argue that for IaaS clouds interference should be expected and benchmarked. Specific focus for this challenge, as an extension of Challenge 8, is to benchmark under a specific multi-tenancy model, from the shared-nothing approach of multi-cluster grids, to shared-hardware and shared-virtualized machine approaches prevalent in today's commercial clouds [48, 52], and possibly others.

4.4 Metrics

Challenge 9. Beyond traditional performance.

Traditional performance metrics—such as utilization, throughput, and makespan—have been defined for statically-sized, homogeneous systems. We have raised in our previous work [35] the challenge of adapting these metrics for distributed on-demand systems, such as the contemporary multi-cluster grids and commercial

IaaS clouds. IaaS clouds raise new challenges in defining cloud-related metrics, such as elasticity [7, 29, 42]; they also require revisiting traditional metrics, including dependability-related [31].

We also argue for revisiting the analysis of results and their refinement into metrics. For example, due to their change over time and imperfect performance isolation, IaaS clouds may require revisiting the concept of variability, beyond the traditional mean (or median) and standard deviation. Our preliminary work [40] on the variability of performance in IaaS and other types of clouds indicates that variability can be high and may vary with time.

Traditionally, system warm-up is excluded from performance evaluation, leaving only the steady-state period of the system for study. However, especially for hybrid and other multi-site cloud architectures, we argue for the need to also measure the transitional period that occurs when a significant fraction of the system resources are in the process of being leased or released.

> **Challenge 10. The cost issue.**

Although cost models were discussed in benchmarking and performance evaluation of both databases and grids, a variety of issues have not been addressed. Specifically, the sub-leasing cost model used in today's commercial IaaS clouds (e.g., Amazon's "spot" instances) provides a new focus. It is also unclear how to define costs for a hybrid cloud infrastructure, especially when the performance of the cloud—throughput, makespan, etc.—does not match the expectation [39, 67]. Last but not least, it is unclear how to define the source of budgets, for example either infrastructural or operational funds, a situation which affects a variety of economic metrics. Early approaches exist [14, 43].

5   Experience Towards IaaS Cloud Benchmarking

In this section, we present our experience in joining a community of experts working on benchmarking IaaS clouds and in conducting independent research on the topic.

5.1   Methodology: The SPEC Cloud Working Group

The SPEC Research Group[2] (RG) is a new group within the Standard Performance Evaluation Corporation (SPEC). Among other activities, the SPEC RG facilitates the interaction between academia and industry by co-organizing the Joint

---

[2]http://research.spec.org/.

ACM/SPEC International Conference on Performance Engineering (ICPE). The
Cloud Working Group[3] (CWG) is a branch of the SPEC RG that aims to develop
the methodological aspects of cloud benchmarking (**Challenges 1–3** in Sect. 4). In
this section we summarize two initiatives of the SPEC RG and CWG.

Beyond Traditional Performance Traditional performance metrics such as utilization and normalized schedule length [50] have been defined for statically
sized systems. Redefining these metrics for dynamic systems, especially in the
context of black-box resources leased from clouds, is a topic of interest for the
CWG (**Challenges 5 and 6**). Beyond performance, the CWG is also interested in
other non-functional metrics, such as elasticity, utility, performance isolation, and
dependability (**Challenges 4, 9, and 15**).

Reproducibility of Experiments (Orthogonal to Our Challenges) Being able to
reproduce experimental results is critical for the validity and lifetime of obtained
results. However, this goal is difficult to achieve when the system under test
is complex, dynamic, or large-scale; IaaS clouds have all these characteristics.
A recent initiative of the RG is to build a repository[4] that can be used to share
experimental results, setups, and other meta-data. Moreover, the call for papers
issued by ICPE 2013 includes a focus on reproducibility of experiments.

5.2 SkyMark: A Framework for IaaS Cloud Benchmarking

We have recently implemented a part of the architecture described in Sect. 3 as our
SkyMark tool for IaaS cloud benchmarking [4]. SkyMark already implements two
of the distinguishing features of our architecture (see Sect. 3.2). First, SkyMark
provide services for managing the incoming stream of requests (jobs) and the
resources leased from the cloud [65]. For the former, SkyMark provides single or
multiple job queues, depending on the configuration of the experiment, and each
queue supports a variety of simple scheduling policies (e.g., FCFS). For the latter,
SkyMark supports several static and dynamic resource provisioning policies.

Second, SkyMark supports complex workloads (**Challenge 7**). Workloads are
split into units. Each unit is defined by the characteristic resource to be stressed (e.g.,
through CPU-intensive jobs), the job arrival pattern (one of uniform, increasing, and
bursty), and the job durations. SkyMark is able, for a given target configuration, to
generate workloads that lead to a user-specified average utilization in the absence of
system overheads.

Using SkyMark, we were able [65] to benchmark three IaaS clouds, including
Amazon EC2. We have used in out benchmarks six provisioning policies and

[3]http://research.spec.org/working-groups/rg-cloud-working-group.html.

[4]ICPE Organizers, Reproducibility repository approved, http://icpe2013.ipd.kit.edu/news/
single_view/article/reproducibility-repository-approved/.

three allocation policies, with provisioning and allocation policies considered either independently or together. We were also able [4] to evaluate, for our OpenNebula private clouds, the interference occurring in various multi-tenancy scenarios (**Challenge 8**).

5.3 Real-World Evaluation of IaaS Cloud Performance

Several of the challenges we formulated in Sect. 4 are the outcome of our previous research conducted from the past three years in benchmarking and understanding the performance of several cloud infrastructures. We summarize in the following some of our main results that motivated this classification.

Challenge 2 We have observed the long-term evolution in performance of clouds since 2007. Then, the acquisition of one EC2 cloud resource took an average time of 50 s, and constantly increased to 64 s in 2008 and 78 s in 2009. The EU S3 service shows pronounced daily patterns with lower transfer rates during night hours (7 PM to 2 AM), while the US S3 service exhibits a yearly pattern with lowest mean performance during the months January, September, and October. Other services have occasional decreases in performance, such as SDB in March 2009, which later steadily recovered until December [40]. Finally, EC2 spot prices typically follow a long-term step function [56].

Challenge 3 Depending on the provider and its middleware abstraction, several cloud overheads and performance metrics can have different interpretation and meaning. In IaaS clouds, resource acquisition is typically the sum of the installation time and boot times, and for Amazon EC2 has a stable value in the order of minutes [39]. Other IaaS providers, such as GoGrid, behave similarly to grids and offer highly variable resource acquisition times, i.e., one order magnitude higher than EC2. In contrast, the Google App Engine (GAE), which offers a higher-level PaaS abstraction, defines the acquisition overhead as the time between the issue of a HTTP request until the HTTP response is returned; the overhead of GAE is in the order of seconds [57], an order of magnitude lower than for EC2. The performance interpretations and differences can have similarly high variations depending on the middleware. The black-box execution approach in IaaS clouds of externally-compiled software encapsulated in VMs generates high degradations from the expected peak performance, up to six to eight times lower than the theoretical maximum of Amazon's "Elastic Compute Unit" (ECU, 4.4 GOPS) [39]. Parallel computing-wise, the performance of today's IaaS is below the theoretical peak of today's dedicated parallel supercomputers even for demanding conveniently parallel applications by 60–70 %. Furthermore, benchmarking the sustained performance of other infrastructures such as GAE is almost prohibited by the sandboxed environment that completely hides the underlying hardware on which the instance is started with no user control, raising the need for **Challenge 6** [57].

The IaaS middleware has a significant impact on the PaaS environments researched on top. An interesting example is Amazon Simple Workflow (SWF)[5] that enables programming and executing workflow applications on the EC2 cloud. Our previous analysis[45] indicates that SWF represents an attractive environment for running traditional workflow applications, especially those consisting of numerous relatively short activities affected by the large grid middleware overheads. In contrast, porting existing grid workflow middleware environments such as ASKALON to the cloud, although effective, exhibit performance losses due to their high middleware stacks required for portability in supporting a wider range of distributed and heterogeneous cluster, grid, and cloud computing infrastructures, as opposed to the SWF restricted, but highly optimized for the EC2 infrastructure.

Challenge 4 With respect to reliability, the payment models and compensations in case of resource failures make clouds a more promising platform than traditional distributed systems, especially grids. Interesting from the reliability point of view are the EC2 spot instances that allow customers to bid on unused capacity and run those instances for as long as their bid exceeds the current spot price. Our analysis on this risk-reward problem between January 2011 and February 2012 demonstrates that spot instances may represent a cheaper but still reliable solution offering up to 99 % availability provided that users make slightly generous bids, such as $0.35 for m1.large instances [56].

Challenge 5 Although multi-cloud environments promise seemingly infinite scalability and performance, our experience revealed that this is not always the case for communicating non-embarrassingly parallel applications. For example, our study on using Amazon EC2 and GoGrid as independent providers[16] illustrated that multi-clouds can help in shortening the makespan for workflow applications which do not require transferring large amounts of data among activities. In situations when data transfers dominate the computation time, the workflow does not benefit from a federation of Clouds and performs better in a single provider configuration. A deeper analysis of the results also reveals that cheap schedules targeting cost minimisation rarely consider federated resources and rather use resources from a single provider. An explanation for this behavior is the hourly based price model offered by the providers, cheap solutions trying to increase resource utilisation instead of launching simultaneous instances.

Challenge 9 Regarding the importance of system warmup, an interesting case is the modern just-in-time (JIT) compilations of Java application running on GAE infrastructure which can boost the performance of interpreted Java byte code by a factor of four in a predictable manner (from the third request onwards in case of GAE) [57].

Challenge 10 The variety of cost models combined with performance variability makes the cloud provider selection a difficult problem for the cloud user. For

---

[5]https://aws.amazon.com/de/swf/.

example, our analysis in [57] shows that computing costs are lower on GAE than in EC2 for very short jobs, mostly due to the cycle-based payment granularity, as opposed to the hourly billing intervals of EC2. The cost model may also vary within one provider. For example, the EC2 reserved instances are cheaper than standard instances if their usage is of about 50 % for for one year reservations, and of about 30 % for three year reservations [56]. In contrast, spot instances on EC2 may represent a 60 % cheaper but equally reliable alternative to standard instances provided that a correct user bet is made [56].

5.4   Statistical Workload Models

Challenge 7 In our previous work, starting from multi-cluster grid traces, we have proposed statistical models of BoTs [38], and characterized BoTs [34, 38] and workflows [34]. We found, notably, that BoTs are the dominant programming model for *compute-intensive* workloads in grids—they account for 80–90 % of both number of tasks and resource consumption. We have characterized and modeled statistically MapReduce workloads, starting from four traces of large clusters, including Google's [13].

A recent trend in *data-intensive* processing is the increasing automation of work, as workflows of inter-dependent tasks. We have modeled conceptually and characterized empirically [28] the workflow of a class of MapReduce applications, where time-stamped data collected from super-nodes in a global-scale deployment of a hundred-million-node distributed computing system are analyzed. This MapReduce use case has challenging features for MapReduce systems such as Hadoop and its successor YARN: small (kilobytes) to large (hundreds of megabytes) data sizes per observed item, very poor (100:1) to excellent (1:1 million) output:input ratio, and short (seconds) to long (hours) individual-job duration. Our findings indicate that traditional benchmarks for MapReduce that rely on single applications, such as PUMA, HiBench, ClueWeb09, and Grid/PigMix, are well complemented by workflow-based benchmarking.

5.5   Open Data: Several Useful Archives

Challenge 7 Workload and operational trace archives are an important tool in developing benchmarks. Although IaaS clouds are new, several online archives could already provide interesting data.

General workload traces for parallel systems and multi-cluster grid are provided by the Parallel Workloads Archive [18] and the Grid Workloads Archive [37], respectively. For an example of domain-specific workload traces, the Game Trace Archive [25] publishes data representative for online gaming.

For operational traces, the Failure Trace Archive [47] and the P2P Trace Archive [70] provide operational information about general and domain-specific (peer-to-peer) distributed systems.

Conclusion

The importance of IaaS cloud benchmarking has grown proportionally to the increased adoption of this technology, from small and medium businesses to scientific HPC users. In contrast to the fragmented field of today, we discuss in this work a more focused, unified approach to IaaS benchmarking, in which the community can join into identifying the main challenges, and then share best-practices and experiences. This approach could greatly benefit (prospective) cloud users with system procurement and performance management.

The unified view includes a generic architecture for IaaS cloud benchmarking, and focuses on ten important methodological, system-, workload-, and metrics-related issues. In our generic architecture, resource and job management can be provided by the testing infrastructure, there is support for black-box systems that change rapidly and can evolve over time, tests are conducted with complex workloads, and various multi-tenancy scenarios can be investigated.

We also discuss four classes of challenges in developing this approach: methodological, system property-related, workload-related, and metric-related. We identify ten main challenges to benchmarking IaaS clouds:

1. Experiment compression. (Methodological)
2. Beyond black-box testing through testing short-term dynamics and long-term evolution. (Methodological)
3. Impact of middleware. (Methodological)
4. Reliability, availability, and related system properties. (System)
5. Massive scale, multi-site benchmarking. Cloud-bursting. Co-allocation. (System)
6. Performance isolation. (System)
7. Realistic yet tunable models of workloads and of system performance. (Workload)
8. Benchmarking performance isolation under different multi-tenancy models. (Workload)
9. Beyond traditional performance. Elasticity and variability. (Metric)
10. The cost issue. Relate with metrics such as utilization, throughput, and makespan. (Metric)

Last, we summarize our experience towards benchmarking IaaS clouds. We have initiated various community-wide efforts via our work in the SPEC Research Group and its Cloud Working Group. We also present here a summary of our work in building models and tools for IaaS cloud benchmarking.

Acknowledgements This work was partially supported by the STW/NWO Veni grant @larGe (11881), EU projects PEDCA and EYE, Austrian Science Fund (FWF) project TRP 237-N23, and the ENIAC Joint Undertaking (project eRAMP).

References

1. Albayraktaroglu K, Jaleel A, Wu X, Franklin M, Jacob B, Tseng CW, Yeung D (2005) Biobench: A benchmark suite of bioinformatics applications. In: ISPASS, IEEE Computer Society, pp 2–9
2. Amaral JN (2012) How did this get published? Pitfalls in experimental evaluation of computing systems. LTES talk, [Online] Available: http://webdocs.cs.ualberta.ca/~amaral/Amaral-LCTES2012.pptx. Last accessed Oct 2012.
3. Amazon Web Services (2012) Case studies. Amazon web site, [Online] Available: http://aws.amazon.com/solutions/case-studies/. Last accessed Oct 2012.
4. Antoniou A, Iosup A (2012) Performance evaluation of cloud infrastructure using complex workloads. TU Delft MSc thesis, [Online] Available: http://repository.tudelft.nl/view/ir/uuid:d8eda846-7e93-4340-834a-de3e4aa93f8b/. Last accessed Oct 2012.
5. Armbrust M, Fox A, Griffith R, Joseph AD, Katz RH, Konwinski A, Lee G, Patterson DA, Rabkin A, Stoica I, Zaharia M (2010) A view of cloud computing. Commun ACM 53(4):50–58
6. Arpaci-Dusseau RH, Arpaci-Dusseau AC, Vahdat A, Liu LT, Anderson TE, Patterson DA (1995) The interaction of parallel and sequential workloads on a network of workstations. In: SIGMETRICS, pp 267–278
7. Brebner P (2012) Is your cloud elastic enough?: performance modelling the elasticity of infrastructure as a service (iaas) cloud applications. In: ICPE, pp 263–266
8. Brebner P, Cecchet E, Marguerite J, Tuma P, Ciuhandu O, Dufour B, Eeckhout L, Frénot S, Krishna AS, Murphy J, Verbrugge C (2005) Middleware benchmarking: approaches, results, experiences. Concurrency and Computation: Practice and Experience 17(15):1799–1805
9. Buble A, Bulej L, Tuma P (2003) Corba benchmarking: A course with hidden obstacles. In: IPDPS, p 279
10. Chapin SJ, Cirne W, Feitelson DG, Jones JP, Leutenegger ST, Schwiegelshohn U, Smith W, Talby D (1999) Benchmarks and standards for the evaluation of parallel job schedulers. In: JSSPP, pp 67–90
11. Chen Y, Ganapathi A, Griffith R, Katz RH (2011) The case for evaluating mapreduce performance using workload suites. In: MASCOTS, pp 390–399
12. Czajkowski K, Foster IT, Kesselman C (1999) Resource co-allocation in computational grids. In: HPDC
13. De Ruiter TA, Iosup A (2012) A workload model for MapReduce. TU Delft MSc thesis, [Online] Available: http://repository.tudelft.nl/view/ir/uuid:1647e1cb-84fd-46ca-b1e1-21aaf38ef30b/. Last accessed Oct 2012.
14. Deelman E, Singh G, Livny M, Berriman JB, Good J (2008) The cost of doing science on the cloud: the Montage example. In: SC, IEEE/ACM, p 50
15. Downey AB, Feitelson DG (1999) The elusive goal of workload characterization. SIGMETRICS Performance Evaluation Review 26(4):14–29
16. Durillo JJ, Prodan R (2014) Workflow scheduling on federated clouds. In: Euro-Par, Springer, LNCS
17. Eeckhout L, Nussbaum S, Smith JE, Bosschere KD (2003) Statistical simulation: Adding efficiency to the computer designer's toolbox. IEEE Micro 23(5):26–38
18. Feitelson D (2013) Parallel Workloads Archive. http://www.cs.huji.ac.il/labs/parallel/workload/
19. Folkerts E, Alexandrov A, Sachs K, Iosup A, Markl V, Tosun C (2012) Benchmarking in the cloud: What it should, can, and cannot be. In: TPCTC, pp 173–188

20. Frachtenberg E, Feitelson DG (2005) Pitfalls in parallel job scheduling evaluation. In: JSSPP, pp 257–282
21. Ganapathi A, Chen Y, Fox A, Katz RH, Patterson DA (2010) Statistics-driven workload modeling for the cloud. In: ICDE Workshops, pp 87–92
22. Genbrugge D, Eeckhout L (2009) Chip multiprocessor design space exploration through statistical simulation. IEEE Trans Computers 58(12):1668–1681
23. Georges A, Buytaert D, Eeckhout L (2007) Statistically rigorous java performance evaluation. In: OOPSLA, pp 57–76
24. Gray J (ed) (1993) The Benchmark Handbook for Database and Transaction Systems, 2nd edn. Mergan Kaufmann
25. Guo Y, Iosup A (2012) The Game Trace Archive. In: NETGAMES, pp 1–6
26. Guo Y, Biczak M, Varbanescu AL, Iosup A, Martella C, Willke TL (2014) How well do graph-processing platforms perform? an empirical performance evaluation and analysis. In: IPDPS
27. Guo Y, Varbanescu AL, Iosup A, Martella C, Willke TL (2014) Benchmarking graph-processing platforms: a vision. In: ICPE, pp 289–292
28. Hegeman T, Ghit B, Capota M, Hidders J, Epema DHJ, Iosup A (2013) The btworld use case for big data analytics: Description, mapreduce logical workflow, and empirical evaluation. In: BigData Conference, pp 622–630
29. Herbst NR, Kounev S, Reussner R (2013) Elasticity in Cloud Computing: What it is, and What it is Not. In: Proceedings of the 10th International Conference on Autonomic Computing (ICAC 2013), San Jose, CA, June 24–28, USENIX, preliminary Version
30. Huber N, von Quast M, Hauck M, Kounev S (2011) Evaluating and modeling virtualization performance overhead for cloud environments. In: CLOSER, pp 563–573
31. Huber N, Brosig F, Dingle N, Joshi K, Kounev S (2012) Providing Dependability and Performance in the Cloud: Case Studies. In: Wolter K, Avritzer A, Vieira M, van Moorsel A (eds) Resilience Assessment and Evaluation of Computing Systems, XVIII, Springer-Verlag, Berlin, Heidelberg, URL http://www.springer.com/computer/communication+networks/book/978-3-642-29031-2, iSBN: 978-3-642-29031-2
32. Iosup A (2013) Iaas cloud benchmarking: approaches, challenges, and experience. In: HotTopiCS, pp 1–2
33. Iosup A, Epema DHJ (2006) GrenchMark: A framework for analyzing, testing, and comparing grids. In: CCGrid, pp 313–320
34. Iosup A, Epema DHJ (2011) Grid computing workloads. IEEE Internet Computing 15(2):19–26
35. Iosup A, Epema DHJ, Franke C, Papaspyrou A, Schley L, Song B, Yahyapour R (2006) On grid performance evaluation using synthetic workloads. In: JSSPP, pp 232–255
36. Iosup A, Jan M, Sonmez OO, Epema DHJ (2007) On the dynamic resource availability in grids. In: GRID, IEEE, pp 26–33
37. Iosup A, Li H, Jan M, Anoep S, Dumitrescu C, Wolters L, Epema DHJ (2008) The grid workloads archive. Future Gener Comput Syst 24(7):672–686
38. Iosup A, Sonmez OO, Anoep S, Epema DHJ (2008) The performance of bags-of-tasks in large-scale distributed systems. In: HPDC, ACM, pp 97–108
39. Iosup A, Ostermann S, Yigitbasi N, Prodan R, Fahringer T, Epema DHJ (2011) Performance analysis of cloud computing services for many-tasks scientific computing. IEEE Trans Par Dist Syst 22(6):931–945
40. Iosup A, Yigitbasi N, Epema DHJ (2011) On the performance variability of production cloud services. In: CCGRID, pp 104–113
41. Iosup A, Prodan R, Epema DHJ (2012) Iaas cloud benchmarking: approaches, challenges, and experience. In: SC Companion/MTAGS
42. Islam S, Lee K, Fekete A, Liu A (2012) How a consumer can measure elasticity for cloud platforms. In: ICPE, pp 85–96
43. Jackson KR, Muriki K, Ramakrishnan L, Runge KJ, Thomas RC (2011) Performance and cost analysis of the supernova factory on the amazon aws cloud. Scientific Programming 19(2–3):107–119

44. Jain R (ed) (1991) The Art of Computer Systems Performance Analysis. John Wiley and Sons Inc.
45. Janetschek M, Prodan R, Ostermann S (2013) Bringing scientific workflows to amazon swf. In: 2013 39th Euromicro Conference Series on Software Engineering and Advanced Applications, IEEE, pp 389–396, DOI 10.1109/SEAA.2013.13
46. Kim K, Jeon K, Han H, Kim SG, Jung H, Yeom HY (2008) Mrbench: A benchmark for mapreduce framework. In: ICPADS, pp 11–18
47. Kondo D, Javadi B, Iosup A, Epema DHJ (2010) The failure trace archive: Enabling comparative analysis of failures in diverse distributed systems. In: CCGrid, pp 398–407
48. Krebs R, Momm C, Kounev S (2012) Architectural concerns in multi-tenant saas applications. In: CLOSER, pp 426–431
49. Krebs R, Momm C, Kounev S (2012) Metrics and techniques for quantifying performance isolation in cloud environments. In: Int'l. ACM SIGSOFT conference Quality of Software Architectures (QoSA), pp 91–100
50. Kwok YK, Ahmad I (1999) Benchmarking and comparison of the task graph scheduling algorithms. J Parallel Distrib Comput 59(3):381–422
51. Mell P, Grance T (2011) The NIST definition of cloud computing. National Institute of Standards and Technology (NIST) Special Publication 800-145, [Online] Available: http://csrc.nist.gov/publications/nistpubs/800-145/SP800-145.pdf. Last accessed Oct 2012.
52. Momm C, Krebs R (2011) A qualitative discussion of different approaches for implementing multi-tenant saas offerings. In: Software Engineering (Workshops), pp 139–150
53. Moreno-Vozmediano R, Montero RS, Llorente IM (2011) Multicloud deployment of computing clusters for loosely coupled mtc applications. IEEE Trans Parallel Distrib Syst 22(6):924–930
54. Oliner AJ, Ganapathi A, Xu W (2012) Advances and challenges in log analysis. Commun ACM 55(2):55–61
55. Oskin M, Chong FT, Farrens MK (2000) Hls: combining statistical and symbolic simulation to guide microprocessor designs. In: ISCA, pp 71–82
56. Ostermann S, Prodan R (2012) Impact of variable priced cloud resources on scientific workflow scheduling. In: Euro-Par 2012 – Parallel Processing, Springer, Lecture Notes in Computer Science, vol 7484, pp 350–362
57. Prodan R, Sperk M, Ostermann S (2012) Evaluating high-performance computing on google app engine. IEEE Software 29(2):52–58
58. Raicu I, Zhang Z, Wilde M, Foster IT, Beckman PH, Iskra K, Clifford B (2008) Toward loosely coupled programming on petascale systems. In: SC, ACM, p 22
59. Saavedra RH, Smith AJ (1996) Analysis of benchmark characteristics and benchmark performance prediction. ACM Trans Comput Syst 14(4):344–384
60. Schroeder B, Wierman A, Harchol-Balter M (2006) Open versus closed: A cautionary tale. In: NSDI
61. Sharkawi S, DeSota D, Panda R, Indukuru R, Stevens S, Taylor VE, Wu X (2009) Performance projection of hpc applications using spec cfp2006 benchmarks. In: IPDPS, pp 1–12
62. Sonmez OO, Mohamed HH, Epema DHJ (2010) On the benefit of processor coallocation in multicluster grid systems. IEEE Trans Parallel Distrib Syst 21(6):778–789
63. Spacco J, Pugh W (2005) Rubis revisited: Why j2ee benchmarking is hard. Stud Inform Univ 4(1):25–30
64. Vahdat A, Yocum K, Walsh K, Mahadevan P, Kostic D, Chase JS, Becker D (2002) Scalability and accuracy in a large-scale network emulator. In: OSDI
65. Villegas D, Antoniou A, Sadjadi SM, Iosup A (2012) An analysis of provisioning and allocation policies for infrastructure-as-a-service clouds. In: CCGrid, pp 612–619
66. Vishwanath KV, Vahdat A, Yocum K, Gupta D (2009) Modelnet: Towards a datacenter emulation environment. In: Peer-to-Peer Computing, pp 81–82
67. Walker E (2009) The real cost of a cpu hour. IEEE Computer 42(4):35–41
68. Wang G, Butt AR, Pandey P, Gupta K (2009) Using realistic simulation for performance analysis of MapReduce setups. In: HPDC Workshops, pp 19–26

69. Zaharia M, Borthakur D, Sarma JS, Elmeleegy K, Shenker S, Stoica I (2010) Delay scheduling: a simple technique for achieving locality and fairness in cluster scheduling. In: EuroSys, pp 265–278

70. Zhang B, Iosup A, Pouwelse J, Epema D (2010) The Peer-to-Peer Trace Archive: design and comparative trace analysis. In: Proceedings of the ACM CoNEXT Student Workshop, CoNEXT '10 Student Workshop, pp 21:1–21:2

GPU-Accelerated Cloud Computing
for Data-Intensive Applications

**Baoxue Zhao, Jianlong Zhong, Bingsheng He, Qiong Luo, Wenbin Fang,
and Naga K. Govindaraju**

Abstract Recently, many large-scale data-intensive applications have emerged
from the Internet and science domains. They pose significant challenges on the
performance, scalability and programmability of existing data management systems.
The challenges are even greater when these data management systems run on
emerging parallel and distributed hardware and software platforms. In this chapter,
we study the use of the GPU (Graphics Processing Units) in MapReduce and general
graph processing in the Cloud for these data-intensive applications. In particular,
we report our experiences in developing system prototypes, and discuss the open
problems in the interplay between data-intensive applications and system platforms.

1 Introduction

In recent years, *Big Data* has become a buzz word in both industry and academia,
due to the emergence of many large-scale data-intensive applications. These data-
intensive applications not only have very large data volume, but may also have
complex data structures and high update rates. All these factors pose significant
challenges on the performance, scalability and programmability of existing data
management systems. We elaborate more details about these challenges in the
following.

B. Zhao • Q. Luo (✉)
Department of Computer Science and Engineering, HKUST, Hong Kong
e-mail: bzhaoad@cse.ust.hk; luo@cse.ust.hk

J. Zhong • B. He
School of Computer Engineering, Nanyang Technological University, Nanyang, Singapore
e-mail: jzhong2@ntu.edu.sg; bshe@ntu.edu.sg

W. Fang
San Francisco, CA, USA
e-mail: wenbin@cs.wisc.edu

N.K. Govindaraju
Microsoft Redmond, Redmond, WA, USA
e-mail: nagag@microsoft.com

© Springer Science+Business Media New York 2014   105
X. Li, J. Qiu (eds.), *Cloud Computing for Data-Intensive Applications*,
DOI 10.1007/978-1-4939-1905-5__5

Performance Many processing tasks are driven by data updates, which require on-line response. Examples include traffic control and video surveillance. The performance issue is crucial for these on-line applications over large amounts of data.

Scalability Also due to the increasing data volume, it is essential for systems to scale with data growth.

Programmability To meet performance and scalability requirement of big data, data management systems are run on parallel and/or distributed platforms. Programming on such systems is much more challenging than sequential programming.

Many data processing algorithms and systems have been developed, including MapReduce [20] and general graph processing. MapReduce was originally proposed by Google for the ease of development of web document processing on a large number of machines. This framework provides two primitive operations (1) a map function to process input key/value pairs and to generate intermediate key/value pairs, and (2) a reduce function to merge all intermediate pairs associated with the same key. With a MapReduce framework, developers can implement their application logic using the two primitives. The MapReduce runtime will automatically distribute and execute the task on a number of computers. MapReduce is mainly for flat-structured data, and can be inefficient for unstructured data [54]. Thus, general graph processing systems are proposed for processing unstructured data such as social networks and graphs. Representative systems include Google's Pregel [54] and Microsoft's Trinity [63].

Both MapReduce and general graph processing platforms have been developed and run on various kinds of distributed and parallel systems. This chapter focuses on two emerging platforms: GPUs (Graphics Processing Units) and the Cloud, as the representatives for many-core and distributed computing platforms, respectively. Specifically, we review the related work for MapReduce and general graph processing on GPUs and Cloud platforms. Moreover, we report our experiences in developing system prototypes: Mars [32] and MarsHadoop [25] for GPU-based MapReduce; Medusa [74,76] and Surfer [16] for GPU-based and Cloud-based graph processing, respectively. Finally, we discuss the open problems in the interplay between data processing systems and system platforms.

Organization The remainder of this chapter is organized as follows. Section 2 reviews the background on GPUs and Cloud Computing, and related work on MapReduce and general graph processing frameworks on GPUs and in the Cloud. Section 3 introduces the MapReduce work on GPU Clusters. Section 4 presents the parallel graph processing techniques on GPUs and the Cloud. We conclude our chapter and discuss the open problems in Sect. 5.

2   Background and Related Work

2.1   Cloud Computing

With the rapid growth of the Internet and other application areas such as finance, biology and astronomy, great amounts of data are produced continuously and need to be processed with high time constraints. To handle data-intensive problems, the concept of *Cloud Computing* has been proposed. A few Internet corporations implemented their own Cloud Computing platforms to provide elastic computing services for their customers. Such as Google Compute Engine, Amazon EC2 and Microsoft Azure. The Cloud Computing services are provided at different levels: Infrastructure as a Service (IaaS), Platform as a Service (PaaS) and Software as a Service (SaaS). Customers who use services at a higher level do not need to know the lower level details of the Cloud, e.g., network topology or resource allocation. In view of these features, Cloud Computing poses new challenges for computing tasks compared with traditional computation platforms such as HPC clusters. In Sect. 4.2 we will discuss the challenges in detail and introduce the solutions for graph processing in the Cloud.

2.2   The GPU

In recent years, GPUs (Graphics Processing Units) have shifted from pure graphics processors to general-purpose parallel processors. A modern GPU can run a massive number of lightweight threads simultaneously to process data in the SIMD (Single Instruction, Multiple Data) style and can provide an order of magnitude speedup over traditional CPU with higher cost-efficiency. GPUs are widely used in desktops, servers and clusters as parallel computing platforms to accelerate various kinds of applications. However, writing a correct and efficient GPU program is challenging in general, and even more difficult for higher level applications. First, the GPU is a many-core processor with massive thread parallelism. To fully exploit the GPU parallelism, developers need to write parallel programs that scale to hundreds of cores. Moreover, compared with CPU threads, the GPU threads are lightweight, and the tasks in the parallel algorithms should be fine-grained. Second, the GPU has a memory hierarchy that is different from the CPU's, and is exposed to the programmer for explicit use. Since applications usually involve irregular accesses to the memory, careful designs of data layouts and memory accesses are key factors to the efficiency of GPU acceleration. Finally, since the GPU is designed as a co-processor, developers have to explicitly perform memory management on the GPU, and deal with GPU specific programming details such as kernel configuration and invocation. All these factors make the GPU programming a difficult task. In this chapter, we will introduce the GPU-accelerated MapReduce system (Sect. 3) and GPU-accelerated graph processing library (Sect. 4.1), both of which ease the effort of developing higher level applications using GPUs.

2.3 MapReduce

MapReduce [20] is a programming model proposed by Google, and has been widely used for large scale data processing. Many researchers and engineers have tried to implement their own MapReduce systems since the publication of the MapReduce paper. Hadoop [3] is the most successful and widely-used open source implementation of MapReduce on the distributed computing platform. There are also some implementations on other platforms, such as multi-core shared-memory systems and GPUs.

Phoenix [62,67,72] is a MapReduce library that runs on shared memory systems leveraging the power of multi-core CPUs. Our previous work Mars [25, 32] is among the first GPU-accelerated MapReduce frameworks. Mars provides a set of higher level programming interfaces, and hides the vendor-specific lower-level details such as thread configurations. The design goal of Mars is to ease the GPU programming effort for MapReduce applications. Since Mars, there has been a number of improvements [11,14,36,40] as well as extended GPU-based MapReduce implementations to support multi-GPUs on a single-machine [17,18,41], integrated architectures [15] and clusters [8,64,65,68].

MapCG [36] is a single-machine MapReduce framework that provides source code portability between CPU and GPU. The users only need to write one version of the code, and the MapCG runtime is responsible for generating both CPU and GPU specific codes and executes them on the corresponding platforms: multi-core CPUs and GPUs. Different from Mars, MapCG does not need the counting step to compute the required memory space on GPUs. Instead, it allocates a large block of GPU memory space, and uses the *atomicAdd* operation to manage and record the memory space required by each thread. Another improvement of MapCG is that it avoids the sorting of intermediate key/value pairs by using a memory efficient hash table. Ji et al. [40] proposed to use the GPU shared memory to buffer the input and output data of the *Map* and *Reduce* stages. Chen et al. [14] proposed to use shared memory in a more efficient way by carrying out reductions in shared memory. Grex [11] is a recent GPU-based MapReduce framework. It provides some new features over Mars and MapCG, including parallel input data splitting, even data distribution to *Map/Reduce* tasks to avoid partitioning skew, and a new memory management scheme. Experiments show that Grex achieves 12.4× and 4.1× speedup over Mars and MapCG, respectively.

Chen et al. [15] designed a MapReduce framework for integrated architectures, i.e. AMD Fusion chip as a representative in their implementation. In their framework, the workload can be partitioned across the CPU cores and GPU cores by two different schemes: the *map-dividing scheme* and the *pipelining scheme*. In the first scheme, each of the *Map/Reduce* stage is executed by both CPU cores and GPU cores simultaneously, whereas in the second scheme, each stage is executed by only one type of cores. To leverage the memory overhead, a *continuous reduction* strategy based on *reduction object* is used in the framework. The strategy is very similar to the optimization work in [14]. Their experiment results show 1.2–2.1× speedup over the best multi-core or discrete GPU-based implementation.

While previous implementations use a single GPU, MGMR [18, 41] is a single-machine MapReduce system supporting multiple GPUs. With the support of host memory, MGMR can handle large-scale data exceeding GPU memory capacity. In addition, MGMR uses the GPUDirect technology to accelerate inter-GPU data transmission. The Pipelined MGMR (PMGPR) [17] is an upgraded version of MGMR. PMGMR takes advantage of the CUDA stream feature on Fermi and Kepler GPUs to achieve the overlap of computation and memory copy. For Fermi GPUs, PMGMR uses a runtime scheduler to resolve the dependency among different CUDA streams to achieve the highest concurrency, whereas for Kepler GPUs, PMGMR exploits Kepler's Hyper-Q feature to automatically reach the best performance. PMGMR achieves 2.5× speedup over MGMR.

To support MapReduce on GPU clusters, MarsHadoop [25] makes a simple extension by integrating single-node Mars into Hadoop using the Hadoop streaming technology [5]. Most of the work on MapReduce on GPU clusters integrates GPU workers into Hadoop [8,27,29,64,68,73], and there is also an implementation using MPI (Message Passing Interface) [65].

MITHRA [27] is a Hadoop-based MapReduce framework for Monte-Carlo simulations. It leverages GPUs for the *Map/Reduce* stage computation. Like MarsHadoop, MITHRA uses Hadoop streaming technology to invoke the GPU kernels written in CUDA. Pamar [68] integrates GPUs into the Hadoop framework using JCUDA API. The main focus of Pamar is to provide a framework that can utilize different types of resources (CPU and GPU) transparently and automatically. Surena [8], on the other hand, uses Java Native Interface (JNI) to invoke CUDA code from the Java-based Hadoop framework. Shirahata et al. [64] proposed a hybrid map task scheduling techniques for MapReduce on GPU clusters by dynamic profiling of the map task running on CPUs and GPUs, and demonstrated a speedup of nearly two times over the original scheduler of Hadoop. Lit [73] and HadoopCL [29] improves previous Hadoop-based works by automatically generating kernel codes for GPU devices, so that they hide the GPU programming complexity from users. Specifically, Lit uses an annotation based approach to generate CUDA kernel code from Java code, whereas HadoopCL generates OpenCL kernel code from Java code using an open source tool called Aparapi [2]. In these Hadoop-based extensions, various features of Hadoop such as reliability, scalability and simplified input/output management through HDFS are inherited while the *Map* and *Reduce* stages are parallelized on the GPUs.

GPMR [65] is a MapReduce library on GPU clusters. It is not based on Hadoop; instead it implements the MapReduce model using MPI. GPMR supports multiple GPUs on each node. Compared with the Hadoop-based GPU MapReduce implementation, GPMR is more flexible and more efficient since it exposes more GPU programming details to the application level. Therefore, users can apply application-specific optimizations. Moreover, GPMR also parallelizes the sort and partitioning modules of MapReduce. The scalability of GPMR to the number of GPUs is limited, as the speedup of most applications decreases dramatically when there are more than 16 GPUs [71].

In addition to the MapReduce frameworks supporting NVIDIA GPUs, there are some efforts using other types of CPUs and GPUs. Among them, StreamMR [23] is a MapReduce framework for AMD GPUs, and CellMR [61] is a MapReduce framework supporting asymmetric Cell-Based Clusters. Our enhanced Mars implementation [25] also supports AMD GPUs and co-processing of different types of processors (Multi-core CPU, NVIDIA GPU and AMD GPU).

2.4   General Graph Processing

Graphs are common data structures in various applications such as social networks, computational chemistry and web link analysis. Graph processing algorithms have been the fundamental tool in such fields. Developers usually apply a series of operations on the graph edges and vertices to obtain the final result. Example operations are breadth first search (BFS), PageRank [58], shortest paths and customized variants (for example, developers may apply different application logics on top of BFS). The efficiency of graph processing is essential for the performance of the entire system. On the other hand, writing every graph processing algorithm from scratch is inefficient and involves repetitive work, since different algorithms may share the same operation patterns, optimization techniques and common software components. A programming framework supporting high programmability for various graph processing applications and providing high efficiency can greatly improve productivity.

Recently, we have witnessed many research efforts in offering parallel graph processing frameworks on multi-core/many-core processors and cloud computing platforms. Those frameworks embrace architecture-aware optimization techniques as well as novel data structure designs to improve the parallel graph processing on the target platform. The most popular paradigm so far is vertex-oriented programming. The introduction of vertex-oriented programming is based on the observations in previous studies [21, 51, 52] that many common graph algorithms can be formulated using a form of the bulk synchronous parallel (BSP) model (we call it *GBSP*). In GBSP, local computations are performed on individual vertices, and vertices are able to exchange data with each other. These computation and communication procedures are executed iteratively with barrier synchronization at the end of each iteration. This common algorithmic pattern is adopted by common parallel graph processing frameworks such as Pregel [54], GraphLab [53] and Medusa [76]. For example, Pregel applies a user-defined function *Compute()* on each vertex in parallel in each iteration of the GBSP execution. The communications between vertices are performed with message passing interfaces.

3 MapReduce on GPU Clusters

In this section, we introduce the MapReduce implementation on GPU clusters. We first give an overview of the previous work: Mars single-machine and MarsHadoop. We also give an alternative of multi-machine implementation of Mars, called Mars-MR-MPI. Finally we study the performance of different implementations.

3.1 Mars Overview

Mars [25, 32] is a GPU-based MapReduce implementation. It hides the programming details of vendor-specific GPU devices, and provides a set of user-friendly higher level programming interfaces. The design of Mars is guided by three goals:

1. *Programmability*. Ease of programming releases programmers' efforts on GPU programming details and makes them more focused on higher-level algorithm design and implementation.
2. *Flexibility*. The design of Mars should be applicable to various kinds of devices including multi-core CPUs, NVIDIA GPUs and AMD GPUs. Moreover, it should be easy for users to customize their workflows.
3. *Performance*. The overall performance of GPU-based MapReduce should be comparable to or better than that of the state-of-the-art CPU-based counterparts.

Mars provides a set of APIs, which are listed in Table 1. These APIs are of two types: user-implemented APIs, which the users should implement, and the system-provided APIs, which is a part of the Mars library implementation and can be called by the users directly. The APIs of Mars are similar to those of other MapReduce frameworks, except that Mars uses two steps for both the *Map* and *Reduce* stages. Firstly, the count functions (MAP_COUNT or REDUCE_COUNT) are invoked to compute the sizes of the key/value pairs and then the MAP or REDUCE is invoked to emit the actual key/value pairs.

Figure 1 shows the workflow of Mars. The Mars workflow contains three stages for a MapReduce job—*Map*, *Group* and *Reduce*. Before the *Map* stage, the input data on the disk is transformed into input records using the CPU and those records are copied from the main memory into the GPU device memory. Both the *Map* and *Reduce* stages use a two-step lock-free scheme, which avoids costly atomic operations and dynamic memory allocation on GPU devices. Take the *Map* stage as an example. In the first step *MapCount* invokes the user-defined MAP_COUNT function to compute the sizes of the intermediate key/value pairs for each thread. Then a prefix sum operation is performed to compute the writing locations for each thread as well as the total sizes of the output. Finally Mars allocates device memory space for the output. In the second step, the user-defined MAP function is invoked on each thread to map the input records to intermediate records and output them to the device memory according to the pre-computed writing locations. The lock-free scheme of the *Reduce* stage is similar to that of the *Map* stage. The *Group* stage sorts

Table 1 Mars APIs [25, 32]

Function name	Description	Type
MAP_COUNT	Calculates the output buffer size of MAP	User
MAP	The map function	User
REDUCE_COUNT	Calculates the output buffer size of REDUCE	User
REDUCE	The reduce function	User
EMIT_INTERMEDIATE_COUNT	Emits the key size and the value size in MAP_COUNT	System
EMIT_INTERMEDIATE	Emits the key and the value in MAP	System
EMIT_COUNT	Emits the key size and the value size in REDUCE_COUNT	System
EMIT	Emits the key and the value in REDUCE	System

the intermediate key/value pairs according to the key field, so that the intermediate key/value pairs with the same key are stored consecutively as a group.

Since the three stages are loosely coupled modules, the Mars framework can fit three kinds of user-customized workflows, according to whether the *Group* and *Reduce* stages are required:

- MAP_ONLY. Only the *Map* stage is required and executed.
- MAP_GROUP. Only the *Map* and *Group* stages are executed.
- MAP_GROUP_REDUCE. All three stages—*Map*, *Group*, and *Reduce* are executed.

The GPU-based Mars single-machine implementation was evaluated in comparison with the CPU-based MapReduce framework Phoenix [62] as well as the native implementation without MapReduce using a set of representative MapReduce applications. The results show that the GPU-based Mars was up to 22 times faster than Phoenix, and Mars applications had a code size reduction of up to 7 times compared with the native implementation. In summary, Mars greatly simplifies the MapReduce programming on CUDA-based GPU and achieves great efficiency.

3.2 MarsHadoop

While the single-GPU Mars makes a showcase of implementing MapReduce using GPU, it cannot handle very large data set due to the limited memory capacity of a single GPU. In many data-intensive applications, the data scale exceeds far beyond the memory capacity of a single computer, let alone the GPU memory, which usually has a much smaller capacity than main memory.

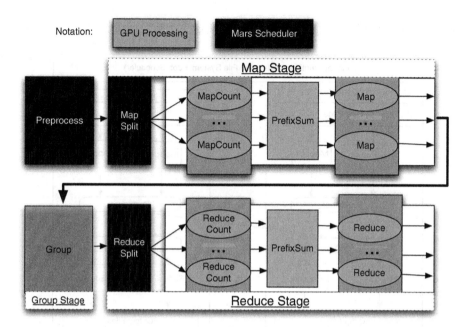

Fig. 1 The workflow of Mars on the GPU [25,32]

We briefly introduce the previous multi-machine implementation of Mars—MarsHadoop [25]. MarsHadoop is implemented by integrating Mars into the widely used Hadoop MapReduce framework. This integration provides an easy way of exploiting computation power of multiple GPUs for MapReduce, while it also inherits the scalability and fault-tolerance features of Hadoop, as well as the distributed file system support.

Figure 2 shows the workflow of MarsHadoop. A Mapper/Reducer in MarsHadoop is executed on either CPU or GPU, depending on the underlying processors. MarsHadoop Mappers and Reducers are integrated using Hadoop streaming technology [5], which enables the developers to use their customized Mapper/Reducer implementation with any programming language in Hadoop. The Mapper/Reducer executable reads data from *stdin* and emit record to the *stdout*, while the actual task execution is the same as on single machine. The preliminary experiments using Matrix Multiplication on three nodes (one master node and two slave nodes) showed that MarsHadoop was up to 2.8 times faster than the Hadoop without GPU.

3.3 Mars-MR-MPI

In the following we present an alternative to MarsHadoop, which we call Mars-MR-MPI.

MapReduce-MPI (MR-MPI) [59, 60] is an open source, lightweight implementation of the MapReduce model using MPI and C/C++. It is designed for

Notation: [GPU Mapper/Reducer]   (CPU Mapper/Reducer)

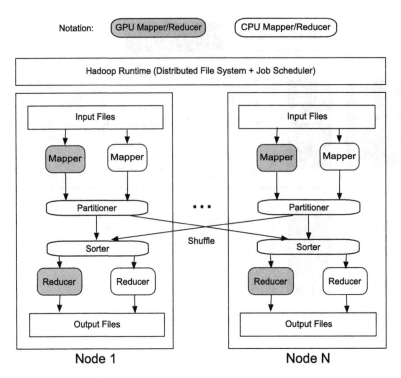

Fig. 2 MarsHadoop workflow [25]. The Map and Reduce tasks are executed on GPUs or CPUs

distributed-memory clusters. MR-MPI has well organized APIs and complete document support. It has been successfully used for SOM [66] and shows good scalability on hundreds of cores. It can process large data sets far exceeding the accumulated memory size of the cluster by using on-disk virtual pages. Moreover, since MR-MPI is implemented using C/C++, the GPU code can be invoked seamlessly with no or little extra runtime cost. We choose MR-MPI as an alternative for extending Mars to multiple machines in view of these features.

The Mars-MR-MPI is implemented as follows.

1. **Initial Data Loading.** Since the MR-MPI framework has no distributed file system support, to avoid the overhead of remote reading, we partition the input data into chunks of equal size and distribute them evenly to the local file system of each node. This approach is comparable with Hadoop since most Hadoop map tasks will read HDFS blocks stored in local node.
2. **The *Map* Stage.** Instead of assigning only one block of data (i.e. 64 MB, which is the default block size of Hadoop) to each map task, we use persistent map tasks for Mars-MR-MPI. In other words, we launch only a small number of map tasks for a job, with each task processing many blocks of input data iteratively. The processing of each data block is the same as the *Map* stage of single-machine Mars, followed by an additional step of organizing the intermediate key/value

pairs generated from this block into an MR-MPI *KeyValue* object and add this object to the MR-MPI runtime framework. The GPU device for each map task is chosen according to the MPI rank of the current process. Using this approach, the number of GPU context switches is reduced with more work done in each context.

3. **The *Reduce* Stage.** In MR-MPI, each time the reduce callback function [6] is called, it will process only one *Key-MultiValues* tuple, which contains a unique key and a list of values. A parallel reduce for one tuple is inefficient if the tuple contains only a small number of values. Therefore, we allocate a global fixed-size memory buffer and pass it to the reduce callback function to accumulate the tuples. Once the size of the accumulated tuples exceeds a threshold ratio of the buffer size, we will perform a parallel reduction on the GPU for all tuples and empty the buffer for accumulating new tuples. In addition to the global buffer, a boolean flag is passed to the callback function, to indicate whether this is the first call on the GPU device. If so, we initialize the GPU device context.

Both the MarsHadoop and the Mars-MR-MPI are based on existing MapReduce frameworks, namely Hadoop and MR-MPI. Compared with Hadoop, MR-MPI provides an interface that is more flexible for integrating the GPU into MapReduce, and the persistent tasks can be used to reduce overhead and better utilize device resources.

3.4 Experiments

We study the performance of the two alternatives of MapReduce on a GPU cluster experimentally.

The experiments are conducted on a 20-node GPU cluster on Amazon EC2. Each node is a Hardware Virtual Machine(HVM)-based instance equipped with 8 Intel Xeon E5-2670 Processors, 15 GB memory, 60 GB local storage and a single NVIDIA Kepler GK104 GPU card (with 1536 CUDA cores and 4 GB memory). The Operating System is Ubuntu 12.04 with CUDA SDK v5.0 installed.

We first study the performance of MarsHadoop using a classic data-intensive MapReduce workload—Inverted Index, which extracts the URL links from a set of HTML files. Each map task takes a block of data as input and emit ⟨*url, filename*⟩ for each URL extracted from the input, whereas each reduce task simply outputs the list of file names for each unique URL. For MarsHadoop streaming job, we parallelize the map tasks on the GPU, whereas the reduce tasks are sequentially executed as they only perform outputting (this kind of reduce task is called IdentityReducer in Hadoop). We implemented the sequential Inverted Index using Hadoop Java API and ran it as Hadoop sequential job as the baseline. We set the number of map slots on each node to 4 in Hadoop configuration. For the sequential job, each map uses one CPU core whereas for the MarsHadoop streaming job, the four map slots on each node share the single GPU to make full use of the GPU computation resources.

We use two Wikipedia web page data sets of different sizes from the Purdue
MapReduce Benchmarks Suite [9], one 50 GB and the other 150 GB. Figure 3
shows the execution time of the map tasks in MarsHadoop streaming jobs and
Hadoop sequential jobs. For both data sets, the MarsHadoop streaming jobs are
more efficient than Hadoop sequential jobs.

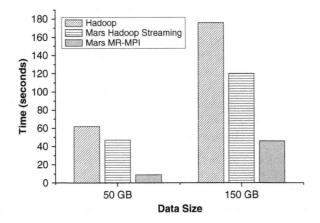

Fig. 3 The execution time of Inverted Index map tasks in MarsHadoop streaming jobs, Hadoop
sequential jobs and Mars-MR-MPI jobs using 50 and 150 GB data sets

Next we study the performance of Mars-MR-MPI, in comparison with MarsHadoop. Figure 3 shows the execution time of map tasks in Mars-MR-MPI and
MarsHadoop for Inverted Index respectively. We observed that for both 50 GB and
150 GB data sets, the map time of Mars-MR-MPI is 3–5× faster than MarsHadoop
streaming. Compared with Mars-MR-MPI, the inefficiency of MarsHadoop streaming is due to the following two factors:

1. Inter-process data communication overhead with Hadoop streaming, since the
   input data are passed into the Mars map executable by *stdin* and the output passed
   out by *stdout*.
2. The latencies from Hadoop internal, such as the latency of a TaskTracker
   requesting new tasks from JobTracker. The GPUs will be idle during the latency
   intervals, leading to under-utilization.

As the Mars-MR-MPI is more efficient, we further study its scalability and
performance bottlenecks. We configure Mars-MR-MPI to process 2.5 GB data on
each node. Figure 4 shows the time consumption of each MR-MPI stage with
the cluster size varied from 2 to 20 nodes. We observe that when the number of
nodes increases, for the stages involving only local operations, including Map stage,
Sort/Hash stage and Reduce stage, the time nearly keeps stable. The reason is that
the local operations are performed independently on each node and the workload on
each node is even. However, for the Network I/O stage which involves large amount
of inter-node communication, the time increases with the cluster size.

We further give the time breakdown of Mars-MR-MPI running Inverted Index with two data sets on the entire cluster (Fig. 5). The result shows that the Network I/O takes 30 and 36 % of the total time on 50 and 150 GB data sets, respectively. We conclude that the network I/O is the performance bottleneck when the cluster size or data size becomes larger.

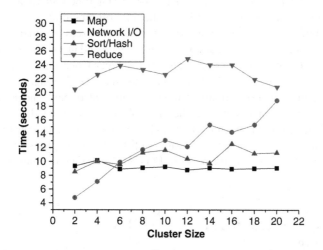

Fig. 4 The time consumption of each MR-MPI stage for Mars-MR-MPI with cluster size varied, running Inverted Index on 50 GB data set

Fig. 5 The time breakdown of Mars-MR-MPI running Inverted Index on the entire cluster

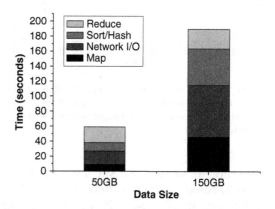

Both MarsHadoop and Mars-MR-MPI are built on top of existing MapReduce frameworks and do not parallelize the internals of the frameworks, such as sort or hash partition. The performance of this type of extension is closely dependent on the performance of the frameworks themselves. We now study the performance of the GPMR, a recent stand-alone MapReduce library based on the GPU. We select two examples enclosed with the GPMR source code: K-means Clustering and Integer Counting. The former example is map-computation-bound, whereas the latter is communication-bound.

To test the GPMR scalability on various number of nodes, we launch one MPI process for each GPU. Due to the limitation of the GPU-based radix sort used in GPMR, we let each process consume 32 million randomly generated integers for Integer Counting, and 32 million randomly generated two-dimensional floating point data for K-means Clustering. The results are shown in Fig. 6. In the K-mean Clustering results in Fig. 6a, we notice that (1) The Map time keeps nearly stable for various number of nodes and it dominates the total running time; (2) The Network I/O, Sort and Reduce stages consume very little time. The reason is that the K-means Clustering needs a lot of computation in the map stage and produces very small size intermediate data. In contrast, in Fig. 6b, since Integer Counting produces a large amount of intermediate result, both the Map and Network I/O stages dominate the total running time. It also requires a moderate amount of Sort and Reduce time to handle the intermediate data, but the time of these operations does not change much with the variation of number of nodes, as these are local operations. We conclude that the GPMR framework scales well to cluster size for compute-bound applications, but suffers from the network I/O bottleneck for communication-bound ones.

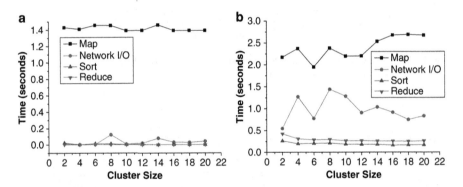

Fig. 6 The time consumption of each MapReduce stage in GPMR with number of nodes varied. (**a**) K-means Clustering with each GPU processing 32 million randomly generated two-dimensional floating points. (**b**) Integer Counting with each GPU processing 32 million randomly generated integers

Finally, we study the GPMR scalability to data size. Due to the limitation of the GPU-based radix sort, GPMR cannot handle more than 32 million integers on each process unless it uses CPU-based sort algorithms. The scalability test is only conducted for K-means Clustering. We use 20 nodes with one process on each node and let each process consume various numbers of points ranging from 32 million to 160 million. The result is shown in Fig. 7. The map time grows linearly to the data size, whereas the Network I/O, Sort and Reduce consumes very little time.

Fig. 7 The time consumption
of each MapReduce stage in
GPMR with data size varied,
running K-means Clustering
on 20 nodes

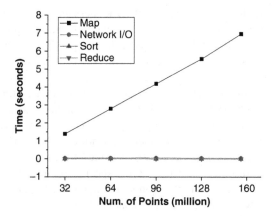

4   Graph Processing on GPUs and the Cloud

In this section, we introduce two representative vertex-oriented programming
frameworks on GPUs and in the Cloud—Medusa and Surfer. Particularly, Medusa
is a parallel graph processing library running on multi-GPUs on a single machine.
It uses a novel graph programming model called "Edge-Message-Vertex" and
simplifies the graph processing using GPUs. Surfer uses a network performance
aware graph partitioning framework to improve the performance of large graph
processing on the Cloud.

4.1   Parallel Graph Processing on GPUs

Recent years have witnessed the increasing adoption of GPGPU (General-Purpose
computation on Graphics Processing Units) in many applications [57], such as
databases [33, 34] and data mining [26]. The GPU has been used as an accel-
erator for various graph processing applications [31, 35, 48, 70]. While existing
GPU-based solutions have demonstrated significant performance improvement
over CPU-based implementations, they are limited to specific graph operations.
Developers usually need to implement and optimize GPU programs from scratch
for different graph processing tasks.

Medusa is the state-of-the-art vertex-oriented graph processing framework on
multiple GPUs in the same machine [76]. Medusa is designed to ease the pain
of leveraging the GPU in common graph computation tasks. Extending the single vertex API of Pregel, Medusa develops a novel graph programming model
called "Edge-Message-Vertex" (EMV) for fine-grained processing on vertices and
edges. EMV is specifically tailored for parallel graph processing on the GPU.
Medusa provides a set of APIs for developers to implement their applications.
The APIs are based on the EMV programming model for fine-grained parallelism.

Medusa embraces an efficient message passing based runtime. It automatically executes user-defined APIs in parallel on all the processor cores within the GPU and on multiple GPUs, and hides the complexity of GPU programming from developers. Thus, developers can write the same APIs, which automatically run on multiple GPUs.

Memory efficiency is often an important factor for the overall performance of graph applications [31, 35, 48, 70]. Medusa has a series of memory optimizations to improve the locality of graph accesses. A novel graph layout is developed to exploit the *coalesced* memory feature of the GPU. A graph aware message passing mechanism is specifically designed for message passing in Medusa. Additionally, Medusa has two multi-GPU-specific optimization techniques, including the cost model guided replication for reducing data transfer across the GPUs and overlapping between computation and data transfer.

Medusa has been evaluated on the efficiency and programmability. Medusa simplifies programming GPU graph processing algorithms in terms of a significant reduction in the number of source code lines. Medusa achieves comparable or better performance than the manually tuned GPU graph operations.

The experiments were conducted on a workstation equipped with four NVIDIA Tesla C2050 GPUs, two Intel Xeon E5645 CPUs (totally 12 CPU cores at 2.4 GHz) and 24 GB RAM. The workloads include a set of common graph processing operations for manipulating and visualizing a graph on top of Medusa. The graph processing operations include PageRank, breadth first search (BFS), maximal bipartite matching (MBM), and single source shortest paths (SSSP). In order to assess the queue-based design in Medusa, we have implemented two versions of BFS: BFS-N and BFS-Q for the implementations without and with the usage of queue-based APIs, respectively. Thus, BFS-Q is work optimal whereas BFS-N is not. Similarly, two versions of SSSP are implemented: SSSP-N and SSSP-Q without and with the usage of queue-based APIs, respectively.

The experimental dataset includes two categories of sparse graphs: real-world and synthetic graphs. Table 2 shows their basic characteristics. We use the GTgraph graph generator [4] to generate power-law and random graphs. To evaluate MBM, we generate a synthetic bipartite graph (denoted as BIP), where vertex sets of two sides have one half of the vertices and the edges are randomly generated. The real world graphs are publicly available [1, 7].

MTGL [13] is used as the baseline for graph processing on multi-core CPUs. The BFS and PageRank implementations are offered by MTGL. We implement the Bellman-Ford SSSP algorithm and a randomized maximal matching algorithm [10] using MTGL. The best result was obtained when the number of threads was 12 on the experiment machine. MTGL running on 12 cores is on average 3.4 times faster than that running on one core. Due to the memory intensive nature of graph algorithms, the scalability of MTGL is limited by the memory bandwidth.

Figure 8 shows the speedup for Medusa over MTGL running on 12 cores. The *speedup* is defined as the ratio between the elapsed time of the CPU-based execution and that of Medusa-based execution. PageRank is executed with 100 iterations. Medusa is significantly faster than MTGL on most comparisons and delivers a

Table 2 Characteristics of graphs used in the experiments

Graph	Vertices (10^6)	Edges (10^6)	Max d	Avg d	σ
RMAT	1.0	16.0	1,742	16	32.9
Random (Rand)	1.0	16.0	38	16	4.0
BIP	4.0	16.0	40	4	5.1
WikiTalk (Wiki)	2.4	5.0	100,022	2.1	99.9
RoadNet-CA (Road)	2.0	5.5	12	2.8	1.0
kkt_power (KKT)	2.1	13.0	95	6.3	7.5
coPapersCiteseer (Cite)	0.4	32.1	1,188	73.9	101.3
hugebubbles-00020 (Huge)	21.2	63.6	3	3.0	0.03

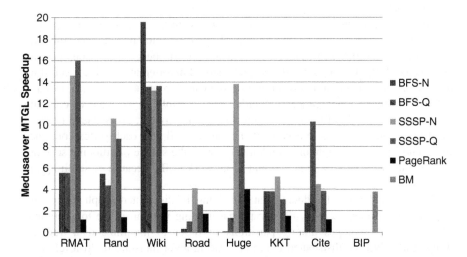

Fig. 8 Performance speedup of Medusa running on the GPU over MTGL [13] running on 12 cores

performance speedup of 1.0–19.6 with an average of 5.5. On some graphs such as Road, BFS-N is notably slower than MTGL-based BFS, because the work-inefficient issue of BFS-N is exaggerated on the graphs with large diameter.

The work-efficient BFS and SSSP algorithms (BFS-Q and SSSP-Q) achieve better performance on the graphs with large diameters, and can degrade the performance in some cases (e.g., Rand, Wiki and KKT) due to the computation and memory overhead in maintaining the queue structure. This is consistent with the previous studies [37].

4.2 Parallel Graph Processing on the Cloud

Large graph processing has become popular for various data-intensive applications on increasingly large web and social networks [43, 44]. Due to the ever increasing size of graphs, application deployments are moving from a small number of HPC servers or supercomputers [28, 46] towards the Cloud with a large number of commodity servers [44, 54]. Early studies on parallel graph processing in the Cloud are to adopt existing distributed data-intensive computing techniques in the Cloud [19,39]. Most of these studies [43,44,77] are built on top of MapReduce [19], which is suitable for processing flat data structure, not particularly for graph structured data. More recently, systems such as Pregel [54], Trinity [63] and Surfer [16] have been developed specifically for large graph processing. These systems support a vertex-oriented execution model and allow users to develop custom logics on vertices. The Medusa system [76] has been extended to support the GPU-enabled cloud environment [75]. In those Cloud-based graph processing systems, network performance optimizations are the key for improving the overall performance.

Most vertex-oriented graph processing systems share the same network performance issue. Take Pregel as an example. Pregel executes user-defined function *Compute*() per vertex in parallel, based on the general bulk synchronous parallel (BSP) model. By default, the vertices can be stored in different machines according to a simple hash function. However, the simple partitioning function leads to heavy network traffic in graph processing tasks. For example, if we want to compute the two-hop friend list for each account in a social network, every friend (vertex) must first send its friends to each of its neighbors, and then each vertex combines the friend lists of its neighbors. Implemented with the simple partitioning scheme, this operation results in a great amount of network traffic because of shuffling the vertices.

A traditional way of reducing data shuffling in distributed graph processing is graph partitioning [22, 45, 49]. Graph partitioning minimizes the total number of cross-partition edges among partitions in order to minimize data transfer. The commonly used distributed graph processing algorithms are multi-level algorithms [46, 47, 69]. These algorithms recursively divide the graph into multiple partitions with bisections according to different heuristics.

It is well understood that large graphs should be partitioned; however, little attention is given to how graph partitioning can be effectively integrated into the processing in the Cloud environment. There are a number of challenging issues in the integration. First, graph partitioning itself is a very costly task, generating lots of network traffic. Moreover, partitioned graph storage and vertex-oriented graph processing need a careful revisit in the context of Cloud. The Cloud network environment is significantly different from those in previous studies [46, 47, 49], e.g., Cray supercomputers or a small cluster. The network bandwidth is often the same for every machine pair in a small cluster. However, the network bandwidth of the Cloud environment is uneven among different machine pairs. Current Cloud infrastructures are often based on tree topology [12, 30, 42]. Machines are first grouped into *pods*, and then pods are connected to higher-level switches. The intra-pod bandwidth is much higher than the cross-pod bandwidth. Even worse, the topology information is usually unavailable to users due to virtualization techniques in the Cloud. In practice, such network bandwidth unevenness has been confirmed by both Cloud providers and users [12,42]. It requires careful network optimizations and tuning on graph partitioning and processing.

We briefly describe the approach adopted by Surfer [16]. Surfer uses a network performance aware graph partitioning framework to improve the network performance of large graph processing on partitioned graphs. Specifically, the graph partitions generated from the framework improve the network performance of graph processing tasks. To capture the network bandwidth unevenness, Surfer models the machines chosen for graph processing as a complete undirected graph (namely *machine graph*): each machine as a vertex, and the bandwidth between any two machines as the weight of an edge. The network performance aware framework recursively partitions the data graph, as well as the machine graph, with bisection correspondingly. That is, the bisection on the data graph is performed with the corresponding set of machines selected from the bisection on the machine graph. The recursion terminates when the data graph partition can fit into main memory. By partitioning the data graph and machine graph simultaneously, the number of cross-partition edges among data graph partitions is gracefully adapted to the aggregated amount of bandwidth among machine graph partitions. To exploit the data locality of graph partitions, Surfer develops *hierarchical combination* to exploit network bandwidth unevenness in order to improve the network performance.

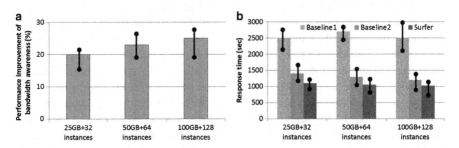

Fig. 9 Network performance aware graph partitioning (**a**) and NR (**b**) on Amazon EC2 with the number of medium instances varied

Surfer has been evaluated on a real-world social network and synthetic graphs of over 100 GB each in a 32-node cluster as well as on Amazon EC2. We briefly discuss the experimental results on network performance aware graph partitioning and graph processing on Amazon EC2.

We compare Surfer with two baselines: "Baseline 1" is the baseline Surfer with local combination, but with graph partition storage distribution generated from ParMetis, and "Baseline 2" is "Baseline 1" with the bandwidth aware graph partitioning, without hierarchical combination. Figure 9a shows the performance improvement of the network bandwidth-aware optimization on graph partitioning, and Fig. 9b compares the response time of *Network ranking* (NR) with different approaches. NR is to generate a ranking on the vertices in the graph using PageRank [58] or its variants. In the experiment, the number of medium instances is increased from 32 to 128 and the size of synthetic graphs is increased from 25 to 100 GB. We measure 100 times of each experiment on the same set of instances, and report the average and the range for the elapsed time of graph partitioning and processing. The variation is acceptable in Amazon EC2. Due to the network bandwidth unevenness in Amazon EC2, the network performance aware optimizations improve both graph partitioning and processing, with 20–25 % performance improvement for graph partitioning and with 49 and 18 % performance improvement for NR over Baseline 1 and 2 respectively. This demonstrates the effectiveness of the network performance aware optimizations of Surfer on the public Cloud environment.

5 Summary and Open Problems

In this chapter, we have introduced the MapReduce implementations on GPU clusters, as well as two state-of-the-art graph processing frameworks running on GPUs and the Cloud.

The MapReduce model is designed originally for big data processing on large clusters, thus scalability is a very important feature. The approaches of integrating GPU parallelism into Hadoop [3] using various technologies such as Hadoop streaming, Hadoop pipes, JCUDA and Java Native Interface can inherit the outstanding scalability and fault-tolerance features of the Hadoop framework. However they usually incur low efficiency due to inter-process communication cost and under-utilization of GPU resources. Moreover, only the map and reduce stages are parallelized whereas the time-consuming sort process remains sequential.

Similar to Hadoop-based work, the Mars-MR-MPI can also process out-of-memory data sets with the support of the MR-MPI framework. Moreover, it is more efficient than the Hadoop-based work using streaming. However, its performance is still limited by the network I/O cost. The stand-alone GPMR framework [65] exposes the GPU programming details to the users, which makes the programming more complex, but can achieve a better performance if the program is well-tuned. GPMR processes input data in chunks. However, due to the lack of a buffer mechanism during the MapReduce pipeline, it cannot handle data sets exceeding the main memory capacity. The scalability of GPMR is still limited, though it involves less overhead and is more optimized than the Hadoop-based GPU MapReduce work.

Graph are very common in data-intensive applications. Compared with other data-intensive applications such as text processing, graph applications are usually more complex and need more computation and communication. To cope with challenges in processing large graphs, several general graph frameworks have been proposed in recent years. Medusa is a representative vertex-oriented graph processing framework on GPUs. It simplifies the graph processing on GPUs and achieves comparable or better performance than the manually tuned GPU graph operations. Surfer focuses on improving the network performance of graph processing on the Cloud by employing network performance-aware graph partitioning strategies. As such, both the graph partitioning and processing efficiency can be improved in a public Cloud environment.

We conclude the chapter with a few open problems as the future research directions.

1. For both MapReduce and general graph processing, data communication i.e., network I/O is the performance bottleneck, which limits the scalability of MapReduce and graph processing algorithms on multi-GPUs and clusters. The experiment results of GPMR show that the speedup of most applications decreases dramatically when there are tens of GPUs. Zhong et al. [76] used up to four GPUs in one machine to accelerate a set of common graph algorithms such as BFS and PageRank. Their study shows that scalability for graph algorithms with light weight computation is poor since the inter-GPU communication cost can easily become the bottleneck, and the scalability issue can be magnified in a distributed environment. To reduce network I/O, we may consider using more advanced communication techniques provided by hardware vendors such as GPUDirect. We can also apply GPU or CPU based data compression algorithms [24] to reduce the amount of data transfer at the cost of increased computation.

2. Out-of-core support is missing in most GPU-based systems. In recent years we have witnessed significant improvement in the computation capability of the GPU, however, the capacity of the GPU memory rarely increases. Yet most data-intensive applications involve data that exceeds the aggregated main memory size. Currently single-GPU MapReduce implementations [14, 25, 32, 36, 40] can only process in-memory data. GPMR processes data in chunks, however, it cannot provide full out-of-core support when data size exceeds main memory capacity. Existing studies on GPU graph processing also mainly deal with in-memory processing of graphs [31, 37, 38, 55, 56, 76]. With several Gigabytes of GPU memory, the size of the maximum input graph is limited to millions of vertices and edges. External memory CPU algorithms have been widely adopted by many applications, including Hadoop shuffle and graph processing [50], for processing data larger than main memory. However, adopting external memory algorithms for GPU is challenging due to the larger gap between GPU memory bandwidth and disk bandwidth, as well as the overhead of PCIe data transfer.

3. For GPU-based MapReduce, variable-length data (keys and values) processing is challenging. To handle variable-length data, Mars uses a lock-free method by pre-computing the key and value length before emitting the actual key/value pair, and some other works use atomic operations. Both approaches bring extra overheads, and the performance of each approach is application dependent. Moreover, variable-length data leads to un-coalesced memory access on GPU.

4. Dynamic Graph Processing. Real world graphs, such as the social networks, are usually evolving. Also, some graph algorithms require changing the graph structure during runtime. However, currently there is little work on GPU-based dynamic graph processing. Narse et al. [56] presented implementations of five graph algorithms which morph structure of the input graph in different ways. They provide a set of basic methods for adding and deleting subgraphs and

require users to make their choices based on the application characteristics and the scale of the problem. The applicability of their methods are application dependent and requires non-trivial programming efforts to implement.

References

1. 10th DIMACS implementation challenge. http://www.cc.gatech.edu/dimacs10/index.shtml
2. AMD Aparapi. http://developer.amd.com/tools-and-sdks/opencl-zone/opencl-libraries/aparapi
3. Apache Hadoop. http://hadoop.apache.org
4. GTGraph generator. http://www.cse.psu.edu/~madduri/software/GTgraph/index.html
5. Hadoop Streaming. http://hadoop.apache.org/docs/stable/streaming.html
6. MapReduce-MPI Documentation. http://mapreduce.sandia.gov/doc/Technical.html/Manual.html
7. Stanford large network dataset collections. http://snap.stanford.edu/data/index.htm
8. Abbasi, A., Khunjush, F., Azimi, R.: A preliminary study of incorporating GPUs in the Hadoop framework. In: 2012 16th CSI International Symposium on Computer Architecture and Digital Systems (CADS'12), pp. 178–185. IEEE (2012)
9. Ahmad, F., Lee, S., Thottethodi, M., Vijaykumar, T.: PUMA: Purdue MapReduce Benchmarks Suite. http://web.ics.purdue.edu/~fahmad/papers/puma.pdf
10. Anderson, T.E., Owicki, S.S., Saxe, J.B., Thacker, C.P.: High-speed switch scheduling for local-area networks. ACM Transactions on Computer Systems (TOCS) 11, 319–352 (1993)
11. Basaran, C., Kang, K.D.: Grex: An efficient MapReduce framework for graphics processing units. Journal of Parallel and Distributed Computing 73(4), 522–533 (2013)
12. Benson, T., Akella, A., Maltz, D.A.: Network traffic characteristics of data centers in the wild. In: Proceedings of the 10th ACM SIGCOMM Conference on Internet Measurement, pp. 267–280. ACM (2010)
13. Berry, J., Hendrickson, B., Kahan, S., Konecny, P.: Software and Algorithms for Graph Queries on Multithreaded Architectures. In: IEEE International Parallel and Distributed Processing Symposium (IPDPS'07), pp. 1–14. IEEE (2007)
14. Chen, L., Agrawal, G.: Optimizing MapReduce for GPUs with effective shared memory usage. In: Proceedings of the 21st international symposium on High-Performance Parallel and Distributed Computing, pp. 199–210. ACM (2012)
15. Chen, L., Huo, X., Agrawal, G.: Accelerating MapReduce on a coupled CPU-GPU architecture. In: Proceedings of the International Conference on High Performance Computing, Networking, Storage and Analysis, p. 25. IEEE Computer Society Press (2012)
16. Chen, R., Yang, M., Weng, X., Choi, B., He, B., Li, X.: Improving Large Graph Processing on Partitioned Graphs in the Cloud. In: Proceedings of the Third ACM Symposium on Cloud Computing (SoCC'12), pp. 3:1–3:13 (2012)
17. Chen, Y., Qiao, Z., Davis, S., Jiang, H., Li, K.C.: Pipelined Multi-GPU MapReduce for Big-Data Processing. In: Computer and Information Science, pp. 231–246. Springer (2013)
18. Chen, Y., Qiao, Z., Jiang, H., Li, K.C., Ro, W.W.: MGMR: Multi-GPU based MapReduce. In: Grid and Pervasive Computing, pp. 433–442. Springer (2013)
19. Dean, J., Ghemawat, S.: MapReduce: Simplified data processing on large clusters. In: Proceedings of the 6th Conference on Symposium on Opearting Systems Design and Implementation (OSDI'04) (2004)
20. Dean, J., Ghemawat, S.: MapReduce: Simplified data processing on large clusters. Communications of the ACM 51(1), 107–113 (2008)

21. Delorimier, M., Kapre, N., Mehta, N., Rizzo, D., Eslick, I., Rubin, R., Uribe, T.E., Knight, T.F., Dehon, A.: GraphStep: A System Architecture for Sparse-Graph Algorithms. In: 2006 14th Annual IEEE Symposium on Field-Programmable Custom Computing Machines (FCCM'06), pp. 143–151. IEEE (2006)
22. Derbel, B., Mosbah, M., Zemmari, A.: Fast distributed graph partition and application. In: IPDPS (2006)
23. Elteir, M., Lin, H., Feng, W.c., Scogland, T.: StreamMR: an optimized MapReduce framework for AMD GPUs. In: 2011 IEEE 17th International Conference on Parallel and Distributed Systems (ICPADS'11), pp. 364–371. IEEE (2011)
24. Fang, W., He, B., Luo, Q.: Database compression on graphics processors. Proceedings of the VLDB Endowment 3(1–2), 670–680 (2010)
25. Fang, W., He, B., Luo, Q., Govindaraju, N.K.: Mars: Accelerating MapReduce with graphics processors. IEEE Transactions on Parallel and Distributed Systems (TPDS) 22(4), 608–620 (2011)
26. Fang, W., Lu, M., Xiao, X., He, B., Luo, Q.: Frequent itemset mining on graphics processors. In: Proceedings of the 5th International Workshop on Data Management on New Hardware (DaMoN'09), pp. 34–42 (2009)
27. Farivar, R., Verma, A., Chan, E.M., Campbell, R.H.: MITHRA: Multiple data independent tasks on a heterogeneous resource architecture. In: 2009 IEEE International Conference on Cluster Computing and Workshops (CLUSTER'09), pp. 1–10. IEEE (2009)
28. Gregor, D., Lumsdaine, A.: The Parallel BGL: A generic library for distributed graph computations. In: Parallel Object-Oriented Scientific Computing (POOSC) (2005)
29. Grossman, M., Breternitz, M., Sarkar, V.: HadoopCL: MapReduce on Distributed Heterogeneous Platforms Through Seamless Integration of Hadoop and OpenCL. In: Proceedings of the 2013 IEEE 27th International Symposium on Parallel and Distributed Processing Workshops and PhD Forum, pp. 1918–1927. IEEE Computer Society (2013)
30. Guo, C., Wu, H., Tan, K., Shi, L., Zhang, Y., Lu, S.: Dcell: a scalable and fault-tolerant network structure for data centers. In: ACM SIGCOMM Computer Communication Review, vol. 38, pp. 75–86. ACM (2008)
31. Harish, P., Narayanan, P.: Accelerating large graph algorithms on the GPU using CUDA. In: High performance computing (HiPC'07), pp. 197–208. Springer (2007)
32. He, B., Fang, W., Luo, Q., Govindaraju, N.K., Wang, T.: Mars: a MapReduce framework on graphics processors. In: Proceedings of the 17th International Conference on Parallel Architectures and Compilation Techniques (PACT'08), pp. 260–269. ACM (2008)
33. He, B., Lu, M., Yang, K., Fang, R., Govindaraju, N.K., Luo, Q., Sander, P.V.: Relational query coprocessing on graphics processors. ACM Transactions on Database Systems (TODS) 34(4), 21:1–21:39 (2009)
34. He, B., Yu, J.X.: High-throughput transaction executions on graphics processors. Proceedings of the VLDB Endowment 4(5), 314–325 (2011)
35. He, G., Feng, H., Li, C., Chen, H.: Parallel SimRank computation on large graphs with iterative aggregation. In: Proceedings of the 16th ACM SIGKDD international conference on Knowledge discovery and data mining, pp. 543–552. ACM (2010)
36. Hong, C., Chen, D., Chen, W., Zheng, W., Lin, H.: MapCG: writing parallel program portable between CPU and GPU. In: Proceedings of the 19th International Conference on Parallel Architectures and Compilation Techniques (PACT'10), pp. 217–226. ACM (2010)
37. Hong, S., Kim, S.K., Oguntebi, T., Olukotun, K.: Accelerating CUDA graph algorithms at maximum warp. In: Proceedings of the 16th ACM symposium on Principles and Practice of Parallel Programming (PPoPP'11), pp. 267–276 (2011)
38. Hong, S., Oguntebi, T., Olukotun, K.: Efficient parallel graph exploration on multi-core CPU and GPU. In: 2011 International Conference on Parallel Architectures and Compilation Techniques (PACT'11), pp. 78–88. IEEE (2011)
39. Isard, M., Budiu, M., Yu, Y., Birrell, A., Fetterly, D.: Dryad: distributed data-parallel programs from sequential building blocks. ACM SIGOPS Operating Systems Review 41(3), 59–72 (2007)

40. Ji, F., Ma, X.: Using shared memory to accelerate MapReduce on graphics processing units. In: 2011 IEEE International Parallel and Distributed Processing Symposium (IPDPS'11), pp. 805–816. IEEE (2011)
41. Jiang, H., Chen, Y., Qiao, Z., Li, K.C., Ro, W., Gaudiot, J.L.: Accelerating MapReduce framework on multi-GPU systems. Cluster Computing pp. 1–9 (2013)
42. Kandula, S., Sengupta, S., Greenberg, A., Patel, P., Chaiken, R.: The nature of data center traffic: measurements & analysis. In: Proceedings of the 9th ACM SIGCOMM conference on Internet Measurement Conference (IMC'09), pp. 202–208. ACM (2009)
43. Kang, U., Tsourakakis, C., Appel, A.P., Faloutsos, C., Leskovec, J.: HADI: Fast diameter estimation and mining in massive graphs with Hadoop. Tech. Rep. CMU-ML-08-117, Carnegie Mellon University (2008)
44. Kang, U., Tsourakakis, C.E., Faloutsos, C.: Pegasus: A peta-scale graph mining system - implementation and observations. In: 2009 9th IEEE International Conference on Data Mining (ICDM'09), pp. 229–238. IEEE (2009)
45. Karypis, G., Kumar, V.: A fast and high quality multilevel scheme for partitioning irregular graphs. SIAM Journal on Scientific Computing 20(1), 359–392 (1998)
46. Karypis, G., Kumar, V.: A parallel algorithm for multilevel graph partitioning and sparse matrix ordering. Journal of Parallel and Distributed Computing 48(1), 71–95 (1998)
47. Karypis, G., Kumar, V.: Parallel multilevel k-way partitioning scheme for irregular graphs. Journal of Parallel and Distributed computing 48(1), 96–129 (1998)
48. Katz, G.J., Kider Jr, J.T.: All-pairs shortest-paths for large graphs on the GPU. In: Proceedings of the 23rd ACM SIGGRAPH/EUROGRAPHICS symposium on Graphics Hardware, pp. 47–55. Eurographics Association (2008)
49. Koranne, S.: A distributed algorithm for k-way graph partitioning. In: Proceedings of the 25th Conference of EUROMICRO (EUROMICRO'99), vol. 2, pp. 446–448. IEEE (1999)
50. Kyrola, A., Blelloch, G., Guestrin, C.: GraphChi: Large-scale graph computation on just a PC. In: Proceedings of the 10th USENIX Symposium on Operating Systems Design and Implementation (OSDI'12), pp. 31–46 (2012)
51. Lin, J., Schatz, M.: Design patterns for efficient graph algorithms in MapReduce. In: Proceedings of the Eighth Workshop on Mining and Learning with Graphs (MLG'10), pp. 78–85. ACM (2010)
52. Low, Y., Gonzalez, J., Kyrola, A., Bickson, D., Guestrin, C., Hellerstein, J.M.: GraphLab: A new parallel framework for machine learning. In: The 26th Conference on Uncertainty in Artificial Intelligence (UAI'10) (2010)
53. Low, Y., Gonzalez, J., Kyrola, A., Bickson, D., Guestrin, C., Hellerstein, J.M.: Distributed GraphLab: A framework for machine learning and data mining in the cloud. Proceedings of the VLDB Endowment 5(8), 716–727 (2012)
54. Malewicz, G., Austern, M.H., Bik, A.J., Dehnert, J.C., Horn, I., Leiser, N., Czajkowski, G.: Pregel: A System for Large-Scale Graph Processing. In: Proceedings of the 2010 ACM SIGMOD International Conference on Management of Data (SIGMOD'10), pp. 135–146. ACM (2010)
55. Merrill, D., Garland, M., Grimshaw, A.: Scalable GPU graph traversal. In: Proceedings of the 17th ACM SIGPLAN symposium on Principles and Practice of Parallel Programming (PPoPP'12), pp. 117–128 (2012)
56. Nasre, R., Burtscher, M., Pingali, K.: Morph algorithms on GPUs. In: Proceedings of the 18th ACM SIGPLAN symposium on Principles and Practice of Parallel Programming (PPoPP'13), pp. 147–156 (2013)
57. Owens, J.D., Luebke, D., Govindaraju, N., Harris, M., Krüger, J., Lefohn, A.E., Purcell, T.J.: A Survey of General-Purpose Computation on Graphics Hardware. In: Computer Graphics Forum, vol. 26, pp. 80–113. Wiley Online Library (2007)
58. Page, L., Brin, S., Motwani, R., Winograd, T.: The PageRank citation ranking: Bringing order to the Web. Stanford InfoLab. Technical report (1999)
59. Plimpton, S.J., Devine, K.D.: MapReduce in MPI for large-scale graph algorithms. Parallel Computing 37(9), 610–632 (2011)

60. Plimpton, S and Devine, K: MapReduce-MPI Library. http://mapreduce.sandia.gov
61. Rafique, M.M., Rose, B., Butt, A.R., Nikolopoulos, D.S.: CellMR: A framework for supporting MapReduce on asymmetric cell-based clusters. In: 2009 IEEE International Parallel and Distributed Processing Symposium (IPDPS'09), pp. 1–12. IEEE (2009)
62. Ranger, C., Raghuraman, R., Penmetsa, A., Bradski, G., Kozyrakis, C.: Evaluating MapReduce for multi-core and multiprocessor systems. In: IEEE 13th International Symposium on High Performance Computer Architecture (HPCA'07), pp. 13–24. IEEE (2007)
63. Shao, B., Wang, H., Li, Y.: Trinity: A distributed graph engine on a memory cloud. In: Proceedings of the 2013 ACM International Conference on Management of Data (SIGMOD'13), New York, New York, USA (2013)
64. Shirahata, K., Sato, H., Matsuoka, S.: Hybrid Map task scheduling for GPU-based heterogeneous clusters. In: 2010 IEEE Second International Conference on Cloud Computing Technology and Science (CloudCom'10), pp. 733–740. IEEE (2010)
65. Stuart, J.A., Owens, J.D.: Multi-GPU MapReduce on GPU clusters. In: 2011 IEEE International Parallel and Distributed Processing Symposium (IPDPS'11), pp. 1068–1079. IEEE (2011)
66. Sul, S.J., Tovchigrechko, A.: Parallelizing BLAST and SOM algorithms with MapReduce-MPI library. In: IEEE International Symposium on Parallel and Distributed Processing Workshops and Phd Forum (IPDPSW'11), pp. 481–489. IEEE (2011)
67. Talbot, J., Yoo, R.M., Kozyrakis, C.: Phoenix++: Modular MapReduce for Shared-Memory Systems. In: Proceedings of the 2nd International Workshop on MapReduce and its Applications, pp. 9–16. ACM (2011)
68. Tan, Y.S., Lee, B.S., He, B., Campbell, R.H.: A Map-Reduce based Framework for Heterogeneous Processing Element Cluster Environments. In: IEEE/ACM 12th International Symposium on Cluster, Cloud and Grid Computing (CCGrid'12), pp. 57–64. IEEE (2012)
69. Trifunović, A., Knottenbelt, W.J.: Parallel Multilevel Algorithms for Hypergraph Partitioning. Journal of Parallel and Distributed Computing 68, 563–581 (2008)
70. Vineet, V., Narayanan, P.J.: CUDA cuts: Fast graph cuts on the GPU. In: IEEE Computer Society Conference on Computer Vision and Pattern Recognition Workshops (CVPRW'08), pp. 1–8. IEEE (2008)
71. Wittek, P., Darányi, S.: Leveraging on High-Performance Computing and Cloud Technologies in Digital Libraries: A Case Study. In: IEEE Third International Conference on Cloud Computing Technology and Science (CloudCom'11), pp. 606–611. IEEE (2011)
72. Yoo, R.M., Romano, A., Kozyrakis, C.: Phoenix rebirth: Scalable MapReduce on a large-scale shared-memory system. In: IEEE International Symposium on Workload Characterization (IISWC'09), pp. 198–207. IEEE (2009)
73. Zhai, Y., Mbarushimana, E., Li, W., Zhang, J., Guo, Y.: Lit: A high performance massive data computing framework based on CPU/GPU cluster. In: IEEE International Conference on Cluster Computing (CLUSTER'13), pp. 1–8. IEEE (2013)
74. Zhong, J., He, B.: Parallel Graph Processing on Graphics Processors Made Easy. Proceedings of the VLDB Endowment 6(12), 1270–1273 (2013)
75. Zhong, J., He, B.: Towards GPU-Accelerated Large-Scale Graph Processing in the Cloud. In: IEEE Third International Conference on Cloud Computing Technology and Science (CloudCom'13), pp. 9–16. IEEE (2013)
76. Zhong, J., He, B.: Medusa: Simplified Graph Processing on GPUs. IEEE Transactions on Parallel and Distributed Systems (TPDS) 25(6), 1543–1552 (2014)
77. Zhou, A., Qian, W., Tao, D., Ma, Q.: DISG: A DIStributed Graph Repository for Web Infrastructure (Invited Paper). Proceedings of the 2008 Second International Symposium on Universal Communication 0, 141–145 (2008)

Adaptive Workload Partitioning and Allocation for Data Intensive Scientific Applications

Xin Yang and Xiaolin Li

Abstract Scientific applications are becoming data intensive, and traditional load-balance solutions require reconsideration for scaling data and computation in various parallel systems. This chapter examines state-transition applications, which is a representative scientific application that handles grand-challenging problems (e.g., weather forecasting and ocean prediction) and relates to intensive data. We propose an adaptive workload partitioning and allocation scheme for parallelizing state-transition applications in various parallel systems. Existing schemes insufficiently balance both computation of complicated scientific algorithms and increasing volumes of scientific data simultaneously. Our solution addresses this problem by introducing a time metric to unify the workloads of computation and data. System profiles in terms of CPU and I/O speeds are considered for embracing system diversity, suggesting accurate estimation of workload. The solution consists of two major components: (1) an adaptive decomposition scheme that uses the quad-tree structure to break up workload and manage data dependency; and (2) a decentralized scheme for distributing workload across processors. Experimental results from real-world weather data demonstrate that the solution outperforms other partitioning schemes, and can be readily ported to diverse systems with satisfactory performance.

1 Introduction

Modern scientific applications are becoming data intensive and increasingly rely on various computing systems to analyze data and discover insights quickly. Low-cost sensors and other scientific technologies (e.g., fine-granularity computing models) drive the increase of scale of scientific data. Scientists start to explore new computing systems such as clouds to scale data and computation in an extended deployment while spending reduced cost. As a consequence, solutions effective in traditional computing settings require reconsideration for performance purpose. In this chapter, we use *state-transition scientific application* as an example to

X. Yang (✉) • X. Li
Department of CISE, University of Florida, Gainesville, FL, USA
e-mail: xin@cise.ufl.edu; andyli@ece.ufl.edu

© Springer Science+Business Media New York 2014   131
X. Li, J. Qiu (eds.), *Cloud Computing for Data-Intensive Applications*,
DOI 10.1007/978-1-4939-1905-5_6

discuss modifications when porting traditional solutions to new computing settings. Specifically, the adaptive partitioning and allocation methods for processing state-transition applications in a load-balance manner are examined.

State-transition applications tackle grand-challenge scientific problems (e.g., weather forecasting [1] and ocean prediction [2]). They simulate the evolvement of environments, named *states*, such as atmosphere, ocean, and so on. Sensors or other scientific instruments are deployed in environments for collecting *observations*. Ideally, these observations can be used to predict the changes of environments directly. But in reality, errors are generally common in them. For example, measurements from scientific instruments might not be accurate, fluctuations exist in environments, or the underlying mathematical models may be inaccurate. As a result, observations need to be calibrated before describing environmental states. State-transition algorithms are applied here for calibrating observations using previous states.

Most applications of interest in this domain are modeled in a 2D or 3D coordinate space, and need to handle two independent datasets (represented as logic arrays) for observations and states. These two arrays need to follow a same decomposition pattern and distribute partitioned blocks across a parallel system (e.g., a cluster, a virtual organization in a grid, or a virtual cluster in clouds). Observations typically reflect fluctuations of the environment and exist in a few local regions where significant phenomena occur, resulting in a sparse array. To address such dynamism, adaptive partitioning solutions [3–7] are typically used to balance the distribution of computation of observations, generating blocks of different sizes for the data of states. While many state-transition applications increasingly use a growing volume of scientific data for high-resolution, extended-coverage and timely results, solutions that balance the computation of observations need to balance the data of states as well.

In addition, to make solutions portable across various parallel computing systems, performance profiles of systems need to be considered. Modern HPC clusters are often built with different hardware configurations, indicating different CPU and I/O speeds [8]. Newly emerging virtual clusters are built using various types of virtual machines to meet various computing needs. New issues due to virtualization, such as network jitters [9] and processor sharing [10] on Amazon EC2, affect the performance as well. As profiles reflect CPU and I/O speeds, we should adjust workload partitioning and allocation schemes accordingly to match different system profiles.

1.1 Summary of Contributions

In this chapter, we present an adaptive partitioning and load-balancing scheme, called Apala, for balancing state-transition applications in a computer cluster system. Apala consists of an adaptive decomposition scheme for decomposing arrays into blocks to maximize parallelism and a decentralized scheme for distributing blocks across processors. Based on the quad-tree [11] structure, blocks are decomposed adaptively and recursively. The distributing scheme distributes the blocks across processors by leveraging the linear representation of the quad-tree structure. Techniques of virtual decomposition and finding-side-neighbor are proposed for organizing data dependencies of updating "halos" (i.e., accessing non-local distributed arrays [12, 13]) between adjacent blocks.

An important feature of Apala is that the decomposition decision is based on both computation and data. Balancing either one independently suggests different decomposition patterns. To consider both jointly, Apala introduces a time metric to unify the workloads of computation and data. More specifically, the workload in terms of time is calculated by adding the time of computing observations (i.e., computation amount/system's CPU speed) and that of loading the data of states (i.e., data amount/system's I/O speed).

1.2 Organization

The rest of this chapter is organized as follows. We discuss related work in Sect. 2. The partitioning problems in parallelizing state-transition applications are described in Sect. 3. Section 4 presents Apala, including unifying the workloads of computation and data with the consideration of system profiles, decomposing unified workloads adaptively, and distributing workloads across processors. Experimental results are given for comparing Apala with other partitioning schemes and showing Apala's portability in Sect. 5. We conclude our work in "Conclusion" section.

2 Related Work

Efficient partitioning and balancing of workloads in parallel systems are both needed to achieve good performance and scalability. The scientific computing community has made significant efforts in partitioning computations using a number of non-overlapping regular blocks while minimizing the maximally loaded block. Adaptive partitioning methods are widely used in the presence of computation skews [3–5, 7, 15].

The GBD [5, 15] partitioning, also called rectilinear partitioning, uses $(M-1)*(N-1)$ lines to decompose a 2D domain into M*N blocks. In case computations distribute non-uniformly in the domain, these blocks are of different sizes but contain the same amount of computations. The GBD partitioning is widely applied [19] due to its approved load-balance effectiveness and easy-to-organize communications of block boundaries. [5] also proposes a semi-GBD partitioning. The semi-GBD first uses $M-1$ lines to divide a 2D domain into M stripes. Then, it either divides every stripe into N blocks (called M×N-way jagged partitioning), or divides each stripe according to the amount of computations the stripe contains (called M-way jagged partitioning) that stripes need not to have the same number of blocks. According to [7], the semi-GBD partitioning has a better load-balance effectiveness in some cases. However, synchronization complexity increases. The HB [3] partitioning is an adaptive and recursive partitioning method similar to the quad-tree structure we use. Different from the quad-tree manner, HB uses a split to divide a block into two sub-blocks every time.

These adaptive partitioning methods require a global view of computations to determine the placement of lines or splits. They also imply a significant overhead of finalizing a decomposition pattern for a domain, i.e., the domain is scanned again and again to determine every partitioning decision. In parallel environments, maintaining a global view for intensive computations and data is hardly feasible, and frequent workload scans incur substantial overheads. Apala overcomes these by presenting a distributed partitioning method that every processor partitions a local block independently. There is no need to maintain a global view of workloads in Apala, and the scan is for the local block only.

Although finding an optimal decomposition plan is NP-hard [20], many parallel frameworks use heuristics to integrate these adaptive partitioning methods for handling computation skews at runtime, such as [21, 22] for the adaptive mesh refinement problem. Apala resembles them but uses a decentralized strategy to partition the workload instead of the centralized mechanisms used in these frameworks.

Data is playing a more important role in state-transition applications. Apala explicitly considers data in its partitioning decisions and uses a time metric to unify computation and data according to system profiles. A related work to Apala is Mammoth [13] that processes state-transition applications using a MapReduce system. For the load imbalance issue, Mammoth relies on a runtime management by launching shadow tasks for heavy blocks. SkewReduce [23] is a specially designed system for feature-extracting scientific applications. SkewReduce defines two cost functions to estimate the costs of the partitioning and merging operations. A block will be bi-partitioned if the performance gain of parallelizing the two parts outweighs the partitioning and merging costs. SkewReduce samples the data to estimate the workload and guide the partitioning. Its MapReduce programming model and runtime make it easy-to-use and efficient. In contrast, Apala still addresses the partitioning and load-balance problem in the conventional MPI programming model.

Fig. 1 Example of parallelizing a state-transition application by equally partitioning the computation (*dark blue*) or by equally partitioning the data (*light blue*). For both scenarios, the computation and the data cannot be equally partitioned simultaneously, and consequently the workloads allocated to processors P1, P2, P3, and P4, are not equal (Color figure online)

3   Problem Description

For state-transition applications, the workloads of computation and data are determined by observations and states, respectively. The data of observations is generally of small size and does not bring in data workloads in terms of I/Os. An efficient parallelization scheme needs to partition and balance both workloads. However, the inconsistent distributions of the two workloads complicate the parallelization work. Consider the example in Fig. 1. The state-transition application of the weather data assimilation is modeled in a 2D coordinate space with a bounding domain, and changes of states (e.g., severe regional weather phenomena) are observed in a small region. Balancing the parallelization of this application's computation may result in the partitioning illustrated by the dash lines. We can see that, although the workload of computation is balanced, the workload of data corresponding to block size is not. Likewise, partitioning with the consideration of balancing data (illustrated by lines) suffers from the imbalanced partitioning of computation.

The partitioning problem becomes more complex if porting the parallelization work across different systems. Although the application's computation scale and data volume are constant, the CPU and I/O times spent on computing and loading data vary as systems have different CPU and I/O speeds. The length of the bars indicating the workloads of computation and data in Fig. 1 will change when porting to different systems due to their different profiles. Consequently, the partitioning strategies should be adjusted accordingly.

4   Apala

Apala features three key design merits: (1) it unifies and balances computation and data requirements; (2) it leverages the quad-tree structure to conduct the adaptive and recursive decomposition; (3) it utilizes a decentralized mechanism to distribute workloads across processors for load balance.

4.1   Unifying Workloads

Apala unifies the workloads of computation and data by quantifying the two in terms of time. Specifically, Apala first estimates the time needed for computing the observations as well as for loading the data of states. The combined time is then considered for partitioning. Ideally, every processor spends an equal amount of time on loading and computing its assigned workload.

Two factors affect the time estimation: the speed of loading the states and the speed of computing the observations. In our work, we mainly consider the system's CPU and I/O speeds. Consider a simple example of processing a block on two

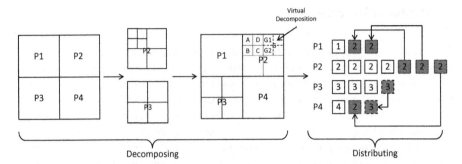

Fig. 2 Apala consists of two major steps: decomposing and partitioning. The decomposing step generates a decomposition plan for the application, and the partitioning step adjusts workload allocations among processors for load balance. The decomposing step involves three detailed substeps. (1) The entire application is uniformly decomposed, and each processor takes one equal-sized block. (2) Each processor independently generates an adaptive decomposition using the quad-tree structure. This decomposition is for the local block only. (3) Some blocks are "virtually" decomposed for finding side neighbors to set up data dependencies across processors

clusters, `cluster1` and `cluster2`. `cluster1` features 2,000 average MOPS (Million Operations Per Second) CPU speed and 100 average MBPS (Megabytes Per Second) I/O speed, while `cluster2` has 1,500 average MOPS CPU speed and 1,000 average MBPS I/O speed. If the block associates with 100 MB data of states and needs 100 million CPU operations to compute observations using state-transition algorithms, its unified workload on `cluster1` is $\frac{100}{100} + \frac{100}{2,000} = 1.05$ s, while that on `cluster2` is $\frac{100}{1,000} + \frac{100}{1,500} = 0.17$ s.

4.2 Decomposing the Unified Workload

Apala decomposes the unified workload into blocks for exposing parallelism as much as possible. In addition, the decomposition should be well structured so that synchronizations among blocks are organizable. Apala exploits the quad-tree structure in its decomposition scheme. A block with an intensive workload will be decomposed into four equal-sized sub-blocks. Each sub-block is checked to determine if further decomposition is needed. The decomposition continues until every block has a bounded workload.

There are two advantages for the quad-tree structure. First, blocks are regularly decomposed in which every decomposition operation generates four equal-sized sub-blocks. The decomposition shape is critical to simplify synchronization complexity and consequently reduce synchronization overhead. Rectangles are the most preferred shape to decompose 2D workloads for such purpose [7, 14], and quad-decomposing blocks can guarantee this. Second, it is easy to follow the quad-tree manner and decompose blocks adaptively and recursively.

Algorithm 1: Local decomposition

Require: L: single-layer workload (2D) of the state-transition application
      N: number of processors
      i: processor id
Ensure: P_i: local decomposition at processor i
1: Threshold $T \leftarrow \frac{L}{N}$
2: Decomposition $Q_i \leftarrow \varnothing$, $P_i \leftarrow \varnothing$
3: block $p \leftarrow$ uniform_decompose(L, i, N)
4: $Q_i \leftarrow Q_i \cup \{p\}$
5: **repeat**
6:      block $p \leftarrow$ choose the first block from Q_i
7:      **if** $p.wl > T$ **then**
8:          blocks $subs \leftarrow$ quad_decompose(p)
9:          **for all** block p' in $subs$ **do**
10:            **if** $p'.wl > T$ **then**
11:              $Q_i \leftarrow Q_i \cup p'$
12:            **else**
13:              $P_i \leftarrow P_i \cup p'$
14:            **end if**
15:          **end for**
16:      **else**
17:          $P_i \leftarrow P_i \cup p$
18:      **end if**
19: **until** $Q_i \neq \varnothing$
20: **return** P_i

Although state-transition applications are typically modeled in a 3D coordinate space, the workload decomposing is conducted layer by layer along the vertical direction (z-axis). All layers apply the same 2D decomposition. So we describe the decomposition scheme based on the 2D array of a single layer in the following.

The decomposition is summarized in Algorithm 1. At the beginning, the 2D array is uniformly decomposed into blocks, one for each processor. Every processor independently decomposes its local block in the adaptive and recursive manner. The block's workload is computed, and the block will be decomposed into four equal-sized sub-blocks if it exceeds the threshold. We define the threshold as the average workload across the system, i.e., the number of processors divides the amount of workloads. This recursive decomposing operation continues for every sub-block until each of them meets the threshold. This procedure is analogous to the construction of a quad-tree: the initial local block corresponds to the root; the sub-blocks that contain heavy workloads and are further decomposed correspond to internal nodes; and the final sub-blocks correspond to the leaves.

Synchronizations between adjacent blocks for swapping "halo" updates also benefit from the quad-tree structure. Data dependencies among blocks can be set up by finding side neighbors for the leaves in the quad-tree, and synchronizations occur when adjacent blocks are distributed to different processors. The algorithm introduced in [11] can be used for side-neighbor-finding, but it is restricted to find side neighbors with equal or larger size. As illustrated in Fig. 2, block G's

---
Algorithm 2: Building block dependencies

Require: P: "virtually decomposed" blocks
       r: node (block that finds neighbors)
       d: direction where to find neighbors
Ensure: S: set of neighbor nodes
 1: set *vdnodes* ← nodes in P decomposed from r
 2: **for** node *sub_r* in *vdnodes* **do**
 3:    node p ← ancestor node of both r and its neighbor
 4:    *addr* ← address of *sub_r* to p
 5:    *addr* ← mirror operation
 6:    node *dest* ← tree traversal from p using *addr*
 7:    $S \leftarrow S \cup \{dest\}$
 8: **end for**
 9: **return** S

---

left-side neighbor will be ambiguous when using this algorithm as there are two such neighbors. We circumvent this restriction by introducing the virtual decomposition technique: large blocks are virtually decomposed as finely as the smallest one. As a result, finding a side neighbor for a large block is split into finding a set of side neighbors for its virtual sub-blocks. The decomposition is virtual because the original block is the minimum unit of distributing workloads. The virtual blocks will not be distributed separately to different processors, nor will there be data dependencies among these virtual blocks.

Building data dependencies for blocks is conducted via the quad-tree traversal. We use node and block interchangeably to ease the understanding of operations related to the quad-tree structure. The concept of *address* is used: except the root, the address of a quad-tree node is defined as its corresponding block's position in its super-block (i.e., *LT* as lefttop, *LB* as leftbottom, *RB* as rightbottom, and *RT* as righttop). Two nodes can concatenate the addresses between them as *path* to refer to each other. The node (or sub-node from the virtual decomposition) locates its side neighbor in three steps: first, finds the path to the common ancestor of the neighbor; second, executes a mirror operation on the path; finally, search down from the ancestor along the mirrored path. The mirror operation replaces every *L/R* with *R/L* if the direction is *left* or *right*, or every *T/B* with *B/T* if the direction is *top* or *bottom*, along the path. Algorithm 2 summarizes the procedure of building dependency. An example is given in Fig. 2 that block G is virtually decomposed for finding its two left side neighbors, i.e., C and D.

4.3   Distributing the Unified Workload

Apala's distributing scheme is responsible for mapping blocks to processors with the consideration of load balance. It is based on the linear representation of the quad-tree at every processor and a decentralized scheme for re-mapping blocks from overloaded processors to underloaded ones.

The linear representation is generated using the in-order traversal of quad-tree leaves. A block's four sub-blocks are mapped in the order of "*TL, BL, BR, TR*" (counterclockwise order from topleft). Further decomposition of any sub-block is represented by replacing it with an expanded mapping of its sub-blocks (e.g., decomposing the topleft in "*TL, BL, BR, TR*" will generate the mapping of "[*TL, BL, BR, TR*], *BL, BR, TR*"). This linear representation eases the distributing work of mapping blocks to processors. The first a few blocks with the total workload approximating the threshold will be reserved for the local processor. The rest will be distributed to underloaded processors. Recall that the quad-tree structure is used for building dependencies for blocks. The block distributed to other processors can explore its neighbor blocks quickly, and subsequently processors can set up communication for swapping "halo" updates.

Overloaded processors distribute their extra workloads to underloaded ones in a decentralized manner. Every processor independently checks the available capacity of every underloaded processor, sorts the blocks to be distributed in the ascending order according to their workloads, and maps every such block to the first underloaded processor that is available.

This decentralized mechanism allows an overloaded processor to complete its distributing action quickly. However, it might also lead to a situation that too many overloaded processors push workloads to the same underloaded processor simultaneously, resulting in a new overloaded processor. To overcome this, we introduce a throttle factor γ to control the amount of workload an overloaded processor can push to an underloaded one. Algorithm 3 outlines this decentralized distributing scheme.

Algorithm 3: Decentralized distributing scheme

Require: P_i: the blocks at processor i
    L: workload amount
    N: number of processors
1: blocks to be distributed $O \leftarrow \varnothing$
2: $P_i^l, P_i^r \leftarrow$ divides P_i that P_i^l are blocks reserved locally and P_i^r are to be distributed.
3: $O \leftarrow O \cup P_i^r$
4: sort(O)
5: $T_a \leftarrow \frac{L}{N}$
6: **for all** underloaded processors j **do**
7:    $j.free \leftarrow \gamma * (T_a - j.wl)$
8: **end for**
9: **for** block p in O **do**
10:    **for all** underloaded processors j **do**
11:      **if** $p.wl \le j.free$ **then**
12:        $p.owner \leftarrow j$;
13:        $j.wl \leftarrow j.wl + p.wl$
14:        $j.free \leftarrow j.free - p.wl$
15:      **end if**
16:    **end for**
17: **end for**

---

5 Evaluation

In this section, we present the experimental evaluation. It includes two parts: (1) comparing Apala with other partitioning schemes (i.e., uniform partitioning, Generalized Block Distribution (GBD) [5, 15], and Hierarchical Bipartition (HB) [3]) in terms of the effectiveness of load balance; (2) evaluating Apala's portability of adjusting its partitioning and load-balance scheme according to system profiles; (3) evaluating Apala's overhead of partitioning.

5.1 Setup

Applications and Datasets The state-transition application of weather data assimilation [16] is used. It models states of the environment and observations of the atmosphere in a 3D bounding box. The data assimilation algorithm is performed layer-by-layer along the z-axis and point-by-point within each layer. At every point, the states and the observations are assimilated for new states. These states will not only update the point itself but also the neighbor points in a 4×4 "halo".

We use two datasets (Fig. 3) in the evaluation. The first contains 75 GB data of states and 25 MB data of observations, while the second contains 19 GB data of

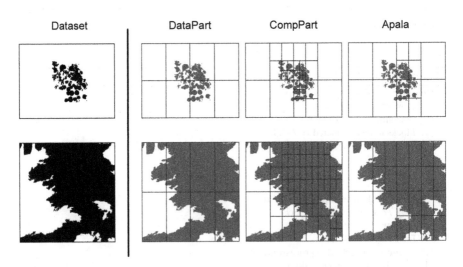

Fig. 3 The datasets we use in the experimental evaluation. The first dataset is from the Center for Analysis and Prediction of Storms at the University of Oklahoma, which described the observations covering the Oklahama state on May 20, 2010. The second one was captured from weather.com, which described the observations covering Gainesville, Florida on January 1, 2012. Both are modeled in the 3D coordinate space but showed with the 2D view. The first is bounded in a $1{,}323 \times 963 \times 10$ box, while the second is bounded in a $400 \times 400 \times 20$ box. The decomposition patterns with different schemes for both datasets are illustrated as well

states and 3 MB data of observations. Both states and observations are stored in the key-value format in plain text files, i.e., *"x,y,z,var1,var2,...,varN"* for states and *"x,y,z,ob"* for observations, where *"x,y,z"* represents the coordinate, *"var1"* represents the environmental variable, and *"ob"* represents the observation.

Computer Clusters We use four clusters for the evaluation: two HPC clusters of Alamo and Sierra at FutureGrid, and two virtual clusters, EC2.Small and EC2.Large, consisting of Amazon EC2 small and large instances, respectively.

Each node at Alamo contains two 2.66 GHz Intel Xeon X5550 processors (four cores per processor) and 12 GB memory and is interconnected via InfiniBand. Alamo uses a NFS-based parallel file system for the shared data storage. Each node at Sierra contains two 2.5 GHz Intel Xeon L5420 processors (four cores per processor) and 32 GB memory and is also interconnected via InfiniBand. Sierra uses a ZFS file system for the shared data storage.

Each small instance in EC2.Small has 1 EC2 compute unit, 1.7 GB memory, and moderate I/O speed, while each large instance in EC2.Large has four EC2 compute units, 7.5 GB memory, and high I/O speed. Due to the virtualization overhead, the two virtual clusters perform much more moderately (particularly the EC2.Small cluster) than the physical HPC clusters. For their data storage, we create an Amazon EBS (Elastic Block Service) volume, attach it to a dedicated instance, and mount it to the cluster using the NFS file system.

Benchmark Tools We use the NAS Parallel Benchmark (NPB) [17] and the IOR HPC benchmark [18] to measure the CPU and I/O speeds for every cluster. The NPB consists of several benchmarks that simulate the computational fluid dynamics applications, and these applications cover various computing patterns. The CPU speeds of these benchmarks are averaged, and the average value is used to represent the CPU speed of the cluster. To measure the I/O speed, the IOR HPC benchmark is used to reproduce the I/O patterns of our data assimilation application, i.e., concurrently and randomly accessing a continuous block of a single file. Table 1 lists the profiles of the CPU and I/O speeds of the four clusters.

Table 1 Profiles of the clusters	Alamo	Sierra	EC2.Large	EC2.Small
I/O (Read, MB/s)	1233	1099	938	478
I/O (Write, MB/s)	391	70	15	16
CPU (MOPS)	824	351	128	33

Implementation Apala is implemented using C++ with the standard MPI-2 library. It reads the benchmark results describing system profiles (i.e., the CPU speed and the I/O speed) from a configure file. The paths to the data of states and observations are contained in this file as well. Apala generates a quad-tree-based decomposition plan using a *partition* method, and allocates the workload to processors using a *distribute* method. For each processor, its workload allocation is organized as a list of rectangular blocks. These blocks are represented using indexes of arrays (i.e., the bottom-left coordinate and the top-right coordinate). State-transition algorithms are programmed from the perspective of an individual point. For updates in "halos" that are out of original blocks, Apala has a *synchronize* method for users to manage synchronizations. Indexes of points and data dependencies are built when generating decomposition plans, and they are used to drive the *synchronize* method. An *aggregate* method is opened for users to define how to finalize the result of a point covered by multiple "halos".

We set the throttle factor γ to 0.5, implying at most half of the processors can push their workloads to an underloaded one. Note that every result in the following figures is the average value of five runs. The error bars are small, indicating performance fluctuations are marginal, even on virtual clusters.

5.2 Decomposition Patterns

Two static partitioning strategies, "DataPart" and "CompPart", are used for the comparison purpose. The "DataPart" partitions the workload according to the data of states only, while the "CompPart" accords to that of observations only. Figure 3 illustrates the decomposition patterns of using "DataPart", "CompPart", and Apala to decompose both datasets for eight processors. We can see that, "DataPart" generates a uniform decomposition as the data of states indicating I/Os distributes evenly, "CompPart" generates a much finer decomposition for the regions with dense observations. In comparison, the decomposition from Apala is in between due to its comprehensive consideration of computation and data.

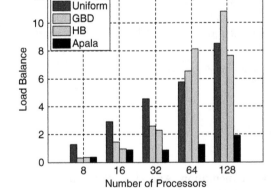

Fig. 4 Comparison of the load balance effectiveness among Uniform, GBD, HB, and Apala, with the first dataset

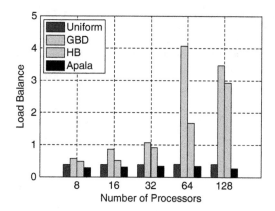

Fig. 5 Comparison of the load balance effectiveness among Uniform, GBD, HB, and Apala, with the second dataset

5.3   Effectiveness of Load Balance

The effectiveness of load balance is measured according to $(Max - Avg)/Avg$, where Max is the execution time of the longest processor, and Avg represents the average execution time of all the processors. Smaller values indicate better load balance.

The results comparing Apala with other partitioning schemes are presented in Figs. 4 and 5 for the two datasets, respectively. We can see that, Apala outperforms the partitioning schemes of uniform, GBD, and HB for both datasets by at most ten times. Uniform, GBD, and HB partition the workload according to the computation only. Ignoring the workload of loading the large volume of states results in load imbalance. The first dataset shows more significant imbalance. That is because the observations in the first dataset mainly concentrate on hot spots, and the block sizes are more diverse after decomposition. However, Apala performs stably because it accounts for both computation and data.

5.4   Portability

When porting to a new computer cluster, the CPU and I/O speeds of the system change, and Apala will adjust its workload estimation and the subsequent partitioning and load-balance scheme. To evaluate Apala's portability, we deploy Apala to the four clusters and compare its performance to static (not portable) partitioning strategies. Due to space limit, only results about the first dataset is presented in this paper.

According to the CPU and I/O speeds listed in Table 1, Alamo and Sierra show excellent CPU and I/O speeds. EC2.Large and EC2.Small are expected to present poor I/O speeds due to using the shared EBS volume. All the I/Os for the data of

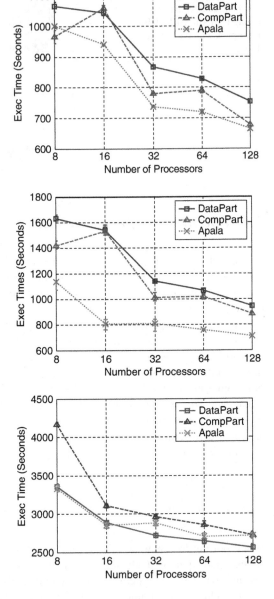

Fig. 6 Comparison of the execution time of "DataPart", "CompPart", and Apala on the Alamo cluster, with the first dataset

Fig. 7 Comparison of the execution time of "DataPart", "CompPart", and Apala on the Sierra cluster, with the first dataset

Fig. 8 Comparison of the execution time of "DataPart", "CompPart", and Apala on the EC2.Large cluster, with the first dataset

states will be directed to the shared EBS storage. EC2.Small also shows a poor CPU speed due to the shared use of physical processors [10].

Intuitively, for the system that has a fast I/O speed, the time spent on loading the data of states is relatively short in the workload estimation, and partitioning using "CompPart" that depends on observations is preferred (and vice versa for the system with a fast CPU speed).

Fig. 9 Comparison of the execution time of "DataPart", "CompPart", and Apala on the EC2.Small cluster, with the first dataset

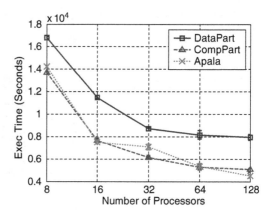

We use "DataPart", "CompPart" and Apala to partition the first dataset for the evaluation of portability. Results are presented in Figs. 6, 7, 8, and 9. As "DataPart" and "CompPart" are static, their partitioning and load-balance schemes are constant across systems. We can observe that, partitioning according to observations outperforms that based on states for Alamo, Sierra and EC2.Small, while partitioning according to states performs better on EC2.Large. This matches our expectation that partitioning according to the weak factor yields a better load balance. In contrast, Apala always shows excellent performance on all systems. It outperforms both static schemes significantly on the HPC clusters and almost performs best on the virtual clusters (ties with "DataPart" on EC2.Large and "CompPart" on EC2.Small). The reason is straightforward, jointly considering computation and data always benefits the partitioning and load-balance scheme.

5.5 Overhead of Partitioning

We measure the partitioning overhead for Apala with the two datasets and show the results in Figs. 10 and 11. Since the results cover all the four clusters, they are normalized to be plotted in the same figure. For each cluster, the execution time with 8 processors is set to 1, and the values with 16, 32, 64, and 128 processors are adjusted proportionally. The "CPU+I/O" parts for Apala include scientific computations and data loads. The "Synchronization" parts represent the time Apala spends on MPI_Isend, MPI_Irecv, and MPI_Barrier. The "Partitioning Overhead" means processors are decomposing their local blocks and distributing the workload to (or receiving from) others for load balance. At each tick, the four bars from the left to the right represent Alamo, Sierra, EC2.Large, and EC2.Small, respectively.

We can see that the partitioning overhead in Apala is minimal for both datasets on all the clusters. This is reasonable as each processor only estimates its local workload, and such estimation is merely based on the data size, the computation

Fig. 10 Comparison of the
CPU+I/O, the
synchronization, and the
partitioning overhead in terms
of time on the four clusters,
the first dataset

Fig. 11 Comparison of the
CPU+I/O, the
synchronization, and the
partitioning overhead in terms
of time on the four clusters,
the second dataset

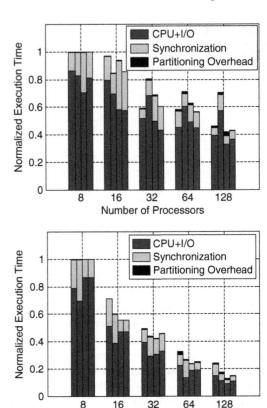

scale, and system profiles. The partitioning overhead increases with respect to the number of processors, as distributing the workloads involves more processors, and the communication complexity increases accordingly.

Conclusion

In this chapter, we presented Apala, an adaptive workload partitioning and allocation scheme for parallelizing data intensive state-transition applications in various parallel systems. State-transition applications are representative data-intensive scientific applications. They generally tackle grand-challenge problems (e.g., weather forecasting, ocean prediction) and involve extremely complex algorithms. Apala considers both computation and data in its workload partitioning and allocation scheme. It introduces a time metric for unifying the workloads of computation and data and profiles systems for accurate workload estimation. The quad-tree structure is used to represent

(continued)

the procedure of breaking up arrays into blocks, and techniques of virtual decomposition and finding-side-neighbors are introduced to organize data dependency. A decentralized distributing strategy is applied for distributing blocks across processors. Experimental results from the real-world data show that, Apala outperforms other partitioning schemes in terms of the effectiveness of load balance by at most ten times. Moreover, it shows excellent portability on diverse systems from HPC clusters to virtual clusters in clouds and incurs marginal overhead of partitioning.

References

1. M. Fisher, J. Nocedal, Y. Trémolet, and S. Wright, "Data assimilation in weather forecasting: a case study in pde-constrained optimization," *Optimization and Engineering*, vol. 10, no. 3, pp. 409–426, 2009.
2. A. Robinson and P. Lermusiaux, "Overview of data assimilation," *Harvard reports in physical/interdisciplinary ocean science*, vol. 62, 2000.
3. M. Berger and S. Bokhari, "A partitioning strategy for nonuniform problems on multiprocessors," *ToC*, vol. 100, no. 5, pp. 570–580, 1987.
4. D. Nicol, "Rectilinear partitioning of irregular data parallel computations," DTIC Document, Tech. Rep., 1991.
5. F. Manne and T. Sørevik, "Partitioning an array onto a mesh of processors," *Applied Parallel Computing Industrial Computation and Optimization*, pp. 467–477, 1996.
6. O. Beaumont, V. Boudet, F. Rastello, and Y. Robert, "Matrix multiplication on heterogeneous platforms," *TPDS*, vol. 12, no. 10, pp. 1033–1051, 2001.
7. E. Saule, E. O. Bas, and U. V. Catalyurek, "Partitioning spatially located computations using rectangles," in *IPDPS*. IEEE, 2011.
8. N. Wright, S. Smallen, C. Olschanowsky, J. Hayes, and A. Snavely, "Measuring and understanding variation in benchmark performance," in *DoD High Performance Computing Modernization Program Users Group Conference (HPCMP-UGC), 2009*. IEEE, 2009, pp. 438–443.
9. T. Zou, G. Wang, M. Salles, D. Bindel, A. Demers, J. Gehrke, and W. White, "Making time-stepped applications tick in the cloud," in *SoCC*. ACM, 2011, p. 20.
10. G. Wang and T. Ng, "The impact of virtualization on network performance of amazon ec2 data center," in *INFOCOM*. IEEE, 2010, pp. 1–9.
11. H. Samet, "The quadtree and related hierarchical data structures," *ACM Computing Surveys (CSUR)*, vol. 16, no. 2, pp. 187–260, 1984.
12. B. H. A. Hoekstra and R. Williams, "High-performance computing and networking."
13. X. Yang, Z. Yu, M. Li, and X. Li, "Mammoth: autonomic data processing framework for scientific state-transition applications," in *Proceedings of the 2013 ACM Cloud and Autonomic Computing Conference*. ACM, 2013, p. 13.
14. J.-R. Sack and J. Urrutia, *Handbook of computational geometry*. North Holland, 1999.
15. B. Aspvall, M. M Halldórsson, and F. Manne, "Approximations for the general block distribution of a matrix," *Theoretical computer science*, vol. 262, no. 1, pp. 145–160, 2001.
16. M. Xue, D. Wang, J. Gao, K. Brewster, and K. Droegemeier, "The Advanced Regional Prediction System (ARPS), storm-scale numerical weather prediction and data assimilation," *Meteorology and Atmospheric Physics*, vol. 82, no. 1, pp. 139–170, 2003.

17. R. Van der Wijngaart and P. Wong, "Nas parallel benchmarks version 2.4," NAS technical report, NAS-02-007, Tech. Rep., 2002.
18. "IOR HPC Benchmark," http://sourceforge.net/projects/ior-sio/.
19. H. P. F. Form, "High performance fortran language specification," 1993.
20. M. Grigni and F. Manne, "On the complexity of the generalized block distribution," *Parallel Algorithms for Irregularly Structured Problems*, pp. 319–326, 1996.
21. M. J. Berger and J. Oliger, "Adaptive mesh refinement for hyperbolic partial differential equations," *Journal of computational Physics*, vol. 53, no. 3, pp. 484–512, 1984.
22. X. Li and M. Parashar, "Hybrid runtime management of space-time heterogeneity for parallel structured adaptive applications," *TPDS*, pp. 1202–1214, 2007.
23. Y. Kwon, M. Balazinska, B. Howe, and J. Rolia, "Skew-resistant parallel processing of feature-extracting scientific user-defined functions," in *SoCC*. ACM, 2010, pp. 75–86.

DRAW: A New Data-gRouping-AWare Data Placement Scheme for Data Intensive Applications with Interest Locality

Jun Wang, Pengju Shang, and Jiangling Yin

Abstract Recent years have seen an increasing number of scientists employ data parallel computing frameworks such as MapReduce and Hadoop to run data intensive applications and conduct analysis. In these co-located compute and storage frameworks, a wise data placement scheme can significantly improve the performance. Existing data parallel frameworks, e.g. Hadoop, or Hadoop-based clouds, distribute the data using a random placement method for simplicity and load balance. However, we observe that many data intensive applications exhibit *interest locality* which only sweep part of a big data set. The data often accessed together results from their *grouping* semantics. Without taking data grouping into consideration, the random placement does not perform well and is way below the efficiency of optimal data distribution. In this paper, we develop a new Data-gRouping-Aware (DRAW) data placement scheme to address the above-mentioned problem. DRAW dynamically scrutinizes data access from system log files. It extracts optimal data groupings and re-organizes data layouts to achieve the maximum parallelism per group subjective to load balance. By experimenting two real-world MapReduce applications with different data placement schemes on a 40-node test bed, we conclude that DRAW increases the total number of local map tasks executed up to 59.8 %, reduces the completion latency of the map phase up to 41.7 %, and improves the overall performance by 36.4 %, in comparison with Hadoop's default random placement.

1 Introduction

The emerging myriad data intensive applications place a demand on high-performance computing resources with massive storage. Academic and industrial pioneers have been developing big data parallel computing frameworks and large-scale distributed file systems to facilitate the high-performance runs of data-intensive applications, such as bio-informatics [26], astronomy [25], and

J. Wang (✉) • P. Shang • J. Yin
EECS, University of Central Florida, Orlando, FL 32826, USA
e-mail: jwang@eecs.ucf.edu; shang@eecs.ucf.edu; jyin@eecs.ucf.edu

© Springer Science+Business Media New York 2014   149
X. Li, J. Qiu (eds.), *Cloud Computing for Data-Intensive Applications*,
DOI 10.1007/978-1-4939-1905-5_7

high-energy physics [23]. Our recent work [27] reported that data distribution in distributed file systems could significantly affect the efficiency of data processing and hence the overall application performance. This is especially true for those with sophisticated access patterns.

In practice, many scientific and engineering applications have *interest locality:* (1) domain scientists are only interested in a *subset* of the whole data set, and (2) scientists are likely to access one subset more frequently than others. For example, in the bioinformatics domain, X and Y chromosomes are related to the offspring's gender. Both chromosomes are often analyzed together in generic research rather than all the 24 human chromosomes [15]. Regarding other mammal's genome data pools, the chimpanzee is usually compared with human [18,28]. Another example is, in the climate modeling and forecasting domain, some scientists are only interested in some specific time periods [29]. In summary, these co-related data have high possibility to be processed as a group by specific domain applications. Here, we formally define the "**data grouping**" to represent the possibility of two or more data (e.g., blocks in Hadoop) to be accessed as a group. Such data grouping can be quantified by a *weight*: a count that these data have already been accessed as a group. The potential assumption is that if two pieces of data have been already accessed together for many times, it is highly possible for them to be accessed as a group in the future [11].

There are two different ways to distribute the grouped data: clustering, or declustering. Each way is optimal for specific type of data intensive applications. In the former case, some applications access binary files [10, 14] or other structured data that have data dependency. Data from the same group must be physically stored together to form a valid input data. Hence, they should be clustered as much as possible so as to reduce the data migration cost [31]. For the latter one, accessed data does not have dependency [2] such as genome indexing [1] and word count [2]. Grouped data could be distributed as evenly as possible to maximize parallelism and performance. In this paper, we focus on the MapReduce framework which splits the input data-set into independent chunks. As one of the most popular MapReduce implementations, Yahoo's Hadoop [2] employs a random data placement scheme in light of load balance and simplicity [4]. This allows the MapReduce [13] programs to access *the whole data set* at full parallelism. Unfortunately, current random placement schemes are inefficient when used on applications with high interest locality—when only a subset of the data is processed—because the grouped data could be clustered into a small number of nodes rather than being evenly distributed.

In this paper, we develop a new Data-gRouping-AWare data placement scheme (**DRAW**) that takes into account the data grouping effects to significantly improve the performance for data-intensive applications with interest locality. Without loss of generality, DRAW is designed and implemented as a Hadoop-version prototype. For a multi-rack Hadoop cluster, DRAW is launched at rack level (inter-rack) to manage the data distribution. DRAW consists of three components: (1) a data access history graph (HDAG) to scrutinize data access history patterns, (2) a data grouping matrix (DGM) derived from HDAG to group related data, and (3) an optimal data placement algorithm (ODPA) generating final data layout. By experimenting with real world genome indexing [1] and astrophysics applications [9], DRAW is able to execute up to 59.8 % more local map tasks in comparison with random placement. In addition, DRAW reduces the completion time of map phase by up to 41.7 %, and the MapReduce task execution time by up to 36.4 %.[1]

The rest of this paper is organized as follow: Sect. 2 explains our motivation. Section 3 describes the design of DRAW. Section 4 theoretically proves the inefficiency of Hadoop's default random placement method. Sections 5 and 6 present experimental methodology and our results and analysis respectively. Section 7 presents related works. Finally, "Conclusion" section concludes the paper.

2   Motivation

The raw data obtained from the scientific simulations/sensors needs to be uploaded to the Hadoop cluster for subsequent MapReduce programs [27]. In these large scale data sets, the accessing frequency and pattern of each data varies because of the applications' interest locality. For example, UCSC Genome Browser [3] hosts the reference sequences and working draft assemblies for a large collection of genomes. It is obvious this different groups will access different subsets of these genome data: mammal [12], insect [19], or vertebrate [33]. Even when in the same category, e.g. mammal, different groups may focus on different species [18, 28].

By using Hadoop's default random data placement strategy, the overall data distribution may be balanced,[2] but there is no guarantee that the data accessed as a group is evenly distributed. To further explore why such clustered data grouping creates performance barriers for the MapReduce program, we need to know how a MapReduce program works. A MapReduce job is split into many map tasks to process in parallel. Map tasks intend to be allocated to the nodes with the needed data locally being stored to achieve "compute-storage co-localit". Without evenly distributed grouping data, some map tasks are either scheduled on other nodes which remotely access the needed data, or they are scheduled on these data holding nodes but have to wait in the queue. These map tasks violate the data locality and could severely drag down the MapReduce program performance [2]. We show an example in Fig. 1: if the grouping data are distributed by Hadoop's random strategy, the shaded map tasks with either remote data access or queueing delay are the performance barriers; whereas if these data are evenly distributed, the MapReduce program can avoid these barriers.

---

[1]These numbers can be affected by the number of launched reduce tasks, the required data size, etc.

[2]If the initial data distribution is not balanced, Hadoop users can start a balancer (an utility in Hadoop), to re-balance the data among the nodes.

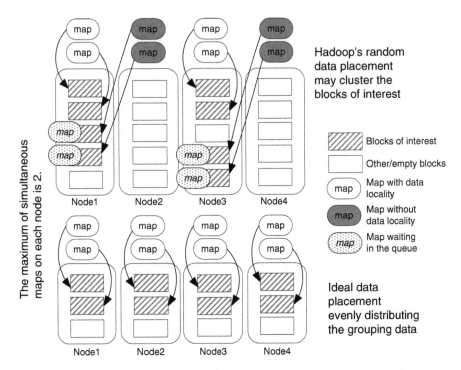

Fig. 1 A simple case showing the efficiency of data placement for MapReduce programs

Therefore, the reason for the inefficiency of Hadoop's random data placement is because the data semantics, e.g. grouping access patterns (caused by applications'interest locality), are lost during the data distribution. On the other hand, dynamic data grouping is an effective mechanism for exploiting the predictability of data access patterns and improving the performance of distributed file systems [11, 16, 22]. In this work, we incorporate data grouping semantics into Hadoop's data distribution policy to improve the MapReduce programs'performance

3 Data-gRouping-AWare Data Placement

In this section, we design DRAW at rack-level, which optimizes the grouping data distribution inside a rack. There are three parts in our design: a data access history graph (HDAG) to exploit system log files learning the data grouping information; a data grouping matrix (DGM) to quantify the grouping weights among the data and generate the optimized data groupings; an optimal data placement algorithm (ODPA) to form the optimal data placement.

3.1 History Data Access Graph (HDAG)

HDAG is a graph describing the access patterns among the files, which can be learned from the history of data accesses. In each Hadoop cluster rack, the NameNode maintains system logs recording every system operation, including the files which have been accessed. A naive solution can be: monitor the files which are being accessed; every two continuously accessed files will be categorized in the same DRAW 5 group. This solution is simple for implementation because it only needs a traversal of the *NameNode* log files. However in practical situations there are two problems: first, the log files could be huge which may result in unacceptable traversal latency; second, the continuously accessed files are not necessarily related, e.g. the last file accessed by task x and the first file accessed by task *x*+1. Therefore, we need to define checkpoint to indicate how far the HDAG will traverse back in the *NameNode* logs; and we also need to exploit the mappings between tasks and files to accurately learn the file access patterns. Note that in Hadoop clusters, files are split into blocks which is the basic data distribution unit; hence we need to translate the grouping information at file level into block level. Fortunately, the mapping information between files and blocks can be found in the *NameNode*. Figure 2 shows an example of HDAG: given three MapReduce tasks, $t1$ accesses $d1$, $d2$, $d3$, $d6$, $d7$, $d8$, here d is block; $t2$ accesses $d2$, $d3$, $d4$, $d7$, $d9$; and $t3$ accesses $d1$, $d2$, $d5$, $d6$, $d7$, $d10$. The accessing information initially generated from the log files is shown as Fig. 2a. Thereafter we can easily translate the table into the HDAG shown as Fig. 2b. This translation step makes it easier to generate the grouping Matrix for the next step.

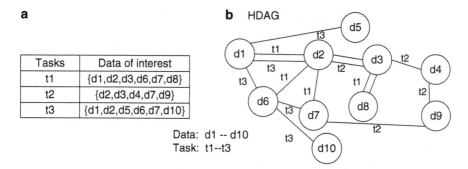

a

Tasks	Data of interest
t1	{d1,d2,d3,d6,d7,d8}
t2	{d2,d3,d4,d7,d9}
t3	{d1,d2,d5,d6,d7,d10}

Data: d1 -- d10
Task: t1--t3

Fig. 2 An example showing the History Data Access Graph (HDAG)

3.2 Data Grouping Matrix (DGM)

Based on HDAG, we can generate a data grouping matrix (DGM) showing the relation between every two data blocks. Given the same example as shown in Fig. 2, we can build the DGM as shown in Fig. 3 (step 1 and step 2), where each element

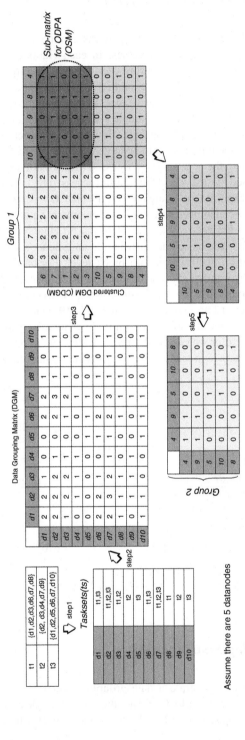

Fig. 3 An example showing the grouping matrix and the overall flow to cluster data based on their grouping weights

$DGM_{i,j} = grouping_{i,j}$ is the grouping weight between data i and j. Every $DGM_{i,j}$ can be calculated by counting the tasks in common between task sets of ts_i and ts_j. The elements in the diagonal of the DGM show the number of jobs that have used this data. In DRAW, DGM is a n by n matrix, where n is the number of existing blocks. As we stated before, one data belonging to group A may belong to group B at the same time; the grouping weight in the DGM denotes "how likely" one data should be grouped with another data.

After knowing the DGM in Fig. 3, we use a matrix clustering algorithm to group the highly related data in step 3. Specifically, Bond Energy Algorithm (BEA) is used to transform the DGM to the clustered data grouping matrix (CDGM). Since a weighted matrix clustering problem is N-P hard, the time complexity to obtain the optimized solution is $O(n^n)$, where n is the dimension. The BEA algorithm saves the computing cost by finding the sub-optimal solution in time $O(n^2)$ [17]; it has been widely utilized in distributed database systems for the vertical partition of large tables [24] and matrix clustering work [17]. The BEA algorithm clusters the highly associated data together indicating which data should be evenly distributed. Assuming there are 5 *DataNodes* in the Hadoop cluster, the CDGM in Fig. 3 indicates data $\{6, 7, 1, 2, 3\}$ (group 1) and $\{4, 9, 5, 10, 8\}$ (group 2) should be evenly distributed when placed on the 5 nodes. Note that we have only 10 pieces of data in our example, after knowing that $\{6, 7, 1, 2, 3\}$ should be placed as a group (horizontally), it is natural to treat the left data $\{4, 9, 5, 10, 8\}$ as another group. Hence step 4 and step 5 in Fig. 3 are not necessary for our case, but when the number of remaining data (after recognizing the first group) is larger than the number of nodes, more clustering steps are needed.

3.3   Optimal Data Placement Algorithm (ODPA)

Knowing the data groups alone is not enough to achieve the optimal data placement. Given the same example from Fig. 3 , random placing of each group, as shown in Fig. 4(1), task 2 and task 3 can only run on 4 nodes rather than 5, which is not optimal.

This is because the above data grouping only considers the horizontal relationships among the data in DGM, and so it is also necessary to make sure the blocks on the same node have minimal chance to be in the same group (vertical relationships). In order to obtain this information, we propose an algorithm named Optimal Data Placement Algorithm (ODPA) to complete our DRAW design, as described in Algorithm 1. ODPA is based on sub-matrix for ODPA (OSM) from CDGM. OSM indicates the dependencies among the data already placed and the ones being placed. For example, the OSM in Fig. 3 denotes the vertical relations between two different groups (group 1: 6, 7, 1, 2, 3 and group 2: 4, 9, 5, 10, 8).

Take the OSM from Fig. 3 as an example, The ODPA algorithm starts from the first row in OSM, whose row index is 6. Because there is only one minimum value 0 in column 9, we assign $DP[6] = \{6, 9\}$, which means data 6 and 9 should be placed

Without ODPA, the parrallelism may be not maximized

node1	node2	node3	node4	node5
d6	d7	d1	d2	d3
d4	d9	d5	d10	d8

Tasks	requried data	Involved nodes
t1	d1,d2,d3,d6,d7,d8	1,2,3,4,5
t2	d2,d3,d4,d7,d9	1,2,4,5
t3	d1,d2,d5,d6,d7,d10	1,2,3,4

Not optimal

(1)

Optimized data layout maximizes the parallelism

node1	node2	node3	node4	node5
d6	d7	d1	d2	d3
d9	d8	d4	d10	d5

Tasks	requried data	Involved nodes
t1	d1,d2,d3,d6,d7,d8	1,2,3,4,5
t2	d2,d3,d4,d7,d9	1,2,3,4,5
t3	d1,d2,d5,d6,d7,d10	1,2,3,4,5

Optimal

(2)

Fig. 4 Without ODPA, the layout generated from CDGM (Clustered Data-Grouping Matrix) may be still non-optimal

---

Algorithm 1: ODPA algorithm

Input: The sub-matrix (OSM) as shown in Fig. 3 : $M[n][n]$; where n is the number of data nodes;
Output: A matrix indicating the optimal data placement: $DP[2][n]$;
Steps:
for each row from $M[n][n]$ **do**
    $R=$ the index of current row;
    Find the minimum value V in this row;
    Put this value and its corresponding column index C into a set ***MinSet***;
    $MinSet = C1, V1, C2, V2,$; // there may be more than one minimum value
    if there is only one tuple $(C1, V1)$ in *MinSet* **then**
        //The data referred by C1 should be placed with the data referred by R on the same
node;
        $DP[0][R] = R$;
        $DP[1][R] = C1$;
        Mark column $C1$ is invalid (already assigned);
        Continue;
    end if
    for each column C_i from *MinSet* **do**
        Calculate $Sum[i] = sum(M[\star][Ci])$; // all the items in C_i column
    end for
    Choose the largest value from Sum array;
    C = the index of the chosen Sum item;
    $DP[0][R] = R$;
    $DP[1][R] = C$;
    Mark column C is invalid (already assigned);
end for

---

on the same data node because 9 is the least relevant data to 6. When checking row 7, there are five equal minimum values, which means any of these five data are equally related on data 7. To choose the optimal candidate among these five candidates, we need to examine their dependencies to other already placed data, which is performed by the FOR loop calculating the Sum for these five columns. In our case, $Sum[8] = 5$

is the largest value; by placing 8 with 7 on the same node, we can, to the maximum extent, reduce the possibility of assigning it onto another related data block. Hence, a new tuple $\{7, 8\}$ is added to DP. After doing the same processes to the rows with index 1, 2, 3, we have a $DP = \{\{6, 9\}, \{7, 8\}, \{1, 4\}, \{2, 10\}, \{3, 5\}\}$, indicating the data should be placed as shown in Fig. 4(2). Clearly, all the tasks can achieve the optimal parallelism (5) when running on the optimal data layout. With the help of ODPA, DRAW can achieve the two goals: maximize the parallel distribution of the grouping data, and balance the overall storage loads.

3.4 Other Considerations

3.4.1 The Cases Without Interest Locality

DRAW is designed for the applications showing interest locality. However there are some real world applications do not have interest locality. In this case, all the data on the cluster belongs to the same group; or the access is not following any specific pattern. Therefore the data grouping matrix contains the same grouping weight for each pair of data (except for the diagonal numbers); the BEA algorithm will not cluster the matrix, all the data blocks will stay on the nodes and distributed as the default random data distribution. Because all the data are equally popular, theoretically random data distribution can evenly balance them onto the nodes. In this case, DRAW has the same performance as Hadoop's random data distribution strategy.

3.4.2 The Cases with Special Interest Locality

The purpose of DRAW is to optimize the performance for the common applications which follow or do not totally deviate from the previous interest locality. However in practice, some applications may have unpredicted access patterns that DRAW did not study yet. These uncommon queries may suffer from bad performance because DRAW cannot guarantee these accessing data are well distributed, but these patterns will be considered into DRAW's future data organization to deal with future occurrences.

3.4.3 Multiple Jobs with Multiple Data Sets

For simplicity, the above design is for the cases when multiple jobs are accessing a single data set on the cluster. It can be easily scaled up to multiple jobs with multiple data sets. Given multiple jobs with special interest on different data sets, there will be NO data affinity among these sets; therefore in these cases, there will be multiple HDAGs, each of which is corresponding to a special data set and processed separately.

3.4.4   Cluster/Datacenter Using Virtualization

Some clusters and data centers may use virtualization to increase utilization efficiency and dramatically lower capital and operating costs. The virtualization layer always make the data locality fuzzy because the relationship between virtual machines and physical machines is not transparent for users and not static. DRAW makes an potential assumption that the distribution of virtual machines among the physical machines is balanced and managed by the virtualization layer [5]. On top of VMs load balancing, DRAW is able to provide optimized data distribution to improve the applications performance. In another word, DRAW is a complimentary benefit no mater whether the cluster/datacenter is virtualized or not.

4   Analysis

In order to reveal the importance and necessity of DRAW, we need to show how inefficient the default random data distribution strategy is. Specifically, we quantify four factors in this section: the possibility for a random data distribution to be an optimal solution, the optimal degree of a given data distribution, how optimal the random data distribution can achieve, and how much improvement the random solution can achieve by using multi-replica in the same rack.

We make two assumptions: (1) uniform block size (64 M) is used; (2) the default InputSplit is used, so the Hadoop block size is treated as the size for each input split [2]. The Hadoop Map/Reduce framework spawns one map task for each InputSplit, hence we assume that the number of map tasks is the same as the number required blocks.

4.1   The Chance That "Random = Optimal"

Given a cluster with N nodes, and a running application accessing M blocks that are distributed on these nodes, the "optimal data placement" should be able to distribute the M data as evenly as possible so that the corresponding M map tasks can also benefit from the maximum parallelism and data locality. However the practical Hadoop cluster's configuration may result in another "optima" case: if the maximum number of simultaneous map tasks on each node is 2, and each node is equipped with a dual-core processor, then the performance of running 2 maps on a single node is the same as running 1 map. Hence we define the "optimal data placemen" as: given a *TaskTracker* running l maps, $l \neq 0$, any other *TaskTracker* running $j \neq 0$ maps has to obey $|l - j| < 2$; any other *TaskTracker* running $j = 0$ map has to obey $|l - j| \leq 2$. As shown in Fig. 5, both data placements are optimal for the corresponding MapReduce programs.

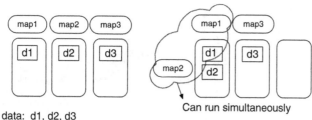

data: d1, d2, d3
The MapReduce job launches 3 maps to access these data

Fig. 5 Two map tasks are allowed run simultaneously; both data layouts are optimal for the MapReduce programs accessing $d1 \sim d3$

We have two cases to analyze: the number of data (M) is less than or equal to the number of nodes (N); and the M is larger than N.

Case 1 $M \leq N$ In this case, all the M blocks can be fit into one stripe on the data nodes, after which there are two ways to achieve the "optimal data placement":

1. M blocks are evenly distributed on M nodes. The possibility for Hadoop's random data placement to achieve this distribution is: C_N^M / N^M , where C_N^M means choosing M nodes from N nodes to hold the M data, N^M means the number of all possible data layouts (each block of M has N possible locations);

2. i nodes hold 1 block each, and other $\frac{M-i}{2}$ nodes are allowed to hold 2 blocks each. The possibility of this case is: $\dfrac{\Sigma_{i=1}^{\frac{M}{2}}[C_N^i.C_M^i.C_{N-i}^{\frac{M-i}{2}}.\Pi_{j=0}^{\frac{M-i}{2}} C_{M-i-2.j}^2]}{N^M}$, where $C_N^i.C_M^i$ means the nodes holding one block each, the rest of the items are for the nodes holding two blocks each.

Hence, when $M \leq N$, the possibility of achieving "optimal data placement" for Hadoop's random data placement is the combination of above two equations:

$$\frac{C_N^M + \Sigma_{i=1}^{\frac{M}{2}}[C_N^i.C_M^i.C_{N-i}^{\frac{M-i}{2}}.\Pi_{j=0}^{\frac{M-i}{2}} C_{M-i-2.j}^2]}{N^M} \qquad (1)$$

Case 2 $M > N$ In this case, $M = kN + d = (k+1).d + k.(N-d)$, where $k \geq 1, d \geq 0$. The "optimal data placement" can be achieved by distributing the blocks in two groups: the first group has d nodes, each of which host $k+1$ blocks; the second group has $N - d$ nodes, each of which hosts k blocks. In this way, each node will be assigned the same number of map tasks. For random data placement, the possibility of achieving this is shown in Eq. (2). The number of all possible data layout is still N^M.

$$\frac{C_N^d \Pi_{j=0}^{d-1} C_{M-(k+1)j}^{k+1}.C_{N-d}^{N-d} \Pi_{j=0}^{N-d-1} C_{M-(k+1)d-k.j}^k}{N^M} \qquad (2)$$

Fig. 6 The Possibility of
achieving "OPtimal data
placement" (POP) for
Hadoop's default data
placement algorithm

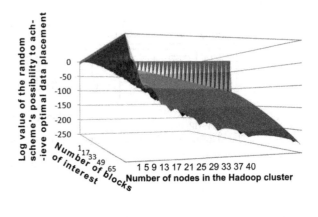

Hence, the Possibility of achieving the "OPtimal data placement" (POP) for
Hadoop's default data placement algorithm is the combination of Eqs. (1) and
(2). It is clear that POP is related to three factors: the number of data(blocks) of
interest, the number of nodes in the Hadoop cluster, and the maximum number of
simultaneous map tasks on a single node. We already assume the last factor as 2
in this paper. We plot the trajectory of POP in Fig. 6. Note that in the z axis, we
show the log value of the POPs for clarity: when $z = 0$, it means the random data
placement is the "optimal data placement"; when $z < 0$, it means the possibility
is 10^z. As Fig. 6 shows, for a specific number of data of interest (>2), along with
the increasing number of nodes in the Hadoop cluster, POP is decreasing; given a
cluster with a specific number of nodes, the increasing number of data of interest
leads to a lower POP as well. Based on our analysis, for a small scale cluster as our
test bed which only has 40 nodes, when the number of data of interest is larger than
5 (320 M), it is highly unlikely that $(POP = 10^{-100})$ the random data placement
will achieve optimal data layout. Unfortunately, most of data-intensive applications
work on large-scale (GB or even PB) data [13].

4.2 The Optimal Degree of a Given Data Distribution

As we already proposed the definition of the optimal data distribution, the ones
which do not satisfy the requirement are not optimal, but it is still interesting to
know "how optimal" they are. Therefore, we propose a concept "optimal degree
of data distribution", denoted as **Degree**. Degree is between [0, 1]: Degree for the
"optimal data placement" in Sect. 3.3 is 1; in the cases when all the interested data
are clustered in one node, Degree is 0.

To calculate Degree, we assume there are N nodes, M data of interest, the
maximum number of simultaneous map tasks on a single node is k, the number
of data of interest on i_{th} node is B_i, so $M = \Sigma_{i=1}^{n} B_i$. As a result, the Degree can
be defined as Eq. (3). The $max(B_i) - B_{opt}$ means the difference between the node
storing the max number of (interest) data in a random distribution and any node

in optimal data distribution; the less this number is, the more efficient the random solution is; *Bopt* can be denoted as $\lceil \frac{M}{N-K} \rceil .k$. Symbol "$\lceil \rceil$" is used because of simultaneous running map tasks ($x \sim x + k - 1$ blocks result in the same number of map cycles to run the maps simultaneously); note that the ks cannot be canceled because of the existence of "$\lceil \rceil$".

$$
\begin{aligned}
Degree &= 1 - \frac{\lceil (max(B_i) - B_{opt})/k \rceil}{\lceil (M - B_{opt})/k \rceil} \\
&= 1 - \frac{\lceil (max(B_i) - \lceil \frac{M}{N.K} \rceil .k)/k \rceil}{\lceil (M - \lceil \frac{M}{N.K} \rceil .k)/k \rceil}
\end{aligned}
\tag{3}
$$

We use an example in Fig. 7 to show how to use Eq. (3). Assume we have $N = 3$ nodes, $M = 5$ data of interest, and $k = 2$ as in previous analysis, Fig. 7 shows four different data distribution. $B_{opt} = \lceil \frac{M}{N.K} \rceil k = 2$, hence in optimal data distribution, the maximum number of blocks on a single node is 2. In practical MapReduce

Fig. 7 An example to show how to use Eq. (4) to calculate the optimal degree of data distribution: *Degree(A)* = 0 (clustered), *Degree(B)* = *Degree(C)* = 0.5 (suboptimal), *Degree(D)* = 1 (optimal)

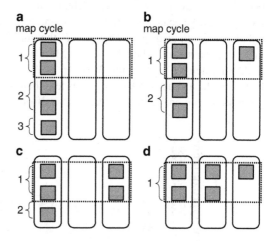

running, (**A**) can finish the five maps on the five blocks in three mapping cycles (because $k = 2$), while (**B**) and (**C**) need two cycles, **D** needs only one cycle. We can calculate the Degrees for these four cases to quantify their efficiency: (**A**), $max(B_i) = M = 5$, hence the *Degree(A)* = 0, which means (*A*) is the least optimal distribution; similarly we also get *Degree(B)* = 0.5, *Degree(C)* = 0.5 (suboptimal) and *Degree(D)* = 1 (optimal).

4.3 The "Optimal-Degree" of the Random Distribution

We already proved random distribution can hardly achieve optimal solution in Sect. 4.1, but it is also necessary to show how close the random and optimal data distributions are. Therefore we quantify the level of approximation (LoA) between random and optimal solutions as shown in Eq. (4)[3]; where $P(Degree)$ means the possibility of a random solution achieving the distributions with the Degree of optimal data distribution, e.g. $P(0)$ is the possibility for random data distribution to cluster all the data of interest onto the same node ($Degree = 0$).

$$LoA = \int_{Degree=0}^{1} Degree.P(Degree)$$

$$= \int_{max(B_i)=M}^{\lceil \frac{M}{N.K} \rceil.k} Degree.P(Degree)$$

(4)

It is observed that LoA is a function related to three factors: M (number of blocks of interest), N (number of nodes in the cluster), and k (number of allowed simultaneous map tasks on a single node). We use sampling technique to obtain the trajectories of LoA to learn how the factors affect the efficiency of random data distribution. We set $N = 40$ in the simulation according to the cluster size of our test bed; $M =10, 30, 60, 80, k =1, 2$. The results are shown in Fig. 8. Larger k always increases LoA because the more simultaneously running map tasks will hide the unbalanced data distribution better; M, the number of data of interest, affects LoA in an uncertain way: when $M \ll N$ (M=10, N=40), increasing M may decrease LoA but when M is close the N or $M > N$, increasing M leads to a larger LoA. However, the average LoA for $k \leq 2$ is less than 45 %, which means the random data distribution can only achieve "less-than-half-optimal" data distribution, on average.

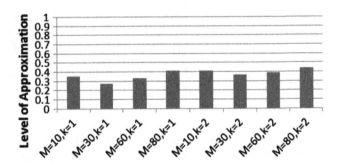

Fig. 8 Level of approximation between random data distributions and the optimal solution, the number of nodes N is set to 40

---

[3]In other words, LoA denotes how sub-optimal the random distribution is, on average. The more *LoA* is close to 1, the closer the random and optimal approaches are.

4.4 Multi-Replica Per Rack

In previous analysis, we assume that there is only one copy of each data existing in each rack. This assumption is derived from the practical Hadoop configurations, e.g. Hadoop with single-replica for each data [7, 32], Hadoop with three replica for each data but put into three different racks [8], etc. However, there are some Hadoop clusters that keep two or even three copies of the same data in the same rack [2] to provide better write performance. As we stated in Sect. 2, the more replica for each data in the same rack, the more optimal data distribution the random strategy can achieve (given that any two replica cannot stay in the same node). In order to prove our DRAW is still necessary for multiple replica Hadoops, we launch intensive experiments as sensitivity study in Sect. 6.3.

5 Methodology

5.1 Test Bed

Our test bed consists of 40 heterogenous nodes in total with Hadoop 0.20.1 installed on it. All these nodes are in a single rack. The cluster and node configurations are shown in the Table 1. In our setup, the cluster's master node is used as the *NameNode* and *JobTracker*, whereas the 39 worker nodes are configured to be *DataNodes* and *TaskTrackers*.

Table 1 CASS cluster configuration

Fourteen compute/data nodes and one head node	
Make & model	Dell PowerEdge 1950
CPU	2 Intel Xeon 5140, Dual Core, 2.33 GHz
RAM	4.0 GB DDR2, PC2-5300, 667 MHz
Internal HD	2 SATA 500 GB (7,200 RPM) or 2 SAS 147 GB (15 K RPM)
Network connection	Intel Pro/1000 NIC
Operating system	Rocks 5.0 (Cent OS 5.1), Kernel: 2.6.18-53.1.14.e15
Twenty-five compute/data nodes	
Make & model	Sun V20z
CPU	2x AMD Opteron 242 @ 1.6 GHz
RAM	2 GB—registered DDR1/333 SDRAM
Internal HD	1x 146 GB Ultra320 SCSI HD
Network connection	c1x 10/100/1000 Ethernet connection
Operating system	Rocks 5.0 (Cent OS 5.1), Kernel: 2.6.18-53.1.14.e15
Cluster network	
Switch make & model	Nortel BayStack 5510-48T Gigabit Switch

5.2   Applications

We launched two applications on the real scientific data in our experiments: one from bio-informatics area, and one from astrophysics research.

Bowtie [1], is a real application from genome research. This application indexes the chromosomes with a Burrows-Wheeler indexing [6] algorithm to keep their memory footprint small. The genome's indexing is a strategy for rapid gene search or alignment. In our experiments, Bowtie's indexing algorithm is implemented in MapReduce framework. The data is about 40 GB of genome data that is downloaded from [3], including human, horse, chimpanzee, etc. 32 species in total. The application is performed on specific species, or random combinations of species (interest locality).

The second application is a mass analyzer working with astrophysics data sets for halo finding [9]. The data sets are comprised of particle positions and velocities. Specifically, each particle has one corresponding file, which has the following content: $position(x, y, z)$, $velocity(V_x, V_y, V_z)$, $particlemass$, and $particletag$. The total size of the download is about 10 GB of particle data in total, and each particle file is exactly 512 MB. The mass analyzer reads the mass data for specific particles, or combinations of particles, and calculates the average mass in each area (interest locality); the area size is pre-defined.

We first run the application 20 times on randomly chosen data sets to build the grouping history. Then DRAW is used to re-organize the data. Finally we re-run the application (which also randomly selects species to do indexing) on the newly distributed data for ten times and record the average performance, which is used to compare with the programs performance on random data distribution.

5.3   Implementation

Data Grouping Learning Data grouping information can be derived from the NameNode log file, which maintains all the system operations. We filter out the file accessing information from the log file first, and the files accessed by the same task (denoted by the same "JobID") are considered as grouping files in HDAG, as shown in Fig. 2. After the log traversal, a matrix showing the data grouping at file-level (file-grouping) can be generated. The mapping between filenames and blocks is exploited[4] to generate the "Data Grouping Matrix (DGM)" at block level (as shown in Fig. 3). In order to improve the log learning efficiency, we set a check point using the time stamp when we used DRAW last time, thus the current log learning starts from the most recent operations back to the check point.

---

[4]By using Hadoop system call "fsck" with parameters "-files -blocks -location" for each file.

Data Grouping Clustering Given the data grouping matrix, Bond Energy Algorithm is used to perform matrix clustering. The size of each group is same as the number of nodes in the cluster. In this way, all the data groups should be placed one after another from right-top to the left-bottom in the clustered DGM(CDGM) (Fig. 3). As we explained in Sect. 3.3, in order to achieve the optimal data placement, we also need ODPA algorithm to generate the final DRAW matrix showing the target data layout.

Data Placement The most challenging part of this work is how to implement the data re-organization according to the "optimal data layout" generated by DRAW. In a Hadoop cluster, all the information about the block locations, and mappings between the files and blocks, are located in the *NameNode*. If we want to re-organize the data in the cluster, we need to, accordingly, modify the information in the *NameNode*. However, the *NameNode* does not provide any functionality that allows the users to modify this information; it just passively updates them based on the periodical reports from the living *DataNodes*. On the other hand, the *DataNodes* only support read, write, and delete operations, but there is no available function to migrate the data among the *DataNodes*. We solve this problem by modifying the Hadoop storage system. Our observations show that each block and its metadata on the *DataNode* are registered in a log file, which reports to the *NameNode* for updating. By logging in each *DataNode* which requires data re-organization, we migrate the data, metadata, and its registration information as a group. After the migration, we extend HDFS to push the DataNodes'updated layout back to the NameNode.

Launching Frequency Obviously, the lower launching frequency of DRAW may slowly respond to the data semantics changes, while higher frequency may cause high data mining and calculating overhead. In practical situations, the value of the time interval should be determined by the workload characteristics. Our current design adopts self-learning launching frequency to achieve the best performance and accuracy as follows: (1) the initial launching frequency is given by a predefined number, e.g. 24 h in our experiments; (2) we monitor the data migration and evaluate the access-pattern changing ratio based on the amount of data relocated; (3) if the changing ratio is high enough to meet our predefined jumping threshold,[5] we increase the frequency by two times (twice more frequently), e.g. 24 h initial value now is 12 h; (4) if the changing ratio is lower than our diving threshold,[6] we will adopt a two times lower frequency, e.g., 48 h in our case; (5) otherwise, we keep the current DRAW launching frequency.

If the launching frequency becomes higher than our pre-defined shutdown threshold, then it means the data has little interest locality (or the data access is not

---

[5]In current version, we define the jumping threshold as 30 %, which means if 30 % or more data are being relocated, a new higher DRAW launching frequency will be generated.

[6]Similar to jumping threshold, we define this diving threshold as 10 %, which means if 10 % or less data are being relocated, we will lower the frequency.

following any specific pattern). In this case, DRAW will be shut down because this application cannot be optimized by data re-organization. This DRAW -shutdown threshold currently is defined as: if the data changing ratio keeps triggering the jump-threshold continuously for five times, we will shut down DRAW until the user manually enable it again.

6   Experimental Results and Analysis

In this section, we present four sets of results: the unbalanced data distribution caused by Hadoop's default random data placement; comparison of the traces of the MapReduce programs on the randomly placed data, and the DRAW's re-organized data; the sensitivity study used to measure the impact of the NR (number of replica for each data block in Hadoop) on DRAW; and the overhead of performing DRAW data re-organization.

6.1   Experiment Results

Intuitively, the data distribution may be related to the way the data is uploaded. There are two ways for the users to upload data: bulkily upload all the data at once; or upload the data based on their categories, e.g. species or particles in our cases. The second way considers the human-readable data grouping information (in our case, data belonging to the same species or particles are assumed to be highly related) rather than the blindly uploading as in the first method. We upload the data to our test bed by using these two data uploading methods, 20 times for each. The overall data distributions are similar in these runs.

First, after bulk uploading the genome data of six species (a subset of our 40 GB genome data), the data distribution (from a randomly picked run) is shown in Fig. 9(1). Given a research group only interested in human [18, 28], the requiring data is clustered as shown in Fig. 9(2). The human data is distributed on only half (51.3 %) of the cluster, which means the parallelism for the future MapReduce job is not optimal.

When using the category-based uploading method, we surprisingly find that the overall data distribution is similar to what is shown in Fig. 9. To highlight the unbalanced distribution of the related data, we quantify the degree of unbalance with $1 - \frac{\# \, of \, nodes \, having \, the \, data}{\# \, of \, nodes}$. With 20 runs using the species-based data uploading method, on average, the data of a specific species is distributed over only 53.2 % nodes of the cluster. The conclusion shows that even when the data is uploaded based on the initial data grouping information, the Hadoop's random data placement is not able to achieve the maximal parallelism for the associate data.

In order to show the efficiency of the DRAW data placement strategy, Fig. 10 plots the balanced data distribution (human) after using DRAW on our Hadoop test bed. The grouping information to generate HDAG is artificially defined as: all

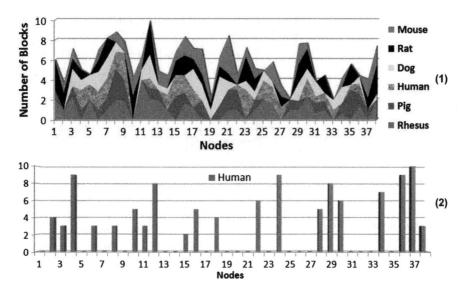

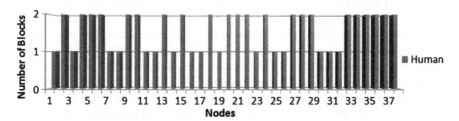

Fig. 9 The data layout after bulk uploading six species'genome data, and the human's genome data layout

Fig. 10 The layout of human genome data after DRAW placement

human data is accessed as a group. Note that we assume the human data is the single grouping data only for Fig. 10, so that to avoid the noise from other data groups. This will be released in the following sections.

6.2 Performance Improvement of MapReduce Programs

6.2.1 Genome Indexing

Based on the DRAW re-organized 40 GB genome data, we run the Bowtie indexing MapReduce program to index the human's chromosomes. Figure 11 shows the traces of two runs on DRAW's re-organized data and Hadoop's randomly placed

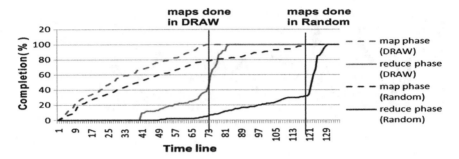

Fig. 11 The running of Genome indexing MapReduce program on human genome data

Table 2 Comparison of two runs of Genome Indexing application

	Total maps	Local maps	Ratio
On DRAW	399	302	76.1 %
On random	399	189	47.1 %

data, respectively. We configure the MapReduce job according to the assumptions described in Sect. 4. The number of reducers is set as large as possible so that the reduce phase will not be the performance bottleneck. In our case, we use 39 reducers. The map phase running on DRAW's data is finished 41.7 % earlier than the one running on randomly placed data, and the job's overall execution time is also improved by 36.4 % when using DRAW's data. The reason is shown in Table 2. The MapReduce job running on the DRAW's re-organized data has 76.1 % maps which benefit from having data locality, compared with 47.1 % from the randomly placed data; the number of local map tasks is increased by $(320 - 189)/189 = 59.8\%$.

Note that there are still 23.9 % maps which are working without having data locality even after the DATA's data re-organization. There are two reasons: first, the data grouping information the BEA algorithm used is generated from all previous.

MapReduce programs rather any specific one, and the ODPA follows *High-WeightFirst-Placed* strategy, which means the data with higher (accumulative) grouping weights will be granted higher priority to be evenly distributed. In other words, the distribution of the non-hottest data is only optimized but may be not 100 % perfect for the corresponding MapReduce programs. Second, the matrix clustering is an N–P hard problem, hence the clustered grouping matrix generated from BEA algorithm, whose time complexity is $O(n^2)$ rather than $O(n^n)$, is a pseudo-optimal solution. Adoption of BEA algorithm is a reasonable tradeoff between efficiency and accuracy. However, since the hottest data will be granted the highest priority to be clustered, the applications interested in these data can achieve the ideal parallelism. Apparently, before we run the human genome indexing application, the human data is not the hottest based on the history information; its data distribution is changed and different from what Fig. 10 shows.

6.2.2 Mass Analyzer on Astrophysics Data

In the above bio-informatics applications, the data size of each species, especially for the mammals, is about 3 GB after decompression. When using Hadoop's default 64 MB block size, about 48 blocks are required to represent one species, which is greater than the 40 nodes in our test bed. In this section, we do experiments on smaller data sets: each particle's data is exactly 512 M, which will be split into only 8 blocks.

Our Mass Analyzer on the astrophysics data tries to calculate the average mass of each area. The results are shown in Fig. 12. DRAW reduces the map phase by 18.2 %, and the overall performance of the MapReduce program is improved by only 11.2 %. It is obvious that the impact of DRAW is linearly related to the size of the required data by the MapReduce program. The less data is being accessed, the more close that random data placement can achieve maximized parallelism (which is already proved in Sect. 4). For example, given 40 nodes in the cluster and 2 maximum simultaneous map tasks on each node, the 8 blocks of each astrophysics data file are more likely to be balanced when compared to the 48 blocks of an mammal's genome data. Hence the conclusion is DRAW works better for the MapReduce programs accessing large-scale data (larger than 3 GB for our hardware configuration).

6.3 Sensitivity Study: The Number of Replica (NR)

The number of replica (NR) for each data block in Hadoop cluster is configurable. For data distribution, the more replica that exist for each block, the higher possibility that the grouping data can be evenly distributed. Hence, the efficiency of DRAW on the MapReduce programs is inverse proportional to NR in the Hadoop.

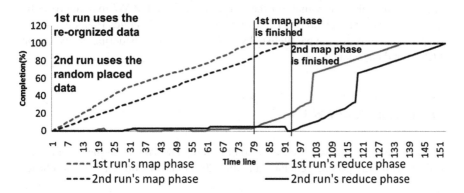

Fig. 12 The running of Mass Analyzer on astrophysics data; the size of interested data for each run is relative small (eight blocks on average)

Table 3 Comparison of the experimental NHD (% of nodes holding the data) and DRAW's ideal NHD

	NR=1			NR=2			NR=3		
	Blks	Experimental _NHD	DRAW _NHD	Blks	E_NHD	D_NHD	Blks	E_NHD	D_NHD
Stickleback	44	44.7%	100%	82	63.2%	100%	122	81.6%	100%
Opossum	48	47.4%	100%	100	73.7%	100%	150	86.8%	100%
Chicken	61	73.7%	100%	122	97.4%	100%	174	89.5%	100%
C. briggsae	13	26.3%	34.2%	23	42.1%	60.5%	34	68.4%	89.5%

In order to quantify the impact of NR on our design, we bulkily upload the 40G genome data to our test bed configured with $NR = 1$, $NR = 2$ and $NR = 3$, respectively. Figure 13 shows the data distributions for four species: Stickleback, Opossum, Chicken from vertebrates, and C. briggsae from nematodes. The "% of nodes holding the data (NHD)" is directly related to the parallelism that the program accessing corresponding species can use. The results prove that, in most cases,[7] NR is linearly related to the parallelism of data distribution; which means a higher degree of replica in Hadoop can mitigate the problem of unbalanced grouping-data distribution. For example, the Stickleback data is only distributed on 44.7% of the nodes in 1-replica Hadoop; when using 3-replica Hadoop, 81.5% of the nodes can provide Stickleback data.

Now we study the efficiency of DRAW for multiple replica Hadoop systems. We still use the above data. Table 3 shows the comparison of the experimental NHD and DRAW's ideal NHD. The NHD difference indicates the possible improvement DRAW can achieve. Note that for the three vertebrates, the number of blocks for each species is larger than the number of nodes in our test bed, hence ideally, DRAW can distributes the grouping data on all the nodes, with 100% NHD; for the C. briggsae whose number of blocks is smaller than 40, the ideal DRAW's NHD is calculated as $\frac{\# \, of \, Blks}{\# \, of \, nodes}$, which is shown in bold font in Table 3. Our experimental results show that, for the 2-replica Hadoop, DRAW may improve the data distribution parallelism by 27.2% on average; for the 3-replica Hadoop, DRAW is expected to improve the parallelism by 17.6% (without considering the exception of Chicken data) on average.

6.4 Overhead of DRAW

In this section, we quantify the overhead of running DRAW (a complete run until it is finished) on the 40 GB genome data after 20 initial runs on our test bed cluster

---

[7]There is one exception for Chicken: the data is more evenly distributed in 2-replica case than 3-replica.

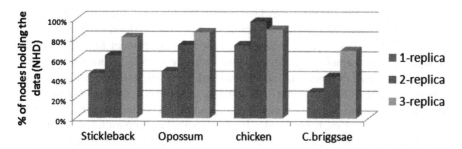

Fig. 13 The data distributions (NHD) of four species, on 1-replica, 2-replica and 3-replica Hadoop

The three parts of DRAW: building HDAG, building and clustering DGM, and re-organizing the data based on ODPA, have different overheads.

Building HDAG The first step is negligible because it only scans the customized log files (only several kilobytes for 20 runs of the genome indexing program) once and records pertinent information in HDAG table.

Building and Clustering DGM Forty GB data will be split into about 640 blocks, and based on our algorithm the memory requirement is 6.7 MB. The BEA algorithm takes 37 s to cluster the 640×640 matrix.

Data Re-organization This is the most time-consuming step in DRAW algorithm, because we have to login every DataNode to migrate the data/metadata/registration information. The data migration time is linearly related to the data size and the network bandwidth among the nodes. In our specific case, after 20 warm-up runs, 497 out of the 640 blocks need to be re-organized. The overall run time of the DRAW tool is 4.7 min.

The overall execution times of our genome indexing program on randomly placed data and DRAW re-organized data are 33 min 43 s and 20 min 37 s, respectively. Hence the above time costs (about 5 min 25 s) are worthy compared to the overall performance improvements, about 13 min. This improvement can be expected for all the subsequent genome indexing programs which follow the previous access patterns.

7   Related Work

Several previous works exploited the grouping-like data semantics and organized data layout in some specific ways to support high-performance data accesses. Ahmed et. al. [11] exploited the file-grouping relation to better manage the distributed file caches. The groupings of files are based on file access history patterns. They fetch these groups of files to improve cache performance rather than single files. The rationale is that group accessed files are likely to be group accessed again. This idea works well in cache management. In our data intensive computing, such grouping behavior is at chunk level rather than file level. It mainly takes place between high-level applications or processes rather than low-level file blocks.

Yuan [31] develops a data dependency-based data placement for the scientific cloud work flows, which clusters the relative data as intensively as possible to effectively reduce data movement during the workflow's execution. However, data access patterns exhibit differently from data parallel frameworks, such as MapReduce. The MapReduce job performance is directly determined by the co-located compute and data locality of each map task [2]. This results in the parallelism degree of data distribution in a Hadoop cluster. In other words, the relevant data needs to be distributed as evenly as possible to favor high-performance runs of MapReduce programs.

Xie et al. [20] takes data locality into account for launching speculative MapReduce tasks in heterogeneous environments. They focus on balancing data processing load based on network topology and disk space utilization of a cluster. In contrast, DRAW focuses on data redistribution based on data semantics; they are two complimentary works.

Our previous work MRAP [27] develops a set of MapReduce APIs for data providers who may be aware of the subsequent access patterns of the data after being uploaded. By specifying the access patterns, the data are distributed in a cor responding way such that the best data access performance can be achieved. However, it requires application developers to specify the data access patterns beforehand. Our DRAW captures grouping patterns by runtime tools.

Ko [21] and Yuan [30] exploit the data provenance of intermediate data in MapReduce framework. This type of data semantics can be used in two ways: (1) to provide better data fault-tolerance [21]: the intermediate data may have different importance, which are quantified as the cost of reproducing them, hence they should be granted different fault-tolerant strategies; (2) to save storage capacity [30]: some times storing of the intermediate data is more expensive than reproducing them, therefore it is better to trade the computation cost with the storage capacity. How ever, the way of storing or reproducing the intermediate data will not affect the application overall performance except when a node failure happens. DRAW exploits data grouping patterns in MapReduce framework for high-performance.

Conclusion

The default random data placement in a MapReduce/Hadoop cluster does not take into account data grouping semantics. This could cluster many grouped data into a small number of nodes, which limits the data parallelism degree and results in performance bottleneck. In order to solve the problem, a new data-grouping-aware data placement (DRAW) scheme is developed. DRAW captures runtime data grouping patterns and distributes the grouped data as evenly as possible. There are three phases in DRAW: learning data grouping information from system logs, clustering the data-grouping matrix,

(continued)

and re-organizing the grouping data. We also theoretically prove that the inefficiency of Hadoop's random placement method. Our experimental results show that for two representative MapReduce applications Genome Indexing and Astrophysics, DRAW can significantly improve the throughput of local map task execution by up to 59.8 %, and reduce the execution time of map phase by up to 41.7 %. The overall MapReduce job response time is reduced by 36.4 %.

Acknowledgements This work is supported in part by the US National Science Foundation Grant CNS-1115665, CCF-1337244 and National Science Foundation Early Career Award 0953946.

References

1. http://bowtie-bio.sourceforge.net/index.shtml.
2. http://developer.yahoo.com/hadoop/tutorial/module1.html.
3. http://genome.ucsc.edu/.
4. http://hadoop.apache.org/common/docs/r0.18.3/hdfs_design.html.
5. http://lbvm.sourceforge.net/.
6. http://michael.dipperstein.com/bwt/.
7. http://sector.sourceforge.net/benchmark.html.
8. https://issues.apache.org/jira/browse/hadoop-2559.
9. http://t8web.lanl.gov/people/heitmann/arxiv/.
10. http://www.unidata.ucar.edu/software/netcdf/docs/.
11. Ahmed Amer, Darrell D. E. Long, and Randal C. Burns. Group-based management of distributed file caches. In *Proceedings of the 22 nd International Conference on Distributed Computing Systems (ICDCS '02)*, ICDCS '02, pages 525-, Washington, DC, USA, 2002. IEEE Computer Society.
12. Anup Bhatkar and J. L. Rana. Estimating neutral divergence amongst mammals for comparative genomics with mammalian scope. In *Proceedings of the 9th International Conference on Information Technology*, pages 3–6, Washington, DC, USA, 2006. IEEE Computer Society.
13. Jeffrey Dean and Sanjay Ghemawat. Mapreduce: simplified data processing on large clusters. *Commun. ACM*, 51:107–113, January 2008.
14. Matthew T. Dougherty, Michael J. Folk, Erez Zadok, Herbert J. Bernstein, Frances C. Bernstein, Kevin W. Eliceiri, Werner Benger, and Christoph Best. Unifying biological image formats with hdf5. *Commun. ACM*, 52:42–47, October 2009.
15. Anna Dumitriu. X and y (number 5). In *ACM SIGGRAPH 2004 Art gallery*, SIGGRAPH '04, pages 28-, New York, NY, USA, 2004. ACM.
16. Gregory Ganger and M. Frans Kaashoek. Embedded inodes and explicit grouping: Exploiting disk bandwidth for small files. In *Proceedings of the 1997 USENIX Technical Conference*, pages 1–17, 1997.
17. Narasimhaiah Gorla and Kang Zhang. Deriving program physical structures using bond energy algorithm. In *Proceedings of the Sixth Asia Pacific Software Engineering Conference*, APSEC '99, pages 359-, Washington, DC, USA, 1999. IEEE Computer Society.
18. Yoonsoo Hahn and Byungkook Lee. Identification of nine human-specific frameshift mutations by comparative analysis of the human and the chimpanzee genome sequences. *Bioinformatics*, 21:186–194, January 2005.

19. Roger S. Holmes and Erwin Goldberg. Brief communication: Computational analyses of mammalian lactate dehydrogenases: Human, mouse, opossum and platypus ldhs.*Comput. Biol. Chem.*, 33:379–385, October 2009.
20. Xie Jiong, Yin Shu, Ruan Xiaojun, Ding Zhiyang, Tian Yun, J. Majors, A. Manzanares, and Qin Xiao. Improving mapreduce performance through data placement in heterogeneous hadoop clusters. April 2010.
21. Steven Y. Ko, Imranul Hoque, Brian Cho, and Indranil Gupta. Making cloud intermediate data fault-tolerant. In *Proceedings of the 1st ACM symposium on Cloud computing*, SoCC '10, pages 181–192, New York, NY, USA, 2010. ACM.
22. Geoffrey H. Kuenning and Gerald J. Popek. Automated hoarding for mobile computers. In *Proceedings of the sixteenth ACM symposium on Operating systems principles*, SOSP '97, pages 264–275, New York, NY, USA, 1997. ACM.
23. Jian Guo Liu, Moustafa Ghanem, Vasa Curcin, Christian Haselwimmer, Yike Guo, Gareth Morgan, and Kyran Mish. Achievements and experiences from a grid-based earthquake analysis and modelling study. In *Proceedings of the Second IEEE International Conference on e-Science and Grid Computing*, E-SCIENCE '06, pages 35-, Washington, DC, USA, 2006. IEEE Computer Society.
24. M. Tamer Özsu and Patrick Valduriez. *Principles of distributed database systems (2nd ed.)*. Prentice-Hall, Inc., Upper Saddle River, NJ, USA, 1999.
25. Manuel Rodriguez-Martinez, Jaime Seguel, and Melvin Greer. Open source cloud computing tools: A case study with a weather application. In *Proceedings of the 2010 IEEE 3rd International Conference on Cloud Computing*, CLOUD '10, pages 443–449, Washington, DC, USA, 2010. IEEE Computer Society.
26. Michael C. Schatz. Cloudburst. *Bioinformatics*, 25:1363–1369, June 2009.
27. Saba Sehrish, Grant Mackey, Jun Wang, and John Bent. Mrap: a novel mapreduce-based framework to support hpc analytics applications with access patterns. In *Proceedings of the 19th ACM International Symposium on High Performance Distributed Computing*, HPDC '10, pages 107–118, New York, NY, USA, 2010. ACM.
28. Matthias Specht, Renaud Lebrun, and Christoph P. E. Zollikofer. Visualizing shape transformation between chimpanzee and human braincases. *Vis. Comput.*, 23:743–751, August 2007.
29. Shivam Tripathi and Rao S. Govindaraju. Change detection in rainfall and temperature patterns over India. In *Proceedings of the Third International Workshop on Knowledge Discovery from Sensor Data*, SensorKDD '09, pages 133–141, New York, NY, USA, 2009. ACM.
30. Dong Yuan, Yun Yang, Xiao Liu, and Jinjun Chen. A cost-effective strategy for intermediate data storage in scientific cloud workflow systems. pages 1–12, May 2010.
31. Dong Yuan, Yun Yang, Xiao Liu, and Jinjun Chen. A data placement strategy in scientific cloud workflows. *Future Gener. Comput. Syst.*, 26:1200–1214, October 2010.
32. Baopeng Zhang, Ning Zhang, Honghui Li, Feng Liu, and Kai Miao. An efficient cloud computing-based architecture for freight system application in china railway. In *Proceedings of the 1st International Conference on Cloud Computing*, CloudCom '09, pages 359–368, Berlin, Heidelberg, 2009. Springer-Verlag.
33. L. Q. Zhou, Z. G. Yu, P. R. Nie, F. F. Liao, V. V. Anh, and Y. J. Chen. Log-correlation distance and fourier transform with Kullback-Leibler divergence distance for construction of vertebrate phylogeny using complete mitochondrial genomes. In *Proceedings of the Third International Conference on Natural Computation - Volume 02*, ICNC '07, pages 304–308, Washington, DC, USA, 2007. IEEE Computer Society

Part II
Resource Management

Auction-based scheduling approach to allocating computational tasks to computing resources. Federation model for cloud systems. Transferring traditional workflow management systems to cloud computing models.

Efficient Task-Resource Matchmaking Using Self-adaptive Combinatorial Auction

Han Zhao and Xiaolin Li

Abstract In loosely coupled distributed computing systems, one of the major duties performed by the scheduler is to efficiently manage the allocation of computational tasks to computing resources. Such matchmaking services become difficult to implement when resources belong to different administrative domains, each of which has unique and diverse valuation for task bundles. In order to cope with the heterogeneity, we introduce a novel combinatorial auction approach that solves the task-resource matchmaking problem in a utility computing environment. This auction based approach is characterized as "self-adaptive" in two senses. First, efficient allocation is achieved through adaptive adjustment of task pricing towards the market equilibrium point. Second, payment accounting is adaptive to the changing auction states at various stages that discourages strategic bidding from egocentric bidders. The objective of the research presented in this chapter is to examine the applicability of the combinatorial auction based approaches in utility computing, and to develop efficient task allocation schemes using the self-adaptive auction. Through simulations, we show that the proposed combinatorial auction approach optimizes allocative efficiency for task-resource matchmaking when valuation functions are concave, and achieves incentive compatibility once the auction process finalizes.

1 Introduction

In loosely coupled distributed computing systems, the goal of task scheduling is to map tasks to resources that are optimal with respect to some performance criteria while subject to certain allocation constraints. Substantial research efforts have been

H. Zhao (✉)
Department of CISE, University of Florida, Gainesville, FL, USA
e-mail: han@cise.ufl.edu;

X. Li
Department of ECE, University of Florida, Gainesville, FL, USA
e-mail: andyli@ece.ufl.edu

© Springer Science+Business Media New York 2014
X. Li, J. Qiu (eds.), *Cloud Computing for Data-Intensive Applications*,
DOI 10.1007/978-1-4939-1905-5_8

directed towards developing efficient task-resource matchmaking algorithms over years. However, the rapid advancing of hardware, software as well as computing paradigms have posed new challenges to the design of efficient task allocation strategies. The first challenge arises from the growing scale of resource deployment. Due to the funding limitation of a single institution, many distributed platforms today involve resource contributions from multiple institutions to tackle computationally demanding scientific problems (e.g., PlanetLab [31], TeraGrid [13], FutureGrid [19], etc.). As the scale expands, task allocation needs to be allocated in a way that maximizes the aggregate utilities of participating resource owners. Second, highly autonomous resource contributors often pursue task allocation results for their own goods. Therefore, an effective design of the allocation strategy should prevent participants from engineering the allocation process at the expense of others. Finally, new computing paradigms such as cloud computing emerge, allowing computing resources to be packaged as services and charged on demand. This paradigm shift associates concern for monetary cost with allocation mechanism design, and highlights cost–benefit analysis for scheduling.

To better address these challenges, applying the so called socioeconomic approaches to the task and resource scheduling problems becomes popular in computer science study. These are established approaches in economic analysis and production management that make dynamic allocation decisions based on the fluctuating demand of self-interested individuals. The socioeconomic approaches are suitable for task and resource scheduling in utility computing due to the following observations: (1) design similarity between market pricing principles and grid/cloud scheduling mechanisms; (2) role similarity between rational economic individuals and resource providers/users seeking for utility maximization. One form of the socioeconomic approaches is to use auction, which introduces competitions for optimal allocation outcomes. There are many variations for auction mechanism design. In this chapter, we are particularly interested in *Combinatorial Auction* [15], which allows bidders to bid for item bundles. Especially, we exploit effective combinatorial auction forms for the task-resource matchmaking problem in the following aspects: (1) defining suitable valuation functions to express preference for task bundle; (2) exposing sufficient information to bidders during the auction process for transparent auction design; (3) providing incentives for bidders to reveal truthful valuations.

In this study, these issues are jointly highlighted. We describe an efficient task-resource matchmaking strategy based on a novel self-adaptive auction form. We observe that valuations for task bundles are likely to be concave due to the effect of diminishing returns. For example, when tasks are interdependent, processing them imposes extra coordination overhead that results in increased cost-to-benefit ratio. Therefore, the marginal valuation is expected to be decreasing. According to this observation, we develop our proposed approach based on a dynamic auction form that iteratively provides feedbacks to both auctioneer and bidders for strategy update. Through multi-round communications, the auction maximizes information that allows bidders to adaptively respond to market prices set by the auctioneer. In addition, the auction achieves incentive compatibility using a non-linear payment calculation strategy originally proposed by Ausubel [4]. This iterative approach presents a departure from existing static auction models which suffer from loss of allocative efficiency and untruthful bidding. For example, in Amazon's spot instance auction model [38], bids collected from resource users are sorted from high to low until the aggregate demand meets supply. Winner determination is statically calculated based on one-shot bid placement. Such one-shot auctions are effective approaches to allocate resources. However, in fear of losing the auction, the bidders are subject to overbid, resulting in overpaying market clearing price. As a result, such a static uniform price auction model greatly impairs the utility of end users as they pay higher price for resource acquisition.

In spite of its appealing advantages, a few hurdles need to be overcome before applying the self-adaptive auction approach. First, due to the iterative nature, the self-adaptive auction features a communication intensive process. The negotiation cost might be too high before a market clearing state is reached. Second, the convergence process to the market equilibrium state might take too long to complete. Both of them are in general undesirable when we wish to simplify the bidding process and make prompt allocation decision whenever possible. In this chapter, we identify appropriate scenarios suitable for the self-adaptive auction. In addition, we refactor the original auction form described in [4] to reduce the communication overhead as well as to speed up the convergence of the auction process. The efficiency of the approach is examined in simulations, and results show that our solution is efficient and amenable to practical implementations in distributed systems.

1.1 Summary of Contributions

We summarize the contributions of the study presented in this chapter as follows: (1) we map the task-resource matchmaking problem in a utility computing environment into an auction based scheduling problem in a competitive economic market, and exploit the solution space for auction based scheduling strategy design; (2) we develop a self-adaptive auction based matchmaking strategy that optimizes allocation efficiency as well as achieves incentive compatibility; (3) with both theoretical and simulation analysis, we validate the properties of our approach, and demonstrate its advantage over other design options.

1.2 Organization

The rest of the chapter is organized as follows. In Sect. 2, we present an overview of the related work. Section 3 introduces the problem background and presents a summary of the auction scheduling design. Section 4 illustrate the design details of the auction approach for the task-resource matchmaking problem and justify the design choices. Section 5 presents the evaluation results. Finally, "Conclusion" section concludes the chapter.

2 Related Work

Game theory and the related economic theories are useful tools to model the behaviors of egocentric agents in a distributed environment, presenting theoretical appealing values to task and resource allocation in loosely coupled distributed systems [1, 10, 23, 27, 33, 35]. In addition to the theoretical development, market-oriented scheduling has been applied to practical distributed system design. Example projects include Spawn [41], POPCORN [32], G-Commerce [43], and Tacoon [25]. In Faucets [24], auction was conducted to determine the optimal placement of tasks on the servers. Another early work was Nimrod/G [9], where grid resources were allocated based on user-negotiated contracts with the resource sellers. The core idea behind these works is to allocate under-utilized resources in a symbolic marketplace coordinated by some management entity in the distributed system. One critical issue in designing such a resource market is resource pricing, and resolving it typically involves searching for game/market equilibrium state. In [21], the authors investigated this issue and derived a Nash bargaining solution to discover resource prices in mobile grids. Another approach is to inspect the supply-to-demand state on the market, and determine the price at Walrasian equilibrium point (when supply equals to demand). For example, Danak and Mannor [16] studied effect of supply adjustment to resource allocation from the seller's perspective. Our self-adaptive auction based algorithm adopts the latter approach in a way that resource prices on the market are dynamically adjusted based on matching of supply and demand.

When translating economic paradigms to task-resource matchmaking mechanism design, auction is of particular interests to researchers as it explicitly defines interactive negotiation rules that are suitable to implement in distributed systems. Due to this reason, various auction models have been examined and applied to task and resource scheduling. One popular model to use is the double auction model. In a double auction, a third-party auctioneer is created to match offers and bids from multiple sellers and bidders simultaneously. Grosu and Das [22] compared the first-price auction, the Vickrey auction, and the double auction from both perspectives of customers and resource owners in grids. They concluded that double auction mostly benefits utilities for both sellers and bidders. The model was further developed by Garg et al. [20] who presented a meta-scheduler implementing continuous double auction for resource mapping in global grids. In this study, we target at a different problem setting. In addition, our auction model addresses the combinatorial valuation of task bundles such that $V(X_1) + V(X_2) \neq V(X_1 \cup X_2)$. A single-item auction model is clearly not applicable to such a task-bundle allocation scenario. The combinatorial auction model has received significant attentions [17, 18, 26]. However, existing works either use a static auction that entraps in the complexity of solving winner determination, or use a uniform pricing policy that overlooks the issue of incentive compatibility. Our study addresses both problems and realizes adaptivity in two senses: (1) market price is adaptively adjusted towards maximum market efficiency; and (2) payment is adaptively calculated to ensure incentive compatibility. Therefore, the analysis conducted in this chapter will help to expand the scope of current research on auction based task-resource matchmaking mechanisms.

Finally, the emerging cloud computing platform opens enormous opportunities to market-oriented task and resource scheduling [8]. In cloud computing, resource management is utility oriented. By commoditizing resources, resource owners are now capable of offering computing services in return of revenues. In a cloud environment, auction models offer a promising solution for task dispatching and resource provisioning. However, existing research [18,28,34,37] leveraging auction models are categorized as "one-shot" auction models that provide no feedback to auction participants, preventing auction participants from changing their strategies towards optimal outcomes. Incentive-compatible auctions were also applied to determine pricing in allocating cloud computing resources [30, 42]. Similar to our work, Zaman et al. [44] proposed to use combinatorial auctions to allocate VM instances in cloud. In their study, allocation was determined by solving a linear program while we take advantage of iterative bid feedback. In this chapter, we examined the application of a dynamic iterative auction model that overcomes the problems of one-shot auction models. In [39], the authors adopted a similar auction model by building an experimental resource market inside Google Inc. The auction was intended to improve the long-term resource utilization within the company. We believe that the research proposed here is greatly beneficial to identify the solution space, and to extend the horizon of auction based task-resource matchmaking in utility and cloud computing.

3   Problem Formulation

In this section, we formulate the task-resource matchmaking problem to be studied in this chapter, clarify assumptions, problem constraints as well as the design goals for the auction based solution. Since our approach builds on a dynamic iterative auction form, a brief introduction to this auction form is presented afterwards to ease the understanding of the solution elaborated in subsequent sections.

3.1   Preliminaries

We aim to design an efficient matchmaking strategy for computational task allocation in a distributed environment. The basic form of the problem is fairly simple: to allocate m tasks to n independent sites such that each site obtains a subset of tasks x_i. The final allocation is expected to be *exhaustive* and *non-overlapping*, i.e., $\sum_{i=1}^{n} |x_i| = m$ and $x_i \cap x_j = \emptyset$ for $i \neq j$. Note that the requirement of non-overlapping does not prevent typical reliability measures. In case of task replication, replicated tasks are treated as distinctive tasks to be allocated in the m task set.

Before we proceed, several assumptions and constraints need to be clarified. First, tasks to be allocated are discrete and indivisible. We consider a data-parallel model categorized as SPMD (Single Program, Multiple Data), where a job is split up to create tasks running on multiple sites with different input. Tasks are considered to be homogeneous when they have similar input size, and heterogeneous otherwise. We will discuss both cases in later analysis. Second, autonomous sites (sites for short hereafter) are those organizations with resources to process computational tasks contained in the assigned task bundle. Each site values the allocated task bundle independently. Let site i's valuation function of bundle x be $V_i(x)$, following the constraints of $V_i(\emptyset) = 0$ and $V_i(x_p) \geq V_i(x_q)$ for all $x_p \supseteq x_q$. The valuation function $V_i(x_i)$ defines the perceived benefits of processing task bundle x_i for site i (e.g., service reward in the form of monetary compensation in commercial platforms, or resource access privilege in volunteer computing). In addition, site i needs to pay certain cost $P_i(x_i)$ for task bundle processing. In the context of task scheduling, such cost typically refers to the cost of dedicated resources allocated by site i for processing task bundle x_i. The utility function $U_i(x_i) = V_i(x_i) - P_i(x_i)$ represents site i's cost–benefit summary of provisioning task processing service. Finally, each site is associated with a budget which limits its maximum bid amount, e.g., π_i defines site i's total available resource. The notations used in our matchmaking strategy design are summarized in Table 1.

Table 1 Notation summary

Notation	Elements in task allocation	Corresponding economic term
$\mathbb{J} = \{1, 2, \ldots, m\}$	Tasks	Items
$\mathbb{S} = \{1, 2, \ldots, n\}$	Sites	Bidders
x_i	Task allocation for site i	Item bundle for bidder i
$V(x)$	Task bundle value	Item value
$P(x)$	Site cost	Bidder payment
$U(x)$	Site utility	Bidder utility
$A = (x_1, \ldots, x_n)$	Task allocation	Item assignment
$Q(A)$	Aggregate resource contribution	Seller revenue
$\lambda = \{1, 2, \ldots, r\}$	Epoch	Round
d_i	Site i's demand	Bidder i's demand
π_i	Resource capacity of site i	Budget of bidder i
p^*	Task price at equilibrium state	Market clearing price

We define *social welfare* $\mathbb{W}$ as the aggregate valuations of all sites. An allocation is considered Pareto-efficient (or simply efficient) if it maximizes the social welfare associated with that allocation.

Definition 1 (Efficient Allocation for Task-Resource Matchmaking). Let $\mathbb{A}$ denote the set of all possible allocations for the general task-resource matchmaking problem. An efficient allocation is an allocation $A = (x_1, x_2, \ldots, x_n)$ of m tasks that maximizes the overall social welfare, i.e., $\mathbb{W} = \max_{A \in \mathbb{A}} \sum_{i=1}^{n} V_i(x_i)$.

Definition 1 corresponds to *Pareto optimality*, which states that no agent is able to get better off without disadvantaging others. In the context of task scheduling, since resource owners receive higher reward if they provide better service quality (note that this statement simplifies the problem formulation because it is difficult to quantify the quality of service in general), this state optimizes the service efficiency by allocating the task bundle to the most suitable sites. We establish a market for trading computational tasks, and attempt to identify an equilibrium state on the market where neither shortage nor surplus of the computational tasks exist. If such an equilibrium state is found, we obtain an exhaustive allocation of the computational tasks while the supply and the demand is balanced on the market. In economic analysis, an important concept called competitive equilibrium characterizes our desired market equilibrium state.

Definition 2 (Competitive Equilibrium). A competitive equilibrium is a state of a price vector $p = [P_1(x_1), \ldots, P_i(x_i), \ldots, P_n(x_n)]$ and an allocation A such that (1) $U_i(p, A) = \max_{A \in \mathbb{A}}[V_i(A) - P_i(A)]$ for every i; and (2) $\Upsilon(p, A) = \max_{A \in \mathbb{A}} \sum_{i=1}^{n} P_i(A)$.

The following theorem reveals that the competitive equilibrium state implies the absence of Pareto improvements, leading to allocative efficiency.

Theorem 1 ([15]). *Allocation A is said to be supported in competitive equilibrium if and only if A is a socially efficient allocation as defined in Definition 1.*

Our objective is to design a task-resource matchmaking strategy that achieves allocative efficiency. One challenge immediately presents itself, however, when self-autonomous sites are unwilling to reveal their true valuations to the task scheduler. As a result, we also target at designing an effective matchmaking strategy that discourages self-interested organizations participating in task allocation from playing strategic maneuvers. In this chapter, we leverage a self-adaptive auction to fulfill these objectives.

3.2 Task-Resource Matchmaking: A Game Theoretic Perspective

To this end, we have delineated the matchmaking problem as an optimization problem. In this section, we rephrase it from the realm of the game theory. Specifically, the task-resource matchmaking problem is abstracted as a dynamic non-cooperative game played by n bidders (autonomous sites). We assign the role of auctioneer to a task scheduler who will coordinate the auction process. Besides the task scheduler, no single site has information of other sites' information. The auction is conducted in discrete rounds (referred to as epochs hereafter): $\lambda = \{1, 2, \ldots, r\}$.

The auction strategy θ_i^j played by site i at epoch j is defined as any function mapping the self-observable bidding history h_i^j (the observable bid of i's opponents from the start of the auction till round j) to the current demand quantities d_i^j conforming to the auction rules, i.e., $\theta_i^j : h_i^j \rightarrow d_i^j$. Accordingly, we define the complete strategy profile Θ_i as the set of all possible θ_i site i adopts during the auction process.

One common assumption in game theory is that agents are rational, i.e., they always choose to perform the actions that lead to optimal outcome for themselves amongst all feasible strategies. We follow this assumption in our problem formulation. In particular, each site determines the desired task quantities d_i^j at epoch j according to its utility function (a positive result indicates that the acquisition is beneficial). Hence, we design our auction based matchmaking strategy by respecting individual rationality of each site.

3.3 Task-Resource Matchmaking: An Illustrative Scenario

Figure 1 describes an illustrative scenario for the task-resource matchmaking problem. In this example, a task scheduling service deployed on a public gateway node accepts task submission from geographically dispersed users, discovers a set of qualified worker sites, and dispatches the tasks to these sites periodically. Users are unaware of the task placement determined by the matchmaking policy. Each worker site is composed of a collection of computational, storage, and networking resources that can be used to process the assigned tasks. The same task bundle might present different values to different sites. For example, in Fig. 1, suppose the input data for task bundle x is locally cached at site A, processing the same task bundle x will consume more networking resources in B, and returns less service reward to B due to the relatively slow processing speed. As a result, task bundle x is valued more by site A than by site B. Based on the reported value information, the task of the scheduler is to periodically allocate tasks to participating sites in an efficient and incentive compatible manner.

3.4 Introduction to Dynamic Iterative Auction

Auction is a useful mechanism to discover the true market value of a set of commodities, and to efficiently allocate them to a set of competitive buyers. In a static auction such as the first-price sealed-bid auction, winner determination is completed in a closed fashion that discourages market competition and ultimately leads to reduced revenues. Therefore, a **Dynamic Iterative Auction** (DIA) [7] gains favors from researchers because it allows auctioneer to take the most advantage of

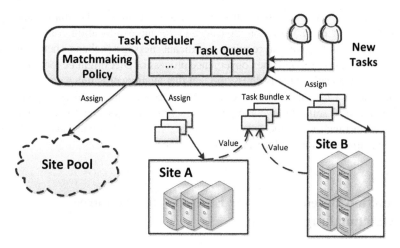

Fig. 1 An illustrate scenario for task-resource matchmaking

market information collected from bidders. By introducing an iterative valuation elicitation process, bidders are able to adjust bidding strategies based on signals from his/her opponents. A DIA has many varying forms. Figure 2 depicts a typical execution cycle for a general DIA process. During the cycle, each bidder responds to auctioneer's outcry of the price with a quantity of the desired commodity bundle. Based on the collected demand from all bidders, the auctioneer adjusts the market price to adapt to the demand changes. This process continues until the terminating condition of the auction is met. In summary, the dynamism brings bidding transparency to bidders, and the iterative process boosts pricing adaptivity for the auctioneer.

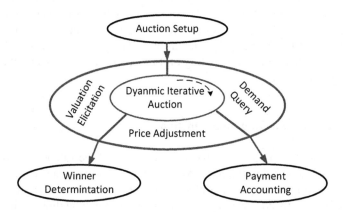

Fig. 2 Flow of a dynamic iterative auction

Although a DIA bears a number of appealing features, the implementation complexity hinders its adoption in task and resource allocation. First, DIA is communication-intensive that requires significant message exchange between auctioneer and bidders. Second, the convergence process of DIA might be too long to be practically acceptable. This is due to the fact that auctioneer is unaware of bidders' demand curves which will otherwise guide the price adjustment. In this chapter, we propose a refined self-adaptive auction approach that allows sites to directly report the valuation functions to the auctioneer. Such a strategy eliminates auction-bidder communications in normal DIA and expedites the convergence.

4 Auction Based Design for Efficient Task-resource Matchmaking Strategy

In this section, we present our strategy design for the task-resource matchmaking problem. We start with the simplest case where all tasks are homogeneous. Next, we expand our analysis to the K-type heterogeneous case where tasks are homogeneous within each category. Finally, we investigate the general heterogeneous case and discuss a potential solution.

4.1 The Homogeneous Case

We start from allocating m equal-size tasks to n sites. Many examples of such tasks exist in distributed computing that involves the same executable to be run with almost equivalent input size. It represents a common pattern in data parallelism computation, and typically involves static chunking of a loop (e.g., image processing, text analysis, etc.). However, although all tasks share similar input size and kernel function, they are dispatched to machines with different processing speeds. This leads to the load balancing problem we are trying to tackle. A bundle of such tasks is often referred to as Bag-of-Tasks (BoT) as tasks within the bundle are communication free.

4.1.1 Selection of the Valuation Function

We assume a private value model that sites do not exchange valuation information when it learns others' bid information. Moreover, in order to guarantee the existence of market clearing price, the marginal valuations of tasks are assumed to be monotonic and strictly concave, i.e., computational tasks exhibit diminishing returns (or marginal values) to sites. This is justified by the following considerations. For tasks with interdependencies, processing more tasks requires excessive resource consumption to deal with the task dependency. As task number grows, the amount of excessive resource consumption increases. Thus the valuation curve grows sublinearly, as shown in Fig. 3. In fact, the phenomena of diminishing returns appears not only in task valuation, but also in resource valuation [29]. For example, for a cloud resource customer who has a flexible resource demand, the valuation for an additional allocated Virtual Machine (VM) instance is decreasing because of the increasing coordination overhead. We argue that the assumption of concavity in valuation function is more common encountered and more flexible than the step valuation functions used in many auction models. This is because the continuous concave valuation function allows bidders to express partial preference over a commodity bundle.

Fig. 3 Tasks with interdependencies present diminishing return to sites due to excessive consumed resources

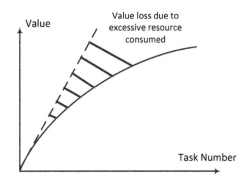

For tasks without interdependencies, any valuation function exhibiting diminishing return would fit our design of task-resource matchmaking strategy. As an example, we propose a simple valuation function for workload balancing while allocating computational tasks. In particular, let π_i be site i's available qualitative computational power (represents the budget of site i), i's valuation for a k-size homogeneous task bundle is given by $V_i(k) = \pi_i/k$. Its meaning can be explained as follows. If site i obtains a k-size task bundle, it will equally distribute its computational resource to the k tasks. Assume that site i acquires one more task assigned from the task queue, it will further divide its resources to meet the computational need. Therefore, the additional $(k + 1)$-th task has a marginal value of $V_i(k + 1) = \pi_i/(k + 1)$. We will show that this setting will lead to optimal workload balance among n sites in Sect. 4.1.4.

4.1.2 Pricing Strategy

In our matchmaking strategy design, we assume that there are always sufficient number of sites to compete for a limited set of tasks. When a new batch of tasks arrive, the task scheduler launches an auction by first pinging a set of qualified sites, and collect qualitative resource capacity information from all sites. We denote these feedbacks as "*v-messages*" because they encapsulate necessary information for the task scheduler to calculate valuations. Note that it is possible for a site to report dishonest information for its own good. However, we will show that sites have no incentives to do so, because of the risk of reduced utility if the payment policy presented in Sect. 4.1.3 is adopted.

Upon receiving v-messages from all sites, the scheduler calculates a valuation matrix. The i-th row of the matrix is given as $v_i = \{v_i^1, \ldots, v_i^m\}$, where $v_i^k = \pi_i / k$ as explained in Sect. 4.1.1. Next, all $n \times m$ elements in the valuation matrix are aggregated, forming a vector V in a non-decreasing sorted order. V represents the complete pricing space where a market clearing price might reside. We use the word "might" simply because a market clearing price may not exist at all if there are duplicate elements in V. Therefore, the scheduler runs a simple randomized algorithm to break ties. In particular, if $n > 1$ elements are identical, then the i-th element is added by the amount of τ / i where τ is a small random integer. Once all ties break, V consists of elements listed in a strictly increasing order. A binary search procedure is then applied to V for locating the market clearing price. Starting with the medium valuation $v^1, v^1 \in$ V, the scheduler shrink its search space by half at each epoch. Suppose at epoch j, v^j is the medium valuation of the current search space, the scheduler calculates a demand quantity for site i based on the following equation:

$$d_i^j = \arg\max_{x \in \mathbb{J}} U_i(x)$$
$$= \arg\max_k | \sum_k v_i^k - k \times v^j > 0 \tag{1}$$

If the aggregate demand $\sum_{i=1}^n d_i^j$ equals to the allocated task number m, the auction terminates and we obtain a market clearing price as well as a feasible allocation. Otherwise, v^j is adjusted according to the relationship of demand and supply, i.e., increase when demand exceeds supply, and decrease otherwise, until the market stabilizes. The final valuation resulting in market equilibrium state is identified as the market clearing price p^*. Note that sites only submit v-messages at the beginning. The price discovery is solely performed by the scheduler based on the collected v-messages. This design effectively eliminates communications between auctioneer and bidders in a conventional DIA design. The complete pricing strategy is summarized in Algorithm 1.

4.1.3   Payment Policy

The pricing strategy presented in Sect. 4.1.2 achieves allocative efficiency in computational task allocation. In this section, we describe a payment policy design helpful for achieving incentive compatibility, an important property for matchmaking mechanism design in the context of utility computing. A common practice in resource and task auction is to let each bidder pay the market clearing

---

Algorithm 1: Task-resource matchmaking: pricing discovery strategy for homogeneous case

---

/∗ **Initialization** ∗/
1: $j \leftarrow 0$
2: **for all** $i \in \mathbb{S}$ **do**
3:      $d_i^j \leftarrow 0$
4:      Sends π_i to scheduler
5: **end for**
6: Calculates sorted acceptable price list V
7: Breaks ties in V when necessary
   {**Iterative Procedure**}
8: **while** $\sum_{i=1}^{n} d_i^j \neq m$ **do**
9:      $j \leftarrow j + 1$
10:     Obtains medium price in V as v^j
11:     Calculates $d_i^j = \arg\max_k \mid \sum_k v_i^k - k \times v^j > 0$ for site i
12:     **if** $\sum_{i=1}^{n} d_i^j > m$ **then**
13:          Discards elements $v \leq v^j$ in V
14:     **else if** $\sum_{i=1}^{n} d_i^\lambda < m$ **then**
15:          Discards elements $v \geq v^j$ in V
16:     **end if**
17: **end while**
    {**Allocation**}
18: Allocates d_i^j to site i

---

price p^*. However, if such a uniform payment policy is employed, rational bidders will have incentives to disclose untruthful demand, which will eventually lead to market inefficiency [4]. To overcome this problem, we use a non-linear payment approach proposed by Ausubel [2]. In a homogeneous task allocation, the payment for site i is calculated periodically. At each epoch, the market supply is compared against the aggregate demand from site i's opponents. If the supply is greater than the aggregate demand, the quantity difference is *credited* to i at current epoch price v^j. On the other hand, suppose at epoch j, the aggregate demand from i's opponent increases compared with that of epoch $j - 1$, the quantity difference is *debited* back at v^j. We define two variables, namely aggregate reserved bundle (e) and epoch reserved bundle (μ) to facilitate the payment calculation process. Their definitions are given out as below.

Definition 3 (Aggregate Reserved Bundle). The aggregate reserved bundle for site i at epoch j is given by:

$$e_i^j = \max\{0, m - \sum_{x \neq i} d_x^j\} \qquad (2)$$

Definition 4 (Epoch Reserved Bundle). The epoch reserved bundle μ_i^j is defined as the difference of the aggregate reserved bundle at adjacent epochs:

$$\mu_i^1 = e_i^1$$
$$\mu_i^j = e_i^j - e_i^{j-1} (j > 1) \tag{3}$$

When $\mu_i^j > 0$, there are μ_i^j tasks "credited" to i at price v^j, and when $\mu_i^j < 0$, μ_i^j tasks are "debited" back to i at v^j. Based on this process, the total payment of i at final epoch r is calculated as follow.

$$P_i(d_i^r) = \sum_{j=1}^{r} v^j \mu_i^j \tag{4}$$

Accordingly, the revenue is given by the following equation.

$$Q(A) = \sum_{i=1}^{n} P_i(d_i^r) \tag{5}$$

Now, we can incorporate the payment calculation procedure into Algorithm 1 as follows. For each site i, the scheduler will use two vectors $\bar{e}_i$ and $\bar{\mu}_i$ to save the historical bundle reservation. After line 16 in Algorithm 1, the scheduler will calculate e_i^j and μ_i^j for every site i. In addition, after the auction procedure is done, the scheduler can calculate a payment amount for every i based on Eq. (4), before line 18 in Algorithm 1. The payment is realized by enforcing committed resources for task processing at all sites.

4.1.4 Strategy Analysis

The auction procedure is self-adaptive, and reaches a market equilibrium state when complete. In this section, we will theoretically analyze the properties of our proposed self-adaptive auction based approach.

Proof of Convergence

Theorem 2. *If the auction proceeds with the iterative updates of demand vector query, as in Algorithm 1: lines 8–17, then the final allocation A converges to a feasible allocation at market clearing price $p^* = v^r$.*

Proof (Proof). The key point to prove the convergence is to ensure the existence of the market equilibrium point. Once we prove its existence, the binary search procedure in lines 8–17 is guaranteed to locate it in V. The existence of the market equilibrium point is illustrated in Fig. 4, where the x-axis stands for the sorted valuations in V, and the y-axis stands for the corresponding aggregate demands given the points lined up on x-axis. Now, suppose the scheduler acting as a virtual auctioneer starts crying out an open price of value 0, and gradually raises the price by following every point on x-axis from left to right. The aggregate demand from all sites decreases, forming a piecewise integer-valued linear function. Each step-wise increase of the cried price will result in exactly one bidder to drop one demanded task, given no tie presents. Therefore, the virtual auction process traverses every possible point in the pricing space. There must exist a market equilibrium point p^* whose corresponding demand intersects with the function $y = m$, where m is the number of total tasks to be allocated.

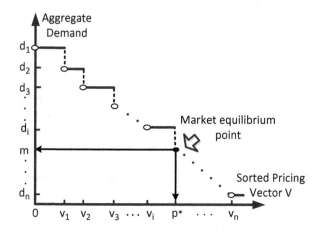

Fig. 4 Convergence proof for the self-adaptive auction based strategy

Proof of Efficiency and Optimal Makespan

Since the self-adaptive auction converges to the market clearing price when supply and demand meets, the resulting market is in the competitive equilibrium state (Definition 2) that renders the final allocation Pareto-efficient. The final allocation would achieve maximum allocative efficiency if elements in the valuation space are distinct.[1] Therefore, tasks are allocated to sites who value them most. In task scheduling, we expect that the auction based matchmaking mechanism could achieve optimal performance with respect to certain system-wide metric. In particular, we are interested in minimizing the processing makespan of the allocated task bundle through efficient allocation, i.e., to minimize the completion time of all tasks. We will show that, using the valuation function defined in Sect. 4.1.1, the self-adaptive auction achieves this by minimizing the maximum task processing time among all sites.

---

[1] However, the task allocation result might incur certain efficiency loss due to possible tie breaks in our strategy design. Compare to the overall efficiency, such efficiency loss is in general negligible.

For the homogeneous case, the allocation corresponding to optimal makespan of task execution can be easily calculated. We show that the self-adaptive auction achieves the same optimal allocation with the valuation function described in Sect. 4.1.1.

Theorem 3. *Let A^{opt} be the optimal makespan allocation of m homogeneous tasks on n sites. Using the auction procedure presented in Algorithm 1, the final allocation A achieves optimal makespan, i.e., $A = A^{opt}$.*

Proof (Proof). If site i $(1 \leq i \leq n)$ acquires d_i^r tasks $(d_i^r > 0)$ at the end of the matchmaking procedure, we have: $V_i(d_i^r) \geq p^* > V_i(d_i^r + 1)$ (according to Eq. (1)). Suppose each task has a fixed workload σ. Since $V_i(k) = \pi_i/k$, the processing time t_i is $t_i = k \times \sigma/\pi_i = \sigma/V_i(k)$. At the final allocation, we assume some site q has the longest processing time t_{max} for its allocated bundle d_q^r, then d_q^r must equal to p^* because $V_i(d_i^r) \geq p^* > V_i(d_i^r + 1)$ holds for every i.

We show that $A = A^{opt}$ by contradiction. If there is some other allocation $A' \neq A$ which achieves shorter task processing makespan than A. This must be achieved by migrating x $(0 < x < d_q^r)$ tasks on site q to some other site, for example, j. The task processing time on j becomes $\sigma/V_j(d_j^r + k)$. Since only two sites swap tasks, the new t'_{max} occurs at j and $t'_{max} < t_{max}$. However, since $V_j(d_j^r + k) < p^* = V_q(d_q^r) < V_j(d_j^r)$, the new makespan t'_{max} is greater than t_{max}. Hence, we prove $A = A^{opt}$.

Proof of Incentive Compatibility

With the payment policy presented in Sect. 4.1.3, site i does not pay the unit price of p^* at the market equilibrium point, but the prices when i is absent from the market. In that sense, the involved payment for i is equivalent to the opportunity cost of assigning the allocated bundle to the winning site. Such a non-linear payment policy has the same effect of multi-unit Vickrey auction which decouples a user's payment with bids. It effectively encourages truthful bidding in a much simpler implementation. Since all sites submit their v-messages to the task scheduler before the auction launches, the task scheduler has the full knowledge of all valuations as well as the full bid information (the complete history of all bids by all bidders). We define truthful bidding as the practice of reporting the actual valuation. For the homogeneous case, truthful bidding means to report π_i sincerely. The following theorem states that the self-adaptive auction achieves incentive compatible.

Theorem 4 (See [2] for Details). *With the aggregate bidding history and the assumption of diminishing marginal valuations, truthful bidding for every site i is a weakly dominant strategy after every epoch, given that payment policy presented in Sect. 4.1.3 is adopted.*

In fact, truthful bidding by every site is a subgame perfect equilibrium, as the strategy profile represents Nash equilibrium of every subgame of the dynamic auction. One thing to notice is that the proposed auction based approach has no guarantee for fairness, because some site reporting high valuations could take over all tasks and starve other sites. A possible solution for this problem is to enforce some allocation cap that limits the maximum task number one could obtain.

4.2 The K-Category Heterogeneous Case

In this section, we present the case when task scheduler wishes to allocate K heterogeneous types of tasks among a set of autonomous sets. Tasks within each type are homogeneous. This scenario is also encountered in cloud resource auction (viewed as the reverse of the task auction) where K types of virtual machine (VM) instances are allocated to n cloud customers. We have developed a prototype middleware platform called CloudBay, which uses a modified Ausubel auction for efficient VM allocation. Readers who are interested to this topic can refer to our work [45] for more details. In general, for the K-category heterogeneous case, we follow the same private value models as in the homogeneous case. The valuation functions are assumed to be monotonic and strictly concave. We need to make a few modifications for Algorithm 1 to work. The task scheduler now runs K parallel auctions, each of which is based on Algorithm 1. A vector of prices is calculated at each epoch and the demand quantities becomes a K-element vector too. This strategy works when the allocated workload is divisible [5]. However, when allocated tasks are discrete, we must enforce the property of substitutes preference, i.e., for any site, increasing the price for one type of task will not decrease the demand for any other task types, to guarantee the existence of market equilibrium state [3].

4.3 The General Heterogeneous Case

Finally, we investigate the general combinatorial case where all tasks are discrete and heterogeneous. The first challenge to deal with is that it is difficult to value and express the exponential number of task bundles at each site. Although a bidding language such as OR or XOR is possible to be employed, it still places significant overheads on both computation and communication. Second, from the perspective of winner determination, an efficient task-resource matchmaking design can be formulated as the following linear programming optimization problem [6].

$$\max \sum_{i \in \mathbb{S}} \sum_{x_i \subseteq A} V_i(x_i)\phi_i(x_i) \tag{6}$$

s.t.

$$\phi_i(x_i) - \sum_{A:x_i \subseteq A} \delta_A = 0, \qquad \forall i \in \mathbb{S}, \forall x_i \subseteq \mathbb{J} \tag{7}$$

$$\sum_{x_i \subseteq \mathbb{J}} \phi_i(x_i) = 1, \qquad \forall i \in \mathbb{S} \tag{8}$$

$$\sum_{A \in \mathbb{A}} \delta_A = 1 \tag{9}$$

$$\phi_i(x_i) \geq 0, \qquad \forall i \in \mathbb{S}, \forall x_i \subseteq \mathbb{J} \tag{10}$$

$$\delta_A \geq 0, \qquad \forall A \in \mathbb{A} \tag{11}$$

In the formulation, $\phi_i(x_i) = 1$ means assigning bundle x_i to site i, and $\delta_i(A) = 1$ is interpreted as selecting allocation A. The objective is to maximize the social welfare subject to bundle and allocation constraints (7)–(11). In [40], the authors proposed a primal-dual algorithm which can be interpreted as an auction process. We will not go further and leave the investigation of the solution space for the general heterogeneous case as a future research direction.

5 Evaluation Results

To validate the properties of the self-adaptive auction based matchmaking strategy, we developed a discrete-event simulator using SimGrid [11], a powerful simulation toolkit for large-scale distributed experiments. The self-adaptive auction was built based on the MSG interfaces that are suitable for simulating a heterogeneous computing environment [36]. We only evaluated the homogeneous case in the simulations.

5.1 Performance of Task Scheduling

In the first set of simulations, we created a distributed platform with 20 sites equipped with different resource capacities, and measured task processing makespan and Jain's fairness index[2] under varying input task number from 10 to 200, with a fixed increasing step of 10. Resource capacity π for all sites were randomly generated following a normal distribution $\mathcal{N}(1, 0.25)$. Each measurement was calculated by averaging ten different runs due to the randomness of the input

---

[2]Jain's fairness index: $f_i = (\sum_{i=1}^n t_i)^2 / n \sum_{i=1}^n t_i^2$, where t_i is i's task processing time. The more f_i is close to 1, the better of fairness.

parameters. The task-resource matchmaking process was implemented according to the strategies described in the homogeneous case (Sect. 4.1). We compare the self-adaptive auction based scheduling with two commonly-used scheduling algorithms.

- **Earliest Completion Time (ECT)**: ECT allocates each task to the site that completes task processing in the quickest time. It represents a set of Gantt chart algorithms (e.g., MaxMin, Sufferage) widely used to schedule BoT tasks [12].
- **Round Robin (RR)**: RR maintains an eligible set of idle sites and matches each task to one site in the set in a round robin manner. A site is removed from the set when it is currently busy, and is inserted back to the set when its current allocated task is completed.

The comparison result is depicted in Figs. 5 and 6. From Fig. 5, we observe that the self-adaptive auction always generate the shortest task makespan, with ECT performs as runner-up. Since RR does not assign high priority to computationally powerful sites, its makespan is constantly bounded by the task processing time on the least powerful site, resulting in the worst makespan performance. On the other hand, RR scores highest in fairness at most sampling points, as shown in Fig. 6, although the advantage is little compared to the other two algorithms. Another observation is that as the number of input task increases, all three algorithms converge to near-optimal f_i value. For ECT and RR, this effect is expected due to their ways of allocation. For the self-adaptive auction, it is because the task processing time on each site is proportional to the valuation closest to the market clearing price p^*. Since we adopt the valuation function defining i's marginal valuation of m tasks to be π_i/m, when m is large, the difference between two consecutive values in v_i becomes smaller. Therefore, variation of fairness becomes less and less as the number of input task increases.

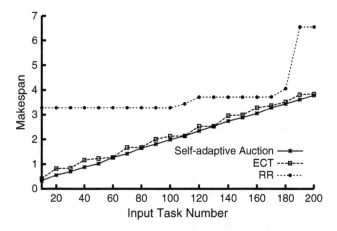

Fig. 5 Performance comparison: makespan

5.2   Validation of Incentive Compatibility

We validate incentive compatibility in Figs. 7 and 8. In this set of simulation, we used a new increasing and concave valuation other than the one described in Sect. 4.1.1. In particular, let the estimated execution time for one task at site i be t_i, we denote the total valuation of j tasks as:

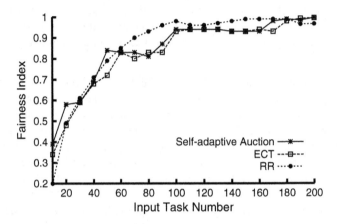

Fig. 6 Performance comparison: fairness index

$$V_i(k) = \sum_k ((1 - \alpha)^{k-1} \times 1/t_i), \tag{12}$$

where α is a parameter to quantify the rate of marginal valuation loss. The reason we used $1/t_i$ is because faster task turnaround time implies higher reward in general. Accordingly, the marginal valuation for the j-th task is formulated as follows.

$$v_i^j = V_i(j) - \sum_{k=1}^{j-1} V_i(j-1) \tag{13}$$

We gradually increased the input task number and set $\alpha = 0.05$. In addition, we randomly selected one site at each run and let it deliberately overbid or underbid. Figure 7 depicts the measured social welfare in all simulations. For comparison we also implemented a random task allocation scheme. We observe that maximum social welfare is achieved when all sites choose to report valuations truthfully. As one site bid strategically with untruthful reported valuations, the social welfare decreases slightly in each round. This result shows that the self-adaptive auction achieves the maximum socially efficient outcome when truthful bidding is used. Next, in Fig. 8, we compare the utility gain of a randomly chosen site using different strategies in the self-adaptive auction. Results show that a site adopting strategic strategies other than truthful bidding experiences utility decrease. Hence, there is no incentive for a single player to not truthfully bid. The conclusion is well aligned with our analysis in Sect. 4.1.4.

5.3 Performance Comparison with Uniform Price Auction

To demonstrate the advantage of the self-adaptive auction proposed for task-resource matchmaking, we implemented a **uniform price auction** algorithm [14] for performance comparison. In a uniform price auction, each bidder submits a demand schedule with an acceptable unit price. The auctioneer decides the market clearing price based on the collected bid information, and reserves resources for winners. An example application of the uniform price auction is Amazon's spot instance auction, where the auctioneer picks user's bid for a VM instance unit from high to low, until supply is depleted. Unlike the self-adaptive auction, the uniform price auction is *static* in nature, and all bidders are asked to pay the same market clearing price for each winning unit. Figure 9 shows the performance comparison result for allocating 1,000 tasks to 100 sites. All results were normalized with respect to the performance of the self-adaptive auction. The result of individual utility was measure by comparing the achieved utility of a randomly selected site. We observe that the self-adaptive auction approach consistently outperforms the uniform price auction approach in all metrics, demonstrating the advantage of introducing dynamism into auction based strategy design. On the one hand, the self-adaptive auction results in better allocative efficiency and higher utility from the perspective of the auctioneer. On the other hand, the self-adaptive auction exhibits advantage to uniform price auction from the perspective of the bidders. In summary, the proposed self-adaptive auction overcomes allocative inefficiency encountered in the commonly adopted uniform price auction.

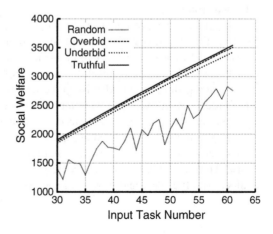

Fig. 7 Validation of incentive compatibility: social welfare

Fig. 8 Validation of
incentive compatibility:
utility for strategic player

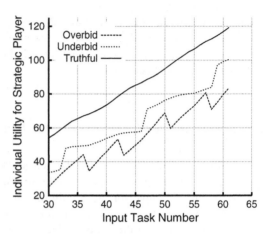

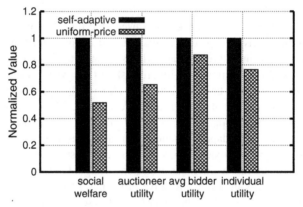

Fig. 9 Performance comparison with uniform price auction

Conclusion

In this chapter, we presented an efficient task-resource matchmaking strategy design that leverages a self-adaptive auction model, and investigated its properties in terms of allocative efficiency and incentive compatibility. The auction based strategy is novel in various respects. First, it enables efficient task pricing through an adaptive price discovery process, without burdening bidders with excessive communications. Second, a non-linear payment accounting approach was introduced to eliminate the incentives of strategic bidding. Finally, we examined the applicability of the proposed auction based approach to K-heterogeneous case, and further, to the general heterogeneous case. The auction based strategy achieves market equilibrium that maximizes allocative efficiency, and provides incentive compatible bidding regulations.

(continued)

To evaluate the performance of the self-adaptive auction approach, we also provided simulation results that reveal new insights to the design of efficient task-resource matchmaking in utility oriented distributed computing platforms.

References

1. Andelman, N., Azar, Y., Sorani, M.: Truthful approximation mechanisms for scheduling selfish related machines. Theor. Comp. Sys. **40**, 423–436 (2007)
2. Ausubel, L.M.: An efficient ascending-bid auction for multiple objects. American Economic Review **94**(5), 1452–1475 (2004)
3. Ausubel, L.M.: An efficient dynamic auction for heterogeneous commodities. American Economic Review **96**(3), 602–629 (2006)
4. Ausubel, L.M., Cramton, P.: Demand reduction and inefficiency in multi-unit auctions. Tech. rep., University of Maryland, Department of Economics (2002)
5. Bharadwaj, V., Ghose, D., Robertazzi, T.G.: Divisible load theory: A new paradigm for load scheduling in distributed systems. Cluster Computing **6**(1), 7–17 (2003)
6. Bikhchandani, S., Ostroy, J.M.: The package assignment model. Journal of Economic Theory **107**(2), 377–406 (2002)
7. Blumrosen, L., Nisan, N.: On the computational power of iterative auctions. In: ACM EC'05, pp. 29–43 (2005)
8. Buyya, R.: Market-Oriented cloud computing: Vision, hype, and reality of delivering computing as the 5th utility. In: IEEE CCGrid'09, p. 1 (2009)
9. Buyya, R., Abramson, D., Giddy, J.: Nimrod/g: an architecture for a resource management and scheduling system in a global computational grid. In: Proceedings of the fourth International Conference/Exhibition on High Performance Computing in the Asia-Pacific Region, pp. 283–289 (2000)
10. Buyya, R., Ranjan, R., Calheiros, R.N.: Intercloud: Utility-oriented federation of cloud computing environments for scaling of application services. In: Proceedings of the 10th International Conference on Algorithms and Architectures for Parallel Processing - Volume Part I (ICA3PP'10), pp. 13–31 (2010)
11. Casanova, H., Legrand, A., Quinson, M.: Simgrid: A generic framework for large-scale distributed experiments. In: UKSIM '08, pp. 126–131 (2008)
12. Casanova, H., Legrand, A., Zagorodnov, D., Berman, F.: Heuristics for scheduling parameter sweep applications in grid environments. In: HCW'00, pp. 349–363 (2000)
13. Catlett, C.: The philosophy of teragrid: Building an open, extensible, distributed terascale facility. In: Proceedings of the 2nd IEEE/ACM International Symposium on Cluster Computing and the Grid (CCGRID '02) (2002)
14. Cramton, P.: Competitive bidding behavior in uniform-price auction markets. In: HICSS'04 (2004)
15. Cramton, P., Shoham, Y., Steinberg, R.: Combinatorial Auctions. MIT Press (2006)
16. Danak, A., Mannor, S.: Resource allocation with supply adjustment in distributed computing systems. In: IEEE ICDCS'10, pp. 498–506 (2010)
17. Das, A., Grosu, D.: Combinatorial auction-based protocols for resource allocation in grids. In: IEEE IPDPS workshop, PDSEC'05, p. 251a (2005)
18. Fujiwara, I., Aida, K., Ono, I.: Applying double-sided combinational auctions to resource allocation in cloud computing. In: IEEE/IPSJ SAINT'10, pp. 7–14 (2010)
19. FutureGrid. https://portal.futuregrid.org/

20. Garg, S.K., Venugopal, S., Buyya, R.: A meta-scheduler with auction based resource allocation for global grids. 14th IEEE International Conference on Parallel and Distributed Systems (ICPADS '08). pp. 187–194 (2008)
21. Ghosh, P., Roy, N., Das, S.K., Basu, K.: A pricing strategy for job allocation in mobile grids using a non-cooperative bargaining theory framework. J. Parallel Distrib. Comput. **65**, 1366–1383 (2005)
22. Grosu, D., Das, A.: Auction-based resource allocation protocols in grids. In: PDCS'04, pp. 20–27 (2004)
23. Guruswami, V., Hartline, J.D., Karlin, A.R., Kempe, D., Kenyon, C., McSherry, F.: On profit-maximizing envy-free pricing. In: ACM SODA'05, pp. 1164–1173 (2005)
24. Kale, L., Kumar, S., Potnuru, M., DeSouza, J., Bandhakavi, S.: Faucets: efficient resource allocation on the computational grid. In: Proceedings of the 2004 International Conference on Parallel Processing (ICPP'04), pp. 396–405 (2004)
25. Lai, K., Rasmusson, L., Adar, E., Zhang, L., Huberman, B.A.: Tycoon: An implementation of a distributed, market-based resource allocation system. Multiagent Grid Syst. **1**, 169–182 (2005)
26. Lau, H.C., Cheng, S.F., Leong, T.Y., Park, J.H., Zhao, Z.: Multi-period combinatorial auction mechanism for distributed resource allocation and scheduling. In: IAT'07, pp. 407–411 (2007)
27. Leme, R.P., Tardos, E.: Pure and Bayes-Nash price of anarchy for generalized second price auction. In: IEEE FOCS'10, vol. 0, pp. 735–744 (2010)
28. Lin, W.Y., Lin, G.Y., Wei, H.Y.: Dynamic auction mechanism for cloud resource allocation. In: IEEE CCGrid'10, pp. 591–592 (2010)
29. Ma, R.T., Chiu, D.M., Lui, J.C., Misra, V., Rubenstein, D.: On resource management for cloud users: A generalized kelly mechanism approach. Tech. rep., Electrical Engineering (2010)
30. Mihailescu, M., Teo, Y.M.: Dynamic resource pricing on federated clouds. In: 2010-10th IEEE/ACM International Conference on Cluster, Cloud and Grid Computing (CCGrid), pp. 513–517 (2010)
31. PlanetLab. http://www.planet-lab.org/
32. Regev, O., Nisan, N.: The POPCORN market. online markets for computational resources. Decision Support Systems **28**(1–2), 177–189 (2000)
33. Rzadca, K., Trystram, D., Wierzbicki, A.: Fair game-theoretic resource management in dedicated grids. In: IEEE CCGrid'07, pp. 343–350 (2007)
34. Shang, S., Jiang, J., Wu, Y., Yang, G., Zheng, W.: A knowledge-based continuous double auction model for cloud market. In: SKG'10, pp. 129–134 (2010)
35. Sherwani, J., Ali, N., Lotia, N., Hayat, Z., Buyya, R.: Libra: A computational economy-based job scheduling system for clusters. Softw. Pract. Exper. **34**(6), 573–590 (2004)
36. SimBoinc. http://simboinc.gforge.inria.fr/
37. Song, B., Hassan, M., Huh, E.N.: A novel cloud market infrastructure for trading service. In: ICCSA'09, pp. 44–50 (2009)
38. Amazon Spot Instance. http://aws.amazon.com/ec2/spot-instances/
39. Stokely, M., Winget, J., Keyes, E., Grimes, C., Yolken, B.: Using a market economy to provision compute resources across planet-wide clusters. In: Proceedings of the 2009 IEEE International Symposium on Parallel&Distributed Processing (IPDPS 2009), pp. 1–8 (2009)
40. de Vries, S., Schummer, J., Vohra, R.V.: On ascending Vickrey auctions for heterogeneous objects. Journal of Economic Theory **132**(1), 95–118 (2007)
41. Waldspurger, C., Hogg, T., Huberman, B., Kephart, J., Stornetta, W.: Spawn: a distributed computational economy. IEEE Transactions on Software Engineering **18**(2), 103–117 (1992)
42. Wang, Q., Ren, K., Meng, X.: When cloud meets ebay: Towards effective pricing for cloud computing. In: 2012 Proceedings IEEE INFOCOM, pp. 936–944 (2012)
43. Wolski, R., Plank, J.S., Brevik, J., Bryan, T.: G-commerce: Market formulations controlling resource allocation on the computational grid. In: IEEE IPDPS'01, pp. 46–53 (2001)
44. Zaman, S., Grosu, D.: Combinatorial auction-based allocation of virtual machine instances in clouds. J. Parallel Distrib. Comput. **73**(4), 495–508 (2013)
45. Zhao, H., Yu, Z., Tiwari, S., Mao, X., Lee, K., Wolinsky, D., Li, X., Figueiredo, R.: Cloudbay: Enabling an online resource market place for open clouds. In: IEEE Fifth International Conference on Utility and Cloud Computing (UCC'12), pp. 135 –142 (2012)

Federating Advanced Cyberinfrastructures with Autonomic Capabilities

Javier Diaz-Montes, Ivan Rodero, Mengsong Zou, and Manish Parashar

Abstract Cloud computing has emerged as a dominant paradigm that has been widely adopted by enterprises. Clouds provide on-demand access to computing utilities, an abstraction of unlimited computing resources, and support for on-demand scale up, scale down and scale out. Clouds are also rapidly joining high performance computing system, clusters and grids as viable platforms for scientific exploration and discovery. Furthermore, dynamically federated Cloud-of-Clouds infrastructure can support heterogeneous and highly dynamic applications requirements by composing appropriate (public and/or private) cloud services and capabilities. As a result, providing scalable and robust mechanisms to federate distributed infrastructures and handle application workflows, that can effectively utilize them, is critical. In this chapter, we present a federation model to support the dynamic federation of resources and autonomic management mechanisms that coordinate multiple workflows to use resources based on objectives. We demonstrate the effectiveness of the proposed framework and autonomic mechanisms through the discussion of an experimental evaluation of illustrative use case application scenarios, and from these experiences, we discuss that such a federation model can support new types of application formulations.

1 Introduction

Cloud computing is revolutionizing the enterprise world, much as the Internet did not so long ago. Clouds are fundamentally changing how enterprises think about IT infrastructure, both internally and externally, by providing on-demand access to always-on computing utilities, an abstraction of unlimited resources, a potential for scale-up, scale-down and scale-out as needed, and for IT outsourcing and automation. Clouds also provide a usage-based payment model where users

J. Diaz-Montes (✉) • I. Rodero • M. Zou • M. Parashar
Rutgers Discovery Informatics Institute, NSF Cloud and Autonomic Computing Center,
Department of Electrical and Computer Engineering, Rutgers University, 96 Frelinghuysen Road,
Piscataway, NJ 08854, USA
e-mail: javidiaz@rdi2.rutgers.edu; irodero@rutgers.edu; mengsong.zou@rutgers.edu;
parashar@rutgers.edu

© Springer Science+Business Media New York 2014   201
X. Li, J. Qiu (eds.), *Cloud Computing for Data-Intensive Applications*,
DOI 10.1007/978-1-4939-1905-5_9

essentially "rent" virtual resources and pay for what they use. Underlying these cloud services are typically consolidated and virtualized data centers that exploit economies of scale to provide attractive cost–benefit ratios. In spite of being in its early stages, cloud computing is already reshaping IT world. In fact, according to The Wall Street Journal, four out of five businesses are moving or planning to move some of their business functions to cloud services.

At the same time that cloud computing is redefining IT, extreme data and compute scales are transforming science and engineering research by enabling new paradigms and practices—those that are fundamentally information/data-driven and collaborative. Cloud abstractions and infrastructures are rapidly becoming part of the overall research cyberinfrastructure, providing viable platforms for scientific exploration and discovery. It is expected that cloud services will join more traditional research cyberinfrastructure components—such as high performance computing (HPC) system, clusters and grids, as part of Cyberinfrastructure Framework for Twenty-First Century Science and Engineering (CIF21) in supporting scientific exploration and discovery. Analogous to their role in enterprise IT, clouds can enable the outsourcing of many of the mundane and tedious aspects research and education, such as deploying, configuring and managing infrastructure, and enable scientists to focus on the science. Computational and Data-enabled Science and Engineering (CDS&E) applications enabled by an advanced cyberinfrastructure (ACI) are providing unprecedented opportunities for understanding and managing natural and engineered systems, and offering unique insights into complex problems and, in addition to support traditional enterprise data analytics services (e.g., those based on MapReduce). For example, clouds can provide a platform for applications when local infrastructure is not available or supplement existing platforms to provide additional capacity or complementary capabilities to meet heterogeneous or dynamic needs [20, 42, 66]. Clouds can also serve as accelerators, or provide resilience to scientific workflows by moving the execution of the workflow on alternative or fewer resources when a failure occurs. The simplicity of the cloud abstraction can alleviate some of the problems scientific applications face in current HPC environments. The analysis of high-dimensional parameter spaces, uncertainty quantification by stochastic sampling, or statistical significance assessment through resampling, are just few examples of a broad class of problems that are becoming increasingly important in a wide range of application domains. These applications can be generally described as many task computing applications [48] and can benefit from the easy access to on-demand elastic customizable resources and the ability to easily scale up, down or out [49]. Clearly, realizing these benefits requires the development of appropriate application platforms and software stacks.

In this chapter, we present a model to support the dynamic federation of resources and the coordinated execution of application workflows on such federated environments. These resources can be of different types of infrastructure including traditional HPC clusters, supercomputers, grids, and clouds. Additionally, the federation provides autonomic scheduling mechanisms that create an abstraction with cloud-like capabilities to elastically provision the resources based on user and application policies and requirements. We discuss the requirements to enable our federation model followed by the description of our federation model and mechanisms. In contrast to previous work such as [52] or [10], which propose models to federate and combine clouds with local resources for cloudbursting, this chapter focuses on providing abstractions to seamlessly federate and provision on-demand a wider range of resources such as high-end systems that are not typically exposed in federated systems or grids. A key aspect of our federation model is the autonomic management and optimization of application execution through cross-layer application/infrastructure adaptation. To demonstrate the effectiveness of the federation model, mechanisms and autonomic management policies we present an experimental evaluation with relevant usage scenarios of the proposed frame-work, including: (1) medical image research, which aims at achieving extended capacity, (2) molecular dynamics simulations using asynchronous replica exchange, which provides adaptivity and elasticity at the application-level, and (3) data analytics workflow based on clustering, which focuses on adaptation to achieve user objectives and requirements. From these use case applications, we discuss ongoing work towards enabling such a federation model to support new types of application formulations such as adaptive workflows where dynamic provisioning and federation is essential to respond to non-deterministic behaviors.

2 State of the Art

This section collects different research efforts aimed to federate resources in the context of grid and cloud computing as well as standards to ease the interoperability among infrastructures. These efforts are mainly focused on providing an infrastructure to compute large scale scientific applications.

2.1 Federating Computational Grids

In the late 1990s, grid computing [16] emerged as the model to support large scientific collaborations by providing their computational resources and the structure behind them. The core concept of grid computing defines an architecture to support shared access to resources provided by members of virtual organizations (VO) [17] that are formed by collaborative data centers and institutions. Some examples of grids are Open Science Grid (OSG) [88] in US, GridX1 in Canada [1], Naregi in Japan [83], APACGrid in Australia [12], Garuda in India [50], Grid'5000 in France [6,78], DAS-3 in the Netherlands [73], D-Grid in Germany [75], e-Science in UK [21], and EGI (following EGEE and DataGrid research efforts) in Europe [76]. Note that the majority of grids result from regional initiatives. However, large dedicated grids have been also built to serve as scientific instruments, such as XSEDE [91] in the US, DEISA [74], HPC-Europa [41] and PRACE [89] in the EU, OSG in US, EGI in Europe, and Grid'5000 in France.

As science was pushing new limits in terms of levels of computation and data and collaboration between scientists from multiple scientific domains across the globe, there was a need for interoperability among different grid systems to create large grid environments that would allow users to access resources of various VOs transparently [54]. Among the grid federation efforts we can find InterGrid [9] along with the work by Assuncao et al. [3] that promotes interlinking different grid systems through economic-based peering agreements to enable inter-grid resource sharing, Gridway [67] through its grid gateways [22] along the work by Leal et al. [35] that proposed a decentralized model for scheduling on federated grids to improve makespan and resource performance, LAGrid meta-scheduling [5, 55, 59] that promotes interlinking different grid systems through peering agreements to enable inter-Grid resource sharing, Koala [39] with the use of delegated matchmaking [24] to obtain the matched resources from one of the peer Koala instances, VIOLA [61] that implements grid interoperability via WS-Agreement [2] and provides co-allocation of multiple resources based on reservations, Grid Meta-Brokering Service (GMBS) [28, 29] proposes an architecture for grid interoperability based on high level abstractions to describe the broker's capabilities and properties using a specific language [30–32, 57], the work by Elmroth et al. [13] that presents a grid resource brokering service based on grid standards, Guim et al. [56] studied scheduling techniques for multi-site grid environments, and within EGEE, efforts to enable interoperability between gLite and UNICORE [14] systems [38, 51].

2.2 Federation in Cloud Computing

Cloud computing has emerged as a dominant paradigm that has been widely adopted by enterprises. Clouds provide on-demand access to computing utilities, an abstraction of unlimited computing resources, and support for on-demand scale up, scale down and scale out. Furthermore, dynamically federated "cloud-of-clouds" infrastructure can support heterogeneous and highly dynamic applications requirements by composing appropriate (public and/or private) cloud services and capabilities. At the same time that cloud computing is redefining IT, it is rapidly joining high-performance computing system, clusters and grids as viable platforms for scientific exploration and discovery. Current cloud platforms can provide effective platforms for certain classes of applications, for example high-throughput computing (HTC) applications. There have been several early projects that have reported successful deployments of applications on existing clouds [11, 18, 27, 68]. Additionally, there are efforts exploring other usage modes [43] and to combine clouds, such as Amazon EC2 [71], with integrated computing infrastructures. Villegas et al. [69] proposed a composition of cloud providers as an integrated (or federated) cloud environment in a layered service model. Assuncao et al. [10] described an approach of extending a local cluster to cloud resources using different scheduling strategies. Along the same lines, Ostermann et al. [42] extended a grid workflow application development and computing infrastructure to include cloud resources, and experimented with Austrian Grid and an academic cloud installation of Eucalyptus using a scientific workflow application. Similarly, Vazquez et al. [66] proposed architecture for an elastic grid infrastructure using the GridWay meta-scheduler, and extended grid resources to Globus Nimbus; Vockler et al. [70] used Pegasus and Condor to execute an astronomy workflow on virtual machine resources drawn from multiple cloud infrastructures based on FutureGrid, NERSC's Magellan cloud and Amazon EC2; Gorton et al. [20] designed a workflow infrastructure for Systems Biology Knowledgebase (Kbase) and built a prototype using Amazon EC2 and NERSC's Magellan cloud; and Bittencourt et al. [4] proposed an infrastructure to manage the execution of service workflows in the hybrid system, composed of the union of a grid and a cloud.

Given the growing popularity of virtualization, many commercial products and research projects, such as OpenNebula [62, 86], OpenStack [87], Nimbus [84], Eucalyptus [40, 77], IBM Smart Cloud [80], Amazon EC2, and VMware vCloud Connector are being developed to dynamically overlay physical resources with virtual machines. Analogously, Riteau et al. [52] proposed a computing model where resources from multiple cloud providers are leveraged to create large-scale distributed virtual clusters. They used resources from two experimental testbeds, FutureGrid in the United States and Grid'5000 in France. In [8], Celesti et al. proposed a cross-federation model based on using a customized cloud manager component placeable inside the cloud architectures. Other example is the Resevoir [53] that aims at contributing to best practices with a cloud and federation architecture. In general, these efforts are intended to extend the benefits of virtualization from a single resource to a pool of resources, decoupling the VM not only from the physical infrastructure but also from the physical location.

2.3 Interoperability Standardization Activities

There are several projects with the goal enabling the interoperability of federated infrastructures. The Open Middleware Infrastructure Institute for Europe (OMII-Europe) aims to significantly influence the adoption and development of open standards that facilitate interoperability between gLite and UNICORE such as OGSA Basic Execution Service (BES) or Job Submission Description Language (JSDL). The Grid Scheduling Architecture Research Group (GSA-RG) of Open Grid Forum (OGF) is currently working on enabling grid scheduler interaction. They are working to define a common protocol and interface among schedulers enabling inter-grid resource usage, using standard tools (e.g., JSDL, OGSA, WS-Agreement). However, the group is paying more attention to agreements. They proposed the Scheduling Description Language (SDL) to allow specification of scheduling policies based on broker scheduling objectives/capabilities (e.g., time constraints, job dependencies, scheduling objectives, preferences). The Grid Interoperation Now Community Group (GIN-CG) of the OGF also addresses the problem of grid interoperability driving and verifying interoperation strategies. They are more focused on infrastructure with five sub-groups: information services, job submission, data movement, authorization, and applications. Aligned with GIN-CG, the OGF Production Grid Infrastructure Working Group (PGI-WG) aims to formulate a well-defined set of profiles and additional specifications. Some recommendations of these initiatives have been considered in existing work which has identified standardization as a key element towards interoperability [15].

There are also two main activities of the OGF for job management: SAGA [19] and DRMAA (Distributed Resource Management Application API) [65]. SAGA provides a set of interfaces used as the application programming model for developing applications for execution in grid environments. DRMAA defines a set of generalized interfaces that applications used to interact with distributed resource management middleware. Both SAGA and DRMAA focus on applications.

Finally, there are other interoperability activities focused in the context of the cloud. We have Siena [90], Open Cloud Computing Interface (OCCI) [85], under the OGF umbrella, that aim at defining standards for cloud interoperability. There is an IEEE Intercloud WG Working Group [81] that is working in standards such as Standard for Intercloud Interoperability and Federation (SIIF) [82].

3   Federation Model to Aggregate Distributed Resources

The federation model that we propose is aimed to orchestrate geographically distributed resources using cloud-like capabilities and abstractions. Our proposed federation model is different from the existing ones, presented in Sects. 2.1 and 2.2, in the sense that we provide a platform to access federated resources using cloud-like capabilities such as on-demand provisioning, dynamic aggregation or cloudbursting. Moreover, we are able to federate various kind of resources (HPC, cloud, and grid) and enable autonomic computing features such as objective-driven workflow execution to efficiently compute large scale problems.

3.1   Requirements

In order to design a federation model to support large scientific and engineering problems, it is imperative to clearly define the characteristics that the resulting system should provide. Having a well determined set of necessary and sufficient requirements simplifies the design process by focusing on the essential functionality. Thus, we used our past and present collaborations with domain scientists to identify key requirements our solution should offer in order to be easy to use and flexible. Next, we describe each one of these requirements.

- **Scalability and Extended Capacity:** Due to the computational requirements of modern scientific applications, it becomes necessary to scale across geographicallydistributed resources. This is because oftentimes a single resource is not sufficient to execute a given scientific workload (e.g. because the resource is of limited scale, or it mismatches application requirements).

- **Interoperability:** While the scalability and extended capacity requirement ensures that diverse resources can be incorporated into the federation, the interoperability requirement guarantees that the federation will be able to interact with these resources. Specifically, the federation must offer mechanisms to interface with common platforms such as personal supercomputers, MPI and MapReduce clusters, massively parallel and shared memory supercomputers, and clouds. At the same time, it must be open such that new platforms can be added in the future.
- **Capability:** By having heterogeneous resources as part of the federation, we can take advantage of their particular characteristics and optimize the resource allocation. In our model tasks and resource allocation can be achieved via a push model with central scheduler, or a pull model where resources obtain tasks via attribute-based queries. Thus, the federation must be aware of the capabilities of each resource to allow optimal usage.
- **Elasticity and On-Demand Access:** The important factor affecting applicability of the federation is its ability to scale up/down or out as needed. For many practical workloads it is difficult to predict computational and storage requirements. Moreover, many applications are dynamic in the sense of convergence, and hence provide no guarantees on the cost of execution. Consequently, the federation must be able to aggregate or drop resources seamlessly. What is important, the resulting elasticity makes the infrastructure resilient and hence improves its ability to sustain computational throughput.
- **Self-discovery:** Having the right monitoring mechanisms in place is important to ensure that the federation provides a realistic view of resources, taking into account their variability over time. Here multiple factors should be taken into account including availability, load, failure-rate, etc. The ability to self-discover strongly affects how the federation manages the offered services and optimizes resources allocation.
- **Democratization:** Users of the federation may have access to a larger number of resources or to specific resources, which enables them to tackle more important scientific challenges. This requires the capability of sharing resources and more importantly controlling their usage to ensure a fair use among all users.

3.2   Federation Architecture

The federation is designed to be dynamically shaped as it is created in a collaborative way, where each site talk with each other to identify themselves, negotiate the terms of adhesion, discover available resources, and advertise their own resources and capabilities. In this way, a federated management space is created on runtime and sites can join and leave at any point. Users can access the federation from any site, see Fig. 1.

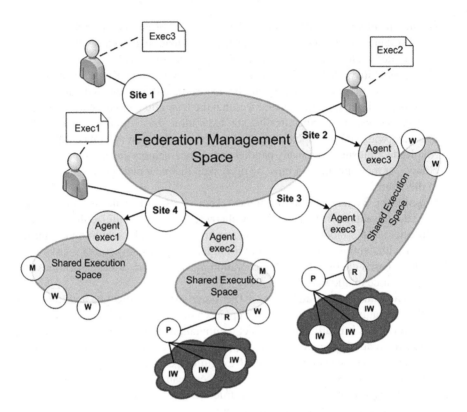

Fig. 1 Federation architecture. Here (M) denotes a master, (W) is a worker, (IW) an isolated worker, (P) a proxy, and (R) is a request handler

The federation model is based on the Comet [36] coordination spaces concept. These Comet spaces are used to coordinate the different aspects of the federation. In particular, we have decided to use two kind of spaces in the federation. First, we have a single federated management space used to create the actual federation and orchestrate the different resources. This space is used to interchange any operational message for discovering resources, announcing changes in a site, routing users' request to the appropriate sites, or initiating negotiations to create ad-hoc execution spaces. On the other hand, we can have multiple shared execution spaces that are created on demand to satisfy computing needs of the users. Execution spaces can be created in the context of a single site to provision local resources and cloudburst to public clouds or external HPC systems. Moreover, they can be used to create a private sub-federation across several sites. This case can be useful when several sites have some common interest and they decide to jointly target certain type of tasks as a specialized community.

As shown in Fig. 1, each shared execution space is controlled by an agent that creates such space and coordinates the resources for the execution of a particular set of tasks. Agents can act as master of the execution or delegate this duty to a dedicated master (M) when some specific functionality is required. Moreover, agents deploy workers to actually compute the tasks. These workers can be in a trusted network and be part of the shared execution space, or they can be part of external resources such as a public cloud and therefore in a non-trusted network. The first type of workers are called secure workers (W) and can pull tasks directly from the space. Meanwhile, the second type of workers are called isolated workers (IW) and cannot interact directly with the shared space. Instead, they have to interact with a proxy (P) and a request handler (R) to be able to pull tasks from the space.

A key aspect of this federation is the autonomic management and optimization (of multiple objectives, including performance, energy, cost, and reliability) of application execution through cross-layer application/infrastructure adaptations. It is essential to be able to adapt to the application's behavior as well as system configuration, which can change at run time, using the notion of elasticity at the application and workflow levels. Hence, the federated infrastructure increases the opportunities to provision appropriate resources for given workflows based on user objectives or policies and different resource classes can be mixed to achieve the user objectives. Resources scale up/down/out based on the dynamic workflow and the given policies. A user objective can be to accelerate application runtime within a given budget constraint, to complete the application in a time constraint, or to select better resources matching to the application type, such as computation-intensive and data-intensive. Furthermore, application requirements and resource status may change, for example, due to workload surges, system failures or emergency system maintenance, and as a result, it is necessary to adapt the provisioning to match these changes in resource and application workload.

3.3   CometCloud

Our federation model is built on top of CometCloud [33, 72] and the concepts that CometCloud is based on. CometCloud is an autonomic computing engine based on the Comet [36] decentralized coordination substrate, and supports highly heterogeneous and dynamic cloud/grid/HPC infrastructures, enabling the integration of public/private clouds and autonomic cloudbursts, i.e., dynamic scale-out to clouds to address extreme requirements such as heterogeneous and dynamics workloads, and spikes in demands.

Conceptually, CometCloud is composed of a programming layer, service layer, and infrastructure layer. The infrastructure layer uses the Chord self-organizing overlay [63] and the Squid [60] information discovery to create a scalable content-based coordination space for wide-area and a content-based routing substrate, respectively. The routing engine supports flexible content-based routing and complex querying using partial keywords, wildcards, or ranges. It also guarantees that all peer nodes with data elements that match a query/message will be located. The service layer provides a range of services to support autonomics at the programming and application level. This layer supports a Linda-like [7] tuple space coordination model, and provides a virtual shared-space abstraction as well as associative access primitives. Dynamically constructed transient spaces are also supported to allow applications to explicitly exploit context locality to improve system performance. Asynchronous (publish/subscribe) messaging and event services are also provided by this layer. The programming layer provides the basic functionality for application development and management. It supports a range of paradigms including the master/worker/BOT. Masters generate tasks and workers consume them. Masters and workers can communicate via virtual shared space or using a direct connection. Scheduling and monitoring of tasks are supported by the application framework. The task consistency service handles lost/failed tasks.

3.4   Autonomic Management

The autonomic management capabilities are provided by the autonomic manager, which is responsible for managing workflows, estimating runtime and scheduling tasks at the beginning of every stage based on the resource view provided by the agents. At each stage, the adaptivity manager monitors tasks runtimes through results, handles the changes of application workloads and resource availability, and adapts resource provisioning if required. Figure 2 shows the architecture of the autonomic management framework. We detail the different components of the autonomic manager below.

Workflow Manager The workflow manager is responsible for coordinating the execution of the overall application workflow, based on user's objectives and status of the infrastructure.

Runtime Estimator The runtime estimator estimates computational runtime and cost of each task. This estimate can be obtained through a computational complexity model or through quick, representative benchmarks. Since performance is strongly affected by the underlying infrastructure (clouds, HPC, or grids) it is more effective to use benchmarks to obtain runtime and cost estimates.

Autonomic Scheduler It uses the information provided by the estimator modules to determine the initial hybrid mix HPC/grids/cloud resources based on user/system-defined objectives, policies and constraints. The autonomic scheduler also profiles the tasks to allow agents to get the most suitable ones for their resources. The scheduler is dynamic and it can update both the allocations and the scheduling policy at runtime.

Elasticity Manager The status of the resources or the performance of the application can change over time and differ from the initial estimation. Thus, the elasticity manager is responsible for preventing the violation of the objectives and policies by elastically adapting the resources allocated to each workflow.

Fig. 2 Architectural
overview of the autonomic
manager framework.
CometCloud creates a cloud
abstraction where all types of
infrastructures are viewed as
elastic clouds that can
provision resources on
demand

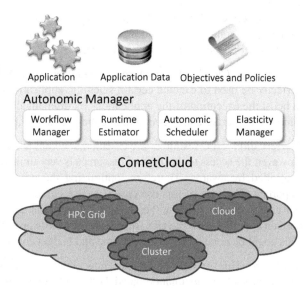

The autonomic manager takes advantage of the cloud abstraction provided by CometCloud to seamlessly interact with any kind of infrastructures. Each infrastructure has specific properties that define the characteristics of its resources. This information is essential to allow the autonomic manager to dynamically federate resources. Since it uses CometCloud, it inherits the support for the master/worker, MapReduce and workflow programming models. Nevertheless, applications are usually described as workflows. Typically, the workflow programming model considers a workflow with multiple stages, where stages should be executed in an order, each stage can run a different application or the same application with different length of tasks, computational requirements, and data.

3.5 Enabling Autonomics

The essence of the autonomic manager resides in the user objectives and policies. They are used to drive the execution of the workflow by provisioning the appropriated number and type of resources. The allocated resources can vary over time, to make sure the application requirements are respected, if a deviation over the estimate execution plan is detected. Deviations on the plan occur due to unexpected failures, performance fluctuation, queue wait time variation, etc. In this Section we present several use cases that represent typical scenarios from the user's perspective and how to achieve them using autonomic techniques.

User Objectives Currently, the autonomic manager supports three main objectives namely acceleration, conservation, and resilience. Nonetheless, new objectives such as energy-efficiency can be easily integrated.

Acceleration Cloud infrastructures provide large amount of resources that can perfectly be used to execute certain scientific applications. Thus, they can be used to boost the execution of the applications by dramatically increasing the number of allocated resources and hence reducing the overall computational time.

Conservation HPC resources are essential to compute many scientific applications. However, the access to this type of resources is very limited and their use is typically controlled by awards. Therefore, optimizing the use of those resources is very important. The idea of this use case is to use clouds to conserve HPC allocations. For example, we could use the cloud to do an initial exploration of the application domain and migrate to the HPC resources only those tasks that progress as expected. This could be done considering runtime and budget constraints.

Resilience This use case investigates how clouds can be used to handle unexpected situations such as an unanticipated HPC/grid downtime, inadequate allocations, unanticipated queue delays or failures of working nodes. Additional cloud resources can be requested to alleviate the impact of the unexpected situations and meet user objectives.

Scheduling Policies To achieve the above user objectives, several policies can be defined. Two of the most representative policies are described as follows.

Deadline The scheduling decision is to select the fastest resource class for each task and to decide the number of nodes per resource class based on the deadline. If the deadline can be achieved with a single node, then only one node will be allocated. When an application needs to be completed as soon as possible, regardless of cost and budget, the largest useful number of nodes is allocated.

Budget When a budget is enforced on the application, the number of allocatable nodes is restricted by the budget. If the budget is violated with the fastest resource class, then the next fastest and cheaper resource class is selected until the expected cost falls within the budget limit.

4   Application Scenarios

This section provides a comprehensive discussion of different representative use case applications and experiences to illustrate the effectiveness of our proposed federation architecture, mechanisms and autonomic strategies. Specifically we discuss different Computational and Data-Enabled Science and Engineering (CDS&E) applications and an enterprise business data analytics workflow. Although the result of these applications is not the goal of this chapter, we believe the discussion of these experiences are useful to define next steps towards advanced cyberinfrastructure and clouds federation for different usage modes [43].

4.1   CDS&E Applications

Two different CDS&E applications are discussed below, namely medical image research and molecular dynamics simulations using asynchronous replica exchange. Both application use cases use federated advanced cyberinfrastructure in combination with clouds, however, they represent different usage modes.

Medical Image Research includes both medical image registration and content-based image retrieval. In the former, we focused on autonomically balancing completion time and cost using federated resources including private data centers, grids and private clouds [34]. In the latter, we use the proposed federation mechanisms to achieve extended capacity to respond to its large computational power requirements, which is described as follows.

Content-based image retrieval (CBIR) has been one of the most active research areas in a wide spectrum of image-related fields over the last few decades. In pathology, hematology already contains a large number of tools to automatically count blood cells. To classify abnormal white blood cells and compare diagnosis between a new case and cases with similar abnormalities is an interesting application. In this application use case we focus on CBIR on digitized peripheral blood smear specimens using low-level morphological features. Specifically, we use CometCloud to execute CBIR in federated heterogenous advanced cyberinfrastructure and cloud resources with the goal of reducing the completion time (i.e., provide answers within minutes or hours rather than weeks). The CBIR code was ported from Matlab to Java as a native CometCloud application to avoid licensing constrains in non-proprietary resources and to enable future implementations of the application on specialized hardware (e.g., accelerators). Since the most computation expensive part is searching query patches within each database image, we chose to use master/worker programming model, thus each image within the database was assigned to a worker. The implementation using the master/worker programming model is shown as Fig. 3. A master and a number of workers (one per physical core) form an overlay at runtime and synchronize using a tuple space (execution space). The master generates tasks (one for each image or subset of images to be processed) and then the workers pull the tasks and process the associated images simultaneously. In order to improve scalability and fault tolerance, workers store intermediate results on disk rather than returning the results back to the master using the comet space. When the workers finish, the intermediate results are consolidated (which represents a small part of the overall execution).

In order to obtain extended capacity, we federated a cluster at Rutgers (a Dell Power Edge system with 256 cores in 8-core nodes) with distributed cyberinfrastructure from NSF Extreme Science and Engineering Discovery Environment (XSEDE), NSF FutureGrid, the National Energy Research Scientific Computing Center (NERSC) and public clouds (Amazon EC2). Specifically, we used Ranger (Sun constellation with 62,976 cores in 16-core nodes) and Lonestar (with 22,656 cores in 12-core nodes) from XSEDE, Hotel (an IBM iDataPlex system with 672 cores in 8-core nodes) from FutureGrid, Hopper (a Cray XE6 system with

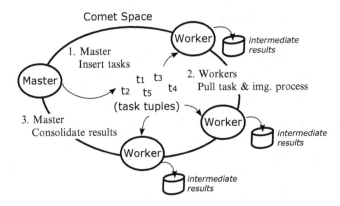

Fig. 3 Master/worker framework implementation in CometCloud

153,216 cores in 24-core nodes) from NERSC, and medium instances from Amazon EC2. The former resources were used through startup awards and the later in pay-as-you-go basis. We used advanced cyberinfrastructure systems "opportunistically" by using short waiting time queues, i.e., queues with limitations such as reduced runtime and number of queued/running jobs. Data transfer was overlapped with computation.

Figure 4 shows the completion time of CBIR algorithm over the database of 925 images for the 50 different configurations (in minutes, using logarithmic scale) and Fig. 5 shows the average throughput (i.e., processed images per minute) that a single node of each of the different platforms can achieve. Completion time for the federated scenario was obtained with real executions while for sequential and local cluster scenarios completion time is an estimation based on the actual execution of the subset of configurations, due to the limitations of very long executions.

The results show that CBIR is dramatically speeded up when using the (dedicated) dell cluster at Rutgers with respect to using a single node (from around two weeks of computation to 12 h). However, using federated infrastructure (i.e., much

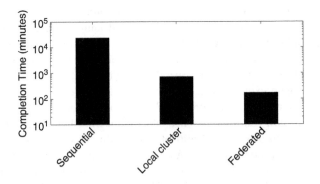

Fig. 4 Completion time using different configurations

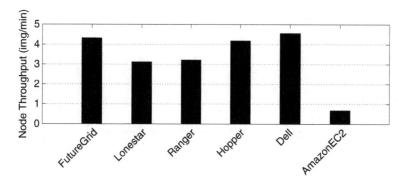

Fig. 5 Average node throughput for different platforms

more resources but not under own control) provides much shorter completion time (about 170 min). In our experiments the jobs used a single node (i.e., up to 24 cores) to run a set of 100 images, however, if we used a smaller set of images per job the penalty due to the queuing times would be higher. In case of Amazon EC2 a job processes a smaller set of images because the nodes have smaller core count. Figure 5 also shows the impact of queuing time on the average throughput in the HPC systems (i.e., Lonestar, Ranger and Hopper). Furthermore, Fig. 6 shows the throughput (i.e., number of processed images per minute) during a time interval of 3 h of the Dell cluster at Rutgers and Hopper, respectively. The Dell cluster shows more stable throughput behavior than Hopper, whose throughput presents spikes over time. Although Hopper nodes are more powerful, the queuing times and the limitation of the number of concurrent running jobs penalizes significantly the throughput.

The proposed federated system presents many opportunities and challenges in the context of medical image research such as exploiting heterogeneous federated resources from the point of view of their capabilities. For example, the Matlab incarnation of CBIR can be run when licenses are available or an incarnation for accelerators (e.g., GPU or Intel MIC) can be run when resources with accelerators are available.

Molecular Dynamics Simulations Using Asynchronous Replica Exchange
Replica exchange [23,64] is a powerful sampling algorithm that preserves canonical distributions and allows for efficient crossing of high-energy barriers that separate thermodynamically stable states. In this algorithm, several copies or replicas, of the system of interest are simulated in parallel at different temperatures using "walkers". These walkers occasionally swap temperatures and other parameters to allow them to bypass enthalpies barriers by moving to a higher temperature. The replica exchange algorithm has several advantages over formulations based on constant temperature, and has the potential for significantly impacting the fields of structural biology and drug design—specifically, the problems of structure based drug design and the study of the molecular basis of human diseases associated

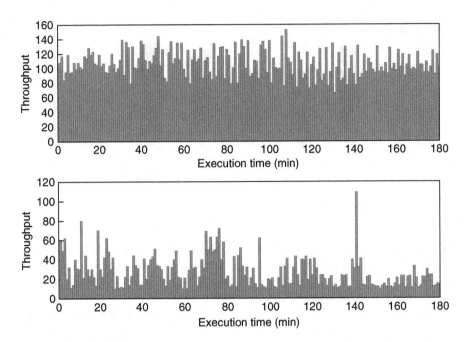

Fig. 6 Throughput (images/minute) for the Dell cluster on *top* and the Hopper supercomputer at the *bottom*

with protein misfolding. Traditional parallel implementations of replica exchange target either tightly coupled parallel systems or relatively small clusters. However, an asynchronous formulation of the replica exchange algorithm was designed and implemented [37, 79], which was proven to be effective, efficient and suitable for grid- based systems. Additionally, it is possible to reformulate the workflow to better utilize the ACI as described below.

Typically molecular dynamics simulations are very static in terms of execution models—the simulations go from start to finish irrespective of whether replicas are progressing towards correct folding. The ability to bias a trajectory by identifying pathways that are progressing towards a fully folded structure and those that are diverging away is an exciting direction for replica exchange formulations. The quality of the protein structure can be monitored by comparing the progress of each replica using secondary structure prediction methods and the radius of gyration. For example, in ubiquitin folding simulation replicas with large radius of gyration would be considered for termination because ubiquitin is a globular protein with a small radius of gyration. However, replicas exhibiting short radius of gyration would remain in the simulation due to the close resemblance to the completely folded ubiquitin protein. In addition to killing diverging replicas, the described application formulation can also spawn new replicas if they are making progress towards correct folding. As a result, the entire simulation would follow a sequence where radius of gyration and secondary structure prediction information will be used to terminate

Fig. 7 NAMD scaling in
different environments

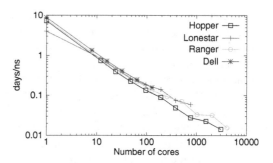

some replicas, cause a conformation to spawn new replicas across a temperature range, and modulate the probability of exchanging to nearby temperatures. By utilizing such a formulation we can dynamically adapt the molecular dynamics simulations, bias trajectories to find pathways towards correct folding and, in doing so, accelerate scientific discovery.

The use of CometCloud provides the opportunity to run simulations on dynamically federated large-scale distributed resources. Thus, what we see is a hierarchical formulation that provides adaptivity and elasticity at the application-level, through asynchronous replica exchange, and at the infrastructure-level, through Comet-Cloud. By utilizing CometCloud's capabilities and its cloud computing abstractions, we can run asynchronous NAMD [44] replica exchange on a federated, distributed environment. From an application perspective, the amount of time a simulation takes is proportional to the size of the protein or system and the desired length of the trajectory. However, by using CometCloud and asynchronous replica exchange scientists can explore the folding of very large proteins and run trajectories at microsecond or potentially even millisecond scale. This larger scale of science also gives rise to interesting scenarios at the CometCloud layer. For example, if we find that the initial allocation of resources is not enough then CometCloud can dynamically federate other distributed sites in order to obtain more resources. Conversely, in the context of protein folding, CometCloud can dynamically kill replicas if it finds that the protein structures being generated by the replicas do not progress towards the known structure or show predicted secondary structure features. By eliminating non-converging replicas we can ensure that CPU cycles are not wasted and speed-up the application.

In order for large-scale simulations to be effective the asynchronous formulation must show good scaling on this heterogeneous distributed environment. Performance evaluation is a necessary tool for understanding the limitations of the various environments provided by CometCloud. This is especially true for commodity and virtualized resources—such as those provided by FutureGrid and Amazon EC2. Thus, the performance of the entire ensemble of simulations depends on the slowest platform. In this case, the slowest platforms correspond to FutureGrid and Amazon EC2 where NAMD replica exchange is deployed on virtual machines. In terms of the simulation, the downward slope shows that the simulation time (in days) for a nanosecond trajectory is decreasing—meaning faster simulations. From Fig. 7 we can conclude that all environments tested exhibit good scalability and consistently report faster simulation times each time the processor count is doubled. More importantly, these results provide justification for a federated architecture where all machines can run simulations in parallel. The close grouping of simulations on large-scale HPC sites (i.e., Ranger, Hopper, Lonestar) also show that distributing replicas across these environments might also be feasible. Combining the fact of the low performance of virtualized environments to run tightly couple simulations [18, 25] and NAMD scaling on HPC infrastructure, we find that there is sufficient motivation for the formulation described above.

4.2 Enterprise Business Data Analytics

Current enterprise business data analytics workflows combine different techniques in their stages such as MapReduce-like applications that aggregate large amounts of data from different sources for business intelligence with clustering techniques. For example, the output of a topic-based text analysis approach such as Latent Dirichlet Allocation (LDA) is represented in a multi-dimensional information space, which includes different topics, information categories, etc. These data points in the multi-dimensional information space can be clustered using Distributed Online Clustering (DOC) to search results and correlate them with known data sources, and allow visualizing and interpreting the results interactively through a GUI. The specific solution in this application use case is a federated hybrid cloud for handling "big data" through DOC.

DOC is a clustering algorithm that targets networked systems in which individual components can monitor their operational status or actions, represent them using sets of globally known attributes, and periodically publish this status or interactions as semantic events that contain a sequence of attribute-value pairs. The algorithm specification, along with details about its implementation and robustness to failures, were the subject of previous publications [47]. Other applications of DOC have been also studied in the context of autonomic resource provisioning [45, 58] and autonomic policy adaptation [46] Here, we explain the main characteristics of the algorithm, and refer the reader to the cited publications for further details.

In DOC, each of the events to be clustered is represented as a point in a multidimensional space, each dimension in this space, referred to as an information space, corresponds to one of the event attributes, and the location of a point within the space is determined by the values for each of its attributes. It is assumed that the range of values of each attribute is an ordered set. For each set, a distance function can be defined in order to measure the similarity between points (i.e., similarity is inversely proportional to distance). This definition is straightforward for quantitative attributes, and can be applied to non-quantitative attributes as well with an appropriate encoding. The notion of similarity based on distance in each dimension extends to the multidimensional information space, for which a

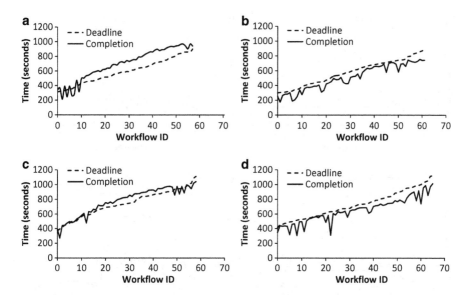

Fig. 8 Deadline and completion time of each workflow with and without cloudburst. (**a**) Only Rutgers (No Cloudburst), deadline 300 s. (**b**) Rutgers+EC2 (CloudBurst), deadline 300 s. (**c**) Only Rutgers (No Cloudburst), deadline 420 s. (**d**) Rutgers+EC2 (CloudBurst), deadline 420 s

distance function can also be defined in terms of the uni-dimensional distances. Conceptually, a cluster is a set of points for which mutual distances are relatively smaller than the distances to other points in the space [26]. However, the approach for cluster detection described in this chapter is not based primarily on evaluating distances between points, but rather on evaluating the relative density of points within the information space. In this case, point similarity is directly proportional to point density.

The approach used for the evaluation of point density, and thus for the detection of clusters and outliers, is dividing the information space into regions and to observe the number of points within each region. If the total number of points in the information space is known, then a baseline density for a uniform distribution of points can be calculated and used to estimate an expected number of points per region. Clusters are recognized within a region if the region has a relatively larger point count than this expected value. Conversely, if the point count is smaller than expected, then these points are potential outliers. However, clusters may cross region boundaries and this must be taken into account when verifying potential outliers. The approach described above lends itself to a decentralized implementation because each region can be assigned to a particular processing node. Nodes can then analyze the points within their region and communicate with nodes responsible for adjoining regions in order to deal with boundary conditions.

As part of this application scenario, we evaluated the autonomic manager by showing how to achieve user objectives such as time constraint and deadline using

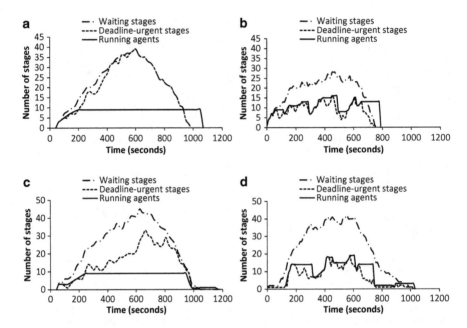

Fig. 9 Number of stages waiting to be executed and number of allocated agents. The required agents are provisioned on-demand by cloudburst regardless of the local resources limitations. (**a**) Only Rutgers (No Cloudburst), deadline 300 s. (**b**) Rutgers+EC2 (CloudBurst), deadline 300 s. (**c**) Only Rutgers (No Cloudburst), deadline 420 s. (**d**) Rutgers+EC2 (CloudBurst), deadline 420 s

cloudbursts to a public cloud when the local resources are limited. We have used Rutgers cluster as a local resource class with 27 nodes where each node has 8 cores, 6 GB memory, 146 GB storage and 1 GB Ethernet connection. For a public cloud, we used Amazon EC2, c1.medium instance type. We are going to use workflows of the DOC application with three different stages each, with different parameters and input files. Therefore, each stage of the workflow has a different execution time. From the point of view of the autonomic manager, each stage is a task and is executed by a single agent. We decided that each agent uses two workers to execute a stage. Hence, the maximum number of agents that can be allocated in the Rutgers cluster is nine because each agent involves three machines (one for the agent and two for the workers). Moreover, each agent can only execute one stage at a time, which means that if there are multiple workflows submitted in a short time, then their stages should wait in the space for some time until they are selected. Therefore, the autonomic manager has to autonomically scale-up/down agents to adapt the provisioned resources to the workload.

User objectives can be set for each stage of the workflow separately as each stage can run a different application with different constraints and the length of computation or the amount of required resources can vary among stages even for the same application. In this experiment, we set a deadline for each stage and we have used shortest deadline first serve (SDFS) policy for task selection. Hence, agents sequentially select stages which have the shortest remaining time to deadline. The number of agents is related to the number of stages which should immediately start to meet the deadline constraint. Thus, the autonomic scheduler starts agents to execute urgent stages. The scheduler tries to allocate resources from the cluster at Rutgers and only if the local cluster does not have enough resources it allocates resources from Amazon EC2 (cloud burst).

The average interval of workflow submission has been set to 10 s during the first 600 s of execution. We show two set of experiments, fixing the deadline for each stage of the workflow to 100 and 140 s, respectively. Since each workflow has a three stages, the deadline for each workflow is 300 and 420 s, respectively. Results are shown in Figs. 8 and 9. Specifically, Fig. 8 shows the deadline and completion time of each workflow for 300 and 420 s. Note that the deadline and completion times of each workflow are relative to the time it was submitted. We can observe that when we executed the workflows using Rutgers resources only (without cloudburst), around a 90 % of the workflow violated deadline constraints, even for a large deadline. However, when we enabled cloudburst to EC2, all workflow were able to meet the deadline constraints by allocating as many EC2 instances as required on-demand.

On the other hand, Fig. 9 shows the number of waiting stages and the number of allocated agents over time. It also shows the deadline-urgent stages, which are those waiting stages that need to be executed immediately to have a chance to meet their deadlines. We can observe in Fig. 9a, c, that local resources were not able to provide the computational power needed to guarantee the deadline constrains. It caused that the waiting time of each stage and the number of deadline-urgent stages to be increased, and therefore deadlines were eventually violated. However, Fig. 9b, d shows that when we enabled cloudburst, the autonomic manager was able to dynamically scale up and down the number of allocated agents to satisfy the demand of deadline-urgent stages. Scaling up the number of allocated agents was immediately done when needed. However, we delayed the deallocation of agents to avoid too much fluctuation. Therefore, by using the autonomic manager, all the workflow stages were able to meet the deadline constraints.

5 Lessons Learned

The different use cases presented in previous sections clearly demonstrate feasibility and capability of an elastic, dynamically federated infrastructure. These use cases have shown how it is possible to use the autonomic capabilities of our framework for different objectives, including acceleration and conservation.

Oftentimes, a single resource is not sufficient to execute a given scientific work-load (e.g. because it is of limited scale, or it mismatches application requirements). Although the majority of researchers with large computational demands have access to multiple infrastructures, such as HPC, computational grids, and clouds, taking advantage of the collective power of these systems is not trivial. Our results show how a federated framework can help to aggregate the computational power (i.e. capacity) of geographically distributed resources and offer them in an elastic way to the users. In the CBIR use case (Sect. 4.1), we shown how the execution can be dramatically sped up, from weeks to minutes. One important element that contributed to the success of this experiment, was the ability of the federation to scale across institutional and geographic boundaries.

As discussed above, it is clear from the state of the art that cloud platforms can effectively support certain classes for CDS&E applications, such as for example, high throughput computing (HTC) applications. However, many other existing CDS&E application formulations are not directly suited for cloud platforms. As a result, it is essential to explore alternate formulations of these applications that could potentially benefit from cloud services. This idea has been demonstrated in the replica exchange use case (Sect. 4.1) where an asynchronous implementation allowed us to take advantage of the capabilities offered by different resources. Therefore, having highly heterogeneous resources as a part of the federation, it is crucial to take advantage of their particular characteristics and optimize resources allocation. This is synergistic with the concept of autonomic computing. In particular, in the replica exchange case we used clouds to complement HPC resources, which allowed us to save HPC allocations.

Finally, one important aspect of clouds is the ability of adapting the resources to the demands of applications and users. In the majority of cases predicting computational and storage requirements is extremely difficult. Therefore, scaling up/down or out as needed becomes essential for dynamic workloads. Our results show that elasticity allows to adapt the number of provisioned resources to the demands. In this way, it is possible to meet the deadline for different applications while utilizing just the appropriated number of resources. This concept is shown in the business data analytics application, Sect. 4.2. Additionally, the elasticity can also be used to make the infrastructure resilient to changes in the federation. Consequently, the federation is able to better sustain computational throughput.

Conclusions

We have presented a federation model that enables the orchestration of hybrid distributed infrastructures and the coordinated execution of application workflows on such federated environments. We experimentally investigated, from an application's perspective, possible usage modes for integrating HPC and clouds as well as how autonomic computing can support these modes. In particular, we used three use case scenarios to highlight different aspects of the federation. First, we showed how medical image research applications can benefit from the federation of distributed resources and their aggregated computational power. Then, we exploited the principles of adaptivity and elasticity at the application level, through asynchronous replica exchange,

(continued)

and at the infrastructure level, through CometCloud, in the context of a molecular dynamics application. We specifically argue how clouds can be beneficial to quickly explore the application domain space saving the HPC allocations to compute only those replicas that were identified as relevant during the exploration. Finally, we performed a deadline objective-driven workflow execution to further study the behavior of the autonomic manager. The workflow was based on a decentralized online clustering application and the results showed autonomic manager is able to achieve deadline constraint by provisioning resources on demand (cloudburst).

Our ongoing work includes the exploration of new scientific application scenarios that require the coordinated used of distributed hybrid infrastructures and supporting new types of application formulations such as adaptive workflows where dynamic provisioning and federation is essential to respond to non-deterministic behaviors. Moreover, we are also working in enabling new cloud-like paradigms to provide a platform where scientist only need to change the application driver to benefit from an existing federation infrastructure. Finally, we would also like to evaluate new ways to manage the different sites of the federation. Currently, it is based on a pull mode and we believe that other mechanisms such as publish/subscribe would bring us many more interesting use cases.

Acknowledgements The research presented in this work is supported in part by US National Science Foundation (NSF) via grants numbers OCI 1310283, OCI 1339036, DMS 1228203 and IIP 0758566, by the Director, Office of Advanced Scientific Computing Research, Office of Science, of the U.S. Department of Energy through the Scientific Discovery through Advanced Computing (SciDAC) Institute of Scalable Data Management, Analysis and Visualization (SDAV) under award number DE-SC0007455, the Advanced Scientific Computing Research and Fusion Energy Sciences Partnership for Edge Physics Simulations (EPSI) under award number DE-FG02-06ER54857, the ExaCT Combustion Co-Design Center via subcontract number 4000110839 from UT Battelle, and by an IBM Faculty Award. We used resources provided by: XSEDE NSF OCI-1053575, FutureGrid NSF OCI-0910812, and NERSC Center DOE DE-AC02-05CH11231. The research and was conducted as part of the NSF Cloud and Autonomic Computing (CAC) Center at Rutgers University and the Rutgers Discovery Informatics Institute (RDI2). We would also like to acknowledge Hyunjoo Kim, Moustafa AbdelBaky, and Aditya Devarakonda for their contributions to the CometCloud project.

References

1. A. Agarwal, M. Ahmed, A. Berman, B. L. Caron, et al. GridX1: A Canadian computational grid. *Future Gener. Comput. Syst.*, 23:680–687, June 2007.
2. A. Andrieux, K. Czajkowski, A. Dan, K. Keahey, H. Ludwig, T. Nakata, J. Pruyne, J. Rofrano, S. Tuecke, and M. Xu. Web Services Agreement Specification (WS-Agreement), GFD-R-P.107. Technical report, GRAAP WG, Open Grid Forum, March 2007.

3. M. D. Assuncao and R. Buyya. Performance analysis of allocation policies for interGrid resource provisioning. *Information and Software Technology*, 51:42–55, January 2009.

4. L. F. Bittencourt, C. R. Senna, and E. R. M. Madeira. Enabling execution of service workflows in grid/cloud hybrid systems. In *Network Operations and Management Symp. Workshop*, pages 343–349, 2010.

5. N. Bobroff, L. Fong, S. Kalayci, Y. Liu, J. C. Martinez, I. Rodero, S. M. Sadjadi, and D. Villegas. Enabling interoperability among meta-schedulers. In *IEEE CCGrid*, pages 306–315, 2008.

6. R. Bolze, F. Cappello, E. Caron, M. Dayde, et al. Grid'5000: a large scale and highly reconfigurable experimental Grid testbed. *International Journal of High Performance Computing Applications*, 20:481–494, November 2006.

7. N. Carriero and D. Gelernter. Linda in context. *Commun. ACM*, 32(4):444–458, 1989.

8. A. Celesti, F. Tusa, M. Villari, and A. Puliafito. How to enhance cloud architectures to enable cross-federation. In *IEEE CLOUD*, pages 337–34, 2010.

9. M. D. de Assuncao, R. Buyya, and S. Venugopal. Intergrid: a case for internetworking islands of grids. *Concurrency Computat. Pract. and Exper.*, 20(8):997–1024, 2008.

10. M. D. de Assuncao, A. di Costanzo, and R. Buyya. Evaluating the cost-benefit of using cloud computing to extend the capacity of clusters. In *ACM HPDC*, pages 141–150, 2009.

11. E. Deelman, G. Singh, M. Livny, B. Berriman, and J. Good. The cost of doing science on the cloud: the montage example. In *Proceedings of the 2008 ACM/IEEE conference on Supercomputing*, SC '08, pages 50:1–50:12, Piscataway, NJ, USA, 2008. IEEE Press.

12. T. Dunning and R. Nandkumar. International cyberinfrastructure: activities around the globe. *Cyberinfrastructure Technology Watch Quarterly*, 2:2–4, February 2006.

13. E. Elmroth and J. Tordsson. A standards-based grid resource brokering service supporting advance reservations, coallocation, and cross-grid interoperability. *Concurr. Comput. : Pract. Exper.*, 21(18):2298–2335, Dec. 2009.

14. D. Erwin and D. Snelling. UNICORE: A Grid Computing Environment. In *International Euro-Par Conference on Parallel Processing*, pages 825–834, Manchester, UK, August 2001.

15. L. Field, E. Laure, and M. W. Schulz. Grid deployment experiences: Grid interoperation. *J. Grid Comput.*, 7(3):287–296, 2009.

16. I. Foster and C. Kesselman. *The Grid: Blueprint for a New Computing Infrastructure*. Morgan-Kauffman, 1999.

17. I. Foster, C. Kesselman, and S. Tuecke. The Anatomy of the Grid: Enabling Scalable Virtual Organizations. *International Journal of High Perfomance Computing Applications*, 15(3):200–222, 2001.

18. G. Fox and D. Gannon. Cloud Programming Paradigms for Technical Computing Applications. Technical report, Indiana University, 2012.

19. T. Goodale, S. Jha, T. Kielmann, A. Merzky, J. Shalf, and C. Smith. A Simple API for Grid Applications (SAGA), GWD-R.72. Technical report, SAGA-CORE Working Group, Open Grid Forum, September 2006.

20. I. Gorton, Y. Liu, and J. Yin. Exploring architecture options for a federated, cloud-based system biology knowledgebase. In *IEEE Intl. Conf. on Cloud Computing Technology and Science*, pages 218–225, 2010.

21. T. Hey and A. Trefethen. The UK e-Science Core Programme and the Grid. *Future Gener. Comput. Syst.*, 18:1017–1031, 2002.

22. E. Huedo, R. Montero, and I. Llorente. A recursive architecture for hierarchical grid resource management. *Future Gener. Comput. Syst.*, 25:401–405, April 2009.

23. K. Hukushima and K. Nemoto. Exchange Monte Carlo method and application to spin glass simulations. *J. Phys. Soc. Jpn.*, 65:1604–1608, 1996.

24. A. Iosup, D. Epema, T. Tannenbaum, M. Farrelle, and M. Livny. Inter-Operable Grids through Delegated MatchMaking. In *International Conference for High Performance Computing, Networking, Storage and Analysis (SC07)*, pages 13:1–13:12, Reno, Nevada, November 2007.

25. A. Iosup, S. Ostermann, N. Yigitbasi, R. Prodan, T. Fahringer, and D. Epema. Performance analysis of cloud computing services for many-tasks scientific computing. *IEEE Trans. Parallel Distrib. Syst.*, 22(6):931–945, 2011.
26. A. K. Jain and R. C. Dubes. *Algorithms for Clustering Data*. Prentice Hall, 1998.
27. K. Keahey and T. Freeman. Science clouds: Early experiences in cloud computing for scientific applications. In *Cloud Computing and Its Applications (CCA-08)*, October 2008.
28. A. Kertesz and P. Kacsuk. Grid Meta-Broker Architecture: Towards an Interoperable Grid Resource Brokering Service. In *CoreGRID Workshop on Grid Middleware in conjunction with Euro-Par, LNCS 4375*, pages 112–116, Desden, Germany, 2008.
29. A. Kertész and P. Kacsuk. Gmbs: A new middleware service for making grids interoperable. *Future Gener. Comput. Syst.*, 26(4):542–553, Apr. 2010.
30. A. Kertesz, I. Rodero, and F. Guim. Bpdl: A data model for grid resource broker capabilities. Technical Report TR-0074, Institute on Resource Management and Scheduling, CoreGRID - Network of Excellence, March 2007.
31. A. Kertesz, I. Rodero, and F. Guim. Meta-Brokering Solutions for Expanding Grid Middleware Limitations. In *Workshop on Secure, Trusted, Manageable and Controllable Grid Services (SGS) in conjunction with International Euro-Par Conference on Parallel Processing*, Gran Canaria, Spain, July 2008.
32. A. Kertžsz, I. Rodero, F. Guim, A. Kertžsz, I. Rodero, and F. Guim. A data model for grid resource broker capabilities. In *Grid Middleware and Services*, pages 39–52, 2008.
33. H. Kim, Y. E. Khamra, I. Rodero, S. Jha, and M. Parashar. Autonomic management of application workflows on hybrid computing infrastructure. *Sci. Program.*, 19(2–3):75–89, 2011.
34. H. Kim, M. Parashar, D. J. Foran, and L. Yang. Investigating the use of autonomic cloudbursts for high-throughput medical image registration. In *IEEE/ACM GRID*, pages 34–41, 2009.
35. K. Leal, E. Huedo, and I. M. Llorente. A decentralized model for scheduling independent tasks in federated grids. *Future Gener. Comput. Syst.*, 25(8):840–852, 2009.
36. Z. Li and M. Parashar. A computational infrastructure for grid-based asynchronous parallel applications. In *HPDC*, pages 229–230, 2007.
37. Z. Li and M. Parashar. Grid-based asynchronous replica exchange. In *IEEE/ACM GRID*, pages 201–208, 2007.
38. M. Marzolla, P. Andreetto, V. Venturi, A. Ferraro, et al. Open Standards-Based Interoperability of Job Submission and Management Interfaces across the Grid Middleware Platforms gLite and UNICORE. In *IEEE International Conference on e-Science and Grid Computing*, pages 592–601, Bangalore, India, December 2007.
39. H. Mohamed and D. Epema. KOALA: a Co-allocating Grid Scheduler. *Concurrency and Computation: Practice & Experience*, 20:1851–1876, November 2008.
40. D. Nurmi, R. Wolski, C. Grzegorczyk, G. Obertelli, S. Soman, L. Youseff, and D. Zagorodnov. The eucalyptus open-source cloud-computing system. In *IEEE/ACM CCGRID*, pages 124–131, 2009.
41. A. Oleksiak, A. Tullo, P. Graham, T. Kuczynski, J. Nabrzyski, D. Szejnfeld, and T. Sloan. HPC-Europa: Towards Uniform Access to European HPC Infrastructures. In *IEEE/ACM International Workshop on Grid Computing*, pages 308–311, November 2005.
42. S. Ostermann, R. Prodan, and T. Fahringer. Extending grids with cloud resource management for scientific computing. In *IEEE/ACM Grid*, pages 42–49, 2009.
43. M. Parashar, M. AbdelBaky, I. Rodero, and A. Devarakonda. Cloud Paradigm and Practices for CDS&E. Technical report, Cloud and Autonomic Computing Center, Rutgers Univ., 2012.
44. J. C. Phillips, R. Braun, W. Wang, J. Gumbart, E. Tajkhorshid, E. Villa, C. Chipot, R. D. Skeel, L. V. Kal, and K. Schulten. Scalable molecular dynamics with NAMD. *J. of Computational Chem.*, pages 1781–1802, 2005.
45. A. Quiroz, H. Kim, M. Parashar, N. Gnanasambandam, and N. Sharma. Towards autonomic workload provisioning for enterprise grids and clouds. In *IEEE/ACM GRID*, 2009.
46. A. Quiroz, M. Parashar, N. Gnanasambandam, and N. Sharma. Autonomic policy adaptation using decentralized online clustering. In *ICAC*, pages 151–160, 2010.

47. A. Quiroz, M. Parashar, N. Gnanasambandam, and N. Sharma. Design and evaluation of decentralized online clustering. *TAAS*, 7(3):34, 2012.
48. I. Raicu, I. Foster, and Y. Zhao. Many-task computing for grids and supercomputers. In *Proc. Workshop on Many-Task Computing on Grids and Supercomputers*, pages 1–11, 2008.
49. I. Raicu, Z. Zhang, M. Wilde, I. Foster, P. Beckman, K. Iskra, and B. Clifford. Towards loosely. coupled programming on petascale systems. In *IEEE/ACM Supercomputing*, 2008.
50. N. Ram and S. Ramakrishran. International cyberinfrastructure: activities around the globe. *Cyberinfrastructure Technology Watch Quarterly*, 2:15–19, February 2006.
51. M. Riedel, A. Memon, M. Memon, D. Mallmann, et al. Improving e-Science with Interoperability of the e-Infrastructures EGEE and DEISA. In *International Convention on Information and Communication Technology, Electronics and Microelectronics (MIPRO)*, pages 225–231, Opatija, Croatia, May 2008.
52. P. Riteau, M. Tsugawa, A. Matsunaga, J. Fortes, and K. Keahey. Large-scale cloud computing research: Sky computing on futuregrid and grid'5000. In *ERCIM News*, 2010.
53. B. Rochwerger, D. Breitgand, E. Levy, A. Galis, et al. The reservoir model and architecture for open federated cloud computing. *IBM Journal of Research and Development*, 53, 2009.
54. I. Rodero, F. Guim, J. Corbalan, L. Fong, Y. Liu, and S. Sadjadi. Looking for an Evolution of Grid Scheduling: Meta-brokering. *Grid Middleware and Services: Challenges and Solutions*, pages 105–119, August 2008.
55. I. Rodero, F. Guim, J. Corbalan, L. Fong, and S. Sadjadi. Broker Selection Strategies in Interoperable Grid Systems. *Future Gener. Comput. Syst.*, 26(1):72–86, January 2010.
56. I. Rodero, F. Guim, J. Corbalan, and A. Goyeneche. The grid backfilling: a multi-site scheduling architecture with data mining prediction techniques. In *Grid Middleware and Services*, pages 137–152, 2008.
57. I. Rodero, F. Guim, J. Corbalan, and J. Labarta. How the JSDL can Exploit the Parallelism? In *IEEE International Symposium on Cluster Computing and the Grid (CCGrid)*, pages 275–282, Singapore, May 2006.
58. I. Rodero, J. Jaramillo, A. Quiroz, M. Parashar, F. Guim, and S. Poole. Energy-efficient application-aware online provisioning for virtualized clouds and data centers. In *Green Computing Conf.*, pages 31–45, 2010.
59. I. Rodero, D. Villegas, N. Bobroff, Y. Liu, L. Fong, and S. M. Sadjadi. Enabling interoperability among grid meta-schedulers. *J. Grid Comput.*, 11(2):311–336, 2013.
60. C. Schmidt and M. Parashar. Squid: Enabling search in dht-based systems. *J. Parallel Distrib. Comput.*, 68(7):962–975, 2008.
61. J. Seidel, O. Waldrich, W. Ziegler, P. Wieder, and R. Yahyapour. Using SLA for Resource Management and Scheduling - a Survey, TR-0096. Technical report, Institute on Resource Management and Scheduling, 2007.
62. B. Sotomayor, R. Montero, I. Llorente, and I. Foster. Virtual infrastructure management in private and hybrid clouds. *IEEE Internet Computing*, 13:14–22, 2009.
63. I. Stoica, R. Morris, D. Liben-Nowell, D. R. Karger, M. F. Kaashoek, F. Dabek, and H. Balakrishnan. Chord: A scalable peer-to-peer lookup protocol for internet applications. In *ACM SIGCOMM*, pages 149–160, 2001.
64. R. Swendsen and J. Wang. Replica Monte Carlo simulation of spin-glasses. *Physical Review Letters*, 57:2607–2609, 1986.
65. P. Troger, H. Rajic, A. Haas, and P. Domagalski. Standardization of an API for Distributed Resource Management Systems. In *Proceedings of the Seventh IEEE International Symposium on Cluster Computing and the Grid*, pages 619–626, Washington, DC, USA, 2007.
66. C. Vazquez, E. Huedo, R. Montero, and I. Llorente. Dynamic provision of computing resources from grid infrastructures and cloud providers. In *Grid and Pervasive Computing Conf.*, pages 113–120, 2009.
67. T. Vazquez, E. Huedo, R. Montero, and I. Lorente. Evaluation of a Utility Computing Model Based on the Federation of Grid Infrastructures. In *International Euro-Par Conference on Parallel Processing*, pages 372–381, Rennes, France, August 2007.

68. C. Vecchiola, S. Pandey, and R. Buyya. High-performance cloud computing: A view of scientific applications. In *Proceedings of the 2009 10th International Symposium on Pervasive Systems, Algorithms, and Networks*, ISPAN '09, pages 4–16, Washington, DC, USA, 2009. IEEE Computer Society.

69. D. Villegas, N. Bobroff, I. Rodero, J. Delgado, et al. Cloud federation in a layered service model. *J. Comput. Syst. Sci.*, 78(5):1330–1344, 2012.

70. J.-S. Vockler, G. Juve, and M. R. Ewa Deelman and. Experiences using cloud computing for a scientific workflow application. In *2nd Workshop on Scientific Cloud Computing in conjunction with ACM HPDC*, pages 402–412, 2011.

71. Amazon EC2. http://aws.amazon.com/ec2/.

72. CometCloud Project. http://www.cometcloud.org.

73. DAS-3 Project. http://www.cs.vu.nl/das.

74. DEISA Project. http://www.deisa.eu.

75. D-Grid Project. http://www.d-grid.de.

76. EGI Europe. http://www.egi.eu.

77. Eucalyptus. http://open.eucalyptus.com/.

78. Grid' 5000 Project. https://www.grid5000.fr.

79. R. Zhang, M. Parashar, and E. Gallichio. Salsa: Scalable asynchronous replica exchange for parallel molecular dynamics applications. In *ICPP*, pages 127–134, 2006.

80. IBM Smart Cloud. http://www.ibm.com/cloud-computing/us/en/.

81. IEEE Intercloud WG (ICWG) Working Group. http://standards.ieee.org/develop/wg/ICWG-2302_WG.html.

82. IEEE Standard for Intercloud Interoperability and Federation. http://standards.ieee.org/develop/project/2302.html.

83. Naregi Project, http://www.naregi.org.

84. Nimbus Project. http://www.nimbusproject.org.

85. Open Cloud Computing Interface (OCCI). http://occi-wg.org/.

86. OpenNebula. http://www.opennebula.org/.

87. OpenStack. http://openstack.org/.

88. Open Science Grid. https://www.opensciencegrid.org/.

89. PRACE Project. http://www.prace-ri.eu.

90. Siena Initiative. http://www.sienainitiative.eu.

91. XSEDE Project. https://www.xsede.org/.

Part III
Programming Models

Comparing high throughput and MapReduce frameworks to handle cloud computing at PaaS levels. Studies of MapReduce as it applies to distributed data centers and datasets; suggests 'push' method to allow separate MapReduce versions to cooperate better. Iterative asynchronous computing algorithm model Maiter performs in distributed data environments.

Migrating Scientific Workflow Management Systems from the Grid to the Cloud

Yong Zhao, Youfu Li, Ioan Raicu, Cui Lin, Wenhong Tian, and Ruini Xue

Abstract Cloud computing is an emerging computing paradigm that can offer unprecedented scalability and resources on demand, and is gaining significant adoption in the science community. At the same time, scientific workflow management systems provide essential support and functionality to scientific computing, such as management of data and task dependencies, job scheduling and execution, provenance tracking, fault tolerance. Migrating scientific workflow management systems from traditional Grid computing environments into the Cloud would enable a much broader user base to conduct their scientific research with ever increasing data scale and analysis complexity. This paper presents our experience in integrating the Swift scientific workflow management system with the OpenNebula Cloud platform, which supports workflow specification and submission, on-demand virtual cluster provisioning, high-throughput task scheduling and execution, and efficient and scalable resource management in the Cloud. We set up a series of experiments to demonstrate the capability of our integration and use a MODIS image processing workflow as a showcase of the implementation.

1 Introduction

Scientific workflow management systems (SWFMS) have been proven essential to scientific computing as they provide functionalities such as workflow specification, process coordination, job scheduling and execution, provenance tracking [61], fault

Y. Zhao • Y. Li • W. Tian • R. Xue
School of Computer Science and Engineering, University of Electronic
Science and Technology of China, Chengdu, China
e-mail: yongzh04@gmail.com; youfuli.fly@gmail.com; tian_wenhong@uestc.edu.cn;
xueruini@gmail.com

I. Raicu (✉)
Department of Computer Science, Illinois Institute of Technology, Chicago, IL, USA
e-mail: iraicu@cs.iit.edu

C. Lin
Department of Computer Science, California State University, Fresno, CA, USA
e-mail: clin@csufresno.edu

© Springer Science+Business Media New York 2014
X. Li, J. Qiu (eds.), *Cloud Computing for Data-Intensive Applications*,
DOI 10.1007/978-1-4939-1905-5__10

tolerance etc. SWFMS in fact represent a subset of Many-Task Computing (MTC) [58] workloads. MTC is reminiscent of High-Throughput Computing, but it differs in the emphasis of using many computing resources over short periods of time to accomplish many computational tasks (i.e. including both dependent and independent tasks), where the primary metrics are measured in seconds (e.g. FLOPS, tasks/s, MB/s I/O rates), as opposed to operations (e.g. jobs) per month. MTC denotes high-performance computations comprising multiple distinct activities, coupled via file system or memory-to-memory transfer operations. Tasks may be small or large, uniprocessor or multiprocessor, compute-intensive or data-intensive. The set of tasks may be static or dynamic, homogeneous or heterogeneous, loosely coupled or tightly coupled. The aggregate number of tasks, quantity of computing, and volumes of data may be extremely large [59]. MTC includes loosely coupled applications that are generally communication-intensive but not naturally expressed using standard message passing interface commonly found in HPC, drawing attention to the many computations that are heterogeneous but not "happily" parallel. [60] There are unprecedented challenges raised for traditional scientific workflows, as the data scale and computation complexity are growing exponentially. The ETL (Extraction-Transformation-Loading), storage, retrieval, analysis and application upon the huge amounts of data are beyond the capability of traditional data processing infrastructures. The community has coined this as Big Data, and it is often associated with the Cloud Computing paradigm.

As an emerging computing paradigm, Cloud computing [6] is gaining tremendous momentum in both academia and industry: not long after Amazon opened its Elastic Computing Cloud (EC2) to the public, Google, IBM, and Microsoft all released their Cloud platforms one after another. Meanwhile, several open source Cloud platforms, such as Hadoop [31], OpenNebula [1], Eucalyptus [32], Nimbus [20], and OpenStack [2], become available with fast growth of their own communities. There are a couple of major benefits and advantages that are driving the widespread adoption of the Cloud computing paradigm: (1) Easy access to resources: resources are offered as services and can be accessed over Internet. For instance, with a credit card, you can get access to Amazon EC2 virtual machines immediately; (2) Scalability on demand: once an application is deployed onto the Cloud, the application can be automatically made scalable by provisioning the resources in the Cloud on demand, and the Cloud takes care of scaling out and in, and load balancing; (3) Better resource utilization: Cloud platforms can coordinate resource utilization according to resource demand of the applications hosted in the Cloud; and (4) Cost saving: Cloud users are charged based on their resource usage in the Cloud, they only pay for what they use, and if their applications get optimized, that will be reflected into a lowered cost immediately.

Theoretically, to address the big data problems in the above scientific computing areas, scientists and application developers may simply refactor all the existing workflow applications into the Cloud computing paradigm, which sounds straightforward but in reality is impractical. As traditional scientific workflow applications have been mature during many years' development and always involve complicated application logic and consist of massive computing processes such as organization, distribution, coordination and parallel processing. Transforming these scientific workflows will not only cost scientists and developers much time, but also require manual handling of all the integration details with various underlying Cloud platforms.

An alternative for researchers is to integrate scientific workflow management systems with Clouds, leveraging the functionalities of both Cloud computing and SWFMSs to provide a Cloud workflow platform as a service for big data processing. In this solution, not only the challenges for traditional scientific workflows can be dealt with, the researchers can also concentrate on applications and utilize the integration platform to process massive data in Clouds. As workflow management systems are diverse in many aspects, such as workflow models, workflow languages, workflow engines, and so on, and each workflow system engine may depend on one specific Distributed Computing Infrastructures (DCIs), porting a workflow management system to run on another DCI may cost a large quantity of extra effort. We would like to free researchers from complicated integration details, such as Cloud resource provisioning, task scheduling and so on, and provide them with the convenience and transparency to a scalable big data processing platform, therefore we propose a service framework to standardize the integration between SWFMSs and Cloud platforms, breaking the limitations that a specific SWFMS is bound to a particular DCI or Cloud environment. We define a series of components and interfaces to normalize the interactions between different workflow management subsystems.

This paper extends earlier work [12] in which we identified various challenges associated with migrating and adapting an SWFMS in the Cloud. In this paper, *we present an end-to-end approach that addresses the integration of Swift, an SWFMS that has broad application in Grids and supercomputers, with the OpenNebula Cloud platform.* The integration covers all the major aspects involved in workflow management in the Cloud, from client-side workflow submission to the underlying Cloud resource management.

This paper's major contributions are:

1. *We analyze the challenges for traditional scientific workflows in the Grid environment, and proposed a structured approach to migrating a SWFMS into the Cloud.*
2. *We integrate Swift with OpenNebula, in order to coordinate and automate scientific analysis and discovery.*
3. *We propose a virtual cluster provisioning mechanism that could recycle Cloud virtual machine instances.*
4. *We present a use case as a showcase of the implementation.*

The rest of the paper is organized as follows: In the next section, we discuss the challenges of traditional scientific workflows and analyze the available solutions to the challenges. In the integration section, we introduce a service framework for the integration of SWFMSs and Cloud platforms and present our end-to-end integration of Swift and OpenNebula. In the performance evaluation section, we set up a series of experiments to analyze the integration and demonstrate the implementation using a NASA MODIS image processing workflow. In the related work section, we discuss related work in migrating scientific workflow management systems from the Grid to the Cloud. In the last section, we draw our conclusions and discuss future work.

2 Challenges and Available Solutions

In this section, we discuss the challenges of utilizing traditional scientific workflows to deal with big data problems and analyze the available solutions to the challenges.

2.1 Challenges for Traditional Scientific Workflows

Scientific workflow systems have been formerly applied over a number of execution environments such as workstations, clusters/Grids, and supercomputers. In contrast to Cloud environment, running workflows in these environments are facing a series of obstacles when dealing with big data problems [43], including data scale and computation complexity, resource provisioning, collaboration in heterogeneous environments, etc.

2.1.1 Data Scale and Computation Complexity

The execution of scientific workflows often consumes and produces huge amounts of distributed data objects. These data objects can be of primitive or complex types, files in different sizes and formats, database tables, or data objects in other forms. At present, the scientific community is facing a "data deluge" [7] coming from experiments, simulations, networks, sensors, and satellites, and the data that needs to be processed generally grows faster than computational resources and their speed. The data scale and management in big data era are beyond the capability of traditional workflows as they depend on traditional infrastructure for resource provisioning, scheduling and computing. For example, in high energy physics, the Large Hadron Collider [4] at CERN can generate more than 100 TB of collision data per second; In bioinformatics, GenBank [3], one of the largest DNA databases, already hosts over 120 billion bases, the European Molecular Biology and Bioinformatics Institute Laboratory (EMBL) hosts 14 PB of data, and the numbers are expected to double every 9–12 months.

In addition to data scale, science analysis and processing complexity is also growing exponentially. Scientists are now attempting calculations requiring orders of magnitude more computing and communication than was possible only a few years ago. For instance, in bioinformatics a protein simulation problem [27] involves running many instances of a structure prediction simulation, each with different random initial conditions and performs multiple rounds. Given a couple of proteins and parameter options, the simulation can easily scale up to 100,000 rounds. In cancer drug design, protein docking can involve millions of 3D structures and have a runtime up to tens of CPU years. To enable the storage and analysis of such large quantities of data and to achieve rapid turnaround, data and computation may need to be distributed over thousands or even tens of thousands of computation nodes.

2.1.2 Resource Provisioning

Resource provisioning represents the functionality and mechanism of allocating computing resource, storage space, network bandwidth, etc., to scientific workflows. As cluster/Grid environments are not adept at providing the workflows with smoothly dynamic resource allocation, the resource provisioned to a scientific workflow is fixed once the workflow has been deployed to execute, which may in return restrict the scale of science problems that can be handled by workflows. Moreover, the scale of resource is upbounded by the size of a dedicated resource pool with limited resource sharing extension in the form of virtual organizations. Meanwhile, the representation of resources in the context of scientific workflows is also bothering the scientists [44], as they must be able to recognize the supported types of resources and tools. For instance, the resource in Taverna is a web service which usually limits the use of many scientific resources that are not represented as web services.

To break through the limitations introduced by traditional resource provisioning strategy, some works have been focused on the approaches for automated provisioning, including the Context Broker [20] from the Nimbus project, which supported the concept of "one-click virtual cluster" that allowed clients to coordinate large virtual cluster launches in simple steps. The Wrangler system [21] was a similar implementation that allowed users to describe a desired virtual cluster in XML format, and send it to a web service, which managed the provisioning of virtual machines and the deployment of software and services. It was also capable of interfacing with many different Cloud resource providers.

2.1.3 Collaboration in Heterogeneous Environments

Collaboration refers to the interactions between a workflow management system and the execution environment, such as resource access, resource status perception, load balance and so on. As more and more scientific research projects become collaborative in nature and involve multiple geographically distributed organizations, which bring a variety of challenges to scientists and application developers to handle the collaboration in heterogeneous environments.

The management of resource, authority authentication, security, etc., can be very complicated, as scientific workflow applications are normally executed in cluster/Grid environments, where accessible computing resources and storage space are located in various management domains. The execution of traditional workflows is also influenced by the heterogeneous performance of computing resource due to the varied configuration of physical machines. In addition, in Grid environment, the status of physical machines is uncontrollable, switching among online (the machine is started up and connected to the Grid), offline (the machine is powered off or disconnected), busy (the machine is executing other tasks), etc., making it extremely difficult to maintain load balance.

2.2   Moving Workflow Applications to the Cloud

Cloud computing has been widely adopted to solve the ever-increasing computing and storage problems arising in the Internet age. To address the challenges of dealing with peta-scale scientific problems in scientific workflow solutions, we can move workflow applications into Cloud, using for instance the MapReduce computing model to reconstruct the formerly applied workflow specifications. MapReduce provides a very simple programming model and powerful runtime system for the processing of large datasets. The programming model is based on just two key functions: "map" and "reduce", borrowed from functional languages. The runtime system automatically partitions input data and schedules the execution of programs in a large cluster of commodity machines. Modified applications to fully leverage the unprecedented scalability and resources on demand offered by the Cloud without introducing extra management overheads.

Despite all the advantages of transforming traditional workflow applications into Cloud-based applications, there are still many drawbacks and unsolved obstacles:

1. Cloud computing cannot benefit from the distinguished features provided by SWFMSs, including management of data and task dependencies, job scheduling and execution, provenance tracking, etc.. The challenges for big data processing in Cloud remain unsolved and are still bothering developers and researchers.
2. Utilizing the certain data flow support offered by MapReduce to refactor traditional workflow applications requires application logic to be rewritten to follow the map-reduce-merge programming model. Scientists and application developers need to fully understand the applications and port the applications before they can leverage the parallel computing infrastructure.
3. Large-scale workflows, especially data-intensive scientific workflows may require far more functionality and flexibility than MapReduce can provide, and the implicit semantics incurred by a workflow specification goes far more than just the "map" and "reduce" operations, for instance, the mapping of computation to compute node and data partitions, runtime optimization, retry on error, smart re-run, etc.
4. Once we decide to migrate workflow applications to Cloud computing, we need to reconstruct the data being processed to be able to be stored in partitioned fashion, such as in GFS, or HDFS, so that the partitions can be operated in parallel, which may introduce a tremendous amount of work to scientists and application developers.

5. Revising workflow applications to be capable of executing in Cloud platforms makes new requests to scientists and application developers, as they need to grasp new programing model and techniques instead of using already-familiar workflow pattern, which may cost large amount of time beyond the research topics. Moreover, the risks associated with vendor lock-in cannot be ignored.

2.3   Migrating Workflow Management into the Cloud

To avoid the disadvantages brought by moving workflow applications directly to the Cloud, we may try to integrate workflow management systems with the Cloud to provide a Cloud workflow platform as a service for big data processing. Once we decide to integrate SWFMS with Cloud computing, we may deploy the whole SWFMS inside the Cloud and access the scientific workflow computation via a Web browser. A distinct feature of this solution is that no software installation is needed for a scientist and the SWFMS can fully take advantage of all the services provided in a Cloud infrastructure. Moreover, the Cloud-based SWFMS can provide highly scalable scientific workflows and task management as services, providing one kind of Software-as-a-Service (SaaS). One concern the user might have is the economic cost associated with the necessity of using Cloud on a daily basis, the dependency on the availability and reliability of the Cloud, as well as the risk associated with vendor lock-in.

To provide a good balance between system performance and usability, an alternative for researchers is to encapsulate the management of computation, data, and storage and other resources into the Cloud, while the workflow specification, submission, presentation and visualization remain outside the Cloud to support the key architectural requirement of user interface customizability and user interaction support. The benefit of adopting the solution to manage and run scientific workflows on top of the Cloud can be multifold:

1. The scale of scientific problems that can be addressed by scientific workflows can be greatly increased compared to cluster/Grid environments, which was previously upbounded by the size of a dedicated resource pool with limited resource sharing extension in the form of virtual organizations. Cloud platforms can offer vast amount of computing resources as well as storage space for such applications, allowing scientific discoveries to be carried out in a much larger scale.
2. Application deployment can be made flexible and convenient. With bare-metal physical servers, it is not easy to change the application deployment and the underlying supporting platform. However with virtualization technology in a Cloud platform, different application environments can be either pre-loaded in virtual machine (VM) images, or deployed dynamically onto VM instances.

3. The on-demand resource allocation mechanism in the Cloud can improve resource utilization and change the experience of end users for improved responsiveness. Cloud-based workflow applications can get resources allocated according to the number of nodes at each workflow stage, instead of reserving a fixed number of resources upfront. Cloud workflows can scale out and in dynamically, resulting in fast turnaround time for end users.

4. Cloud computing provides much larger room for the trade-off between performance and cost. The spectrum of resource investment now ranges from dedicated private resources, a hybrid resource pool combining local resource and remote Clouds, and full outsourcing of computing and storage to public Clouds. Cloud computing not only provides the potential of solving larger-scale scientific problems, but also brings the opportunity to improve the performance/cost ratio.

5. Although migrating scientific workflow management to Cloud may introduce extra management overheads, Cloud computing now can leverage the advantages carried about with SWFMSs (e.g. workflow management, provenance tracking, etc.).

3 Integration of Swift and OpenNebula

In this section, we talk about our end-to-end approach in integrating Swift with the OpenNebula Cloud platform. Before we go into further details of the integration, we will first introduce the reference service framework that we propose to migrate scientific workflows to various Cloud platforms.

3.1 The Service Framework

We propose a reference service framework that addresses the above mentioned challenges and covers all the major aspects involved in the migration and integration of SWFMS into the Cloud, from client-side workflow specification, service-based workflow submission and management, task scheduling and execution, to Cloud resource management and provisioning. As illustrated in Fig. 1, the service framework includes four layers, seven components and six interfaces. Detailed description of the service framework is made public at our website.[1]

The first layer is the Infrastructure Layer, which consists of multiple Cloud platforms with the underlying server, storage and network resources. The second layer is called the Middleware Layer. This layer consists of three subsystems: Cloud Resource Manager, Scheduling Management Service and Task Scheduling Frameworks. The third layer, called the Service Layer, consists of Cloud Workflow

---

[1]http://www.cloud-uestc.cn/projects/serviceframework/index.html.

Management Service and Workflow Engines. Finally, the fourth layer—the Client Layer, consists of the Workflow Specification & Submission and the Workflow Presentation & Visualization subsystem. The service framework would help to break through workflows' dependence on the underlying resource environment, and take advantage of the scalability and on-demand resource allocation of the Cloud.

We present a layered service framework for the implementation and application of integrating SWFMS into manifold Cloud platforms, which can also be applicable when deploying a workflow system in Grid environments. The separation of each layer enables abstractions and different independent implementations for each layer, and provides the opportunity for scientists to develop a stable and familiar problem solving environment where rapid technologies can be leveraged but the details of which are shielded transparently from the scientists who need to focus on science itself. The Interfaces defined in the framework is flexible and customizable for scientists to expand or modify according to their own specified requirements and environments.

3.2 Integration Architecture and Implementation

Based on the service framework, we devise an end-to-end integration approach that addresses the aforementioned challenges. We call it end-to-end because it covers all the major aspects involved in the integration, including a client side workflow submission tool, a Cloud workflow management service that accepts the submissions, a Cloud Resource Manager (CRM) that accepts resource requests from the workflow service and dynamically instantiates a Falkon virtual cluster, and a cluster monitoring service that monitors the health of the acquired Cloud resources.

As illustrated in Fig. 2, the integration architecture consists of four layers. At the client layer, we provide a client-side development and submission tool for application specification and submission. At the service layer, a Cloud workflow service based on the Swift workflow management system [30] is presented as a gateway to the Cloud platform underneath. At the middleware layer, a few components are integrated seamlessly to bridge the gap between the service layer and the underlying infrastructure layer. The components include a Cloud resource manager, a virtual cluster provisioner, and a task execution service. The Cloud workflow service accepts workflowsubmissions from the client tool, and makes resource requests to the Cloud resource manager, which in turn provisions a virtual cluster on-demand and also deploys the Falkon [25] execution service into the cluster. Individual jobs from the workflow service are then passed onto the Falkon service for parallel execution within the virtual cluster, and results delivered back to the workflow service. At the infrastructure layer, we choose the OpenNebula Cloud platform to manage Cloud datacenter resources such as servers, network and storage.

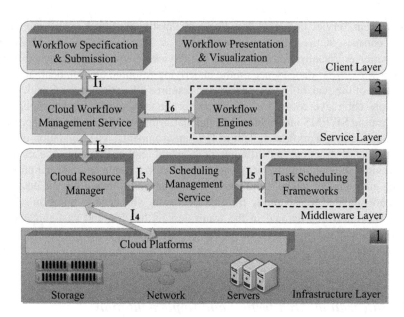

Fig. 1 The service framework

3.2.1 The Swift Workflow Management System

Swift is a system that bridges scientific workflows with parallel computing. It is a parallel programming tool for rapid and reliable specification, execution, and management of large-scale science and engineering workflows. Swift takes a structured approach to workflow specification, scheduling, and execution. It consists of a simple scripting language called SwiftScript for concise specification of complex parallel computations based on dataset typing and iterations [29], and dynamic dataset mappings for accessing large-scale datasets represented in diverse data formats. The runtime system provides an efficient workflow engine for scheduling and load balancing, and it can interact with various resource management systems such as PBS and Condor for task execution.

The Swift system architecture consists of four major components: Program Specification, Scheduling, Execution, and Provisioning, as illustrated in Fig. 3. Computations are specified in SwiftScript, which has been shown to be simple yet powerful. SwiftScript programs are compiled into abstract computation plans, which are then scheduled for execution by the workflow engine onto provisioned resources. Resource provisioning in Swift is very flexible, tasks can be scheduled to execute on various resource providers, where the provider interface can be implemented as a local host, a cluster, a multi-site Grid, or the Amazon EC2 service.

The four major components of the Swift system can be easily mapped into the four layers in the reference architecture: the specification falls into the Presentation Layer, although SwiftScript focuses more on the parallel scripting aspect for user

interaction than on Graphical representation; the scheduling components correspond
to the Workflow Management Layer; the execution components maps to the Task
Management layer; and the provisioning layer can be thought as mostly in the
Operational Layer.

Fig. 2 The integration
architecture

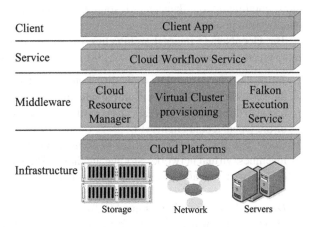

3.2.2   The OpenNebula Cloud Platform

We integrate Swift with the OpenNebula Cloud platform. We choose OpenNebula
for our implementation because it has a flexible architecture and is easy to
customize, and also because it provides a set of tools and service interfaces that
are handy for the integration. We have also integrated with other Cloud platforms
such as Amazon EC2 and Eucalyptus in similar means.

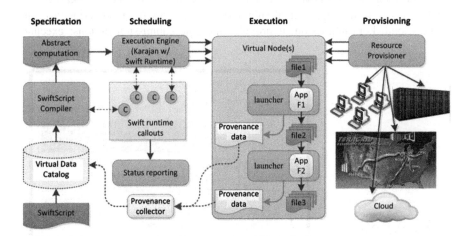

Fig. 3 Swift system architecture

OpenNebula is a fully open-source toolkit to build IaaS private, public and hybrid Clouds, and a modular system that can implement a variety of Cloud architectures and can interface with multiple datacenter services. OpenNebula orchestrates storage, network, virtualization, monitoring, and security technologies to deploy multi-tier services [36, 37] as virtual machines on distributed infrastructures, combining both datacenter resources and remote Cloud resources, according to allocation policies.

The OpenNebula internal architecture (as shown in Fig. 4) can be divided into three layers: *Drivers, Core and Tools* [38]:

1. *Tools:* This layer contains tools distributed with OpenNebula, such as the CLI, the scheduler, the libvirt API implementation or the Cloud RESTful interfaces, and also third party tools that can be easily created using the XML-RPC interface or the OpenNebula client API.
2. *Core:* The core consists of a set of components to control and monitor virtual machines, virtual networks, storage and hosts. The management of VMs, storage devices and virtual network is implemented in this layer by invoking a suitable driver.
3. *Drivers:* This layer is responsible for directly interacting with specific middleware (e.g. virtualization hypervisor, file transfer mechanisms or information services). It is designed to plug-in different virtualization, storage and monitoring technologies and Cloud services into the core.

3.2.3   Key Components

The Client Submission Tool The client submission tool is a standalone java application that provides an IDE for workflow development, and allows users to edit, compile, run and submit SwiftScripts. Scientists and application developers can write their scripts in this environment and also test run their workflows on local host, before they make final submissions to the Swift Cloud service to run in the Cloud. For submission, it provides multiple submission options: execute

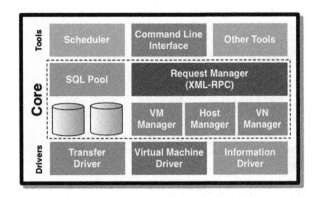

Fig. 4 The OpenNebula architecture

immediately, execute at a fixed time point, or execute recurrently (per day, per week etc.). We give a screenshot of the tool in Fig. 5, which shows the current status of workflows submitted to the Cloud service.

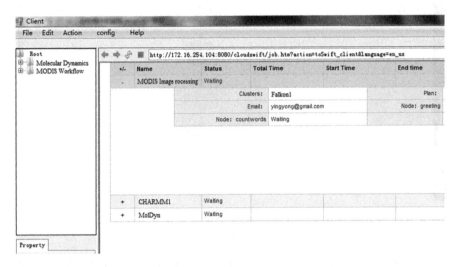

Fig. 5 The client tool

One of the key components of the system is the *Swift Cloud workflow management service* that acts as an intermediary between the workflow client and the backend Cloud Resource Manager. The service has a Web interface for configuration of the service, the resource manager and application environments. It supports the following functionalities: SwiftScript programming, SwiftScript compilation, workflow scheduling, resource acquisition, and status monitoring. In addition, the service also implements fault-tolerance mechanism. A screenshot of the service that visualizes workflow execution progress is shown in Fig. 6.

The *Cloud Resource Manager (CRM)* accepts resource requests from the Cloud workflow management service, and is in charge of interfacing with OpenNebula and provisioning Falkon virtual clusters dynamically to the workflow service. The process is illustrated in Fig. 7. In addition, it also monitors the virtual clusters. The process to start a Falkon virtual cluster is as follows:

1. CRM provides a service interface to the workflow service, the latter makes a resource request to CRM.
2. CRM initializes and maintains a pool of virtual machines, the number of virtual machines in the pool can be set via a config file, Ganglia is started on each virtual machine to monitor CPU, memory and IO.
3. Upon a resource request from the workflow service:

   (a) CRM fetches a VM from the VM pool and starts the Falkon service in that VM.

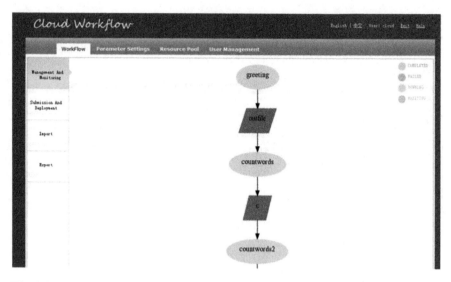

Fig. 6 The cloud Workflow management service

    (b) CRM fetches another VM and starts the Falkon worker in that VM, and also makes that worker register to the Falkon service.

    (c) CRM repeats step (b) until all the Falkon workers are started and registered.

    (d) If the VMs in the pool are not enough, then CRM will make resource request to the underlying OpenNebula platform to create more VM instances.

4. CRM returns the end point reference of the Falkon server to the workflow service, and the workflow service can now dispatch tasks to the Falkon execution service.

5. CRM starts the Cluster Monitoring Service to monitor the health of the Falkon virtual cluster. The monitoring service checks heartbeat from all the VMs in the virtual cluster, and will restart a VM if it goes down. If the restart fails, then for a Falkon service VM, it will get a new VM and start Falkon service on it, and have all the workers register to the new service. For a Falkon worker VM, it will replace the worker, and also delete the failed VM.

6. Note that we also implement an optimization technique to speed up the Falkon virtual cluster creation. When a Falkon virtual cluster is decommissioned, we change its status to "standby", and it can be re-activated.

7. When CRM receives resource request from the workflow service, it checks if there is a "standby" Falkon cluster, if so, it will return the information of the Falkon service directly to the workflow service, and also checks the number of the Falkon workers already in the cluster.

    (a) If the number is more than requested, then the surplus workers are deregistered and put into the VM pool.

    (b) If the number is less than required, then VMs will be pulled from the VM pool to create more workers.

As for the management of VM images, VM instances, and VM network, CRM interacts with and relies on the underlying OpenNebula Cloud platform. Our resource provisioning approach takes into consideration not only the dynamic creation and deployment of a virtual cluster with a ready-to-use execution service, but also efficient instantiation and re-use of the virtual cluster, as well as the monitoring and recovery of the virtual cluster. We demonstrate the capability and efficiency of our integration using a small scale experiment setup.

4 Performance Evaluation

In this section, we demonstrate and analyze our integration approach using a NASA MODIS image processing workflow. The NASA MODIS dataset [28] we use is a set of satellite aerial data blocks, each block is of size around 5.5 MB, with digits indicating the geological feature of each point in that block, such as water, sand, green land, urban area, etc.

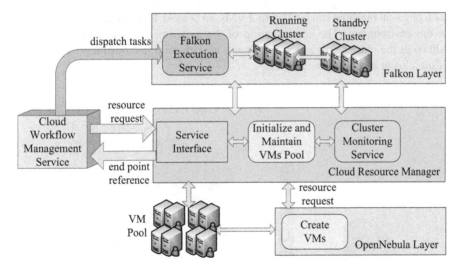

Fig. 7 The cloud resource manager

4.1 The MODIS Image Processing Workflow

The workflow (illustrated in Fig. 8) takes a set of such blocks, gets the size of the urban area in each of the blocks, analyzes and picks the top 12 of the blocks that have the largest urban area, converts them into displayable format, and assembles them into a single PNG file.

Fig. 8 MODIS image
processing workflow

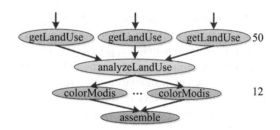

4.2 Experiment Configuration

We use a small cluster setting for the experiments, which includes 6 machines, each configured with Intel Core i5 760 with 4 cores at 2.8 GHZ, 4 GB memory, 500 GB HDD, and connected with Gigabit Ethernet LAN. The operating system is Ubuntu 10.04.1, with OpenNebula 2.2 installed. The configuration for each VM is 1 core, 1.5 GB memory, 20 GB HDD, and we use KVM as the hypervisor. One of the machines is used as the frontend which hosts the workflow service, the CRM, and the monitoring service. The other five machines are used to instantiate VMs, and each physical machine can host up to 2 VMs, so at most 10 VMs can be instantiated in the environment. The configuration of the experiment is illustrated in Fig. 9. Although the cluster size is not significant, we believe it demonstrates the essence of our cluster recycling mechanism.

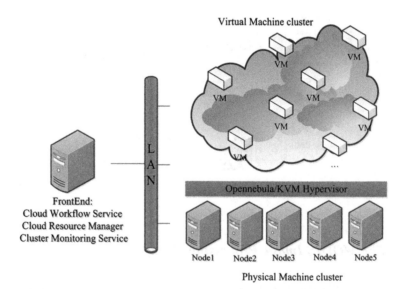

Fig. 9 Experiment configuration

4.3   Experiment Results

In our experiment, we control the workload by changing the number of input data blocks, the resource required, and the submission type (serial submission or parallel submission). So there are three dependent variables. We design the experiment by making two of the dependent variables constant, and changing the other. We run three types of experiments:

1. The serial submission experiment
2. The parallel submission experiment
3. The different number of data blocks experiment

In all the experiments, VMs are pre-instantiated and put in the VM pool. The time to instantiate a VM is around 42 s and this doesn't change much for all the VMs created.

4.3.1   The Serial Submission Experiment

In the serial submission experiment, we first measure the base line for server creation time, worker creation time and worker registration time. We create a Falkon virtual cluster with one server, and varying number of workers, and we don't reuse the virtual cluster.

In Fig. 10, we can observe that the server creation time is quite stable, around 4.7 s every time. Worker creation time is also stable, around 0.6 s each, and for worker registration, the first one takes about 10 s, and for the rest, about 1 s each.

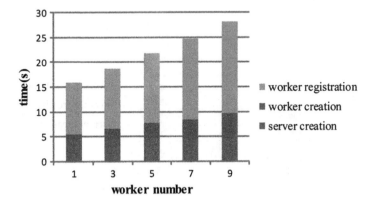

Fig. 10 The base line for cluster creation

For the rest of the serial submission, we submit a workflow after the previous one has finished to test virtual cluster recycling, where the input data blocks remain fixed.

In Fig. 11, the resources required are one Falkon server with five workers, one server with three workers and one server with one worker. We can see that for the second and third submissions, the worker creation and server creation time are zero, only the surplus workers need to de-register themselves.

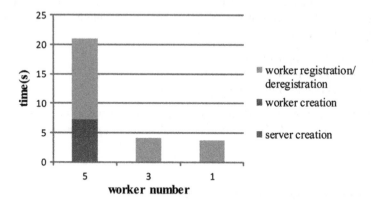

Fig. 11 Serial submission, decreasing resource required

In Fig. 12, the resources required are in the reverse order of those in Fig. 11. Each time two extra Falkon workers need to be created and registered, and the time taken are roughly the same. These experiments show that the Falkon virtual cluster can be re-used after it is being created, and worker resources can be dynamically removed or added.

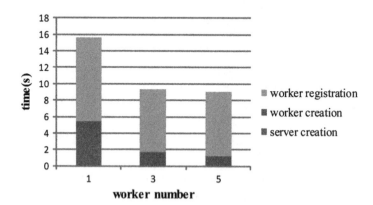

Fig. 12 Serial submission, increasing resource required

In Fig. 13, we first request a virtual cluster with one server and nine workers, we then make five parallel requests for virtual clusters with one server and one worker. We can observe that one of these requests is satisfied using the existing virtual cluster, where the other 4 are created on-demand. In this case, it takes some time to de-register all the eight surplus workers, which makes the total time comparable to on-demand creation of the cluster.

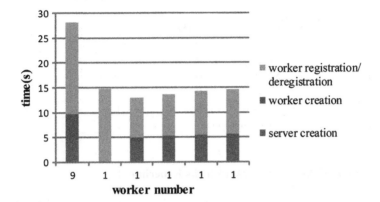

Fig. 13 Serial submission, mixed resource required

4.3.2 The Parallel Submission Experiment

In the parallel submission experiment, we submit multiple workflows at the same time in order to measure the maximum parallelism (the number of concurrent workflows that can be hosted in the Cloud platform) in the environment.

First, we submit resource requests with one server and two workers, and the maximum parallelism is up to three. In Table 1, we show the results for the experiment, in which we make resource requests for one virtual cluster, two virtual clusters, three virtual clusters and four virtual clusters.

For the request of two virtual clusters, it can re-use the one released by the early request, and the time to initialize the cluster is significantly less than fresh creation (445 ms vs. 4,696 ms). It has to create the second cluster on-demand. For the four-virtual-cluster request, since all the VM resources are used up by the first three clusters, the fourth cluster creation would fail as expected. When we change resource requests to one server and four workers, the maximum parallelism is two, and the request to create a third virtual cluster also fails. Since our VM pool has a maximum of ten virtual machines, it's easy to explain why this has happened. This experiment shows that our integrated system can maximize the cluster resources assigned to workflows to achieve efficient utilization of resources.

Table 1 Parallel submission, one server and two workers

# of clusters	Server creation	Worker creation	Worker registration
1	4,624 ms	1,584 ms	11,305 ms
2	4,696 ms	2,367 ms	11,227 ms
	445 ms	0	0
3	4,454 ms	1,457 ms	11,329 ms
	488 ms	0	0
	548 ms	0	0
4	521 ms	0	0
	585 ms	0	0
	686 ms	0	0
	Submission failed		

4.3.3 Different Number of Data Blocks Experiment

In this experiment, we change the number of input data blocks from 50 blocks to 25 blocks, and measure the total execution time with varying number of workers in the virtual cluster.

In Fig. 14, we can observe that with the increase of the number of workers, the execution time decreases accordingly (i.e. execution efficiency improves), however at five workers to process the workflow, the system reaches efficiency peak. After that, the execution time goes up with more workers. This means that the improvement can't subsidize the management and registration overhead of the added worker. The time for server and worker creation, and worker registration remain unchanged when we change the input size (as have been shown in Fig. 10). The experiment indicates that while our virtual resource provisioning overhead is well controlled, we do need to carefully determine the number of workers used in the virtual cluster to achieve resource utilization efficiency.

5 Related Work

Systems such as Taverna [11], Kepler [9], Vistrails [10], Pegasus [8], Swift [30], and VIEW [24] have seen wide adoption in various disciplines such as Physics, Astronomy, Bioinformatics, Neuroscience, Earth Science, and Social Science. In Table 2, we list some use cases that focused on applying SWFMSs to execute data-intensive applications.

There are some early explorers that try to evaluate the feasibility, performance, and adaptation of running data intensive and HPC applications on Clouds or hybrid Grid/Cloud environments. Palankar et al. [17] evaluated the feasibility, cost, availability and performance of using Amazon's S3 service to provide storage support to data intensive applications, and also identified a set of additional functionalities that storage services targeting data-intensive science applications should support.

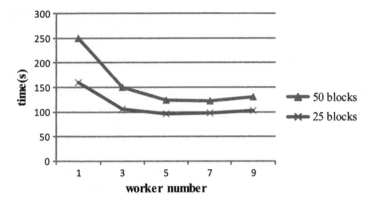

Fig. 14 Different input sizes

Table 2 Use cases of SWFMSs

SWFMSs	Application fields	Use cases
Swift	Climate science	Climate data analysis [13]
Taverna	Bioinformatics	Single nucleotide polymorphisms analysis [14]
Vistrails	Earth science	NASA Earth Exchange [15]
Kepler	Physics	Hyperspectral image processing [35]
VIEW	Medical science	Neurological disorder diagnosis [45]

Oliveira et al. [33] evaluated the performance of X-Ray Crystallography workflow using SciCumulus middleware with Amazon EC2. Wang et al. [34] presented their early definition and experience of scientific Cloud computing in the Cumulus project by merging existing Grid infrastructures with new Cloud technologies. These studies provide good source of information about Cloud platform support for science applications. Other studies investigated the execution of real science applications on commercial Clouds [18, 19], mostly being HPC applications, and compared the performance and cost against Grid environments. While such applications indeed can be ported to a Cloud environment, Cloud execution doesn't show significant benefit due to the applications' tightly coupled nature.

There have been a couple of researcher that have been investigating techniques for deploying data-intensive workflows in the cloud using unique architectures that are difficult to deploy on traditional platforms, such as grids [52–54]. Meanwhile, some other researches focused on developing new algorithms for workflows to take advantage of the unique pricing model and elasticity of infrastructure clouds [46–50],and investigating new cloud workflow-scheduling algorithms that optimize for cost, performance, and other quality-of-service metrics [55–57].

Gideon Juve et al. have studied the cost and performance of workflows in the cloud via simulation [22], using an experimental Nimbus cloud [23], individual Elastic Compute Cloud (EC2) nodes [26], and a variety of different intermediate storage systems on EC2 [41]. Christian Vecchiola et al. have done similar investigations on EC2 and Grid5000 [51]. These studies primarily analyzed the performance and cost of workflows in the cloud, rather than the practical experience of deploying workflows in the cloud. To address the shortages, Gideon Juve et al [39] also related the practical experience of trying to run a nontrivial scientific workflow application on three different infrastructures and compare the benefits and challenges of each platform.

Kozlovszky et al. [40] introduced a convenient way for sharing, integrating and executing different workflows in heterogeneous infrastructure environments. The paper explained in detail how to enable generic DCI compatibility for grid workflow management systems (such as ASKALON, MOTEUR, gUSE/WS-PGRADE, etc.) on job level and indirectly on workflow level. The generic DCI Bridge service enables the execution of jobs onto existing major DCI platforms (such as Service Grids, Desktop Grids, Web services, or even Cloud based DCIs). The CODA framework [16] was designed and implemented to support big data analytics in Cloud computing. Important functions, such as workflow scheduling, data locality, resource provisioning, and monitoring functions, had been integrated into the framework. Through the CODA framework, the workflows could be easily composed and efficiently executed in Amazon EC2. In order to address performance and cost issues of big data processing on Clouds, Long Wang et al. [5] presented a novel design of adaptive workflow management system which included a data mining based prediction model, workflow scheduler, and iteration controls to optimize the data processing via iterative workflow tasks.

Those works mentioned above are important as they provide valuable experience on migrating traditional scientific workflows to various Cloud platforms. However, a normalized, end-to-end integration approach is still missing. We present an end-to-end approach that addresses the integration of Swift, an SWFMS that has broad application in Grids and supercomputers, with the OpenNebula Cloud platform. The integration covers all the major aspects involved in workflow management in the Cloud, including a client side workflow submission tool, a Cloud workflow management service, a Cloud Resource Manager (CRM), and a cluster monitoring service.

Conclusion and Future Work

As more and more scientific applications are migrating into Cloud, it is imperative to also migrate SWFMSs into Cloud to take advantage of Cloud scalability, and also to handle the ever increasing data scale and analysis complexity of such applications. Cloud offers unprecedented scalability to workflow systems, and could potentially change the way we perceive and conduct scientific experiments. The scale and complexity of the science problems that can be handled can be greatly increased on the Cloud, and the on-demand nature of resource allocation on the Cloud will also help improve resource utilization and user experience.

(continued)

We first introduce our service framework for integrating SWFMSs into Cloud computing platforms. Then we present our early effort in integrating the Swift workflow management system with the OpenNebula Cloud platform, in which a Cloud workflow management service, a Cloud resource manager, and a cluster monitoring service are developed. We also demonstrate the functionality and efficiency of our approach using a set of experiments and a real-world scientific workflow.

For future work, we are working on a common interface that will facilitate the integration of Swift with other Cloud platforms such as Amazon EC2 and Open-stack. We will also investigate commonality in migrating other SWFMSs into Cloud, i.e. ways to offer SWFMSs as a service and to enable them to interact with the underlying Cloud resources. We will also leverage distributed storage for VM images for more efficient access, and conduct large scale experiments to look at ways to improve VM instantiation, virtual cluster creation and workflow execution. We are also exploring redesigning workflow systems from the ground up using Cloud Computing building blocks, such as EC2 [65], SQS [63], DynamoDB [64], S3 [62], and CloudWatch [65], in order to deliver a light-weight, fast, and distributed workflow system that should scale along with the largest cloud infra-structures [42].

Acknowledgements This paper is supported by the key project of National Science Foundation of China No. 61034005 and No. 61272528.

References

1. OpenNebula, [Online]. Available: http://www.OpenNebula.org, 2014
2. Openstack, [Online]. Available: http://www.openstack.org, 2014
3. GenBank, [Online]. Available: http://www.ncbi.nlm.nih.gov/genbank, 2014
4. Large Hadron Collider, [Online]. Available: http://lhc.web.cern.ch, 2014
5. Wang L, Duan R, Li X, et al. An Iterative Optimization Framework for Adaptive Workflow Management in Computational Clouds[C]//Trust, Security and Privacy in Computing and Communications (TrustCom), 2013 12th IEEE International Conference on. IEEE, 2013: 1049–1056.
6. I. Foster, Y. Zhao, I. Raicu, S. Lu. Cloud Computing and Grid Computing 360-Degree Compared, IEEE Grid Computing Environments (GCE08) 2008, co-located with IEEE/ACM Supercomputing 2008. Austin, TX. pp. 1–10
7. G. Bell, T. Hey, A. Szalay, Beyond the Data Deluge, Science, Vol. 323, no. 5919, pp. 1297–1298, 2009.
8. E. Deelman et al. Pegasus: A framework for mapping complex scientific workflows onto distributed systems, Scientific Programming, vol. 13, iss. 3, pp. 219–237. July 2005.
9. B. Ludäscher, I. Altintas, C. Berkley, D. Higgins, E. Jaeger, M. Jones, E. A. Lee, J. Tao, Y. Zhao, Scientific workflow management and the Kepler system, Concurrency and Computation: Practice and Experience, Special Issue: Workflow in Grid Systems, vol. 18, iss. 10, pp. 1039–1065, 25 August 2006.

10. J. Freire, C. T. Silva, S. P. Callahan, E. Santos, C. E. Scheidegger and H. T. Vo, Managing Rapidly-Evolving Scientific Workflows, Provenance and Annotation of Data, Lecture Notes in Computer Science, 2006, vol. 4145/2006, 10–18, DOI: 10.1007/11890850_2
11. D. Hull, K. Wolstencroft, R. Stevens, C. Goble, M. Pocock, P. Li, and T. Oinn, Taverna: a tool for building and running workflows of services, Nucleic Acids Research, vol. 34, iss. Web Server issue, pp. 729–732, 2006.
12. Y. Zhao, X. Fei, I. Raicu, S. Lu, Opportunities and Challenges in Running Scientific Workflows on the Cloud, IEEE International Conference on Cyber-enabled distributed computing and knowledge discovery (CyberC), pp. 455–462, 2011.
13. Woitaszek, M., Dennis, J., Sines, T. Parallel High-resolution Climate Data Analysis using Swift. 4th Workshop on Many-Task Computing on Grids and Supercomputers 2011.
14. Damkliang K, Tandayya P, Phusantisampan T, et al. Taverna Workflow and Supporting Service for Single Nucleotide Polymorphisms Analysis[C]//Information Management and Engineering, 2009. ICIME'09. International Conference on. IEEE, 2009: 27–31.
15. Zhang J, Votava P, Lee T J, et al. Bridging VisTrails Scientific Workflow Management System to High Performance Computing[C]//Services (SERVICES), 203 IEEE Ninth World Congress on. IEEE, 2013: 29–36.
16. Chaisiri S, Bong Z, Lee C, et al. Workflow framework to support data analytics in cloud computing[C]//Cloud Computing Technology and Science (CloudCom), 2012 IEEE 4th International Conference on. IEEE, 2012: 610–613.
17. M. Palankar, A. Iamnitchi, M. Ripeanu, S. Garfinkel. Amazon S3 for science grids: a viable solution? In Proceedings of the 2008 international workshop on Data-aware distributed computing (DADC '08), pp. 55–64, 2008.
18. E. Deelman, G. Singh, M. Livny, B. Berriman, and J. Good. The cost of doing science on the Cloud: the Montage example. In Proceedings of the 2008 ACM/IEEE conference on Supercomputing, SC '08, pp. 50:1–50:12, Piscataway, NJ, USA, 2008.
19. C. Vecchiola, S. Pandey, and R. Buyya. High-Performance Cloud Computing: A View of Scientific Applications. In International Symposium onParallel Architectures, Algorithms, and Networks, pp. 4–16, 2009.
20. Keahey, K., and T. Freeman. Contextualization: Providing One-click Virtual Clusters. in eScience. 2008, pp. 301–308. Indianapolis, IN, 2008.
21. G. Juve and E. Deelman. Wrangler: Virtual Cluster Provisioning for the Cloud. In HPDC, pp. 277–278, 2011.
22. Deelman E, Singh G, Livny M, et al. The cost of doing science on the cloud: the montage example[C]//Proceedings of the 2008 ACM/IEEE conference on Supercomputing. IEEE Press, 2008: 50.
23. Hoffa C, Mehta G, Freeman T, et al. On the use of cloud computing for scientific workflows[C]//eScience, 2008. eScience'08. IEEE Fourth International Conference on. IEEE, 2008: 640–645.
24. C. Lin, S. Lu, Z. Lai, A. Chebotko, X. Fei, J. Hua, F. Fotouhi, Service-Oriented Architecture for VIEW: a Visual Scientific Workflow Management System, In Proc. of the IEEE 2008 International Conference on Services Computing (SCC), pp. 335–342, Honolulu, Hawaii, USA, July 2008.
25. I. Raicu, Y. Zhao, C. Dumitrescu, I. Foster, M. Wilde. Falkon: a Fast and Light-weight tasK executiON framework, IEEE/ACM SuperComputing 2007, pp. 1–12.
26. Juve G, Deelman E, Vahi K, et al. Scientific workflow applications on Amazon EC2[C]// E-Science Workshops, 2009 5th IEEE International Conference on. IEEE, 2009: 59–66.
27. M. Wilde, I. Foster, K. Iskra, P. Beckman, Z. Zhang, Allan Espinosa, Mihael Hategan, Ben Clifford, Ioan Raicu, Parallel Scripting for Applications at the Petascale and Beyond, IEEE Computer Nov. 2009 Special Issue on Extreme Scale Computing, vol. 42, iss. 11, pp. 50–60, 2009.
28. NASA MODIS dataset, [Online]. Available: http://modis.gsfc.nasa.gov/, 2013.
29. Y. Zhao, J. Dobson, I. Foster, L. Moreau, M. Wilde, A Notation and System for Expressing and Executing Cleanly Typed Workflows on Messy Scientific Data, SIGMOD Record, vol. 34, iss. 3, pp. 37–43, September 2005.

30. Y. Zhao, M. Hategan, B. Clifford, I. Foster, G. v. Laszewski, I. Raicu, T. Stef-Praun, M. Wilde. Swift: Fast, Reliable, Loosely Coupled Parallel Computation, IEEE Workshop on Scientific Workflows 2007, pp. 199–206.
31. Hadoop, [Online]. Available: http://hadoop.apache.org/, 2012
32. D. Nurmi, R. Wolski, C. Grzegorczyk, G. Obertelli, S. Soman, L. Youseff, D. Zagorodnov. The Eucalyptus Open-Source Cloud-Computing System, 9th IEEE/ACM International Symposium on Cluster Computing and the Grid, CCGRID '09, pp. 124–131, 2009.
33. Oliveira, D. Ocaña, K., Ogasawara, E., Dias, J., Baião, F., Mattoso, M., A Performance Evaluation of X-Ray Crystallography Scientific Workflow Using SciCumulus. IEEE CLOUD 2011, pp. 708–715.
34. L. Wang, J. Tao, M. Kunze, A. C. Castellanos, D. Kramer, and W. Karl. Scientific Cloud Computing: Early Definition and Experience, in 10th IEEE International Conference on High Performance Computing and Communications, HPCC '08. , pp. 825–830, 2008.
35. Zhang J. Ontology-driven composition and validation of scientific grid workflows in Kepler: a case study of hyperspectral image processing[C]//Grid and Cooperative Computing Workshops, 2006. GCCW'06. Fifth International Conference on. IEEE, 2006: 282–289.
36. R. Moreno-Vozmediano, R.S. Montero, I.M. Llorente. Multi-Cloud Deployment of Computing Clusters for Loosely-Coupled MTC Applications, IEEE Transactions on Parallel and Distributed Systems. 22(6), pp. 924–930, 2011.
37. R. S. Montero, R. Moreno-Vozmediano, and I. M. Llorente. An Elasticity Model for High Throughput Computing Clusters, J. Parallel and Distributed Computing. 71(6), pp. 750–757, 2011.
38. OpenNebula Architecture, http://www.opennebula.org/documentation:archives:rel2.2: architecture, 2013.
39. Juve G, Rynge M, Deelman E, et al. Comparing FutureGrid, Amazon EC2, and Open Science Grid for Scientific Workflows[J]. Computing in Science & Engineering, 2013, 15(4): 20–29.
40. M. Kozlovszky, K. Karóczkai, I. Márton, A. Balasko, A. C. Marosi, and P. Kacsuk, Enabling Generic Distributed Computing Infrastructure Compatibility for Workflow Management Systems, Computer Science, vol. 13, no. 3, p. 61, 2012.
41. Juve G, Deelman E, Vahi K, et al. Data sharing options for scientific workflows on amazon ec2[C]//Proceedings of the 2010 ACM/IEEE International Conference for High Performance Computing, Networking, Storage and Analysis. IEEE Computer Society, 2010: 1–9.
42. I. Sadooghi, I. Raicu. CloudKon: a Cloud enabled Distributed tasK executiON framework, Illinois Institute of Technology, Department of Computer Science, PhD Oral Qualifier, 2013
43. Juve G, Deelman E. Scientific workflows in the cloud[M]//Grids, Clouds and Virtualization. Springer London, 2011: 71–91.
44. Lacroix Z, Aziz M. Resource descriptions, ontology, and resource discovery[J]. International Journal of Metadata, Semantics and Ontologies, 2010, 5(3): 194–207.
45. Lin C, Lu S, Lai Z, et al. Service-oriented architecture for VIEW: a visual scientific workflow management system[C]//Services Computing, 2008. SCC'08. IEEE International Conference on. IEEE, 2008, 1: 335–342.
46. Lin C, Lu S. Scheduling scientific workflows elastically for cloud computing[C]//Cloud Computing (CLOUD), 2011 IEEE International Conference on. IEEE, 2011: 746–747.
47. Mao M, Humphrey M. Auto-scaling to minimize cost and meet application deadlines in cloud workflows[C]//Proceedings of 2011 International Conference for High Performance Computing, Networking, Storage and Analysis. ACM, 2011: 49.
48. Oliveira D, Ogasawara E, Ocaña K, et al. An adaptive parallel execution strategy for cloud-based scientific workflows[J]. Concurrency and Computation: Practice and Experience, 2012, 24(13): 1531–1550.
49. Papuzzo G, Spezzano G. Autonomic management of workflows on hybrid grid-cloud infrastructure[C]//Proceedings of the 7th International Conference on Network and Services Management. International Federation for Information Processing, 2011: 230–233.

50. Reynolds C J, Winter S, Terstyanszky G Z, et al. Scientific workflow makespan reduction through cloud augmented desktop grids[C]//Cloud Computing Technology and Science (CloudCom), 2011 IEEE Third International Conference on. IEEE, 2011: 18–23.
51. Vecchiola C, Pandey S, Buyya R. High-performance cloud computing: A view of scientific applications[C]//Pervasive Systems, Algorithms, and Networks (ISPAN), 2009 10th International Symposium on. IEEE, 2009: 4–16.
52. Yuan D, Yang Y, Liu X, et al. On-demand minimum cost benchmarking for intermediate dataset storage in scientific cloud workflow systems[J]. Journal of Parallel and Distributed Computing, 2011, 71(2): 316–332.
53. Çatalyürek Ü V, Kaya K, Uçar B. Integrated data placement and task assignment for scientific workflows in clouds[C]//Proceedings of the fourth international workshop on Data-intensive distributed computing. ACM, 2011: 45–54.
54. Wang J, Korambath P, Altintas I. A physical and virtual compute cluster resource load balancing approach to data-parallel scientific workflow scheduling[C]//Services (SERVICES), 2011 IEEE World Congress on. IEEE, 2011: 212–215.
55. Tolosana-Calasanz R, BañAres J Á N, Pham C, et al. Enforcing QoS in scientific workflow systems enacted over Cloud infrastructures[J]. Journal of Computer and System Sciences, 2012, 78(5): 1300–1315.
56. Bessai K, Youcef S, Oulamara A, et al. Bi-criteria workflow tasks allocation and scheduling in Cloud computing environments[C]//Cloud Computing (CLOUD), 2012 IEEE 5th International Conference on. IEEE, 2012: 638–645.
57. Ostermann S, Prodan R. Impact of variable priced cloud resources on scientific workflow scheduling[M]//Euro-Par 2012 Parallel Processing. Springer Berlin Heidelberg, 2012: 350–362.
58. Ioan Raicu. Many-Task Computing: Bridging the Gap between High Throughput Computing and High Performance Computing, Computer Science Department, University of Chicago, Doctorate Dissertation, March 2009
59. Ioan Raicu, Ian Foster, Yong Zhao, Alex Szalay, Philip Little, Christopher M. Moretti, Amitabh Chaudhary, Douglas Thain. Towards Data Intensive Many-Task Computing, book chapter in Data Intensive Distributed Computing: Challenges and Solutions for Large-Scale Information Management, IGI Global Publishers, 2009
60. Michael Wilde, Ioan Raicu, Allan Espinosa, Zhao Zhang, Ben Clifford, Mihael Hategan, Kamil Iskra, Pete Beckman, Ian Foster. Extreme-scale scripting: Opportunities for large task-parallel applications on petascale computers, Scientific Discovery through Advanced Computing Conference (SciDAC09) 2009
61. Dongfang Zhao, Chen Shou, Tanu Malik, Ioan Raicu. Distributed Data Provenance for Large-Scale Data-Intensive Computing, IEEE Cluster 2013
62. Ioan Raicu, Pete Beckman, Ian Foster. Making a Case for Distributed File Systems at Exascale, ACM Workshop on Large-scale System and Application Performance (LSAP), 2011
63. Dharmit Patel, Faraj Khasib, Iman Sadooghi, Ioan Raicu. Towards In-Order and Exactly-Once Delivery using Hierarchical Distributed Message Queues, 1st International Workshop on Scalable Computing For Real-Time Big Data Applications (SCRAMBL'14) 2014
64. Tonglin Li, Xiaobing Zhou, Kevin Brandstatter, Dongfang Zhao, Ke Wang, Anupam Rajendran, Zhao Zhang, Ioan Raicu. ZHT: A Light-weight Reliable Persistent Dynamic Scalable Zero-hop Distributed Hash Table, IEEE International Parallel & Distributed Processing Symposium (IPDPS) 2013
65. Iman Sadooghi, Sandeep Palur, Ajay Anthony, Isha Kapur, Karthik Belagodu, Pankaj Purandare, Kiran Ramamurty, Ke Wang, Ioan Raicu. Achieving Efficient Distributed Scheduling with Message Queues in the Cloud for Many-Task Computing and High-Performance Computing, 14th IEEE/ACM International Symposium on Cluster, Cloud and Grid Computing (CCGrid) 2014

Executing Storm Surge Ensembles on PAAS Cloud

Abhirup Chakraborty, Milinda Pathirage, Isuru Suriarachchi, Kavitha
Chandrasekar, Craig Mattocks, and Beth Plale

Abstract Cloud computing services are becoming increasingly viable for scientific
model execution. As a leased computational resource, cloud computing enables
a computational modeler at a smaller university to carry out sporadic large-scale
experiments, and allows others to pay for CPU cycles as needed, without incurring
high maintenance costs of a large compute system. In this chapter, we discuss the
issues involved in running high throughput ensemble applications on a Platform-
as-a-Service cloud. We compare two frameworks deploying and running these
applications, namely Sigiri and MapReduce. We motivate the need for a pipelined
architecture to application deployment, and discus a couple of methodologies to
balance the loads, minimize storage overhead, and reduce overall execution time.

1 Introduction

Cloud computing brings immense opportunity to democratize research by rendering
computing power available to a vast majority of researchers and scientists who
cannot afford to buy or run a large cluster or HPC resource. By providing a flexible
framework to rapidly deploy computational resources, cloud computing makes it
feasible for a researcher to lease (from a data center) the resources based on their
need. With the emergence of several cloud computing vendors (e.g., Amazon EC2,
Microsoft Windows Azure, etc.), researchers and scientists from different domains
have recently started to explore the cloud environments for supporting their scientific endeavors or research computing. However, the applicability of cloud platforms
for various applications across the scientific computing landscape is not readily
realizable due to diverse bandwidth and latency sensitivities (i.e., performance

A. Chakraborty (✉) • M. Pathirage • I. Suriarachchi • K. Chandrasekar • B. Plale
School of Informatics and Computing, Indiana University, Bloomington, IN 47408, USA
e-mail: achakrab@indiana.edu; mpathira@indiana.edu; isuruara@indiana.edu;
kavchand@indiana.edu; plale@indiana.edu

C. Mattocks
Rosenstiel School of Marine and Atmospheric Science,
Miami University, Miami, FL 33149, USA
e-mail: cmattock@rsmas.miami.edu

© Springer Science+Business Media New York 2014   257
X. Li, J. Qiu (eds.), *Cloud Computing for Data-Intensive Applications*,
DOI 10.1007/978-1-4939-1905-5__11

requirements) of the applications [8, 10]. In this chapter, we study the execution of a particular class of computational science application, namely ensemble model runs, which are part of the larger class of high throughput applications.

Accurate and timely prediction of the impact of a hurricane's storm surge is a computational and scientific grand challenge problem. Accurate predictions can prevent substantial loss of life and to a lesser extent property. However, this requires a computational model that accurately captures the physical systems (i.e., oceanic systems, atmospheric systems, geographic terrains). The National Oceanographic and Atmospheric Association (NOAA) developed a hydrodynamic coastal ocean model called Sea, Lake and Overland Surges from Hurricanes (SLOSH) [5]. The SLOSH model estimates storm surge height and coastal inundation. The model takes as input a basin, which is a geographical region with known values of topography and bathymetry, topography/bathymetry data that can represent barriers, gaps, passes, and other local features [1]. A second input to the storm surge model is a hurricane track (through a "track file"). The hurricane track is identified by several parameters (i.e., air pressure, radius of maximum winds, location, direction and forward speed).

As a hurricane approaches a coast, the National Hurricane Center (NHC) will hand off the general parameters of the storm to a storm surge unit who will then create an ensemble of several hundred instances of SLOSH varying the model's input parameters. Storm surge results can additionally be integrated with road networks and traffic flow information, precipitation models and river-flow models to aid emergency response.

More specifically, hurricane forecasts that are made even in the final 12–24 h before a storm reaches landfall are usually not very accurate given the unpredictability of the storm. Thus storm surge forecasters run ensembles of SLOSH runs (e.g., several hundred model instances) with varying storm track parameters based on both the forecast storm track parameters and knowledge of the past errors. From the ensemble of runs, an aggregate of the resulting data is produced, capturing the Maximum Envelope of Water (MEOW) and Maximum of the MEOWs (MOM) for each of output groups (an output group is specified by storm direction, storm category and forward motion). Off season, modelers will run SLOSH ensembles whenever there is a change in a basin definition (i.e., topography or bathymetry). A single instance of the SLOSH model takes on average a few minutes to complete for unoptimized code. An average ensemble run is either 300–400 in-season or during off season the ensemble can grow as large as 15,000 instances. Such an application can be characterized as a high throughput parallel computing (HPTC) task with modest (<10 GB) volume of data input and data output. HPTC jobs have an inherently high level of parallelism, in other words, there is low task-to-task communication. This makes the use of cloud resources for in-season and off-season a question that storm surge forecasters are evaluating.

In this chapter, we present the techniques to deploy, run, and monitor a large SLOSH ensemble within a Platform-as-a-Service (PAAS) cloud environment. A SLOSH instance forms an indivisible task while deployed in virtual machines. Executing a large number of such small tasks needs mechanisms to pipeline the tasks in a number of virtual machines, and to balance the loads across the virtual machines. We present two approaches to deploying and running the SLOSH ensemble in the Azure Cloud, using a MapReduce framework *Twister4Azure* [7] and the Sigiri middleware [17], the latter an abstraction for managing jobs in grid and cloud environments. We discuss a framework for balancing computational loads across the different nodes to reduce the total makespan (i.e., maximum node usage) and to effectively utilize the cloud resources.

The remainder of the chapter is organized as follows. Section 2 gives an overview of the cloud environments and the middleware tools used in the paper. Section 3 describes the detailed execution model of the SLOSH application workflow considered in this paper. Section 4 outlines the execution technique and associated optimizations while processing the SLOSH ensemble. Section 5 presents a technique to minimize storage overheads with large-scale ensemble deployment by distributing the loads across the VMs based on the output groups of each of the SLOSH instances. Section 6 discusses the computation model to estimate the execution time of a SLOSH ensemble within the Azure cloud. Section 7 presents experimental studies. Section 8 presents the related work and "Conclusion" section concludes the paper.

2 Architecture/System Overview

The logical architecture model has three layers: a workflow client, the middleware services layer, and a cloud platform. The workflow client may be located either in the cloud or at a researcher's desktop. The middleware services layer is a web-service layer hosted at the researcher's institution or on the cloud. For the cloud platform, we use Windows Azure. We provide an overview of the cloud platform, middleware framework and processing models used in this paper.

2.1 *Windows Azure*

Azure is used in our study as a Platform-as-a-Service (PAAS) in that we utilize its computation model (e.g., worker nodes) and other higher level services. A PAAS also supports development and access to these services through a number of languages. For instance, Azure supports C#, .NET, C++, and Java. Through its .NET-based hosting platform, developers develop applications for Azure using Visual Studio.

Windows Azure is made up of three parts: a server instance that supports application processes, a storage service, and a fabric integrating both the compute and storage services. Developers deploy Windows applications by allocating a number of *server instances* that can be classified as two different roles: the web service hosting instances called *web roles* and the computational instances called compute roles. There are two types of *compute role* instances: *Worker roles* and *VM roles*. In case of the Worker roles, Azure supplies and configures Virtual Hard Disks (VHDs) and Virtual Machines (VMs) behind the scene. Developers interact with the Azure cloud by supplying application packages to the Azure administrative portal. Whereas, in case of the VM roles, the developers need to manage explicitly the VM images by creating necessary OS and application packages for applications. Developers can specify the number of instances with various roles during the application deployment, and also can dynamically adjusts the number of instances during run time.

As persistent storage, Windows Azure provides three types of storage services:

- *Blob*: highly available and scalable storage service for large data.
- *Azure Queue*: reliable, asynchronous message delivery across the worker roles.
- *Table*: scalable, structured, table-like storage and supports simple queries on partitions, row keys, and attributes.

In this study, we use the Azure Worker Role instead of the VM role because the former does not need explicit user efforts in managing the machine instances. Too, worker roles support communication amongst each other and with other middleware services through Azure Queues [10]. VM roles support neither.

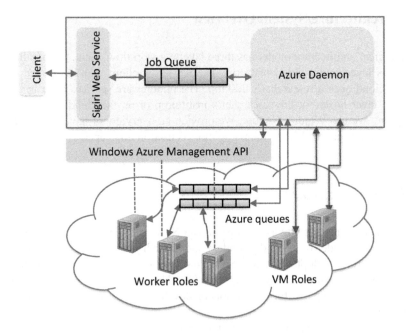

Fig. 1 Pipeline framework using Sigiri middleware and Azure worker role

2.2   Sigiri Middleware

Sigiri is resource abstraction middleware that communicates with and integrates multiple computational resources (e.g., cloud and grid resources) through a unified job management service [17]. A new computational platform is added to Sigiri by a system administrator who adds a daemon for each computational resource and runs the daemon in the system or inside the newly integrated computational resource. A workflow client can submit a job via a Sigiri web service. The jobs are stored in a queue and are executed on the computational resources using the daemon process that manages job execution on the computational resource or interacts with a local scheduler to manage the jobs. Sigiri provides data movement facilities to stage-in and stage-out data from the computational platform.

Figure 1 shows the components of the Sigiri middleware when integrated with only one computational resource, Windows Azure. The Sigiri's daemon for Windows Azure supports both the Azure VM role and the worker role. We use the worker role as described earlier in this section. To run an executable with the worker role, the user simply packages their application as a zipped file (which includes the configuration file describing the application) and registers the application to Sigiri using its web service API. The Sigiri daemon takes care of moving executables and the data to the Worker roles that carry out the actual execution.

2.3   MapReduce: Twister4Azure

Twister4Azure [7] is a distributed MapReduce runtime for executing MapReduce jobs within Windows Azure platform. It copes with the eventual data availability within cloud storage by re-trying the map/reduce task execution and by incorporating a design that does not assume the immediate data availability across all the distributed workers. Twister4Azure uses Azure Queues in scheduling Map and Reduce tasks, Azure Tables for storing metadata and monitoring data usages, and Azure Blobs for storing input, output and intermediate data. To support computations, it uses Worker-Role instances within the Azure Cloud. The MapReduce runtime schedules the tasks stored in the global Queue by periodically pulling the tasks from the Queue and assigning them to a map task. Once all the queued tasks for a job are processed by the map tasks, the reduce tasks start to execute taking the intermediate results of the map tasks. Using the MapReduce runtime, users can dynamically vary (increase or decrease) the number of worker roles in the system.

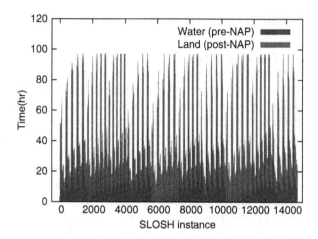

Fig. 2 Logical run time (i.e., "simulation interval") with the amount of time (logical) spent over water as shown for 14,700 parameterized instances

3 The SLOSH Ensemble

SLOSH model, developed by NOAA and evolved from earlier models in 1960s, is in use by the National Hurricane Center (NHC) for forecasting storm surge in real time and for assessing the level of flooding by the storm surge. By running in ensemble mode, this can be done accurately even when the storm's track is in doubt. Also, the SLOSH model is used in several other ways, for example, to assist in "hazard analysis" portion of evacuation planning, to develop structural design criteria based on hurricane winds and surge etc. The SLOSH model is applied to around 38 specific coastal areas, called *basins*, along the Atlantic and Gulf of Mexico coasts of the US, Oahu (Hawai), Puerto Rico and the Virgin Islands. Each of the basins is a geographical region with known values of topography and bathymetry, and it covers, on the average, a few hundred miles of the coastline. The SLOSH model divides a basin into a number of grid cells and estimates the water elevations caused by the storm surge at each of the grid cells.

A SLOSH instance over a basin is represented by a track file with 100 data points along a storm track and each of the points provides a number of parameters associated with the storm (e.g., latitude, longitude, wind-speed, storm direction, pressure drop, radius of maximum winds, etc.); the distance between two successive points is one logical hour. The track file also records the range of the points within the track files over which the SLOSH model would run. So, for a SLOSH instance, the SLOSH model simulates the storm for a duration that is denoted as the *simulation interval*.

To overcome the huge potential for serious errors that could occur if a storm surge forecaster were to issue a warning based on a single, deterministic SLOSH instance, the forecaster will instead run SLOSH as an ensemble that consists of model instances that are configured from different storm track parameters (e.g., forward speed, direction and category). We observe that the execution time for each SLOSH instance within the ensemble varies from a few seconds to more than 10 min when run unoptimized on an Intel Xeon Processor with 2 GHz and 16 GB of memory. We compile the SLOSH code with `gcc 4.1.2` compiler using the default optimization option (-O). Figure 2 shows the significant variations of the simulation intervals within a SLOSH ensemble.

To better understand the performance optimization potential of the SLOSH ensemble, we study the parameters contained in the storm track files for their impact on model instance execution time. Through examination of the storm track files for 14,700 SLOSH instances, we identify two potential parameters. The first one is the total logical execution time of the instance. As can be seen from Fig. 2, this parameter varies from 10 to 100 h. We call this parameter as "simulation interval". The second parameter is the point in (logical) time at which the hurricane hits land; this is called the Nearest Approach Point (NAP), and we refer to it as the "NAP event". The portions of a simulation interval spanned in the water (pre-NAP) and on the land (post-NAP) are shown separately in the figure.

We do experiments to determine the effect of the NAP event, if any, on total model instance execution time for a SLOSH instance. The storm surge model is purported to run faster after the storm reaches the NAP event. Therefore, we study whether the model execution time is uniform or not across the water and the land. If model execution time is uniform, we can ignore the NAP event and use only the simulation interval in estimating the total execution time for a slosh instance. For this measurement, we profile the execution time for 20 SLOSH instances. We select SLOSH instances with a significant time interval spent both over the land and the water. The SLOSH instances are run on an Intel Xeon E7540, 2 GHz processor with 16 GB memory. We look at the actual execution time for SLOSH for different logical hour intervals before and after the NAP event. It the NAP event does not have any impact of the run time, the average execution time (per hour) will be uniform across different SLOSH instances.

As shown in Fig. 3, out of 20 SLOSH instances, there are only 3 outliers that deviate by 4 % from the horizontal line that fits into the rest of the points. Therefore, the model execution time per unit length of simulation interval remains almost uniform among the SLOSH instances. Such an uniform per-unit execution time implies that we can use the simulation interval as the only parameter to estimate (with high accuracy) the total physical execution time for any given SLOSH instance.

The workflow, after execution of the SLOSH ensemble, merges the output files for each SLOSH instance to create aggregate Maximum Envelope of Winds (MEOWs) and Maximum of MEOWs (MOMs) results. MEOWs record the maximum water level recorded at each grid cell; to facilitate interactive visualization and analysis, scientists generate output files (recording MEOWs and MOMs) for a number of groups, which are identified by three parameters: storm direction, forward motion/speed, storm category (on Saffir-Simpson scale [16]).

Fig. 3 Analysis of the impact of NAP event on SLOSH model execution. Each point in the graph corresponds to one SLOSH instance. The average per-unit execution time is nearly uniform among the different SLOSH instances

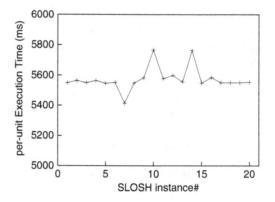

The SLOSH model is run as a command-line program that can be executed in any OS environment. The program is a standalone executable that takes, as input parameters, a basin definition (a geographic area to be modeled) and a set of track files with various storm parameters, i.e., location, storm speed, wind speed, air pressure drop, etc.; each track file defines a SLOSH instance.

Typical execution of the SLOSH model in a parallel or distributed environment is shown in Fig. 4. Here, the SLOSH instances or track files are distributed among a number of instance sets, and each of the instance sets is fed into a replica of the SLOSH program that carries out the computation over the basin. The SLOSH program generates intermediate output files and identifies the output files into groups based on three parameters of the SLOSH instance (or, track file): forward speed, storm direction and storm category. The intermediate output files are envelope files (that records the water level elevation in each of the grid files in the basin) and track files (that are constructed from the input track file). After processing all the instance sets, the output files are merged together to form one pair of output files (i.e., an envelope file and a track file) for each group. The output can be visualized using the SLOSH display program [2].

4   Ensemble Deployment and Execution

Forecasters build an ensemble workflow by defining the track file suite and the basin to run the SLOSH model on. To balance loads across the nodes, we divide the SLOSH instances with the ensemble in a number of instance sets or partitions. A partition is specified as a list of track files. To achieve fine-grained load balancing, we ensure that the number of partitions is a few times larger than the total nodes in the system. In this section, we describe the basic techniques to schedule jobs in the Azure cloud using both the Sigiri middleware and the Twister4Azure MapReduce runtime. In the our scheduling technique, we partition the SLOSH ensemble using the simulation intervals of the instances. The number of partitions is chosen such

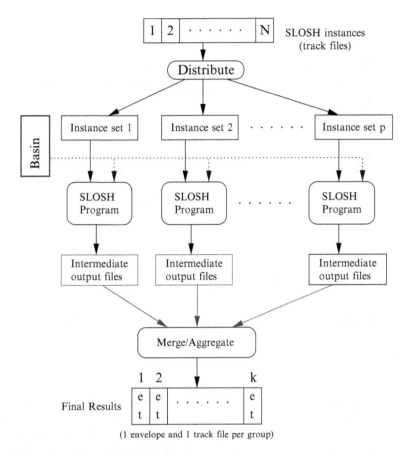

Fig. 4 Slosh ensemble execution workflow

that the total loads for a partition is small enough to allow fine-grained load-balancing across the worker nodes. A user submits a job by providing the SLOSH ensemble and the basin definition as the inputs. The middleware takes the job from the job queue and applies a partitioning algorithm using the simulation intervals as the partitioning metric; each of the partitions forms a task that should be executed the worker nodes. We now describe the detailed systems for processing the SLOSH ensemble using Sigiri middleware and MapReduce runtime.

4.1 Sigiri Middleware

As mentioned earlier, the workflow client, located at the scientist's desktop, submits a job to the cloud via the web service portal. The SLOSH job specifies the directories that contains the SLOSH instances (track files) and the associated basin definitions.

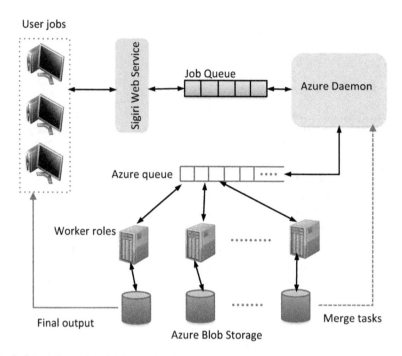

Fig. 5 Scheduling tasks with Sigiri Middleware

Figure 5 shows the details of the job execution with Sigiri middleware. The web service, located in Sigiri Middleware, pulls the required data (track file directory and the basin directory) and stores the data in Azure Blobs. The jobs submitted at the web service are pushed into a global queue. The Azure daemon receives the jobs from the queue and execute the jobs in the worker VMs within the Azure cloud. After receiving a job from the queue, the Azure daemon partitions the SLOSH instances based on the metric simulation intervals of the track files. The number of partitions is determined based on the total worker roles that are going to be used for executing the job. Each partition in the partition definition file contains a list of SLOSH instances or track files, and each partition corresponds to a task. The Azure daemon submits the tasks to an Azure queue. The worker roles pull tasks from the Azure queue and execute the tasks by reading the required data (track files/basins) from the Azure Blobs. Each of the SLOSH instances executed within a worker generates an envelop file and a track file. After processing a SLOSH instance, a worker node locally merges the output files with the previous output files from the same group. Therefore, each worker role maintains only two output files (one envelope and one track file) for each of the groups.

Each of the worker nodes might maintain overlapping groups; therefore, the output files within each of the worker roles should be merged at the end. Instead of waiting for all the worker nodes to finish processing all the tasks in the Azure queue, we pipeline the merge process with the task execution within the worker

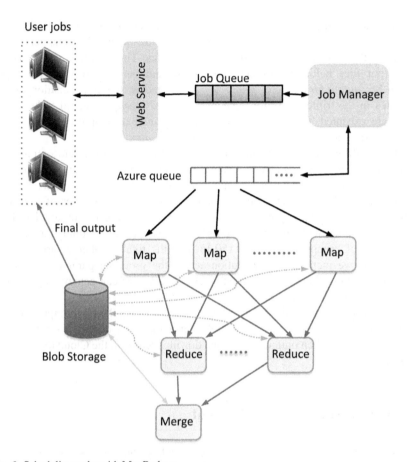

Fig. 6 Scheduling tasks with MapReduce

nodes. When a certain fraction of the worker nodes become idle, the Azure daemon pushes a merge task on the Azure queue, which are grabbed by an idle worker node in the cloud. Such pipelining of the merge process reduces the total makespan while executing a job. Once a job is executed, the Azure daemon notifies the client, and the client downloads the resulting output files from the Azure Blobs.

4.2 MapReduce Runtime

With the MapReduce runtime, similar to the Sigiri Middleware, the workflow client submits jobs via a web service that stores the jobs in a global queue. Figure 6 outlines the job deployment process with MapReduce runtime. A Job Manager (Twister4Azure Client) partitions the SLOSH instances in a job and creates tasks, one for each of the partitions. The Twister4Azure client pushes the tasks in a Map-task-queue which is maintained within a Azure queue. The mappers fetch jobs from the map-task-queue and process the tasks. The mappers locally merge the output files belonging to the same group and generate data as the triple $\langle group\text{-}key, output\,files \rangle$. Here, $group\text{-}key$ is denoted as the concatenation of the attributes in the triple $\langle direction, category, forward\,speed \rangle$. Once all tasks in the queue are executed, the mappers shuffle the intermediate output data across the reducers using the $group\text{-}key$ as the key of the map output.

After shuffling the intermediate output data, all the intermediate output data for the same group is mapped to a single reducer. Therefore, after executing the reducers, we get the final merged output files for each group. Here, we assume that the number of distinct groups is at least equal to the number of reducers. Otherwise, some reducers might not receive any intermediate output files. In a SLOSH ensemble, with current resolution across each of the grouping parameters, the number of groups varies from 150 to 300; the total number of groups even increases as we increase the resolution across the grouping parameters. As the merging of output files is a very lightweight process, we can achieve high merge throughput using only a few reducers.

The *Merge* process of the MapReduce runtime collects the final output files for all the groups and writes them to the Blobs. Once the job is done, the service agent notifies the client. Then output data is then downloaded from the Cloud to the user's desktop.

5   Output-Aware Job Deployment

In case of the a large-scale SLOSH ensemble with large output files, both the storage overheads at each of the worker nodes and the loads for merge/aggregation process increase significantly. We present a load distribution technique that is aware of the output groupings and minimizes the number of intermediate output files to be maintained (at the worker nodes) and be merged (at the aggregator).

While executing the tasks, each worker node generates a number of intermediate output files depending on the groups of the SLOSH instances assigned to the worker node. Within each worker node, all the output files belonging to the same group are merged together and a pair of intermediate output files (an envelop file and a track file) is generated for each group. Therefore, total number of intermediate files generated by the worker nodes depends on the distribution of the SLOSH instances across the worker nodes. In the best case, where all the worker nodes are assigned with SLOSH instances from disjoint groups, the total intermediate files is $2k$, where k is the total groups within the SLOSH ensemble. In this scenario, the *merge* process simply accumulates the files by storing in Azure Blobs; and the process does not require any computation. However, distributing the SLOSH instances based only on the group might lead to high load imbalances across the worker nodes, increasing the makespan. On the other hand, partitioning and distributing the SLOSH instances based on the simulation intervals might lead to a scenario where each worker node receives at least one SLOSH instance from each of the groups; and in such a case, each worker node needs to maintain $2k$ intermediate files. So, the total intermediate files maintained across all the worker nodes is $2pk$, where p is the total workers. Also, in such a scenario, the *merge* process should merge p pairs of files from each group, generating a total of $2k$ final output files.

5.1 Load Partitioning

In output-aware job deployment, we consider both the simulation intervals and output groups when partitioning the SLOSH instances and distributing the partitions across the worker nodes. We first determine the average partition load by dividing the total loads (i.e., sum of the simulation intervals of all the SLOSH instances) by the number of partitions. We arrange the SLOSH instances according to their groups. We start forming partitions by considering the SLOSH instances in the order of their groups, and we assign a SLOSH instance to the current (open) partition until the total load of the partition closely matches with the average partition load; at this point, we commit (or, close) the partition and start to form a another partition in the same way by assigning subsequent SLOSH instances on it. We repeat the process until we create all partitions (T). If we arrange the partitions according to the order they are formed, adjacent partitions may have SLOSH instances from similar groups. So, while assigning the partitions (or tasks) across the worker nodes, the locality (or the order) of the partitions should be considered. Such a deployment scheme needs a fine-grained, load diffusion (through work-stealing) mechanism; hence, such a scheme is not feasible with Twister4Azure, but can be deployed in a Cloud using a Sigiri middleware.

5.2 Work-Stealing with Sigiri

To deploy the tasks (T) across the worker nodes(p), we maintain a total of p Azure queues, one for each worker node. Each queue $i\,(1 \leq i < p)$ is filled with the tasks in the range $\left[(i - 1) \times \frac{T}{p}, i \times \frac{T}{p}\right]$, and the queue p is assigned with the remnant tasks $\left[(p - 1) \times \frac{T}{p}, T\right]$. Each worker node then fetch the tasks from its queue and executes them. If the queue of a worker node i is empty, the worker node tries to steal tasks from another worker's queue.

While a worker node attempts to steal job, the worker node with the largest number of pending tasks might be the candidate to steal tasks from. However, such an approach of stealing tasks from the most-loaded queue, might lead to a large number of overlapping groups within each worker nodes: when several worker nodes try to steal tasks from other queues, the worker nodes might end up selecting the same most-loaded queue, and a batch of worker nodes might be hopping around the queues until all the queues are empty. To reduce such traversals across multiple queues, we use the notion of *normalized load* while selecting the victim queue to seal the tasks from. The normalized load within a queue indicates the current pending tasks in the queue divided by the number of worker nodes currently assigned to the queue. An worker node assigned to the queue with the maximum normalized loads; the worker node consumes tasks from that selected queue until the queue is empty; the worker node select another victim queue and the process repeats until all the queues are empty.

6   Modeling the Execution Time

We develop a computational model to measure the execution time of a SLOSH ensemble within a cloud environment. Such a model can predict the execution time of a large SLOSH ensemble within a cloud with a given number of VMs. Such a prediction before deploying the SLOSH ensemble within the cloud is necessary to provision computational resources within the cloud to meet a user-defined deadline. Also, the computational model can be used to estimate the cost of executing a SLOSH ensemble within the cloud.

Dissecting the execution time of a SLOSH ensemble, we find that the computational (processing) time within each VM is the major component of the total execution, with the time to merge the intermediate output files (Fig. 4) being insignificant. We use a few input parameters to model the execution time of a SLOSH ensemble. We use the parameter per-unit execution time (Fig. 3) to model the computation time for a SLOSH instance. We use the parameters of a storage device (e.g., access time, bandwidth) to model the fetch time from input buffer and total time in a merge process. To get the value for the parameter per-unit execution time, we observe the execution time per a unit of simulation interval for a number of SLOSH instances and take the average value for the parameter. The span of the execution or the total execution time is measured by the latest completion of the VM with the highest loads.

7   Performance Evaluation

We implement two systems to run the SLOSH ensembles using the Twister4Azure MapReduce runtime and the Sigiri middleware. In our experimental setup, the web service interface, Sigiri Daemon and MapReduce clients are hosted on an Intel Xeon E7540 with 2 GHz processor, 16 GB memory, and 1 Gbps connection to an Ethernet switch. Each Azure worker role is created from small compute instances in Azure Cloud. Each of the small compute instances (or worker role VMs) has the

Table 1 Windows Azure compute instance

Parameters	Azure instance
CPU	1.6 GHz X64 Equivalent Processor
Memory	1.75 GB
Disk space	225 GB
Network	100 Mbps
OS	Windows Azure Guest OS 3.1

Fig. 7 Total execution time using 20 worker VMs, varying number of track files, for Twister4Azure

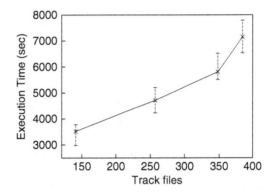

configuration as given in Table 1. We use Azure Queues to communicate among the Sigiri Daemon (or the MapReduce client) and the worker VMs that execute the SLOSH tasks.

We submit jobs to the Cloud through the web Service Interface. The Sigiri daemon (for Sigiri middleware) and the MapReduce client (for Twister4Azure) fetch the submitted jobs, form tasks for each of the jobs, and place the tasks in an Azure Queue. In case of the Sigiri, the Worker role VMs fetch the tasks from the Queue and execute them within the worker. For Twister4Azure, a MapReducer adapter retrieves the tasks from the Queue and sends them to the mappers that execute the tasks. In our experiments, we run up to 400 SLOSH instances. We evaluate the performance of the system by observing the execution time for each of the worker (or mappers) and skewness in the execution. The skewness is measured by the deviation between the maximum and minimum execution time across all the participating VMs. We show in each graph the default parameters for each of the experiments.

7.1 Vary Workloads

Figures 7 and 8 show execution time with varying SLOSH instances for the Twister4Azure and Sigiri Middleware frameworks, respectively. As we increase the number of track files, the average execution time (shown over the line) also increases linearly. The sharp increase in execution time at the end of the line (after 350 SLOSH instances) is due to the large simulation intervals of the track

Fig. 8 Total execution time using 20 worker VMs, varying number of track files, for Sigiri

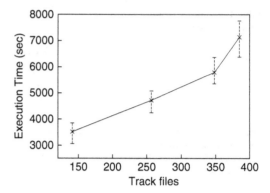

files; hence, a fewer track files contribute to a larger workload. The vertical bar at the point indicates the minimum and maximum execution time across all the VM used the system. If you look the maximum execution time points, we note that the upper bound of the execution time increase only linearly; this is a normal phenomenon as increasing the total workloads linearly would also result in linear increment of the per-worker loads in the system. Also, the skew parameter or the length of the vertical bar increases only a little, which suggests that the skewness remains within a bound. The execution times for both Sigiri Middleware and the MapReduce framework are almost similar. For the experiments, we set the number of total worker VMs to 20. The number of SLOSH instances is varied from 141 to 385, and each point in the graph the track files are partitioned into 60, 80, 100 and 120 partitions, respectively. Each of the partitions form a task for the worker VMs (mappers) in Sigiri Middleware (Twister4Azure). Execution times in both Figs. 7 and 8 are identical, because the application is compute intensive, and the overhead in merging the intermediate results and fetching tasks from the task queue is insignificant compared to the total job execution time.

7.2 Vary Parallelism

We do experiments with varying the number of VMs allocated to the system. Figures 9 and 10 show the effects of varying the number of the worker VMs in Twister4Azure and Sigiri Middleware. Here, as we increase the number of VMs in the cloud, the average execution time (as shown by the line in the graph) decreases linearly. This shows the scalability of the system. The vertical error bar shows the minimum and maximum execution time across the participating VMs. Here, we note that the difference between the maximum and the minimum execution times remain almost similar as we increase the number of VMs. This shows that the total loads of the system in balanced almost uniformly across the worker roles. In the experiment, we use 141 track files which are divided into 60 partitions.

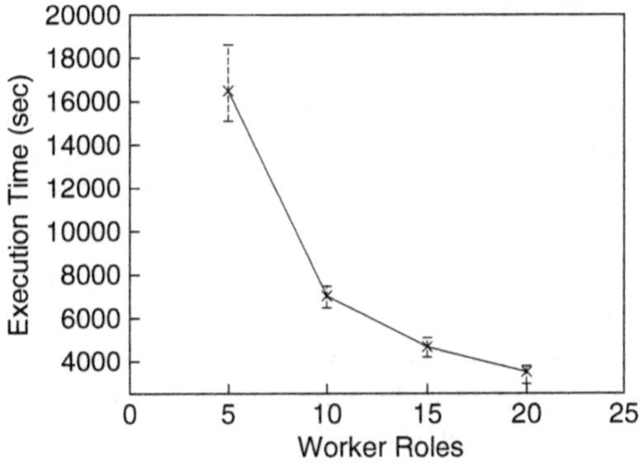

Fig. 9 Total execution time using 141 track files, varying number of Worker Roles, for Twister4Azure

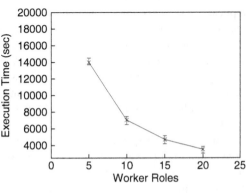

Fig. 10 Total execution time with using 141 track files, varying number of Worker Roles, for Sigiri

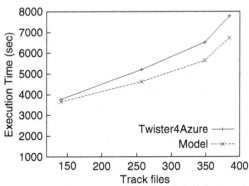

Fig. 11 Execution time of Twister4Azure compared to theoretical computed results

7.3 Evaluating the Model

Figure 11 presents comparative results of execution time using the Twister4Azure framework and the theoretical model as presented in Sect. 6. We show the execution time for varying number of track files. As shown in the figure, the gap between the two lines increases after a certain load (150 track files); however, the deviation is stable beyond 250 track files. For 385 track files, the inaccuracy of the model is near 15 %.

8 Related Work

There are several existing frameworks for executing scientific applications on cloud. SciCumulus [14] is workflow middleware for executing pleasingly parallel tasks with CloudSim, a cloud simulator. The study evaluates the performance in a cloud simulation environment for parametric sweep and data parallel applications. The middleware requires replacement of workflow components by SciCumulus components at the Desktop level, in order to use SciCumulus to run parallel processes using the workflow system. Sigiri, HPC Scheduler and Daytona on the other hand provide a decoupled architecture for execution of parallel jobs by providing a web service interface.

Thilina et al. [6] analyze the performance of two pleasingly parallel bio-medical applications (i.e., assembling genome sequence and dimensionality reduction chemical analysis) in a few cloud frameworks: MapReduce, Apache Hadoop and Microsoft DryadLINQ frameworks. AzureBlast [10] implements a computationally intensive algorithm called BLAST within Azure cloud. Li et al. [9] present the design and implementation of a data processing (i.e., data reprojection, and data reduction) application that integrates ground-based sensor data with the data from a satellite instrumented with a MODIS (or, Moderate Resolution Imaging Spectroradiometer).

Moretti et al. [13] consider a genome assembly application that processes a large collection of sequence data. The authors present a framework to parallelize the genome assembly application over a large number of commodity machines that are harnessed from clusters, clouds and grids. In [12], the authors study the suitability of using a cloud environment (Amazon EC2) to support NASA's HPC workloads. The authors select a representative set of applications from science and engineering domains, and compare the performance of Amazon EC2 to NASA's Pleiades supercomputer. The paper observes that the Cloud system cannot compete with the HPC supercomputer system for tightly-coupled applications with high communication requirements among the code modules.

The Cloudbus toolkit [15] proposes a middleware solution for using Amazon Cloud infrastructure from the Cloudbus workflow engine. This architecture uses different plugins in the workflow system to execute jobs on different cloud resources. These resource plugins are tightly coupled with the workflow system. In this paper, we analyze middleware solutions that are loosely coupled from the workflow system, allowing different workflow systems to execute on cloud resources, with minimum effort.

Wei et al. [11] discuss executing AzureBlast on Azure by evaluating Cirrus, a general parametric sweep service on Azure. The paper addresses issues like fault-handling by reconfiguring and resuming jobs, and dynamic scaling. Our previous workshop paper [4] analyzes the feasibility of cloud environments in supporting the SLOSH applications. Reference [3] addresses load balancing issues to minimize the skewness of the execution times across the worker nodes, considering a batch-mode framework of task execution.

Conclusion

In this chapter, we present the issues in deploying and parallelizing a scientific application (simulating a SLOSH ensemble) in Windows Azure. We present the methodology to balance loads across the worker nodes by partitioning the SLOSH instances. We present the implementation using both a Sigiri Middleware and a Twister4Azure MapReduce runtime. Our experimentations with the two alternate systems show the scalability of the techniques with the number of VMs. Below we outline a few interesting areas of further research.

Fault Tolerant, Elastic Execution with Spot Instances   A number of cloud environments provide spot instances that are activated automatically when instantaneous prices of compute instances fall below a user-specified price. To execute a SLOSH ensemble with spot instances, the execution framework should proactively replicate the computation state to safeguard against the sudden unavailability of the spot instances. To ensure the fault tolerance, the framework should create checkpoints for the SLOSH execution and use the checkpoints to recover from virtual machine failures.

Provenance Collection   An important dimension of science is reproducibility and provenance of results. For a middleware framework to be optimally useful in a world of big data, it must also aid in the capture of provenance and metadata in non-obtrusive yet useful ways. Metadata and provenance capture for this application class, its completeness and quality, are the open issues for future research.

Acknowledgements   This work is funded by the National Science Foundation under grant OCI 1148359. We are grateful to Microsoft for sponsored access to Azure compute resources.

References

1. National Hurricane Center. http://www.nhc.noaa.gov/surge/faq.php#4x
2. NOAA SLOSH display program. http://slosh.nws.noaa.gov/sloshPub/#sloshDsp
3. Chakraborty, A., Pathirage, M., Suriarachchi, I., Chandrasekar, K., Mattocks, C., Plale, B.: Storm surge simulation and load balancing in azure cloud. In: Proc. 21st High Performance Computing Symposium (HPC'13), HPC'13, pp. 1–9. SCS and ACM (2013)
4. Chandrasekar, K., Pathirage, M., Wijeratne, S., Mattocks, C., Plale, B.: Middleware alternatives for storm surge predictions in windows azure. In: Proc. 3rd workshop on Scientific Cloud Computing Date, ScienceCloud '12, pp. 3–12 (2012)
5. Glahn, B., Taylor, A., Kurkowski, N., Shaffer, W.: The role of the slosh model in national weather service storm surge forecasting. National Weather Digest **33**(1), 3–14 (2009)
6. Gunarathne, T., Wu, T.L., Qiu, J., Fox, G.: Cloud computing paradigms for pleasingly parallel biomedical applications. In: Proc. 19th ACM Int. Symposium on High Performance Distributed Computing, HPDC '10, pp. 460–469. ACM, New York, NY, USA (2010)
7. Gunarathnea, T., Qiu, J., Fox, G.: Iterative mapreduce for azure cloud. In: Proc. Cloud Computing and Its Applications, CCA, CCA '11 (2011)

8. Lee, C.A.: A perspective on scientific cloud computing. In: Proc. 19th ACM Int. Symposium on High Performance Distributed Computing, HPDC '10, pp. 451–459 (2010)

9. Li, J., Humphrey, M., Agarwal, D.A., Jackson, K.R., van Ingen, C., Ryu, Y.: eScience in the cloud: A modis satellite data reprojection and reduction pipeline in the windows azure platform. In: IPDPS, pp. 1–10 (2010)

10. Lu, W., Jackson, J., Barga, R.: AzureBlast: a case study of developing science applications on the cloud. In: Proc. 19th ACM Int. Symposium on High Performance Distributed Computing, HPDC '10, pp. 413–420 (2010)

11. Lu, W., Jackson, J., Ekanayake, J., Barga, R.S., Araujo, N.: Performing large science experiments on azure: Pitfalls and solutions. In: CloudCom, pp. 209–217 (2010)

12. Mehrotra, P., Djomehri, J., Heistand, S., Hood, R., Jin, H., Lazanoff, A., Saini, S., Biswas, R.: Performance evaluation of amazon EC2 for NASA HPC applications. In: Proceedings of the 3rd workshop on Scientific Cloud Computing Date, pp. 41–50. New York, NY, USA (2012)

13. Moretti, C., Thrasher, A., Yu, L., Olson, M., Emrich, S.J., Thain, D.: A framework for scalable genome assembly on clusters, clouds, and grids. IEEE Trans. Parallel Distributed Systems 23(12), 2189–2197 (2012)

14. de Oliveira, D., Ogasawara, E., Baião, F., Mattoso, M.: Scicumulus: A lightweight cloud middleware to explore many task computing paradigm in scientific workflows. In: Proc. IEEE 3rd Int. Conf. on Cloud Computing, CLOUD '10, pp. 378–385. IEEE Computer Society, Washington, DC, USA (2010)

15. Pandey, S., Karunamoorthy, D., Buyya, R.: Workflow engine for clouds. In: Cloud Computing, Principles and Paradigms, Wiley Series on Parallel and Distributed Computing, pp. 321–344 (2011)

16. Simpson, R., Saffir, H.: Tropical cyclone destructive potential by integrated kinetic energy. Bull. Amer. Meteor. Soc. 88, 1799–1800 (2007)

17. Withana, E.C., Plale, B.: Sigiri: uniform resource abstraction for grids and clouds. Concurrency and Computation: Practice and Experience 24(18), 1532–0626 (2012)

Cross-Phase Optimization in MapReduce

Benjamin Heintz, Abhishek Chandra, and Jon Weissman

Abstract MapReduce has proven remarkably effective for a wide variety of data-intensive applications, but it was designed to run on large single-site homogeneous clusters. Researchers have begun to explore the extent to which the original MapReduce assumptions can be relaxed including skewed workloads, iterative applications, and heterogeneous computing environments. This chapter continues this exploration by applying MapReduce across widely distributed data over distributed computation resources. This problem arises when datasets are generated and stored at multiple sites as is common in many scientific domains and increasingly e-commerce applications. It also occurs when multi-site resources such as geographically separated data centers are applied to the same application. Using Hadoop, we show that the absence of network and node homogeneity and locality of data lead to poor performance. The problem is that interaction of MapReduce phases becomes pronounced in the presence of heterogeneous network behavior. In this paper, we propose new cross-phase optimization techniques that enable independent MapReduce phases to influence one another. We propose techniques that optimize the push and map phases to enable push-map overlap and to allow map behavior to feed back into push dynamics. Similarly, we propose techniques that optimize the map and reduce phases to enable shuffle cost to feed back and affect map scheduling decisions. We evaluate the benefits of our techniques in both Amazon EC2 and PlanetLab. The experimental results show the potential of these techniques as performance is improved from 7 to 18 % depending on the execution environment and application.

1 Introduction

Recent years have seen increasing amounts of data being generated and stored in a geographically distributed manner for a large variety of application domains. Examples include social networking, Web and Internet service providers, as well

B. Heintz (✉) • A. Chandra • J. Weissman
University of Minnesota, Keller Hall 4-192, 200 Union Street SE,
Minneapolis, MN 55455, USA
e-mail: heintz@cs.umn.edu; chandra@cs.umn.edu; jon@cs.umn.edu

© Springer Science+Business Media New York 2014   277
X. Li, J. Qiu (eds.), *Cloud Computing for Data-Intensive Applications*,
DOI 10.1007/978-1-4939-1905-5__12

as large content distribution networks (CDNs) that serve the content for many of these services. For instance, Facebook has more than one billion users, more than 80 % of whom are outside the US or Canada,[1] while Google has developed storage systems [9,14] that manage data partitioned across globally distributed data centers. A large CDN such as Akamai [30] that currently serves 15–30 % of the global web traffic uses over 100,000 servers deployed in over 1,000 locations in 75 countries around the world.

This trend toward distributed generation and storage is unlikely to stop in the foreseeable future. Wide-area network latency can have a pronounced adverse effect on user experience for Web applications, so there is pressure to distribute infrastructure closer to clients at the edge of the Internet [34]. As a result, many applications collect data from their users—for example in the form of photo uploads or edits to a cloud-hosted document—in an inherently distributed manner. Additionally, wide-area network costs have decreased over time, but not at the same rate as storage and compute costs [7]. At the global scale, wide-area network bandwidth is fundamentally limited by transoceanic cable bandwidth, which has historically grown much more slowly than storage and compute capability [32]. These trends suggest that data will continue to be generated in a distributed manner, and will increasingly be stored close to the distributed data sources rather than transferred across costly wide-area links to a centralized location.

Many modern applications relying on such data need to process large amounts of *highly distributed data* on a *highly distributed platform* with *low latency*. As a motivating example, consider a CDN such as Akamai. Content providers use CDNs to deliver web content, live and on-demand videos, downloads, and web applications to users around the world. The servers of a CDN are deployed in clusters in hundreds or even thousands of data centers around the world. Each server of a CDN records detailed data about each user that it interacts with: every web object that is served, each stream that is played, each application that is accessed, as well as each user action such as playing or pausing a stream. Besides user access information, each server also records network-level and system-level data such as TCP connection statistics [30]. In aggregate, the servers produce tens of billions of lines of log data originating from over a thousand locations each day.

A number of applications must *process voluminous distributed data* to extract useful information. For instance, an analytics application must extract detailed information about who is accessing the content, from which networks and from which geographies. It must also combine access data with network performance data to depict the quality of experience for users, including page download speeds, video startup times, and application transaction times. At the same time, *the processing must be done with minimum latency*. The analytics application must complete processing with a delay of no more than several minutes so that content providers can understand and act upon the key indicators that relate to their users and their business.

---

[1]http://newsroom.fb.com.

A key question for efficient processing of such distributed data is *where* to carry out the computation. As Jim Gray noted, "you can either move your questions or the data" [25]. These two options, however, represent two extreme possibilities. At one extreme, sending massive data from its diverse origin locations to a centralized location may be too slow to meet the requirements of low latency [3, 32]. Further, the cost may be prohibitive, in terms of both data transfer costs and the need to build a single large dedicated data center for application processing. Finally, a centralized solution is intrinsically less fault-tolerant than a distributed one, since failure of the single centralized data center can cause a complete outage that is unacceptable for critical applications such as analytics and monitoring.

At the other extreme, if we map computation onto each input datum *in situ*, the results of these subcomputations comprise intermediate data that must be aggregated to generate the final analysis results. If such intermediate data are large, then aggregating them may be more costly than moving input data to a centralized location. Further, the various locations may differ in their compute capacities, resulting in imbalanced resource utilization.

Between the two extremes of moving all the data to a centralized location for processing and moving all the computation to the sources of data, there is a rich spectrum of possibilities that may in fact be more efficient. Systems for highly distributed data-intensive computing must intelligently decide where along this spectrum leads to the best performance.

In this chapter, we explore how MapReduce systems in particular can make such intelligent decisions. Because MapReduce was originally designed [16] for the relatively homogeneous single-datacenter setting, it is natural to ask whether MapReduce is well suited for data analysis in environments where both data and compute resources are highly distributed. Indeed, as we show through experiments in Sect. 1.1, under a widely distributed environment with high network heterogeneity, Hadoop does not always perform well. We find that the main reason for this performance degradation is the interaction and heavy dependency across different MapReduce phases. This happens because the data placement and task execution are highly coupled in the MapReduce paradigm (because MapReduce attempts to assign tasks to nodes that already host input data for those tasks[2]). Thus, the decisions on where to place data severely impact the scheduling decision on where map and reduce tasks are executed, and vice versa. In a heterogeneous environment, particularly one with slow wide-area links, such coupling can severely impact the end-to-end performance by creating bottleneck links and nodes in the execution. We show that Hadoop's default data placement and scheduling mechanisms do not take such cross-phase interactions into account, and while they may try to optimize individual phases, they could result in globally bad decisions, resulting in poor overall performance. The problem is not that a given phase cannot take into account

---

[2]When this is not possible, tasks must read their inputs remotely, and scarce network bandwidth becomes a limiting factor.

decisions made by a prior phase, but rather the opposite. Upstream decisions may limit the flexibility of later phases, and thus, earlier phase decisions must account for their impact later on.

In spite of these weaknesses of popular MapReduce implementations, the MapReduce abstraction itself is remarkably powerful, and implementing the abstraction in highly distributed settings is a worthy objective. MapReduce, in particular the open-source Hadoop [21] implementation, has been applied to a surprising variety of data-intensive computing applications, and many data scientists have gained MapReduce application development expertise. Further, a rich ecosystem has been built on top of Hadoop, including for example Pig [18], Hive [35], Impala [1], Scalding [2], Mahout [29] and many more. There is tremendous value in bringing this expertise and infrastructure to highly distributed environments.

From a higher level, relaxing the assumptions of the original MapReduce in terms of execution domain and suitable applications is an active area of pursuit by many researchers. Our line of inquiry continues along this path.

1.1 *MapReduce Performance in Widely Distributed Environments*

In this section, we empirically demonstrate the challenge of efficiently executing MapReduce over a widely distributed environment through experiments conducted on the PlanetLab and Amazon EC2 platforms. We present only a subset of results from our experiments here due to space constraints; more details are available in another paper [11].

A typical MapReduce job executed in a cluster environment consists of three main phases: (a) *Map*, where map tasks execute on their input data; (b) *Shuffle*, where the output of map tasks (intermediate key-value pairs) are disseminated to reduce tasks; and (c) *Reduce*, where reduce tasks are executed on the intermediate data to produce the final outputs. It is typically assumed that the input data are already available on the compute nodes before the job execution is started. Such *data push* is usually achieved through file system mechanisms such as those provided by HDFS. However, when data sources are geographically distributed, such as across multiple data centers, the process of pushing data to the compute nodes may itself be costly, and hence, must be considered as a separate phase of the overall computation.

To illustrate this problem, we compare three possible architectures for MapReduce execution: (a) *Local MapReduce (LMR)*, where all data are first moved into a centralized cluster followed by the execution of a local MapReduce job within that cluster; (b) *Global MapReduce*, where all the widely distributed compute resources are considered as a single MapReduce cluster without considering the network heterogeneity; and (c) *Distributed MapReduce (DMR)*, where multiple MapReduce jobs are first executed close to the data sources, followed by a final centralized combination of their outputs. Note that LMR is the typical way in which MapReduce computation is done today.

In our experimental setup, we used a total of eight PlanetLab nodes in two widely separated clusters—four nodes in the US, and four nodes in Europe. In addition, we used one node in each cluster as a data source. For each cluster, we chose tightly coupled machines with high inter-node bandwidth (i.e., they were either co-located at the same site or share some network infrastructure). The intra-cluster bandwidth was between 1.5 and 2.5 MB/s, while the inter-cluster bandwidth between any pair of nodes (between US and EU) was around 300–500 KB/s.

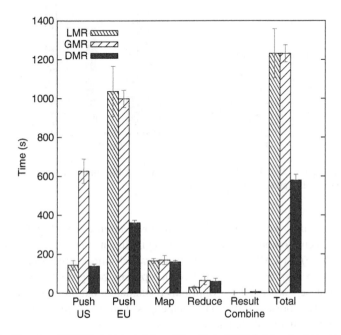

Fig. 1 WordCount on 800 MB plain-text data on PlanetLab. DMR finishes the fastest by avoiding the transfer of large input data over slow links

Figures 1 and 2 (reproduced from [11]) show the results of executing WordCount on plain-text and random input data respectively in this environment. These two scenarios correspond to different application/data characteristics: one—WordCount with plain-text—where input data are aggregated into much smaller intermediate data, and the other—WordCount with random data—where input data expand into larger intermediate data, increasing the shuffle costs. Within each graph, we show the time of individual phases: Push US/EU corresponding to data push from the US and EU data sources respectively, followed by the map and reduce phases. The Result Combine phase is the combine phase for the DMR architecture only, comprising the data transmission plus combination costs, and this phase corresponds to a logical shuffle/reduce of the intermediate results.

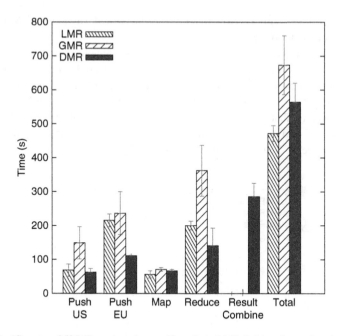

Fig. 2 WordCount on 250 MB random data on PlanetLab. LMR finishes faster since it minimizes the larger intermediate and output data transfer costs

From the results, we make the following observations. From Fig. 1, we see that in a wide-area environment, the cost of moving input data to the compute nodes (the data push phase) for LMR can be significant, which impacts the overall execution time of the job despite the map and reduce phases being relatively efficient. In fact, these datasets are small by MapReduce standards, but the size of data and its distributed nature present orthogonal challenges; here we focus on the challenges arising from widely distributed data.

Since the choice of mapper nodes depends on where data are pushed, pushing data to nearby nodes (as for DMR) is much more efficient when the volume of intermediate data is small relative to that of the input data. On the other hand, from Fig. 2, we see that when the volume of intermediate data is much larger than that of the input data, the cost of combining intermediate results can be the dominant factor. In particular, in this case, shuffling and merging the intermediate results close to the mappers (as for LMR) is much more efficient. GMR performs poorly in both cases, as it does not use network locality either in the push or the result combine phases. Our experiments on the Amazon EC2 environment showed similar results [11].

Overall, these results illustrate the close interdependency between the different stages of a MapReduce execution. In particular, the choice of mapper nodes to which inputs are pushed impacts both how long the data push takes, as well as where the intermediate data are generated. This in turn impacts the performance of the data shuffle to the reducers. This problem is particularly severe for wide-area environments, since they are typically heterogeneous in terms of node and link capacities. Therefore, it is important to optimize the overall end-to-end computation as a whole while taking into account the network and platform characteristics.

1.2 Cross-Phase Optimization

In order to overcome these limitations, we first present a modeling and optimization framework that allows us to explore the spectrum between centralized and distributed computation, and derive an optimal *execution plan* describing the best placement of computation (Sect. 2). This framework serves as an oracle, showing us how we could solve this problem if we had complete information. We apply several high-level insights from this oracle toward a practical implementation in a real MapReduce system where information is more limited. The key idea behind our proposed implementation techniques is to consider not only the execution cost of an individual task or computational phase, but also its impact on the performance of subsequent phases. Specifically we propose two sets of techniques:

Map-Aware Push (Sect. 3) Traditional MapReduce assumes that the input data are pushed to compute nodes before execution starts. We instead propose making the input data push aware of the cost of map execution, based on the source-to-mapper link capacities as well as mapper node computation speeds. We achieve this by overlapping the data push with map execution, which provides us with two benefits. The first benefit is a pipelining effect which hides the latency of data push with the map execution. The second benefit is a dynamic feedback between the map and push that enables nodes with higher speeds and faster links to process more data at runtime.

Shuffle-Aware Map (Sect. 4) In traditional MapReduce, the typical shuffling of intermediate data from mappers to reducers is an all-to-all operation. However, in a heterogeneous environment, a mapper with a slow outgoing link can become a bottleneck in the shuffle phase, slowing down the downstream reducers. We propose map task scheduling based on the estimated shuffle cost from each mapper to enable faster shuffle and reduce execution.

We have implemented these techniques in the Hadoop framework, and evaluated their benefits in both Amazon EC2 and PlanetLab (Sect. 5). The experimental results show the potential of these techniques as performance is improved from 7 to 18 % depending on the execution environment and application.

2 Oracle: Model-Driven Optimization

We now consider a model-driven optimization framework that allows us to explore the spectrum between purely distributed and purely centralized computation. The core of this framework is a model of MapReduce job execution time in a highly distributed setting. This model takes a number of inputs describing the distributed data, distributed compute resources and their interconnections, as well as application characteristics. In particular, the model takes as input the set of distributed data sources as well as the amount of input data stored at each of these sources. To predict computation time, it also takes the set of mappers and reducers along with the rates at which they can perform map and reduce computation. In order to predict time spent in wide-area communication, the model requires knowledge of network bandwidth between all pairs of sources and mappers, and between all pairs of mappers and reducers. Application characteristics are described by a parameter α, which defines the ratio of intermediate data size to input data size.

In a real-world MapReduce implementation, the applicability of such a model may be limited by the need to gather all of these inputs ahead of time. For example, the number of network links to measure may be large, and conditions may vary over time. Alternatively, the computation time required by a new application may not be known without prior profiling. In spite of these practical limitations, such a model is still very valuable, as it can provide insights to guide the design of more lightweight optimization mechanisms, as it does in this section.

2.1 Model and Optimization

We model the distributed platform available for executing the MapReduce application as a tripartite graph with a vertex set of $V = S \cup M \cup R$, where S is the set of data sources, M is the set of mappers, and R is the set of reducers (see Fig. 3). The edge set E of the tripartite graph is the complete set of edges, $(S \times M) \cup (M \times R)$.

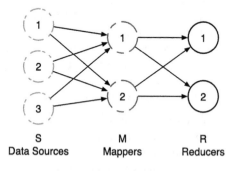

Fig. 3 A tripartite graph model for distributed MapReduce with three data sources, two mappers and two reducers

Each *node* represents a physical resource; either a data source providing inputs, or a computation resource available for executing map or reduce computational processes. A node can therefore represent a single physical machine or even a single map or reduce *slot* in a small Hadoop cluster, or it can represent an entire rack, cluster, or data center of machines in a much larger deployment. Each edge represents the communication path connecting a pair of such nodes. The *capacity of a node* $i \in M \cup R$ is denoted by C_i, and captures the computational resources available at that node in units of bits of incoming data that it can process per second. Note that C_i is also application-dependent as different MapReduce applications are likely to require different amounts of computing resources to process the same amount of data. Likewise, the *capacity of an edge* $(i, j) \in E$ is denoted by B_{ij}, representing the bandwidth (in bits/second) that can be sustained on the communication link that the edge represents.

Application characteristics are captured by two key parameters: the *amount of data* D_i (in bits) that originates at data source i, for each $i \in S$; and the *expansion factor* α that represents the ratio of the size of the output of the map phase to the size of its input. Note that α can take values less than, greater than, or equal to 1, depending on whether the output of the map operation is smaller than, larger than, or equal in size to the input, respectively. Many applications perform extensive aggregation in the map phase, for example by filtering records according to a predicate, or by projecting only a subset of fields from complex records. These applications have α much less than 1. On the other hand, some applications augment the input data in the map phase (e.g., relational join), or they emit multiple copies of intermediate records (e.g., to compute an aggregate at city, state, and national levels), yielding $\alpha > 1$. This parameter has a strong impact on optimal placement decisions, as shown earlier in the experimental results in Sect. 1.1.

In addition to a description of the platform and application, the model also requires a description of the *execution plan* describing where each data source pushes its inputs as well as how the intermediate keys are partitioned across reducers. Given the platform, application, and execution plan, the amount of data flowing through each mapper and reducer and across each network link is known. Combined with knowledge of link bandwidths and compute rates, it is therefore possible to estimate completion time for the full MapReduce job.

Using this model, we formulate a mixed integer program to find an execution plan that minimizes end-to-end job execution time. For more details, see our technical report [22].

2.2   Key Insights

We use this model-driven optimization to derive a number of insights that inform the development of optimization mechanisms in a real-world MapReduce implementation. Using measurements of compute speeds and network links from PlanetLab nodes distributed around the world, we generate optimization inputs corresponding to a globally distributed environment spanning eight nodes in the US, Europe, and Asia. Computing optimal execution plans in this environment shows that it is essential to optimize with the objective of minimizing end-to-end execution time. Specifically, we find that tolerating suboptimality within individual phases (e.g., push, map, shuffle, or reduce) may be necessary to achieve end-to-end optimality. As an example, an optimization that aims to minimize end-to-end execution time leads to execution times 54–81 % lower than an optimization that aims to minimize push and shuffle time. In other words, our model-driven optimization framework shows that *optimizing across phases* with an end-to-end objective is more effective than optimizing with the more local—even myopic—objective of shortening specific phases.

We also use our model-driven optimization to compare the benefit from controlling a single phase (e.g., push or shuffle) of the execution plan to that from controlling both the push and shuffle phases. Our results show that, while controlling only the bottleneck phase is better than controlling only the non-bottleneck phase, controlling (i.e., optimizing) both phases is much better. In particular, *optimizing both phases* leads to execution times 37–52 % lower than optimizing only a single phase. In other words, it is important that we control both phases, answering both where each data source should push its data, as well as how the intermediate data should be partitioned across reducers.

In the following sections, we apply these insights to mechanisms that are more suitable to a real-world MapReduce implementation where the dynamic nature of network, compute, and application characteristics might render a static optimization approach infeasible.

3   Map-Aware Push

The first opportunity for cross-phase optimization in MapReduce lies at the boundary between the push and map phases. A typical practice is what we call a *push-then-map* approach, where input data are imported in one step, and computation begins only after the data import completes. This approach has two major problems. First, by forcing all computation to wait for the slowest communication link, it introduces waste. Second, separating the push and map phases deprives mappers of a way to demand more or less work based on their compute capacity. This makes scheduling the push in a map-aware manner more difficult. To overcome these challenges, we propose two changes: first, overlapping—or pipelining—the push and map phases; and second, inferring locality information at runtime and driving scheduling decisions based on this knowledge.

Before discussing how we implement our proposed approach in Hadoop and showing experimental results, we describe in more detail the problems of a push-then-map approach and how our proposed *Map-aware Push* technique addresses them. To begin, consider the simple example environment shown in Fig. 4, comprising two data sources S_1 and S_2 and two mappers M_1 and M_2.[3] Assume that each data source initially hosts 15 GB of data and that the link bandwidths and mapper computation rates are as shown in the figure.

---

[3]This and the remaining figures and tables from this chapter are reproduced from [23].

3.1   Overlapping Push and Map to Hide Latency

With these network links, the following push distribution would optimize the push (i.e., minimize push time): S_1 pushes 10 GB to M_1 and 5 GB to M_2, and S_2 pushes 3 GB to M_1 and 12 GB to M_2. If we were to use this distribution with a push-then-map approach, then the entire push would finish after 500 s even though source S_2 would finish its part after only 300 s. Map computation would begin after 500 s and continue until 1,350 s.

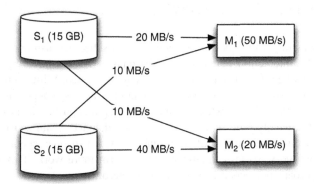

Fig. 4 A simple example network with two data sources and two mappers

If we instead were to overlap the push and map, allowing map computation to begin at each mapper as soon as data begin to arrive, then we could avoid this unnecessary waiting. For example, assuming that we used this same optimal push distribution, then mapper M_2, with slower compute capacity than its incoming network links, would be the bottleneck, finishing after 850 s. By simply overlapping the map and push phases, we could reduce the total push and map runtime by about 37 % in this example.

3.2   Overlapping Push and Map to Improve Scheduling

The second problem arises due to the lack of feedback from the map phase to the push phase. Without this feedback, and absent any *a priori* knowledge of the map phase performance, we are left with few options other than simply optimizing the push phase in isolation. Such a single-phase optimization favors pushing more data to mappers with faster incoming network links. In our example, however, it is the mapper with *slower* network links (M_1) that is actually better suited for map computation. Unfortunately, by pursuing an optimal push phase, we end up with more data at M_2 and in turn roughly 3.3× longer map computation there than at

M_1. For better overall performance, we need to weigh the two factors of network bandwidth and computation capacity and trade off between faster push and faster map. Continuing with our simple example, we should tolerate a slightly slower push in order to achieve a significantly faster map by sending more data to mapper M_1. In fact, in an optimal case, we would send 60 % of all input data there, yielding a total push-map runtime of only 600 s, or a 55 % reduction over the original push-then-map approach.

3.3 Map-Aware Push Scheduling

Of course, this raises the question of how we can schedule push and map jointly, respecting the interaction between the two phases. As we have argued, this is difficult to do when the push and map phases are separated. With overlapped push and map, however, the distribution of computation across mapper nodes can be demand-driven. Specifically, whereas push-then-map first pushes data from sources, our approach logically *pulls* data from sources on-demand. Using existing Hadoop mechanisms, this on-demand pull is initiated when a mapper becomes idle and requests more work, so faster mappers can perform more work. This is how our proposed approach respects map computation heterogeneity.

To respect network heterogeneity, our *Map-aware Push* technique departs from the traditional Hadoop approach of explicitly modeling network topology as a set of racks and switches, and instead infers locality information at runtime. It does this by monitoring source-mapper link bandwidth at runtime and estimating the push time for each source-mapper pair. Specifically, let d be the size of a task in bytes (assume for ease of presentation that all task sizes are equal) and let $L_{s,m}$ be the link speed between source node s and mapper node m in bytes per second. Then we estimate the push time $T_{s,m}$ in seconds from source s to mapper m as

$$T_{s,m} = \frac{d}{L_{s,m}} . \tag{1}$$

Let S denote the set of all sources that have not yet completed their push. Then when mapper node m requests work, we grant it a task from source $s^* = \arg\min_{s \in S} T_{s,m}$. Intuitively, this is equivalent to selecting the closest task in terms of network bandwidth. This is a similar policy to Hadoop's default approach of preferring *data-local* tasks, but our overall approach is distinguished in two ways. First, rather than *reacting* to data movement decisions that have already been made in a separate push phase, it *proactively* optimizes data movement and task placement in concert. Second, it discovers locality information dynamically and automatically rather than relying on an explicit user-specified model.

3.4 Implementation in Hadoop

Now we can discuss how we have implemented our approach in Hadoop 1.0.1. First, the overlapping itself is possible using existing Hadoop mechanisms, but a more creative deployment. Specifically, we set up a Hadoop Distributed File System (HDFS) instance comprising the data source nodes, which we refer to as the "remote" HDFS instance and use directly as the input to a Hadoop MapReduce job. Map tasks in Hadoop typically read their inputs from HDFS, so this allows us to directly employ existing Hadoop mechanisms.[4]

Our scheduling enhancements, on the other hand, require modification to the Hadoop task scheduler. To gather the bandwidth information mentioned earlier, we add a simple network monitoring module which records actual source-to-mapper link performance and makes this information accessible to the task scheduler. For Hadoop MapReduce jobs that read HDFS files as input, each map task corresponds to an InputSplit which in turn corresponds to an HDFS file block. HDFS provides an interface to determine physical block locations, so the task scheduler can determine the source associated with a particular task and compute its $T_{s,m}$ based on bandwidth information from the monitoring module. If there are multiple replicas of the file block, then $T_{s,m}$ can be computed for each replica, and the system can use the replica that minimizes this value. The task scheduler then assigns tasks from the closest source s^* as described earlier.

3.5 Experimental Results

We are interested in the performance of our approach, which overlaps push and map and infers locality at runtime, compared to a baseline push-then-map approach. To implement the push-then-map approach, we also run an HDFS instance comprising the compute nodes (call this the "local" HDFS instance). We first run a Hadoop DistCP job to copy from the remote HDFS to this local HDFS, and then run a MapReduce job directly from the local HDFS. We compare application execution time using these two approaches. Because we are concerned primarily with push and map performance at this point, we run the Hadoop example WordCount job on text data generated by the Hadoop example randomtextwriter generator, as this represents a map-heavy application.

We run this experiment in two different environments: Amazon EC2 and PlanetLab. Our EC2 setup uses eight EC2 nodes in total, all of the m1.small instance type. These nodes are distributed evenly across two EC2 regions: four in the US and the other four in Europe. Each node hosts one map slot and one reduce slot.

---

[4]To improve fault tolerance, we have also added an option to cache and replicate inputs at the compute nodes. This reduces the need to re-fetch remote data after task failures or for speculative execution.

Two PlanetLab nodes, one in the US and one in Europe, serve as distributed data sources. Table 1 shows the bandwidths measured between the multiple nodes in this setup.

Figure 5 shows the execution time[5] of the WordCount job on 2 GB of input data, and it shows that our approach to overlapping push and map reduces the total runtime of the push and map phases by 17.7 %, and the total end-to-end runtime by 15.2 % on our EC2 testbed.

Next, we run the same experiment on PlanetLab. We continue to use two nodes as distributed data sources, and we use four other globally distributed nodes as compute nodes, each hosting one map slot and one reduce slot. Table 2 shows the bandwidths measured between the multiple nodes in this setup. Due to the smaller cluster size in this experiment, we use only 1 GB of text input data.

Table 1 Measured bandwidths in the EC2 experimental setup

From	To	Bandwidth (MB/s)
Source EU	Worker EU	8
Source EU	Worker US	3
Source US	Worker EU	3
Source US	Worker US	4
Worker EU	Worker EU	16
Worker EU	Worker US	2
Worker US	Worker EU	5
Worker US	Worker US	2

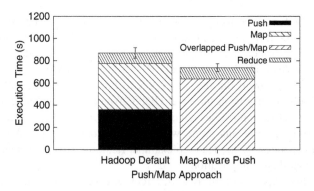

Fig. 5 Runtime of a Hadoop WordCount job on 2 GB text data on a globally distributed Amazon EC2 environment for the push-then-map and *Map-aware Push* approaches

---

[5]Throughout this chapter, error bars indicate 95 % confidence intervals.

From	To	Bandwidth (MB/s)
All sources	All workers	1–3
Workers A–C	Workers A–C	4–9
Workers A–C	Worker D	2
Worker D	Workers A–C	0.2–0.4

Table 2 Measured bandwidths in the PlanetLab experimental setup

Figure 6 shows that push-map overlap can reduce runtime of the push and map phases by 21.3 % and the whole job by 17.5 % in this environment. We see a slightly greater benefit from push-map overlap on PlanetLab than on EC2 due to the increased heterogeneity of the PlanetLab environment.

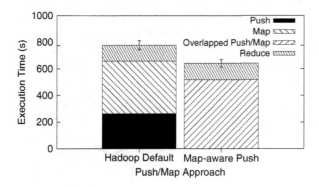

Fig. 6 Runtime of a Hadoop WordCount job on 1 GB text data on a PlanetLab environment for the push-then-map and *Map-aware Push* approaches

4 Shuffle-Aware Map

In the previous section, we showed how the map phase can influence the push phase, in terms of both the volume of data each mapper receives as well as the sources from which each mapper receives its data. In turn, the push determines, in part, when a map slot becomes available for a mapper. Thus, from the perspective of the push and map phases, a set of mappers and their data sources are decided. This decision, however, ignores the downstream cost of the shuffle and reduce as we will show. In this section, we show how the set of mappers can be adjusted to account for the downstream shuffle cost. This was also motivated in Sect. 1.1 as we illustrated the importance of shuffling and merging intermediate results close to mappers, particularly for shuffle-heavy jobs.

In traditional MapReduce, intermediate map outputs are shuffled to reducers in an all-to-all communication. In Hadoop, one can control the granularity of reduce

tasks and the amount of work each reducer will obtain. However, these decisions
ignore the possibility that a mapper–reducer link may be very poor. For example, in
Fig. 7, the links between mapper C and reducers D and E are poor, thus raising the
cost of shuffle. For applications in which shuffle is dominant, this phenomenon can
greatly impact performance, particularly in heterogeneous networks.

Two solutions are possible: changing the reducer nodes, or reducing the amount
of work done by mapper C and in turn reducing the volume of data traversing the
bottleneck links. We present an algorithm that takes the latter approach. In this way,
the downstream shuffle (or reduce) can impact the map. This is similar to the *Map-
aware Push* technique where the map influenced the push.

As in typical MapReduce, we assume the reducer nodes are known *a priori*.
We also assume that we know the approximate distribution of reducer tasks: i.e., we
know the fraction of intermediate data allocated to each reducer node. This allows us
to know how much data must travel on the link from a mapper node to each reducer,
which our algorithm utilizes. The distribution can be estimated using a combination
of reducer node execution power and mapper–reduce link speed, pre-profiled. This
estimate can be updated during the map phase if shuffle and reduce are overlapped.

Fig. 7 An example network
where links from mapper C to
reducers D and E are shuffle
bottlenecks

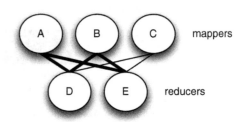

4.1 Shuffle-Aware Map Scheduling

To estimate the impact of a mapper node upon the reduce phase, we first estimate
the time taken by the mapper to obtain a task, execute it, and deliver intermediate
data to all reducers (assuming parallel transport). The intuition is that if the shuffle
cost is high then the mapper node should be throttled to allow the map task to be
allocated to a mapper with better shuffle performance. We estimate the finish time
T_m for a mapper m to execute a map task as follows: $T_m = T_m^{map} + T_m^{shuffle}$, where
T_m^{map} is the estimated time for the mapper m to execute the map task, including the
time to read the task input from a source (using the *Map-aware Push* approach), and
$T_m^{shuffle}$ is the estimated time to shuffle the accumulated intermediate data D_m up to
the current task, from mapper m to all reducer nodes $r \in R$, where R is the set of all
reducer nodes. Let $D_{m,r}$ be the portion of D_m destined for reducer r, and $L_{m,r}$ be
the link speed between mapper node m and reducer node r. Then, we can compute

$$T_m^{shuffle} = \max_{r \in R} \left(\frac{D_{m,r}}{L_{m,r}} \right). \tag{2}$$

The *Shuffle-aware Map* scheduling algorithm uses these T_m estimates to determine a set of *eligible mappers* to which to assign tasks. The intuition is to throttle those mappers that would have an adverse impact on the performance of the downstream reducers. The set of eligible mappers M_{Elig} is based on the most recent T_m values and a tolerance parameter β:

$$M_{Elig} = \{m \in M \,|\, T_m \leq \min_{m \in M} T_m + \beta\}, \tag{3}$$

where M is the set of all mapper nodes.

The intuition is that if the execution time for a mapper (including its shuffle time) is too high, then it should not be assigned more work at present. The value of the tolerance parameter β controls the aggressiveness of the algorithm in excluding slower mappers (in terms of their shuffle performance) from being assigned work. At one extreme, $\beta = 0$ would enforce assigning work only to the mapper with the earliest estimated finish time, intuitively achieving good load balancing, but leaving all other mappers idle for long periods of time. At the other extreme, a high value of $\beta > (\max_{m \in M} T_m - \min_{m \in M} T_m)$ would allow all mapper nodes to be eligible irrespective of their shuffle performance, and would thus reduce to the default MapReduce map scheduling. We select an intermediate value:

$$\beta = \frac{(\max_{m \in M} T_m - \min_{m \in M} T_m)}{2}. \tag{4}$$

The intuition behind this value is that it biases towards mappers with better shuffle performance. This is but one possible threshold; future research will explore other possibilities.

We note that the algorithm makes its decisions dynamically, so that over time, a mapper may become eligible or ineligible depending on the relation between its T_m value and the current value of $\min_{m \in M} T_m$. As a result, this algorithm allows a discarded mapper node to be re-included later should other nodes begin to offer worse performance. Similarly, a mapper may be throttled if its performance starts degrading over time.

4.2 Implementation in Hadoop

We have implemented this *Shuffle-aware Map* scheduling algorithm by modifying the task scheduler in Hadoop. The task scheduler now maintains a list of estimates T_m for all mapper nodes m, and updates these estimates as map tasks finish. It also uses the mapper-to-reducer node pair bandwidth information obtained by the network monitoring module to update the estimates of shuffle times from each mapper node. Every time a map task finishes, the task tracker on that node asks the task scheduler for a new map task. At that point, the scheduler uses (3) to determine the eligibility of the node to receive a new task. If the node is eligible, then it is assigned a task from the best source determined by the *Map-aware Push* algorithm described in Sect. 3. On the other hand, if the node is not eligible, then it is not assigned a task. However, it can request for work again periodically by piggybacking on heartbeat messages, when its eligibility will be checked again.

4.3   Experimental Results

We now present some results that show the benefit of *Shuffle-aware Map*. Here we run our InvertedIndex application, which takes as input a set of eBooks from Project Gutenberg [20] and produces, for each word in its input, the complete list of positions where that word can be found. This application shuffles a large volume of intermediate data, so it is an interesting application for evaluating our *Shuffle-aware Map* scheduling technique.

First, we run this application on our EC2 multi-region cloud as described in Table 1. In this environment, we use 1.8 GB of eBook data as input, and this produces about 4 GB of intermediate data to be shuffled to reducers. Figure 8 shows the runtime for a Hadoop baseline with push and map overlapped, as well as the runtime of our *Shuffle-aware Map* scheduling technique, also with push and map overlapped.

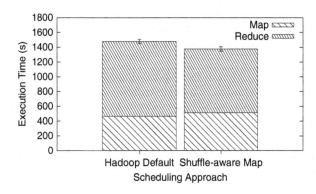

Fig. 8 Runtime of the InvertedIndex job on 1.8 GB eBook data for the default Hadoop scheduler and our *Shuffle-aware Map* scheduler—both with overlapped push and map—on EC2

The reduce time shown includes shuffle cost. Note that in *Shuffle-aware Map* the shuffle and reduce time (labeled "reduce" in the figure) are smaller than in stock Hadoop. Also observe that in *Shuffle-aware Map* the map times go up slightly—this algorithm has decided to make this tradeoff resulting in overall better performance.

On our wider-area PlanetLab setup (see Table 2) we use 800 MB of eBook data and see a similar pattern, as Fig. 9 shows. Again, an increase in map time is tolerated to reduce shuffle cost later on. This may mean that a slower mapper is given more work since it has faster links to downstream reducers. For this application, we see performance improvements of 6.8 and 9.6 % on EC2 and PlanetLab, respectively.

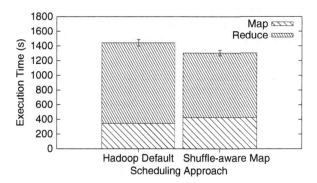

Fig. 9 Runtime of the InvertedIndex job on 800 MB eBook data for the default Hadoop scheduler and our *Shuffle-aware Map* scheduler—both with overlapped push and map—on PlanetLab

5   Putting It All Together

To determine the complete end-to-end benefit of our proposed techniques, we run experiments comparing a traditional Hadoop baseline, which uses a push-then-map approach, to an alternative that uses our proposed *Map-aware Push* and *Shuffle-aware Map* techniques. Taken together, we will refer to our techniques as the *End-to-end* approach. We carry out these experiments on the same PlanetLab and EC2 test environments introduced in Tables 1 and 2, respectively. We focus here on the InvertedIndex application from Sect. 4 as well as a new Sessionization application. This Sessionization application takes as input a set of Web server logs from the WorldCup98 trace [6], and sorts these records first by client and then by time. The sorted records for each client are then grouped into a set of "sessions" based on the gap between subsequent records. Both the InvertedIndex and Sessionization applications are relatively shuffle-heavy, representing a class of applications that can benefit from our *Shuffle-aware Map* technique.

5.1   Amazon EC2

First, we explore the combined benefit of our techniques on our EC2 test environment (see Sect. 3 for details), comprising two distributed data sources and eight worker nodes spanning two EC2 regions. Figure 10 shows results for the InvertedIndex application, where we see that our approaches reduce the total execution time by about 9.7 % over the traditional Hadoop approach. There is little difference in total push and map time, so most of this reduction in runtime comes from a faster shuffle and reduce (labeled "reduce" in the figure). This demonstrates the effectiveness of our *Shuffle-aware Map* scheduling approach, as well as the ability of our techniques to automatically determine how to tradeoff between faster push and map phases or faster shuffle and reduce phases.

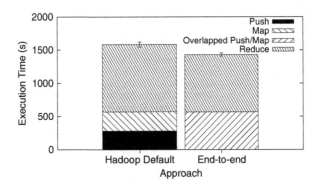

Fig. 10 Runtime of the InvertedIndex job on 1.8 GB eBook data for traditional Hadoop compared with our proposed *Map-aware Push* and *Shuffle-aware Map* techniques (together, *End-to-end*) on EC2

Now consider the Sessionization application, which has a slightly lighter shuffle and slightly heavier reduce than does the InvertedIndex application. Figure 11 shows that for this application on our EC2 environment, our approaches can reduce execution time by 8.8 %. Again most of the reduction in execution time comes from more efficient shuffle and reduce phases. Because this application has a slightly lighter shuffle than does the InvertedIndex application, we would expect a slightly smaller performance improvement, and our experiments confirm this.

5.2   PlanetLab

Now we move to the PlanetLab environment, which exhibits more extreme heterogeneity than the EC2 environment. For this environment, we consider only the InvertedIndex application, and Fig. 12 shows that our approaches can reduce execution time by about 16.4 %. Although we see a slight improvement in total push and map time using our approach, we can again attribute the majority of the performance improvement to a more efficient shuffle and reduce.

To more deeply understand how our techniques achieve this improvement, we record the number of map tasks assigned to each mapper node, as shown in Table 3. We see that both Hadoop and our techniques assign fewer map tasks to Mapper D, but that our techniques do so in a much more pronounced manner.

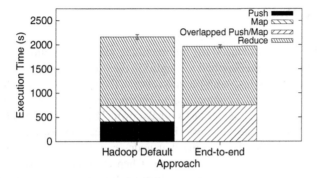

Fig. 11 Runtime of the Sessionization job on 2 GB text log data for traditional Hadoop compared with our proposed *Map-aware Push* and *Shuffle-aware Map* techniques (together, *End-to-end*) on EC2

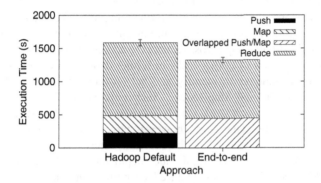

Fig. 12 Execution time for traditional Hadoop compared with our proposed *Map-aware Push* and *Shuffle-aware Map* techniques (together, *End-to-end*) for for the InvertedIndex application with 800 MB eBook data on our PlanetLab test environment

Table 3 Number of map tasks assigned to each mapper node in our PlanetLab test environment

Scheduler	Mapper A	Mapper B	Mapper C	Mapper D
Hadoop default	5	4	5	3
End-to-end	5	5	6	1

Network bandwidth measurements reveal that this node has much slower outgoing network links than do the other mapper nodes; only about 200–400 KB/s compared to about 4–9 MB/s for the other nodes (see Table 2). By scheduling three map tasks at that node, Hadoop has effectively "trapped" intermediate data there, resulting in a prolonged shuffle phase. Our *Shuffle-aware Map* technique, on the other hand, has the foresight to avoid this problem, and it does so by refusing to grant Mapper D additional tasks even when it becomes idle and requests more work.

6   Related Work

Traditionally, the MapReduce [16] programming paradigm assumes a tightly coupled homogeneous cluster applied to a uniform data-intensive application. Previous
work has shown that if this assumption is relaxed, then performance suffers. Zaharia
et al. [37] show that, under computational heterogeneity, the mechanisms built into
Hadoop for identifying straggler tasks break down. Their LATE scheduler provides
better techniques for identifying, prioritizing, and scheduling backup copies of slow
tasks. In our work, we also assume that nodes can be heterogeneous since they
belong to different data centers or locales. Chen et al. [12] report techniques for
improving the accuracy of progress estimation for tasks in MapReduce. Ahmad
et al. [4] demonstrate that despite straggler optimizations, the performance of
MapReduce frameworks on clusters with computational heterogeneity remains poor
as the load balancing used in MapReduce causes excessive and bursty network
communication and the heterogeneity further amplifies the load imbalance of
reducers. Their Tarazu system uses a communication-aware balancing mechanism
and predictive load-balancing across reducers to address these problems. Mantri [5]
explores various causes of outlier tasks in further depth, and develops cause- and
resource-aware techniques to identify and act on outliers earlier, and to greater
benefit, than in traditional MapReduce. Such improvements are complementary
to our techniques. Previous work mainly focuses on computational heterogeneity
within a single cluster. Our work, however, targets more loosely coupled and
dispersed collections of resources with bandwidth heterogeneity and constraints.

Several works have targeted MapReduce deployments in loosely coupled environments. MOON [27] explores MapReduce performance in volatile, volunteer
computing environments and extends Hadoop to improve performance under
loosely coupled networks with unreliable slave nodes. In our work, we do not focus
on solving reliability issues; instead we are concerned with performance issues of
allocating compute resources to MapReduce jobs and relocating source data. Costa
et al. [15] propose MapReduce in a global wide-area volunteer setting. However,
this system is implemented in the BOINC framework with all input data held by the
central scheduler. In our system, we have no such restrictions. Luo et al. [28] propose
a multi-cluster MapReduce deployment, but they focus on more compute-intensive
jobs that may require resources in multiple clusters for greater compute power. In
contrast, we consider multi-site resources not only for their compute power, but also
for their locality to data sources.

Other papers have addressed MapReduce data flow optimization and locality.
Gadre et al. [17] optimize the reduce data placement according to map output
locations, which might still end up trapping data in nodes with slow outward links.
Kim et al. [26] present a similar idea of shuffle-aware scheduling, but do not
consider widely distributed data sources that are not co-located with computation
clusters. Their ICMR algorithm could make use of our mechanisms to improve
the performance of MapReduce under such environments. Pipelining MapReduce
has been proposed in MapReduce Online [13] to modify the Hadoop workflow

for improved responsiveness and performance. It assumes, however, that input data are located with the computation resources, and it does not address the issue of pipelining push and map. MapReduce Online would be a complementary optimization to our techniques since it enables the shuffling of intermediate data without storing it to disk. Our mechanisms could be used to decide where data should flow and their technique could be used to optimize the transfer. Similarly, Verma et al. [36] discuss the specific challenges associated with pipelining the shuffle and reduce stages. Our *Map-aware Push* technique could also be applied to pipeline shuffle and reduce, though we have not yet done so. The Purlieus system [31] considers MapReduce in a single cloud, but is unique in that it focuses on locality in the shuffle phase. It emphasizes the coupling between the placement of tasks (in their case virtual machines) and data. However, these works do not provide an end-to-end overall improvement of the MapReduce data flow.

Other work has focused on fine-tuning MapReduce parameters or offering scheduling optimizations to provide better performance. Sandholm et al. [33] present a dynamic prioritization system for improved MapReduce runtime in the context of multiple jobs. Our work is concerned with optimizing a single job relative to data source and compute resource locations. Babu [8] proposes algorithms for automatically fine-tuning MapReduce parameters to optimize job performance. Starfish [24] proposes a self-tuning architecture which monitors runtime performance of Hadoop and tunes the configuration parameters accordingly. Such work is complementary to ours, however, as we focus on mechanisms to directly change task and data placement rather than tune configuration parameters.

Finally, work in wide-area data transfer and dissemination includes GridFTP [19] and BitTorrent [10]. GridFTP is a protocol for high-performance data transfer over high-bandwidth wide-area networks, and BitTorrent is a peer-to-peer file sharing protocol for wide-area distributed systems. These protocols could act as middleware services to further reduce data transfer costs and make wide-area data more accessible to wide-area compute resources.

Conclusion and Future Work

Many emerging data-intensive applications are widely distributed, either due to the distribution and collection of datasets, or by the provision of multi-site resources such as multiple geographically separated data centers. We show that in such heterogeneous environments, MapReduce/Hadoop performance suffers, as the impact of one phase upon another can severely impact performance along bottleneck links. We show that Hadoop's default data placement and scheduling mechanisms do not take such cross-phase interactions into account, and while they may try to optimize individual phases, they can result in globally bad decisions, resulting in poor overall performance. To overcome these limitations, we first use an oracle—a model-driven optimiza-

(continued)

tion framework—to derive high-level insights. For example, we show that application characteristics can significantly influence the optimal data and computation placement, and that optimizing across both the push and shuffle phases yields the best performance. Applying these insights, we propose techniques to implement cross-phase optimization in a real-world MapReduce system. The key idea behind our proposed techniques is to consider not only the execution cost of an individual task or computational phase, but also its impact on the performance of subsequent phases. We propose two sets of techniques. *Map-aware Push* enables push-map overlap to hide latency and enable dynamic feedback between the map and push phases. Such feedback enables nodes with higher speeds and faster links to process more data at runtime. *Shuffle-aware Map* enables a shuffle-aware scheduler to feed back the cost of a downstream shuffle into the map process and affect the map phase. Mappers with poor outgoing links to reducers are throttled, eliminating the impact of mapper–reducer bottleneck links. For a range of heterogeneous environments (multi-region Amazon EC2 and PlanetLab) and diverse data-intensive applications (WordCount, InvertedIndex, and Sessionization) we show the performance potential of our techniques, as runtime is reduced by 7–18 % depending on the execution environment and application.

Acknowledgements The authors would like to acknowledge Professor Ramesh Sitaraman (ramesh@cs.umass.edu) for his contributions to our model-driven optimization approach (Sect. 2), as well as Chenyu Wang (chwang@cs.umn.edu) for his contributions to the cross-phase optimization techniques. They would further like to acknowledge NSF Grants IIS-0916425 and CNS-0643505, which supported this research.

References

1. Cloudera impala. Http://www.cloudera.com/impala
2. Scalding. Http://github.com/twitter/scalding
3. A conversation with Jim Gray. Queue **1**(4), 8–17 (2003). DOI 10.1145/864056.864078. URL http://doi.acm.org/10.1145/864056.864078
4. Ahmad, F., Chakradhar, S., Raghunathan, A., Vijaykumar, T.N.: Tarazu: Optimizing MapReduce on heterogeneous clusters. In: Proceedings of ASPLOS, pp. 61–74 (2012)
5. Ananthanarayanan, G., Kandula, S., Greenberg, A., Stoica, I., Lu, Y., Saha, B.: Reining in the outliers in map-reduce clusters using mantri. In: Proceedings of OSDI, pp. 265–278 (2010)
6. Arlitt, M., Jin, T.: Workload characterization of the 1998 World Cup Web Site. Tech. Rep. HPL-1999-35R1, HP Labs (1999)
7. Armbrust, M., Fox, A., Griffith, R., Joseph, A.D., Katz, R.H., Konwinsky, A., Lee, G., Patterson, D.A., Rabkin, A., Stoica, I., Zaharia, M.: Above the clouds: A Berkeley view of cloud computing. Tech. Rep. UCB/EECS-2009-28, Electrical Engineering and Computer Sciences, University of California at Berkeley (2009)
8. Babu, S.: Towards automatic optimization of MapReduce programs. In: Proceedings of ACM SoCC, pp. 137–142 (2010)

9. Baker, J., et al.: Megastore: Providing scalable, highly available storage for interactive services. In: Proceedings of CIDR, pp. 223–234 (2011)
10. BitTorrent. Http://www.bittorrent.com
11. Cardosa, M., Wang, C., Nangia, A., Chandra, A., Weissman, J.: Exploring MapReduce efficiency with highly-distributed data. In: Proceedings of MapReduce, pp. 27–33 (2011)
12. Chen, Q., Zhang, D., Guo, M., Deng, Q., Guo, S., Guo, S.: SAMR: A self-adaptive MapReduce scheduling algorithm in heterogeneous environment. In: Proceedings of IEEE CIT, pp. 2736–2743 (2010)
13. Condie, T., Conway, N., Alvaro, P., Hellerstein, J.M., Elmeleegy, K., Sears, R.: MapReduce online. In: Proceedings of NSDI, pp. 313–327 (2010)
14. Corbett, J.C., et al.: Spanner: Google's globally-distributed database. In: Proceedings of OSDI, pp. 251–264 (2012)
15. Costa, F., Silva, L., Dahlin, M.: Volunteer cloud computing: MapReduce over the internet. In: Proceedings of IEEE IPDPSW, pp. 1855–1862 (2011)
16. Dean, J., Ghemawat, S.: MapReduce: Simplified data processing on large clusters. In: Proceedings of OSDI, pp. 137–150 (2004)
17. Gadre, H., Rodero, I., Parashar, M.: Investigating MapReduce framework extensions for efficient processing of geographically scattered datasets. In: Proceedings of ACM SIGMETRICS, pp. 116–118 (2011)
18. Gates, A.F., Natkovich, O., Chopra, S., Kamath, P., Narayanamurthy, S.M., Olston, C., Reed, B., Srinivasan, S., Srivastava, U.: Building a high-level dataflow system on top of map-reduce: the pig experience. Proceedings of the VLDB Endowment 2(2), 1414–1425 (2009). URL http://dl.acm.org/citation.cfm?id=1687553.1687568
19. GridFTP. Http://globus.org/toolkit/docs/3.2/gridftp/
20. Free eBooks by Project Gutenberg. http://www.gutenberg.org/
21. Hadoop. http://hadoop.apache.org
22. Heintz, B., Chandra, A., Sitaraman, R.K.: Optimizing MapReduce for highly distributed environments. Tech. Rep. TR 12-003, Department of Computer Science and Engineering, University of Minnesota (2012)
23. Heintz, B., Wang, C., Chandra, A., Weissman, J.: Cross-phase optimization in MapReduce. In: IEEE International Conference on Cloud Engineering (IC2E), pp. 338–347 (2013)
24. Herodotou, H., Lim, H., Luo, G., Borisov, N., Dong, L., Cetin, F.B., Babu, S.: Starfish: A self-tuning system for big data analytics. In: Proceedings of CIDR, pp. 261–272 (2011)
25. Hey, T., Tansley, S., Tolle, K. (eds.): The Fourth Paradigm: Data-Intensive Scientific Discovery. Microsoft Research, Redmond, Washington (2009). URL http://research.microsoft.com/en-us/collaboration/fourthparadigm/
26. Kim, S., Won, J., Han, H., Eom, H., Yeom, H.Y.: Improving Hadoop performance in intercloud environments. Proceedings of ACM SIGMETRICS 39(3), 107–109 (2011)
27. Lin, H., Ma, X., Archuleta, J., Feng, W.c., Gardner, M., Zhang, Z.: MOON: MapReduce on opportunistic environments. In: Proceedings of ACM HPDC, pp. 95–106 (2010)
28. Luo, Y., Guo, Z., Sun, Y., Plale, B., Qiu, J., Li, W.W.: A hierarchical framework for cross-domain MapReduce execution. In: Proceedings of ECMLS, pp. 15–22 (2011)
29. Hadoop. http://mahout.apache.org
30. Nygren, E., Sitaraman, R., Sun, J.: The Akamai network: A platform for high-performance internet applications. ACM SIGOPS Oper. Syst. Rev. 44(3), 2–19 (2010)
31. Palanisamy, B., Singh, A., Liu, L., Jain, B.: Purlieus: locality-aware resource allocation for MapReduce in a cloud. In: Proceedings of SC, pp. 58:1–58:11 (2011)
32. Rabkin, A., Arye, M., Sen, S., Pai, V., Freedman, M.J.: Making every bit count in wide-area analytics. In: Proceedings of the 14th Workshop on Hot Topics in Operating Systems (2013)
33. Sandholm, T., Lai, K.: MapReduce optimization using dynamic regulated prioritization. In: Proceedings of ACM SIGMETRICS, pp. 299–310 (2009)
34. Satyanarayanan, M., Bahl, P., Caceres, R., Davies, N.: The case for VM-based cloudlets in mobile computing. IEEE Pervasive Computing 8, 14–23 (2009)

35. Thusoo, A., Sarma, J.S., Jain, N., Shao, Z., Chakka, P., Anthony, S., Liu, H., Wyckoff, P., Murthy, R.: Hive: a warehousing solution over a map-reduce framework. Proceedings of the VLDB Endowment **2**, 1626–1629 (2009)
36. Verma, A., Zea, N., Cho, B., Gupta, I., Campbell, R.H.: Breaking the MapReduce stage barrier. In: Proceedings of IEEE Cluster, pp. 235–244 (2010)
37. Zaharia, M., Konwinski, A., Joseph, A.D., Katz, R.H., Stoica, I.: Improving MapReduce performance in heterogeneous environments. In: Proceedings of OSDI, pp. 29–42 (2008)

Asynchronous Computation Model for Large-Scale Iterative Computations

Yanfeng Zhang, Qixin Gao, Lixin Gao, and Cuirong Wang

Abstract Iterative algorithms are widely existed in machine learning and data mining applications. These algorithms have to be implemented in a large-scale distributed environment in order to scale to massive data sets. While *synchronous* iterations might result in unexpected poor performance due to some particular stragglers in a heterogeneous distributed environment, especially in a cloud environment. To bypass the synchronization barriers in iterative computations, this chapter introduces an *asynchronous* iteration model, *delta-based accumulative iterative computation* (DAIC). Different from traditional iterative computations, which iteratively update the result based on the result from the previous iteration, DAIC asynchronously updates the result by accumulating the "changes" between iterations. This chapter presents a general asynchronous computation model to describe DAIC and introduces a distributed framework for asynchronous iteration, Maiter. The experimental results show that Maiter outperforms many other state-of-the-art frameworks.

1 Asynchronous Iteration

The advances in data acquisition, storage, and networking technology have created huge collections of high-volume, high-dimensional data. Making sense of these data is critical for companies and organizations to make better business decisions and even bring convenience to our daily life. Recent advances in data mining, machine learning, and applied statistics have led to a flurry of data analytic techniques that

Y. Zhang (✉)
Northeastern University, Lane 3, No. 11, Wenhua Road, Shenyang, Liaoning 110819, China
e-mail: zhangyf@cc.neu.edu.cn

Q. Gao • C. Wang
Northeastern University at Qinhuangdao, 143 Taishan Road, Qinhuangdao,
Hebei 066004, China
e-mail: gaoqx@mail.neuq.edu.cn; wangcr@mail.neuq.edu.cn

L. Gao
University of Massachusetts Amherst, 151 Holdsworth Way, Amherst, MA 01003, USA
e-mail: lgao@ecs.umass.edu

© Springer Science+Business Media New York 2014   303
X. Li, J. Qiu (eds.), *Cloud Computing for Data-Intensive Applications*,
DOI 10.1007/978-1-4939-1905-5_13

typically require an iterative refinement process [1, 4, 17, 26]. These algorithms are referred to as iterative algorithms.

Iterative algorithms typically perform the same operations on a data set for several iterations. In iteration k, an update function F^k is utilized to update the data set v.

$$v^k = F^k(v^{k-1}), \tag{1}$$

where the data set v contains n elements, i.e., $v = \{v_1, v_2, \ldots, v_n\}$, where v^k represents the kth iteration's result.

The update function F^k could be consistent across all iterations or be different in different iterations. For example, in the PageRank computation [5], the update function is shown as follows:

$$R = dWR + (1 - d)E, \tag{2}$$

where R is the ranking score vector, d is a damping factor, W is a square matrix that represents the web linkage graph, E is a vector denoting the page preference. The update function in PageRank is the same for all iterations. On the other hand, the update function F^k could be different in different iterations. For example, Non-Negative Matrix Factorization (NMF) [16] aims to find an approximate factorization $V \approx WH$, where V is the given non-negative matrix, W and H are two resulted non-negative matrices. NMF iteratively updates H and W as follows:

$$
\begin{cases}
H^k = H^{k-1} \cdot \dfrac{(W^{k-1})^T V}{(W^{k-1})^T W^{k-1} H^{k-1}} & k = 1, 3, 5, \ldots \\
W^k = W^{k-1}
\end{cases}
$$

$$
\begin{cases}
H^k = H^{k-1} & \\
W^k = W^{k-1} \cdot \dfrac{V(H^k)^T}{W^{k-1} H^k (H^k)^T} & k = 2, 4, 6, \ldots
\end{cases} \tag{3}
$$

H combining with W can be seen as a unique iterated data set v. Therefore, the update function in odd iterations and the update function in even iterations are different.

Based on Eq. (1), we can further represent $F(v^k)$ by a set of functions of the form $f_j^k(v_1, v_2, \ldots, v_n)$, each of which performs the update on an element j. That is,

$$v_j^k = f_j^k(v_1^{k-1}, v_2^{k-1}, \ldots, v_n^{k-1}). \tag{4}$$

In distributed computing, multiple processers perform the updates in parallel. For simplicity of exposition, we assume that there are n processors and processor j performs an update for data element j (we will generalize this model in Sect. 2.5). *Synchronous iteration* requires that all processors perform the update in lock steps.

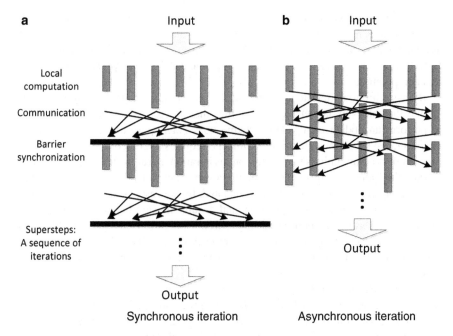

Fig. 1 Synchronous iteration vs. asynchronous iteration

At step k, processor j first collects v_i^{k-1} from all processors, followed by performing the update function f_j based on v_i^{k-1}, $i = 1, 2, \ldots, n$. The main drawback of implementing synchronous iteration in a distributed fashion is that all the update operations in the $(k-1)^{th}$ iteration have to be completed before any of the update operations in the kth iteration starts. Clearly, synchronization is required in each step. These synchronizations might degrade performance, especially in heterogeneous distributed environments.

To avoid the synchronization barriers, *asynchronous iteration* was proposed [8]. Performing update operations asynchronously means that processor j performs the update

$$v_j = f_j(v_1, v_2, \ldots, v_n) \qquad (5)$$

at any time based on the most recent values of all data elements, $\{v_1, v_2, \ldots, v_n\}$. The convergence properties of asynchronous iterations have been studied in [2,3,8].

Figure 1 shows the intuitive difference between synchronous iteration and asynchronous iteration in distributed computing. The computation workload is distributed to processors. The length of the vertical bars denotes the computation time. Since different processors might have different performance and the workload might be distributed unevenly, the processors might have different computation time on their assigned data. Each processor completes its local computation and then starts communication with other processors. In synchronous iteration, there is a synchronization barrier in each iteration. While in asynchronous iteration, each processor does not wait for the other processors and performs computation on its assigned data as much as it can. No idle time exists in asynchronous iteration. The faster processors perform more computations, and the slower processors perform less computations.

By asynchronous iteration, as processor j is activated to perform an update, it "pulls" the values of data elements from the other processors, and uses these values to perform an update on v_j. This scheme does not require any synchronization. However, asynchronous iteration intuitively requires more communications and more useless computations than synchronous iteration. An activated processor needs to pull the values from all the other processors, but not all of them have been updated, or even worse none of them is updated. In that case, asynchronous iteration performs a meaningless computation and results in significant communication overhead. Accordingly, "pull-based" asynchronous iteration is only applicable in an environment where the communication overhead is negligible, such as shared memory systems. In a distributed environment or in a cloud, "pull-based" asynchronous model cannot be efficiently utilized.

As an alternative, after processor i updates v_i, it "pushes" v_i to every other processor j, and v_i is buffered as $B_{i,j}$ on processor j. When processor j is activated, it uses the buffered values $B_{i,j}$, $i = 1, 2, \ldots, n$, to update v_j. In this way, the redundant communications can be avoided. However, the "push-based" asynchronous iteration results in considerable memory overhead. Each processor has to buffer n values, and the system totally needs $O(n^2)$ space.

This chapter will introduce a novel iterative computation model, which can be executed asynchronously while reducing memory consumption.

2 Delta-Based Accumulative Iterative Computation (DAIC)

In this section, we present *delta-based accumulative iterative computation*, DAIC. By DAIC, the iterative algorithms can be executed asynchronously and more efficiently.

2.1 DAIC Introduction

We first give the following 2-step update function of DAIC:

$$
\begin{cases}
v_j^k = v_j^{k-1} \oplus \Delta v_j^k, \\
\Delta v_j^{k+1} = \sum_{i=1}^{n} \oplus g_{\{i,j\}}(\Delta v_i^k).
\end{cases}
\tag{6}
$$

$k = 1, 2, \ldots$ is the iteration number. v_j^k is the state of vertex j after k iterations. Δv_j^k denotes the change from v_j^{k-1} to v_j^k in the '$\oplus$' operation manner, where '$\oplus$' is an abstract operator. $\sum_{i=1}^{n} \oplus x_i = x_1 \oplus x_2 \oplus \ldots \oplus x_n$ represents the accumulation of the "changes".

The first update function says that a vertex state v_j^k is updated from v_j^{k-1} by accumulating the change (i.e., Δv_j^k). The second update function says that the change Δv_j^{k+1}, which will be used in the next iteration, is the accumulation of the received values $g_{\{i,j\}}(\Delta v_i^k)$ from j's various in-neighbors i. The propagated value from i to j, $g_{\{i,j\}}(\Delta v_i^k))$, is generated in terms of vertex i's state change Δv_i^k. Note that, all the accumulative operation is in the '$\oplus$' operation manner.

However, not all iterative computation can be converted to the DAIC form. To write a DAIC, the update function should satisfy four sufficient conditions.

The **first condition** is that,

- update function $v_j^k = f(v_1^{k-1}, v_2^{k-1}, \ldots, v_n^{k-1})$ can be written in the form:

$$v_j^k = g_{\{1,j\}}(v_1^{k-1}) \oplus g_{\{2,j\}}(v_2^{k-1}) \oplus \ldots \oplus g_{\{n,j\}}(v_n^{k-1}) \oplus c_j \qquad (7)$$

where $k = 1, 2, \ldots$ is the iteration number, c_j is a constant, '$\oplus$' is an abstract operator, and $g_{\{i,j\}}(v_i)$ is a function applied on vertex j's in-neighbor i, which denotes the value passed from vertex i to vertex j. In other words, vertex i passes value $g_{\{i,j\}}(v_i)$ (instead of v_i) to vertex j. On vertex j, these $g_{\{i,j\}}(v_i)$ from various vertices i and c_j are aggregated (by '$\oplus$' operation) to update v_j.

For example, the well-known PageRank algorithm satisfies this condition. It iteratively updates the PageRank scores of all pages. In each iteration, the ranking score of page j, R_j, is updated as follows:

$$R_j^k = d \cdot \sum_{\{i|(i \to j) \in E\}} \frac{R_i^{k-1}}{|N(i)|} + (1 - d), \qquad (8)$$

where d is a damping factor, $|N(i)|$ is the number of outbound links of page i, $(i \to j)$ is a link from page i to page j, and E is the set of directed links. The update function of PageRank is in the form of Eq. (7), where $c_j = 1 - d$, '$\oplus$' is '+', and for any page i that has a link to page j, $g_{\{i,j\}}(v_i^{k-1}) = d \cdot \frac{v_i^{k-1}}{|N(i)|}$.

Next, since Δv_j^k is defined to denote the "change" from v_j^{k-1} to v_j^k in the '$\oplus$' operation manner. That is,

$$v_j^k = v_j^{k-1} \oplus \Delta v_j^k, \qquad (9)$$

In order to derive Δv_j^k we pose the **second condition**:

- function $g_{\{i,j\}}(x)$ should have the *distributive property* over '$\oplus$', i.e., $g_{\{i,j\}}(x \oplus y) = g_{\{i,j\}}(x) \oplus g_{\{i,j\}}(y)$.

By replacing v_i^{k-1} in Eq. (7) with $v_i^{k-2} \oplus \Delta v_i^{k-1}$, we have

$$
\begin{aligned}
v_j^k = & g_{\{1,j\}}(v_1^{k-2}) \oplus g_{\{1,j\}}(\Delta v_1^{k-1}) \oplus \ldots \oplus \\
& g_{\{n,j\}}(v_n^{k-2}) \oplus g_{\{n,j\}}(\Delta v_n^{k-1}) \oplus c_j.
\end{aligned}
\tag{10}
$$

Further, let us pose the **third condition**:

- operator '$\oplus$' should have the *commutative property*, i.e., $x \oplus y = y \oplus x$;
- operator '$\oplus$' should have the *associative property*, i.e., $(x \oplus y) \oplus z = x \oplus (y \oplus z)$;

Then we can combine these $g_{\{i,j\}}(v_i^{k-2})$, $i = 1, 2, \ldots, n$, and c_j in Eq. (10) to obtain v_j^{k-1}. Considering Eq. (9), the combination of the remaining $g_{\{i,j\}}(\Delta v_i^{k-1})$, $i = 1, 2, \ldots, n$ in Eq. (10), which is $\sum_{i=1}^{n} \oplus g_{\{i,j\}}(\Delta v_i^{k-1})$, will result in Δv_i^k. Then, we have the 2-step DAIC as shown in (6).

To initialize a DAIC, we should set the start values of v_j^0 and Δv_j^1. v_j^0 and Δv_j^1 can be initialized to be any value, but the initialization should satisfy $v_j^1 = v_j^0 \oplus \Delta v_j^1$, which is the **fourth condition**.

The PageRank's update function as shown in Eq. (8) satisfies all the conditions. $g_{\{i,j\}}(v_i^{k-1}) = d \cdot \frac{v_i^{k-1}}{|N(i)|}$, which has distributive property and satisfies the second condition. '$\oplus$' is '+', which satisfies the third condition. In order to satisfy the fourth condition, v_j^0 can be initialized to 0, and Δv_j^1 can be initialized to $c_j = 1 - d$.

To sum up, DAIC can be described as follows. Vertex j first updates v_j^k by accumulating Δv_j^k (by '$\oplus$' operation) and then updates Δv_j^{k+1} with $\sum_{i=1}^{n} \oplus g_{\{i,j\}}(\Delta v_i^k)$. We refer to Δv_j as the *delta value* of vertex j and $g_{\{i,j\}}(\Delta v_i^k)$ as the *delta message* sent from i to j. $\sum_{i=1}^{n} \oplus g_{\{i,j\}}(\Delta v_i^k)$ is the accumulation of the received delta messages on vertex j since the kth update. Then, the delta value Δv_j^{k+1} will be used for the $(k + 1)^{\text{th}}$ update. Apparently, this still requires all vertices to start the update synchronously when all the vertices have received these delta messages. That is, Δv_j^{k+1} has to accumulate all the delta messages $g_{\{i,j\}}(\Delta v_i^k)$ sent from j's in-neighbors, at which time it is ready to be used in the $(k + 1)^{\text{th}}$ iteration. Therefore, we refer to the 2-step iterative computation in (6) as **synchronous DAIC**.

2.2 Asynchronous DAIC

DAIC can be performed asynchronously. That is, a vertex can start update at any time based on whatever it has already received. We can describe **asynchronous DAIC** as follows, on each vertex j, there are two operations:

$$
\text{receive:} \begin{cases} \text{Whenever receiving } m_j, \\[2mm] \Delta\check{v}_j \leftarrow \Delta\check{v}_j \oplus m_j. \end{cases}
$$

$$
\text{update:} \begin{cases} \check{v}_j \leftarrow \check{v}_j \oplus \Delta\check{v}_j; \\[2mm] \text{For any } h, \text{ if } g_{\{j,h\}}(\Delta\check{v}_j) \neq \mathbf{0}, \\[2mm] \quad \text{send value } g_{\{j,h\}}(\Delta\check{v}_j) \text{ to } h; \\[2mm] \Delta\check{v}_j \leftarrow \mathbf{0}, \end{cases} \tag{11}
$$

where m_j is the received delta message $g_{\{i,j\}}(\Delta\check{v}_i)$ sent from any in-neighbor i. The *receive* operation accumulates the received delta message m_j to $\Delta\check{v}_j$. $\Delta\check{v}_j$ accumulates the received delta messages between two consecutive update operations. The *update* operation updates $\check{v}_j$ by accumulating $\Delta\check{v}_j$, sends the delta message $g_{\{j,h\}}(\Delta\check{v}_j)$ to any of j's out-neighbors h, and resets $\Delta\check{v}_j$ to $\mathbf{0}$. Here, operator '$\oplus$' should have the *identity property* of abstract value $\mathbf{0}$, i.e., $x \oplus \mathbf{0} = x$, so that resetting $\Delta\check{v}_j$ to $\mathbf{0}$ means that the received value is cleared. Additionally, to avoid useless communication, it is also necessary to check that the sent delta message $g_{\{j,h\}}(\Delta\check{v}_j) \neq \mathbf{0}$ before sending.

For example, in PageRank, each page j has a buffer ΔR_j to accumulate the received delta PageRank scores. When page j performs an update, R_j is updated by accumulating ΔR_j. Then, the delta message $d \frac{\Delta R_j}{|N(j)|}$ is sent to page j's linked pages, and ΔR_j is reset to 0.

By asynchronous DAIC, the two operations on a vertex, receive and update, are completely independent from those on other vertices. Any vertex is allowed to perform the operations at any time. There is no lock step to synchronize any operation between vertices.

2.3 Convergence

To study the convergence property, we first give the following definition of the convergence of asynchronous DAIC.

Convergence   Asynchronous DAIC as shown in (11) converges as long as that after each element has performed the receive and update operations an infinite number of times, $\check{v}_j^\infty$ converges to a fixed value $\check{v}_j^*$.

Then, we have the following theorem to guarantee that asynchronous DAIC will converge to the same fixed point as synchronous DAIC. Further, since synchronous DAIC is derived from the traditional form of iterative computation, i.e., Eq. (4), the asynchronous DAIC will converge to the same fixed point as traditional iterative computation.

Theorem 1. *If v_j in (4) converges, $\check{v}_j$ in (11) converges. Further, they converge to the same value, i.e., $v_j^\infty = \check{v}_j^\infty = \check{v}_j^*$.*

The formal proof of Theorem 1 can be found in [33]. We explain the intuition behind Theorem 1 as follows. Consider the process of DAIC as information propagation in a graph. Element i with an initial value c_i propagates delta message $g_{\{i,j\}}(c_i)$ to its out-neighbor j, where $g_{\{i,j\}}(c_i)$ is accumulated to v_j and a new delta message $g_{\{j,h\}}(g_{\{i,j\}}(c_i))$ is produced and propagated to any of j's out-neighbors h. By synchronous DAIC, the delta messages propagated from all vertices should be received by all their neighbors before starting the next round propagation. That is, the delta messages originated from an element are propagated strictly hop by hop. In contrast, by asynchronous DAIC, whenever some delta messages arrive, an element accumulates them to $\check{v}_j$ and propagates the newly produced delta messages to its neighbors. No matter synchronously or asynchronously, the spread delta messages are never lost, and the delta messages originated from each element will be eventually spread along all paths. For a destination node, it will eventually collect the delta messages originated from all vertices along various propagating paths. All these delta messages are eventually received and contributed to any v_j. Therefore, synchronous DAIC and asynchronous DAIC will converge to the same result.

2.4 Effectiveness

As illustrated above, v_j and $\check{v}_j$ both converge to the same fixed point. By accumulating Δv_j (or $\Delta \check{v}_j$), v_j (or $\check{v}_j$) either monotonically increases or monotonically decreases to a fixed value $v_j^* = v_j^\infty = \check{v}_j^\infty$. In this section, we show that $\check{v}_j$ converges faster than v_j.

To simplify the analysis, we first assume that the DAIC is performed in a single processor environment. That is, we perform the element update serially, and the transmission delay is ignored. The delta message sent from element i, i.e., $g_{\{i,j\}}(\Delta v_i)$ (or $g_{\{i,j\}}(\Delta \check{v}_i)$), is directly accumulated to Δv_j (or $\Delta \check{v}_j$). Then, the workload can be seen as the number of performed updates. Let *update sequence* represent the update order of the vertices. By synchronous DAIC, all the vertices have to perform the update once and only once before starting the next round of updates. Hence, the update sequence is composed of a series of *subsequences*. The length of each subsequence is $|V|$, i.e., the number of vertices. Each element occurs in a subsequence once and only once. We call this particular update sequence as *synchronous update sequence*. While in asynchronous DAIC, the update sequence can follow any update order. For comparison, we will use the same synchronous update sequence for asynchronous DAIC.

By DAIC, no matter synchronously and asynchronously, the propagated delta messages of an update on element i in subsequence k, i.e., $g_{\{i,j\}}(\Delta v_i^k)$ (or $g_{\{i,j\}}(\Delta \check{v}_i)$), are directly accumulated to Δv_j^{k+1} (or $\Delta \check{v}_j$), $j = 1, 2, \ldots, n$. By synchronous DAIC, Δv_j^{k+1} cannot be accumulated to v_j until the update of element j in subsequence $k + 1$. In contrast, by asynchronous DAIC, $\Delta \check{v}_j$ is accumulated to $\check{v}_j$ immediately whenever element j is updated after the update of element i in subsequence k. The update of element j might occur in subsequence k or in subsequence $k + 1$. If the update of element j occurs in subsequence k, $\check{v}_j$ will accumulate more delta messages than v_j after k subsequences, which means that $\check{v}_j$ is closer to v_j^* than v_j. Otherwise, $\check{v}_j = v_j$. Therefore, we have Theorem 2. The formal proof of Theorem 2 can be found in [33].

Theorem 2. *Based on the same update sequence, after k subsequences, we have $\check{v}_j$ by synchronous DAIC and v_j by asynchronous DAIC. $\check{v}_j$ is closer to the fixed point v_j^* than v_j is, i.e., $|v_j^* - \check{v}_j| \le |v_j^* - v_j|$.*

In a distributed environment, the data elements are distributed to multiple processors. Each processor performs the update for a subset of elements. (The single processor environment is an extreme case, which requires processing all the elements). By synchronous DAIC, the high-cost synchronization barriers in distributed environment will even degrade the performance. Therefore, in a distributed environment, asynchronous DAIC should perform even better than synchronous DAIC.

2.5 Scheduling in Asynchronous DAIC

By asynchronous DAIC, we should control the update order of the elements, i.e., specifying the scheduling policies. In reality, a subset of elements are assigned to a processor, and multiple processors are running in parallel. The processor can perform the update for the assigned elements in a round-robin manner, which is referred to as *round-robin scheduling*. Moreover, it is possible to schedule the update of these local elements dynamically by identifying their importance, which is referred to as *priority scheduling*. It has been found that selectively processing a subset of the elements has the potential of accelerating iterative computation [31]. Some of the elements can play an important decisive role in determining the final converged outcome. Giving an update execution priority to these elements can accelerate the convergence.

In order to show the progress of the iterative computation, we quantify the iteration progress with L_1 norm of $\check{v}$, i.e., $||\check{v}||_1 = \sum_i \check{v}_i$. Asynchronous DAIC either monotonically increases or monotonically decreases $||\check{v}||_1$ to a fixed point $||v^*||_1$. According to (11), an update of element j, i.e., $\check{v}_j = \check{v}_j \oplus \Delta \check{v}_j$, either increases $||\check{v}||_1$ by $(\check{v}_j \oplus \Delta \check{v}_j - \check{v}_j)$ or decreases $||\check{v}||_1$ by $(\check{v}_j - \check{v}_j \oplus \Delta \check{v}_j)$. Therefore, by priority scheduling, element $j = arg \max_j |\check{v}_j \oplus \Delta \check{v}_j - \check{v}_j|$ is scheduled first. In other words, The bigger $|\check{v}_j \oplus \Delta \check{v}_j - \check{v}_j|$ is, the higher update priority element j has. For example, in PageRank, we set each page j's scheduling priority based on $|R_j + \Delta R_j - R_j| = \Delta R_j$. Then, we will schedule page j with the largest ΔR_j first. To sum up, by priority scheduling, the element $j = arg \max_j |\check{v}_j \oplus \Delta \check{v}_j - \check{v}_j|$ is scheduled for update first.

Theorem 3 guarantees the convergence of asynchronous DAIC under the priority scheduling. The proof of Theorem 3 can be found in [33]. Furthermore, according to the analysis presented above, we have Theorem 4 to support the effectiveness of priority scheduling.

Theorem 3. *By priority scheduling, $\check{v}'_j$ in (11) converges to the same fixed point v^*_j as v_j in (6) converges to, i.e., $\check{v}'^{\infty}_j = v^{\infty}_j = v^*_j$.*

Theorem 4. *Based on asynchronous DAIC, after the same number of updates, we have $\check{v}'_j$ by priority scheduling and $\check{v}_j$ by round-robin scheduling. $\check{v}'_j$ is closer to the fixed point v^*_j than $\check{v}_j$ is, i.e., $|v^*_j - \check{v}'_j| \leq |v^*_j - v_j|$.*

3   Write Asynchronous DAIC Algorithms

In this section, we provide the guidelines of writing DAIC algorithms and show a series of examples. For those algorithms that cannot be directly converted to DAIC form, we also give examples on how to convert the algorithm to satisfy DAIC conditions.

3.1   Guidelines

Given an iterative algorithm, the following steps are recommended for converting it to a DAIC algorithm.

- **Step 1: Formation Check**. Check whether f is in the form of Eq. (7)? If not, the algorithm cannot be converted to a DAIC algorithm. If yes, identify the sender-based function $g_{\{i,j\}}(v_i)$ applied on sender vertex i, the abstract operator '$\oplus$' for accumulating the received delta messages on receiver vertex j, and the constant c_j on each vertex j.
- **Step 2: Properties Check**. Check whether $g_{\{i,j\}}(v_i)$ has the distributive property and whether operator '$\oplus$' has the commutative property, the associative property? If not, the algorithm cannot be converted to a DAIC algorithm.
- **Step 3: Initialization**. According to (6), initialize v^0_j and Δv^1_j to satisfy $v^1_j = v^0_j \oplus \Delta v^1_j$, and write the iterative computation in the 2-step DAIC form.
- **Step 4: Priority Assignment** (Optional). Specify the scheduling priority of each vertex j as $|\check{v}_j \oplus \Delta \check{v}_j - \check{v}_j|$ for scheduling the asynchronous updates.

To support implementing a DAIC algorithm in a large-scale distributed manner and in a highly efficient asynchronous manner, we propose a distributed framework. Users only need to follow the guidelines to specify the function $g_{\{i,j\}}(v_i)$, the abstract operator '$\oplus$', and the initial values v^0_j and Δv^1_j. The framework will automatically deploy the DAIC application in a distributed environment and perform asynchronous iteration efficiently. Before presenting the framework, we first show a broad class of DAIC algorithms.

3.2 Examples

Besides the PageRank algorithm, there are many graph algorithms can be written in DAIC model.

3.2.1 Single Source Shortest Path

The *single source shortest path* algorithm (SSSP) has been widely used in online social networks and web mapping. Given a source node s, the algorithm derives the shortest distance from s to all the other nodes on a directed weighted graph. Initially, each node j's distance d_j^0 is initialized to be ∞ except that the source s's distance d_s^0 is initialized to be 0. In each iteration, the shortest distance from s to j, d_j, is updated with the following update function:

$$d_j^k = \min\{d_1^{k-1} + w(1, j), d_2^{k-1} + w(2, j), \ldots, d_n^{k-1} + w(n, j), d_j^0\}, \quad (12)$$

where $w(i, j)$ is the weight of an edge from node i to node j, and $w(i, j) = \infty$ if there is no edge between i and j. The update process is performed iteratively until convergence, where the distance values of all nodes no longer change.

Following the guidelines, we identify that operator '$\oplus$' is 'min', function $g_{\{i,j\}}(d_i) = d_i + w(i, j)$. Apparently, the function $g_{\{i,j\}}(d_i) = d_i + w(i, j)$ has the distributive property, and the operator 'min' has the commutative and associative properties and the identity property of ∞. The initialization can be $d_j^0 = \infty$ and $\Delta d_j^1 = 0$ if $j = s$, or else $\Delta d_j = \infty$. Therefore, SSSP can be performed by DAIC. Further, suppose Δd_j is used to accumulate the received distance values by 'min' operation, the scheduling priority of node j would be $d_j - \min\{d_j, \Delta d_j\}$.

3.2.2 Linear Equation Solvers

Generally, DAIC can be used to solve systems of linear equations of the form

$$A \cdot \chi = b, \quad (13)$$

where A is a sparse $n \times n$ matrix with each entry a_{ij}, and χ, b are size-n vectors with each entry χ_j, b_j respectively.

One of the linear equation solvers, *Jacobi method*, iterates each entry of χ as follows:

$$\chi_j^k = -\frac{1}{a_{jj}} \cdot \sum_{i \neq j} a_{ji} \cdot \chi_i^{k-1} + \frac{b_j}{a_{jj}}. \quad (14)$$

The method is guaranteed to converge if the spectral radius of the iteration matrix is less than 1. That is, for any matrix norm $||\cdot||$, $\lim_{k\to\infty}||B^k||^{\frac{1}{k}} < 1$, where B is the matrix with $B_{ij} = -\frac{a_{ij}}{a_{ij}}$ for $i \neq j$ and $B_{ij} = 0$ for $i = j$.

Following the guidelines, we identify that operator '$\oplus$' is '$+$', function $g_{\{i,j\}}(\chi_i) = -\frac{a_{ji}}{a_{jj}} \cdot \chi_i$. Apparently, the function $g_{\{i,j\}}(\chi_i) = -\frac{a_{ji}}{a_{jj}} \cdot \chi_i$ has the distributive property, and the operator '$+$' has the commutative and associative properties and the identity property of 0. The initialization can be $\chi_j^0 = 0$ and $\Delta\chi_j^1 = \frac{b_j}{a_{jj}}$. Therefore, the Jacobi method can be performed by DAIC. Further, suppose $\Delta\chi_j$ is used to accumulate the received delta message, the scheduling priority of node j would be $\Delta\chi_j$.

3.2.3 Adsorption

Adsorption [1] is a graph-based label propagation algorithm that provides person-alized recommendation for contents (e.g., video, music, document, product). The concept of *label* indicates a certain common feature of the entities. Given a weighted graph $G = (V, E, W)$, where V is the set of nodes, E is the set of edges, and W is a column normalized matrix (i.e., $\sum_i W(i, j) = 1$) indicating that the sum of a node's inbound links' weight is equal to 1. Node j carries a probability distribution L_j on label set L, and each node j is initially assigned with an *initial distribution* I_j. The algorithm proceeds as follows. For each node j, it iteratively computes the weighted average of the label distributions from its neighboring nodes, and then uses the random walk probabilities to estimate a new label distribution as follows:

$$L_j^k = p_j^{cont} \cdot \sum_{\{i|(i\to j)\in E\}} W(i, j) \cdot L_i^{k-1} + p_j^{inj} \cdot I_j, \tag{15}$$

where p_j^{cont} and p_j^{inj} are constants associated with node j. If Adsorption converges, it will converge to a unique set of label distributions.

Following the guidelines, we identify that operator '$\oplus$' is '$+$', $g_{\{i,j\}}(x) = p_j^{cont} \cdot W(i, j) \cdot x$. Apparently, the function $g_{\{i,j\}}(x) = p_j^{cont} \cdot W(i, j) \cdot x$ has the distributive property, and the operator '$+$' has the commutative and associative properties. The initialization can be $L_j^0 = 0$ and $\Delta L_j^1 = p_j^{inj} \cdot I_j$. Therefore, Adsorption can be performed by accumulative updates. Further, suppose ΔL_j is used to accumulate the received distance values, the scheduling priority of node j would be ΔL_j.

3.2.4 Other Algorithms

We have shown several typical DAIC algorithms. Following the guidelines, we can rewrite them in DAIC form. In addition, there are many other DAIC algorithms.

Table 1 A list of DAIC algorithms

Algorithm	$g_{\{i,j\}}(x)$	$\oplus$	v_j^0	Δv_j^1
SSSP	$x + w(i,j)$	min	∞	$0\ (j = s)$ or $\infty\ (j \neq s)$
Connected components	x	max	-1	j
PageRank	$d \cdot \frac{x}{|N(j)|}$	$+$	0	$1 - d$
Adsorption	$p_i^{cont} \cdot W(i,j) \cdot x$	$+$	0	$p_j^{inj} \cdot I_j$
HITS (*authority*)	$d \cdot A^T A(i,j) \cdot x$	$+$	0	1
Katz metric	$\beta \cdot x$	$+$	0	$1\ (j = s)$ or $0\ (j \neq s)$
Jacobi method	$-\frac{a_{ji}}{a_{jj}} \cdot x$	$+$	0	$\frac{b_j}{a_{jj}}$
Rooted PageRank	$P(j,i) \cdot x$	$+$	0	$1\ (j = s)$ or $0\ (j \neq s)$

Table 1 shows a list of such algorithms. Each of their update functions is represented with a tuple $(g_{\{i,j\}}(x), \oplus, v_j^0, \Delta v_j^1)$.

The *Connected Components* algorithm [12] finds connected components in a graph. Each node updates its component id with the largest received id and propagates its component id to its neighbors, so that the algorithm converges when all the nodes belonging to the same connected component have the same component id. *Hyperlink-Induced Topic Search* (HITS) [14] ranks web pages in a web linkage graph A by a 2-phase iterative update, the *authority update* and the *hub update*. Similar to Adsorption, the authority update requires each node i to generate the output values damped by d and scaled by $A^T A(i,j)$, while the hub update scales a node's output values by $AA^T(i,j)$. The *Katz metric* [13] is a proximity measure between two nodes in a graph. It is computed as the sum over the collection of paths between two nodes, exponentially damped by the path length with a damping factor β. *Rooted PageRank* [26] captures the probability for any node j running into node s, based on the node-to-node proximity, $P(j,i)$, indicating the probability of jumping from node j to node i.

4 Maiter: A Framework Supporting Asynchronous DAIC

This section presents Maiter. Maiter is an asynchronous graph processing framework that supports DAIC. It is implemented by modifying Piccolo [24] and relies on message passing for communication. Piccolo is designed with a distributed table structure, which can be easily utilized to implement distributed state table in Maiter. Maiter framework is also open-source on Google Code.[1]

---

[1]http://code.google.com/p/maiter/.

4.1 System Design

Maiter system is composed of a master and multiple workers. The master
coordinates the workers and monitors the status of workers. The workers run in
parallel and communicate with each other through MPI. Each worker performs the
update for a subset of local elements.

4.1.1 Local State Table

Each worker loads a subset of data elements in memory for processing. Each vertex
is indexed by a global unique *key*. The assignment of a data element to a worker
depends solely on the key. A data element with key j is assigned to worker $h(j)$,
where $h()$ is a hash function applied on the key. Besides, preprocessing for smart
graph partition can be useful. For example, one can use a lightweight clustering
algorithm to preprocess the input data, assigning the strongly related data elements
to the same worker, which can reduce communication.

Fig. 2 Worker overview

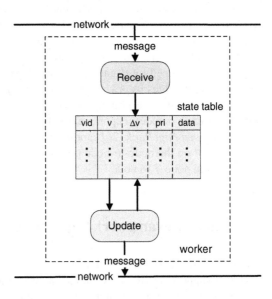

The data elements in a worker are maintained in a local in-memory key-value
store, *state table*. Each state table entry corresponds to a data element indexed by its
key. As depicted in Fig. 2, each table entry contains five fields. The 1st field stores
the key j of a data element; the 2nd field stores v_j; the 3rd field stores Δv_j; the 4th
field stores the priority value of data element j for priority scheduling; the 5th field
stores the input data associated with data element j, such as the adjacency list.

Before iterative computation starts, the input graph is partitioned into multiple
shards, and each of them is assigned to a worker. Several workers parse the input

graph in parallel. The input data associated with data element j is sent to worker $h(j)$. Then worker $h(j)$ fills entry j's data field (i.e. with data element j's input data. Users are responsible for initializing the v fields and the Δv fields through the provided API (will be described in Sect. 4.2). The priority fields are automatically initialized based on the values of the v fields and Δv fields.

4.1.2 Receive Thread and Update Thread

As described in Eq. (11), DAIC is accomplished by two key operations, the receive operation and the update operation. In each worker, these two operations are implemented in two threads, the *receive thread* and the *update thread*. The receive thread performs the receive operation for all local data elements. Each worker receives the delta messages from other workers and updates the Δv fields by accumulating the received delta messages. The update thread performs the update operation for all local data elements. When operating on a data element, it updates the corresponding entry's v field and Δv field, and sends messages to other data elements. The update of the priority field will be discussed in Sect. 4.1.3. The data field is never changed during the iterative computation.

The receive thread writes the Δv field, while the update thread both reads and writes the Δv field. In order to avoid the read-write and write-write conflict risks on a table entry's Δv field, the update operation on a table entry has to be atomic, where the read and write on the Δv field are implemented in critical section. The update thread selects the table entries to perform the update according to a scheduling policy. We will describe the scheduling policies and their implementations in Sect. 4.1.3.

4.1.3 Scheduling Within Update Thread

The simplest scheduling policy is to schedule the local data elements for update operation in a round robin fashion. The update thread performs the update operation on the table entries in the order that they are listed in the local state table and round-by-round. The static scheduling is simple and can prevent starvation.

However, as discussed in Sect. 2.5, it is beneficial to provide priority scheduling. In addition to the static round-robin scheduling, Maiter supports dynamic priority scheduling. A *priority queue* in each worker contains a subset of local keys that have larger priority values. The update thread dequeues the key from the priority queue, in terms of which it can position the entry in the local state table and performs an update operation on the entry. Once all the data elements in the priority queue have been processed, the update thread extracts a new subset of high-priority keys for next round update. The extraction of keys is based on the priority field of each table entry. Each entry's priority field is initially calculated based on its initial v value and Δv value. During the iterative computation, the priority field is updated whenever the Δv field is changed (i.e., whenever some delta messages are received).

The number of extracted keys in each round, i.e., the priority queue size, balances the tradeoff between the gain from accurate priority scheduling and the cost of frequent queue extractions. We have provided an optimal queue size analysis in [31]. The priority queue size is set as a portion of the state table size. For example, if the queue size is set as 1 % of the state table size, we will extract the top 1 % high priority entries in the state table for processing. In addition, we also use the sampling technique proposed in [31] for efficient queue extraction, which only needs $O(N)$ time, where N is the number of entries in local state table.

4.1.4 Message Passing

Maiter implements message passing based on OpenMPI.[2] A message contains a key indicating the message's destination data element and a value. Suppose that a message's destination key is k. The message will be sent to worker $h(k)$, where $h()$ is the partition function for data partition (Sect. 4.1.1), so the message will be received by the worker where the destination data element resides.

A naive implementation of message passing is to send the output messages as soon as they are produced. This will reach the asynchronous iteration's full potential. However, initializing message passing leads to system overhead. To reduce this overhead, Maiter buffers the output messages and flushes them to remote workers after a timeout. If a message's destination worker is the host worker, the output message is directly applied to the local state table. The time interval to flush the buffered messages, i.e., *flush interval* or T_f, balances the gains of asynchrony and the cost of frequent message passing. There is an optimal T_f that minimizes the running time. It depends on applications and data sets. We will set T_f empirically in the experiment section.

The output messages are buffered in multiple *msg table*s, each of which corresponds to a remote destination worker. The reason why Maiter exploits this table buffer design is that we can leverage early aggregation to reduce network communications. Each msg table entry consists of a destination key field and a value field. As mentioned in Sect. 2, the associative property of operator '$\oplus$', i.e., $(x \oplus y) \oplus z = x \oplus (y \oplus z)$, indicates that multiple messages with the same destination can be aggregated at the sender side or at the receiver side. Therefore, by using the msg table, Maiter worker combines the output messages with the same key by '$\oplus$' operation before sending them.

4.1.5 Master Design

The master maintains a list of alive workers and is responsible for coordinating these workers. The master accepts the user-submitted jobs and responds to user's

---

[2]Open MPI. http://www.open-mpi.org/.

requests such as job status query or job interruption. The master is also responsible for terminating an iterative computation. The master collects the local progress reports from all workers and makes a global termination decision based on these progress reports. The detail will be described in Sect. 4.1.6. In addition, in order to support fault tolerance, the master globally controls the checkpointing, including the saving of checkpoints and the resuming from checkpoints, which will be described in Sect. 3 of the supplementary file.

4.1.6 Iteration Termination

To terminate iteration, Maiter exploits *progress estimator* in each worker and a global *terminator* in the master. The master periodically broadcasts a *progress request signal* to all workers. Upon receipt of the termination check signal, the progress estimator in each worker measures the iteration progress locally and reports it to the master. The users are responsible for specifying the progress estimator to retrieve the iteration progress by parsing the local state table.

After the master receives the local iteration progress reports from all workers, the terminator makes a global termination decision in respect of the global iteration progress, which is calculated based on the received local progress reports. If the terminator determines to terminate the iteration, the master broadcasts a *terminate signal* to all workers. Upon receipt of the terminate signal, each worker stops updating the state table and dumps the local table entries to HDFS, which contain the converged results. Note that, even though we exploit a synchronous termination check periodically, it will not impact the asynchronous computation. The workers proceed the iterative computation after producing the local progress reports without waiting for the master's feedback.

A commonly used termination check approach compares the two consecutive global iteration progresses. If the difference between them is minor enough, the iteration is terminated. For example, to terminate the SSSP computation, the progress estimator in each worker calculates the sum of the v field values (the sum of the shortest distance values of all the local nodes) and sends a report with the summed value to the master. Based on these local sums, the terminator in the master calculates a global sum, which indicates the iteration progress. If there is no change between the two global sums collected during a termination check period (i.e., no node's distance is changed during that period), the SSSP computation is considered converged and is terminated.

4.1.7 Fault Tolerance

The fault tolerance support for synchronous computation models can be performed through checkpointing, where the state data is checkpointed on the reliable HDFS every several iterations. If some workers fail, the computation rolls back to the most recent iteration checkpoint and resumes from that iteration. Unfortunately, this fault tolerance mechanism cannot be utilized in asynchronous framework.

Maiter can exploit Chandy-Lamport [7] algorithm to design asynchronous iteration's fault tolerance mechanism. The checkpointing in Maiter is performed at regular time intervals rather than at iteration intervals. The state table in each worker is dumped to HDFS every period of time. However, during the asynchronous computation, the information in the state table might not be intact, in respect that the messages may be on their way to act on the state table. To avoid missing messages, not only the state table is dumped to HDFS, but also the msg tables in each worker are saved. Upon detecting any worker failure (through probing by the master), the master restores computation from the last checkpoint, migrates the failed worker's state table and msg tables to an available worker, and notifies all the workers to load the data from the most recent checkpoint to recover from worker failure. For detecting master failure, Maiter can rely on a secondary master, which restores the recent checkpointed state to recover from master failure.

4.2 Maiter API

Users can implement a Maiter program using Maiter API, which is written in C++ style. A DAIC algorithm is specified by implementing three components, `Partitioner`, `IterateKernel`, and `TermChecker` as shown in Fig. 3.

```
template <class K, class D>
struct Partitioner {
  virtual void parse_line(string& line, K* vid, D* data) = 0;
  virtual int partition(const K& vid, int shards) = 0;
};

template <class K, class V, class D>
struct IterateKernel {
  virtual void init(const K& vid, V* v, V* delta) = 0;
  virtual void accumulate(V* a, const V& b) = 0;
  virtual void send(const V& delta, const D& data,
                    list<pair<K, V> >* output) = 0;
};

template <class K, class V>
struct TermChecker {
  virtual double estimate_prog(LocalTableIterator<K, V>*
                               table_itr) = 0;
  virtual bool terminate(list<double> local_reports) = 0;
};
```

Fig. 3 Maiter API summary

K, V, and D are the template types of data element keys, data element values (v and Δv), and associate data respectively. Particularly, for each entry in the state table, K is the type of the key field, V is the type of the v field/Δv field/priority field, and D is the type of the data field. The `Partitioner` reads an input partition line by line. The `parse_line` function extracts data element id and the associate data by parsing the given line string. Then the `partition` function applied on the key (e.g., a MOD operation on integer key) determines the host worker of the data element (considering the number of workers/shards). Based on this function, the framework will assign each data element to a host worker and determines a message's destination worker. In the `IterateKernel` component, users describe a DAIC algorithm by specifying a tuple $(g_{\{i,j\}}(x), \oplus, v_j^0, \Delta v_j^1)$. We initialize v_j^0 and Δv_j^1 by implementing the `init` interface; specify the '$\oplus$' operation by implementing the `accumulate` interface; and specify the function $g_{\{i,j\}}(x)$ by implementing the `send` interface with the given Δv_i and data element i's associate data, which generates the output pairs $\langle j, g_{\{i,j\}}(\Delta v_i) \rangle$ to data element i's out-neighbors. To stop an iterative computation, users specify the `TermChecker` component. The local iteration progress is estimated by specifying the `estimate_prog` interface given the local state table iterator. The global terminator collects these local progress reports. In terms of these local progress reports, users specify the `terminate` interface to decide whether to terminate.

4.3 Maiter Program Example

For better understanding, we walk through how the PageRank algorithm is implemented in Maiter.[3] Suppose the input graph file of PageRank is line by line. Each line includes a node id and its adjacency list. The input graph file is split into multiple slices. Each slice is assigned to a Maiter worker. In order to implement PageRank application in Maiter, users should implement three functionality components, `PRPartitioner`, `PRIterateKernel`, and `PRTermChecker`.

In `PRPartitioner`, users specify the `parse_line` interface and the `partition` interface. The implementation code is shown in Fig. 4. In

```
class PRPartitioner : public Partitioner<int,vector<int> >{

    void parse_line(string& line, int* key, vector<int>* data) {
        node = get_source(line);
        adjlist = get_adjlist(line);

        *key = node;
        *data = adjlist;
    }

    int partition(const int& key, int shards) {
        return key % shards;
    }
}
```

Fig. 4 PageRankPartitioner implementation

[3]More implementation example codes are provided on Maiter's Google Code website http://code.google.com/p/maiter/.

```
class PRIterateKernel : public IterateKernel<int, float, vector<int> > {

    void initialize(const int& k, float* value, float* delta){
        *value = 0;
        *delta = 0.2;
    }

    void accumulate(float* a, const float& b){
        *a = *a + b;
    }

    void send(const float& delta, const vector<int>& data, vector<pair<int, float> >* output){
        int size = (int) data.size();
        float outdelta = delta * 0.8 / size;
        for(vector<int>::const_iterator it=data.begin(); it!=data.end(); it++){
            int target = *it;
            output->push_back(make_pair(target, outdelta));
        }
    }
}
```

Fig. 5 PRIterateKernel implementation

Fig. 6 PRTermChecker
implementation

```
class PRTermChecker : public TermChecker<int, float> {

    double prev_prog = 0.0;
    double curr_prog = 0.0;

    double estimate_prog(LocalTableIterator<int, float>* statetable){
        double partial_curr = get_sum_v(statetable);
        return partial_curr;
    }

    bool terminate(list<double> local_sums){
        curr_prog += get_sum_v(local_sums);

        if(abs(curr_prog - prev_prog) < term_threshold){
            return true;
        }else{
            prev_prog = curr_prog;
            return false;
        }
    }
}
```

`parse_line`, users parse an input line to extract the node id as well as its adjacency list and use them to initialize the state table's key field (`key`) and data field (`data`). In `partition`, users specify the partition function by a simple *mod* operation applied on the key field (`key`) and the total number of workers (`shards`).

In `PRIterateKernel`, users specify the asynchronous DAIC process by implementing the `init` interface, the `accumulate` interface, and the `send` interface. The implementation code is shown in Fig. 5. In `init`, users initialize node k's v field (`value`) as 0 and Δv field (`delta`) as 0.2. Users specify the `accumulate` interface by implementing the '$\oplus$' operator as '$+$' (i.e., $a = a + b$). The `send` operation is invoked after each update of a node. In `send`, users generate the output messages (contained in output) based on the node's Δv value (delta) and data value (data).

In PRTermChecker, users specify the *estimate_prog* interface and the terminate interface. The implementation code is shown in Fig. 6. In estimate_prog, users compute the summation of v value in local state table. The *estimate_prog* function is invoked after each period of time. The resulted local sums from various workers are sent to the global termination checker, and then the terminate operation in the global termination checker is invoked. In terminate, based on these received local sums, users compute a global sum, which is considered as the iteration progress. It is compared with the previous iteration's progress to calculate a progress difference. The asynchronous DAIC is terminated when the progress difference is smaller than a pre-defined threshold.

5   Performance

In this section, we show Maiter's performance to illustrate asynchronous DAIC's benefit. The experiments are performed on a 4-node local cluster as well as on Amazon EC2 Cloud. The Amazon EC2 cluster includes 100 m1.medium instances. The experiment is performed in the context of four applications, including PageRank, SSSP, Adsorption, and Katz metric. We use Google Webgraph[4] for PageRank computation. Besides this small real data set, we also generate massive synthetic data sets for PageRank and other applications.[5]

Figure 7 shows the running time of different frameworks for PageRank computation on our local cluster. By using Hadoop, we need 27 iterations and more than 800 s to converge.

iMapReduce [32] (iMR-file) separates the iteration-variant state data from the static data, which can reduce the running time of Hadoop by around 50 %. iMapReduce's memory-based version (iMR-mem) further reduces it by providing faster memory access.

Spark [30], with efficient data partition and memory caching techniques, can reduce Hadoop time to less than 100 s.

PrIter [31] identifies the more important nodes to perform the update and ignores the useless updates, by which the running time is reduced. As expected, PrIter's memory-based version (PrIter-mem) converges faster than PrIter's file-based version (PrIter-file).

Piccolo [24] utilizes MPI for message passing to realize fine-grained updates, which improves the performance.

GraphLab [18] provides both synchronous execution engine (*GraphLab-Sync*) and asynchronous execution engine (*GraphLab-AS*). Moreover, under the

---

[4]http://snap.stanford.edu/data/.

[5]The details of synthetic data sets can be found in [33].

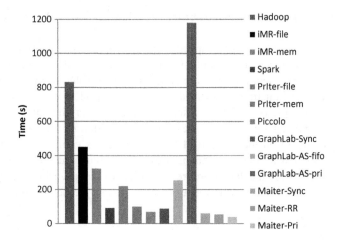

Fig. 7 Running time of PageRank on Google Webgraph on local cluster

asynchronous execution engine, GraphLab supports both fifo scheduling (*GraphLab-AS-fifo*) and priority scheduling (*GraphLab-AS-pri*). GraphLab-Sync uses a synchronous engine and completes the iterative computation with less than 100 s. GraphLab-AS-fifo uses an asynchronous engine and schedules the asynchronous updates in a FIFO queue, which consumes much more time. The reason is that the cost of managing the scheduler (through locks) tends to exceed the cost of the main PageRank computation itself. Even worse, the cost of maintaining the priority queue under asynchronous engine seems much larger. Retrieving the global highest priority item requires to synchronize the global state. Therefore, GraphLab-AS-pri takes longer time to converge.

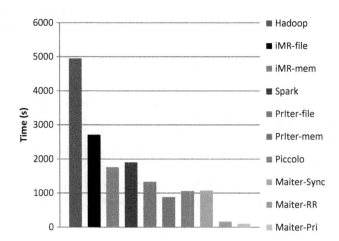

Fig. 8 Running time of PageRank on 100-million-node synthetic graph on EC2 cluster

Fig. 9 Running time of other applications (SSSP, adsorption, and Katz metric) on EC2 cluster

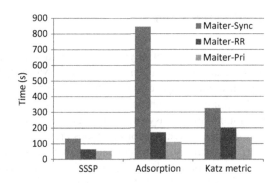

Our synchronous DAIC framework, Maiter-Sync, filters the neglectable updates (ΔR is 0) and performs accumulative updates without concurrency control, which can reduce the running time to about 60 s. Further, the asynchronous DAIC frameworks, Maiter-RR (Maiter with round-robin scheduling) and Maiter-Pri (Maiter with priority scheduling), can even converge faster by avoiding the synchronous barriers. Note that, our priority scheduling mechanism does not result in high cost thanks to the approximate sampling technique [31].

To show the performance under large-scale distributed environment, we run PageRank on the 100-million-node synthetic graph on EC2 cluster. Figure 8 shows the running time result. We can see the similar results as that of local cluster. One thing that should be noticed is that the asynchronous frameworks (Maiter-RR and Maiter-Pri) in large-scale cluster performs much better than that in small cluster. The result is under expectation. As the cluster size increases and the heterogeneity in cloud environment becomes apparent, the problem of synchronous barriers is more and more serious. With the asynchronous execution engine, Maiter-RR and Maiter-Pri can bypass the high-cost synchronous barriers. As a result, Maiter-RR and Maiter-Pri significantly reduce the running time comparing with other synchronous frameworks. Specifically, Maiter-Pri can achieve 60× speedup over Hadoop.

To show that Maiter can support more applications, we also run other applications on EC2 cluster. We perform SSSP, Adsorption, and Katz metric computations with Maiter-Sync, Maiter-RR, and Maiter-Pri. We generate weighted/unweighted 100-million-node synthetic graphs for these applications respectively. Figure 9 shows the running time of these applications. For SSSP, the asynchronous DAIC SSSP (Maiter-RR and Maiter-Pri) reduces the running time of synchronous DAIC SSSP (Maiter-Sync) by half. For Adsorption, the asynchronous DAIC Adsorption is 5× faster than the synchronous DAIC Adsorption. Further, by priority scheduling, Maiter-Pri further reduces the running time of Maiter-RR by around 1/3. For Katz metric, we can see that Maiter-RR and Maiter-Pri also outperform Maiter-Sync.

6   Related Work

The original idea of asynchronous iteration, chaotic iteration, was introduced by Chazan and Miranker in 1969 [8]. Motivated by that, Baudet proposed an asynchronous iterative scheme for multicore systems [2], and Bertsekas presented a distributed asynchronous iteration model [3]. These early stage studies laid the foundation of asynchronous iteration and have proved its effectiveness and convergence. Asynchronous methods are being increasingly used and studied since then, particularly so in connection with the use of heterogeneous workstation clusters. A broad class of applications with asynchronous iterations have been correspondingly raised [10, 22], such as PageRank [15, 20] and pairwise clustering [28]. Our work differs from these previous works and provides a novel asynchronous iteration scheme, DAIC, which exploits accumulative property.

On the other hand, to support iterative computation, a series of distributed frameworks have emerged. In addition to the frameworks we compared in Sect. 5, many other synchronous frameworks are proposed recently. HaLoop [6], a modified version of Hadoop, improves the efficiency of iterative computations by making the task scheduler loop-aware and employing caching mechanisms. CIEL [23] supports data-dependent iterative algorithms by building an abstract dynamic task graph. Pregel [19] aims at supporting graph-based iterative algorithms by using BSP model. REX [25] focuses on supporting iterative computations in which changes, in the form of deltas, are propagated from iteration to iteration, and state is efficiently updated in an extensible way. Twister [9] employs a lightweight iterative MapReduce runtime system by logically constructing a reduce-to-map loop. Naiad [21] is recently proposed to support incremental iterative computations.

All of the above described works build on the basic assumption that the synchronization between iterations is essential. A few proposed frameworks also support asynchronous iteration. The partial asynchronous approach proposed in [11] investigates the notion of partial synchronizations in iterative MapReduce applications to overcome global synchronization overheads.GraphLab [29] supports asynchronous iterative computation with sparse computational dependencies while ensuring data consistency and achieving a high degree of parallel performance. GRACE [27] executes iterative computation with asynchronous engine while letting users implement their algorithms with the synchronous BSP programming model. Our work is the first that proposes to perform DAIC for iterative algorithms. We also identify a broad class of iterative algorithms that can perform DAIC.

7   Summary

This chapter introduces a novel computation model under large-scale distributed environment, DAIC. The DAIC algorithms can be performed asynchronously and converge with much less workload. To support DAIC model, Maiter is designed, which is running on top of hundreds of commodity machines and relies on message passing to communicate between distributed machines. By asynchronous DAIC, Maiter is shown to have better performance than many of state-of-the-art frameworks.

Acknowledgements This work was partially supported by U.S. NSF grants (CNS-1217284, CCF-1018114), National Natural Science Foundation of China (61300023), Fundamental Research Funds for the Central Universities (N120416001, N120416001).

References

1. S. Baluja, R. Seth, D. Sivakumar, Y. Jing, J. Yagnik, S. Kumar, D. Ravichandran, and M. Aly. Video suggestion and discovery for youtube: taking random walks through the view graph. In *Proc. Int'l Conf. World Wide Web (WWW '08)*, pages 895–904, 2008.
2. G. M. Baudet. Asynchronous iterative methods for multiprocessors. *J. ACM*, 25:226–244, April 1978.
3. D. P. Bertsekas. Distributed asynchronous computation of fixed points. *Math. Programming*, 27:107–120, 1983.
4. S. Brin and L. Page. The anatomy of a large-scale hypertextual web search engine. *Comput. Netw. ISDN Syst.*, 30:107–117, April 1998.
5. S. Brin and L. Page. The anatomy of a large-scale hypertextual web search engine. In *Proc. Seventh Int'l Conf. World Wide Web (WWW '98)*, pages 107–117, 1998.
6. Y. Bu, B. Howe, M. Balazinska, and D. M. Ernst. Haloop: Efficient iterative data processing on large clusters. *Proc. VLDB Endow.*, 3(1), 2010.
7. K. M. Chandy and L. Lamport. Distributed snapshots: determining global states of distributed systems. *ACM Trans. Comput. Syst.*, 3(1):63–75, Feb. 1985.
8. D. Chazan and W. Miranker. Chaotic relaxation. *Linear Algebra and its Applications*, 2(2):199–222, 1969.
9. J. Ekanayake, H. Li, B. Zhang, T. Gunarathne, S.-H. Bae, J. Qiu, and G. Fox. Twister: a runtime for iterative mapreduce. In *Proc. IEEE Int'l Workshop MapReduce (MapReduce '10)*, pages 810–818, 2010.
10. A. Frommer and D. B. Szyld. On asynchronous iterations. *J. Comput. Appl. Math.*, 123:201–216, November 2000.
11. K. Kambatla, N. Rapolu, S. Jagannathan, and A. Grama. Asynchronous algorithms in mapreduce. In *Proc. IEEE Conf. Cluster (Cluster' 10)*, pages 245 –254, 2010.
12. U. Kang, C. Tsourakakis, and C. Faloutsos. Pegasus: A peta-scale graph mining system implementation and observations. In *Proc. IEEE Int'l Conf. Data Mining (ICDM '09)*, pages 229 –238, 2009.
13. L. Katz. A new status index derived from sociometric analysis. *Psychometrika*, 1953.
14. J. M. Kleinberg. Authoritative sources in a hyperlinked environment. *J. ACM*, 46:604–632, 1999.
15. G. Kollias, E. Gallopoulos, and D. B. Szyld. Asynchronous iterative computations with web information retrieval structures: The pagerank case. In *PARCO*, volume 33 of *John von Neumann Institute for Computing Series*, pages 309–316, 2005.
16. D. Lee and S. Seung. Learning the parts of objects by non-negative matrix factorization. *Nature*, 401:788–791, 1999.
17. D. Liben-Nowell and J. Kleinberg. The link-prediction problem for social networks. *J. Am. Soc. Inf. Sci. Technol.*, 58:1019–1031, May 2007.

18. Y. Low, J. Gonzalez, A. Kyrola, D. Bickson, C. Guestrin, and J. M. Hellerstein. Distributed graphlab: A framework for machine learning and data mining in the cloud. *Proc. VLDB Endow.*, 5(8), 2012.

19. G. Malewicz, M. H. Austern, A. J. Bik, J. C. Dehnert, I. Horn, N. Leiser, and G. Czajkowski. Pregel: a system for large-scale graph processing. In *Proc. ACM SIGMOD*, pages 135–146, 2010.

20. F. McSherry. A uniform approach to accelerated pagerank computation. In *Proc. Int'l Conf. World Wide Web (WWW '05)*, pages 575–582, 2005.

21. F. McSherry, D. Murray, R. Isaacs, and M. Isard. Differential dataflow. In *Proc. Biennial Conf. Innovative Data Systems Research (CIDR '13)*, 2013.

22. J. C. Miellou, D. El Baz, and P. Spiteri. A new class of asynchronous iterative algorithms with order intervals. *Math. Comput.*, 67:237–255, January 1998.

23. D. G. Murray, M. Schwarzkopf, C. Smowton, S. Smith, A. Madhavapeddy, and S. Hand. Ciel: A universal execution engine for distributed data-flow computing. In *Proc. USEINX Symp. Networked Systems Design and Implementation (NSDI '11)*, 2011.

24. R. Power and J. Li. Piccolo: Building fast, distributed programs with partitioned tables. In *Proc. USENIX Symp. Opearting Systems Design and Implementation (OSDI '10)*, 2010.

25. M. S. R., I. G. Ives, and G. Sudipto. Rex: Recursive, deltabased datacentric computation. *Proc. VLDB Endow.*, 5(8), 2012.

26. H. H. Song, T. W. Cho, V. Dave, Y. Zhang, and L. Qiu. Scalable proximity estimation and link prediction in online social networks. In *Proc. Int'l Conf. Internet Measurement (IMC '09)*, pages 322–335, 2009.

27. G. Wang, W. Xie, A. Demers, and J. Gehrke. Asynchronous large-scale graph processing made easy. In *Proc. Biennial Conf. Innovative Data Systems Research (CIDR '13)*, 2013.

28. E. Yom-Tov and N. Slonim. Parallel pairwise clustering. In *Proc. SIAM Intl. Conf. Data Mining (SDM '09)*, pages 745–755, 2009.

29. L. Yucheng, G. Joseph, K. Aapo, B. Danny, G. Carlos, and M. H. Joseph. Graphlab: A new framework for parallel machine learning. In *Proc. Int'l Conf. Uncertainty in Artificial Intelligence (UAI '10)*, 2010.

30. M. Zaharia, M. Chowdhury, T. Das, A. Dave, J. Ma, M. McCauley, M. J. Franklin, S. Shenker, and I. Stoica. Resilient distributed datasets: A fault-tolerant abstraction for. in-memory cluster computing. In *Proc. USEINX Symp. Networked Systems Design and Implementation (NSDI'12)*, 2012.

31. Y. Zhang, Q. Gao, L. Gao, and C. Wang. Priter: a distributed framework for prioritized iterative computations. In *Proc. ACM Symp. Cloud Computing (SOCC '11)*, 2011.

32. Y. Zhang, Q. Gao, L. Gao, and C. Wang. imapreduce: A distributed computing framework for iterative computation. *J. Grid Comput.*, 10(1):47–68, 2012.

33. Y. Zhang, Q. Gao, L. Gao, and C. Wang. Maiter: A message-passing distributed framework for accumulative iterative computation, http://faculty.neu.edu.cn/cc/zhangyf/papers/maiter-full.pdf. Northeastern university techical report, 2012.

Part IV
Cloud Storage

Challenges and solutions to cloud-related Big Data. FRIEDA: storage and data management framework for IaaS. Data transfer issues addressed using managed file transfer system StorkCloud. Analyzing and storing social media data with IndexedHBase indexing framework.

Big Data Storage and Processing on Azure Clouds: Experiments at Scale and Lessons Learned

Radu Tudoran, Alexandru Costan, Gabriel Antoniu, and Brasche Goetz

Abstract Data-intensive computing is now starting to be considered as the basis for a new, fourth paradigm for science. Two factors are encouraging this trend. First, vast amounts of data are becoming available in more and more application areas. Second, the infrastructures allowing to persistently store these data for sharing and processing are becoming a reality. This allows to unify knowledge acquired through the previous three paradigms for scientific research (theory, experiments and simulations) with vast amounts of multidisciplinary data. The technical and scientific issues related to this context have been designated as the "Big Data" challenges. In this landscape, building a functional infrastructure for the requirements of Big Data applications is critical and is still a challenge. An important step has been made thanks to the emergence of cloud infrastructures, which are bringing the first bricks to cope with the challenging scale of the Big Data vision. Clouds bring to life the illusion of a (more-or-less) infinitely scalable infrastructure managed through a fully outsourced ICT service. Instead of having to buy and manage hardware, users "rent" outsourced resources as needed. However, cloud technologies have not reached yet their full potential. In particular, the capabilities available now for data storage and processing are still far from meeting the application requirements. In this work we investigate several hot challenges related to Big Data management on clouds. We discuss current state-of-the-art solutions, their limitations and some ways to overcome them. We illustrate our study with a concrete application study from the area of joint genetic and neuroimaging data analysis. The goal of this chapter is to present the conclusions of this study performed through a large-scale experiment carried out across three data centers of Microsoft's Azure cloud platform during 2 weeks, which consumed approximately 200.000 compute hours.

R. Tudoran • A. Costan (✉) • G. Antoniu
INRIA Rennes, Campus de Beaulieu, 35042 Rennes, France
e-mail: Radu.Tudoran@irisa.fr; alexandru.costan@inria.fr; Gabriel.Antoniu@inria.fr

B. Goetz
Huawei Technologies, Duesseldorf GmbH, Düsseldorf, Germany, WA, USA
e-mail: goetz.brasche@huawei.com

© Springer Science+Business Media New York 2014   331
X. Li, J. Qiu (eds.), *Cloud Computing for Data-Intensive Applications*,
DOI 10.1007/978-1-4939-1905-5_14

1 Introduction

Data-intensive computing is now starting to be considered as the basis for a new, fourth paradigm for science. Two factors are encouraging this trend. First, vast amounts of data are becoming available in more and more application areas. Second, the infrastructures allowing to persistently store these data for sharing and processing are becoming a reality. This allows unifying knowledge acquired through the previous three paradigms for scientific research (theory, experiments and simulations) with vast amounts of multidisciplinary data. The technical and scientific issues related to this context have been designated as the Big Data challenges and have been identified as highly strategic by major research agencies.

In this landscape, building a functional infrastructure for the requirements of Big Data applications is critical and is still a challenge. An important step has been made thanks to the emergence of cloud infrastructures, which are bringing the first bricks to cope with the challenging scale of the Big Data vision. Clouds bring to life the illusion of a (more-or-less) infinitely scalable infrastructure managed through a fully outsourced ICT service. Instead of having to buy and manage hardware, users rent outsourced resources as needed. However, cloud technologies have not yet reached their full potential. In particular, the capabilities available now for data storage and processing are still rudimentary and rather far from meeting the more and more demanding application requirements.

In this chapter we investigate several hot challenges related to Big Data management on clouds. We focus on the specific needs of data-intensive applications, where huge amounts of data are concurrently shared and processed by a large number of processes. We introduce state-of-the-art solutions for data storage and processing on clouds as they are made available by major cloud storage providers, we discuss their limitations and some ways to overcome them. We illustrate our study with a concrete application study from the area of joint genetic and neuroimaging data analysis, performed through a large-scale experiment carried out across three data centers of Microsoft's Azure cloud platform during 2 weeks, for an overall usage of approximatively 200.000 compute hours.

2 Cloud Storage for Data-Intensive Applications: Challenges

The overwhelming data volumes to be handled by today's data-intensive applications generate several requirements which translate into real challenges for cloud storage systems. Several of these major challenges are discussed below.

Support for Massive Unstructured Data Most data available nowadays is unstructured: pictures, sound, movies, documents, experimental measurements are often represented as raw unstructured blobs (Binary Large Objects) in the first stage, as they are captured by sensors or synthetically generated. According to a 2011 study, unstructured data will account for 90 % of all data generated in the upcoming decade [3]. They serve as input to data-analysis applications and their size tends to grow fast in time (in the order of PB/year) in more and more scenarios. Such data are typically stored as huge objects which are continuously updated by running applications. Traditional databases or file systems can hardly cope with objects that grow to huge sizes efficiently. Emerging cloud storage technologies have not solved this issue yet: the maximum data size supported by object-based cloud data stores is much smaller than required by applications (typically in the order of Gigabytes, less frequently up to 1 Terabyte for some providers). When applications need to handle larger blobs, an extra-level of complexity is generated in order to split data and manage the corresponding set of smaller objects.

Support for Operations on Multiple Files In the context of data collection for science experiments, the number of generated data objects by experiment (usually stored as files) may be high (e.g. monitor files, log files, temporary files, experimental results etc.). Current cloud storage systems do not support even simple operations on multiple such files/blobs (e.g. *grep*, select/filter, compress, aggregate). To perform such operations, one needs to implement its own procedures that will download the files (individually) and go through them (at client side), which leads to long and expensive data movements. This current approach is clearly inefficient: a better approach where the operations could be sent for execution in-place where data are stored (i.e. on the server side), *on multiple files at once* would clearly be more appealing.

High Throughput Under Heavy Access Concurrency Most cloud storage systems available today have been designed to be accessed by a single client at a time and do not favor efficient sharing. However, Big Data processing naturally requires a high degree of parallelism for data analysis (i.e. many compute nodes concurrently process subsets of the input data). This leads to many clients accessing the cloud storage system to read the input data, to write the results, to report their state for monitoring and fault tolerance purposes and to write the log files of their computation. Since data-intensive applications spend considerable time to perform I/O, achieving a high data throughput in spite of heavy access concurrency is an important property that impacts on the total application execution time. Typically, the data storage system must efficiently deal with thousands of concurrent processes to data, both for reading and writing.

Fine Grain Access to Data Subsets Even if many applications use huge blobs as input data, data-intensive applications typically consist of many parallel processes which concurrently access small parts of that input data. Typically, this pattern arises when splitting the initial workload among multiple workers which process small input data sets. Another example regards status checking for compute processes in the log/monitor files. In such cases, the cloud storage system must enable an efficient access to data *at a fine grain*. The goal is to improve the overall data access performance by avoiding useless locking or unnecessary data transfers and sparing the expensive and limited network bandwidth.

Monitoring and Logging Services Large-scale experiments require constant
monitoring of their progress. Monitoring functionalities are rather limited on
clouds and usually only focus on general parameters such as CPU load, disk
accesses or network activity. Such parameters, although useful, do not offer a
complete vision on how the simulation or experiment progresses. To meet such
a goal, a dedicated system able to support more specific monitoring functions is
required in order to identify and qualify shared file accesses, concurrent appends
to shared blobs, job reporting, log aggregation, filtering mechanisms etc.

Support for Highly Parallel Data Workflows More and more data-intensive
applications consist of multiple phases including data acquisition, data curation,
data pre-processing, data storage, offline data-analysis, data visualization, etc.
This can generically be expressed as highly parallel data workflows. Moreover,
such workflows may be geographically distributed across multiple data centers
with specific facilities for certain parts of the global workflows. Synchronizing
concurrent accesses to data under these circumstances is difficult, hence scalable
mechanisms addressing this issue at the level of the cloud storage service are
needed.

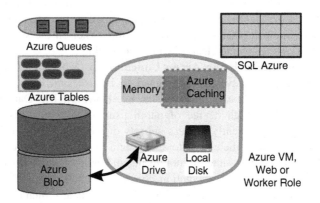

Fig. 1 An overview of the Azure storage services

3   A Case Study: Data Storage and Management
   on Azure Clouds

Currently, the options for sharing data are the cloud object stores, the local resources
of the compute nodes (e.g. memory, disks) or some hybrid approaches between
these two. Each one is geared for various types of data and maximizes a different
(typically conflicting) set of constraints. For instance, storing data within the

deployment increases the throughput but has an ephemeral lifetime, while using the cloud storage provides persistence at the price of high latencies.

In the Microsoft Azure Cloud [2, 4, 5] the data handling solutions range from the classical SQL data bases to blob storage. Figure 1 presents an overview of the data-handling services offered by the Azure cloud. Most of these are designed to support both cloud and on-premises applications (e.g. Blobs, Tables, Queues, SQL), while others only support the cloud compute nodes (e.g. ephemeral disk, drives and caching). Next, we detail all these services.

3.1 Storing Unstructured Data: Azure Blobs

The standard cloud offering for sharing application data consists of storage services accessed by compute nodes via simple, data-centric interfaces. Under the hood, these are distributed storage systems running complex protocols to ensure that data is always available and durable, even when machines, disks and networks fail. This makes them good candidates for persistently storing input/output data.

Azure Blobs is the main storage service of the Azure cloud, able to hold massive amounts of data from many different applications [4, 7]. Users can create multiple storage accounts, which are accessed and protected using a SHA256 authentication system. A user storage account is bounded to a geographical location (i.e. a data center), but for fault tolerance reasons, its data is replicated across multiple data centers.

At its core, Azure Blobs is a distributed storage system, organized as a two layer namespace consisting of *containers* and *blobs*. The system is built on top of specialized data clusters, each cluster having a capacity of tens of petabytes of data. These storage nodes are different than the ones used for the computation service. A REST API provides basic *PUT* and *GET* operations, implemented on top of HTTP/HTTPS. There are two types of blobs based on the elementary working unit: page and block. The block has a size limit of 4 MB and the total data size of a block blob cannot exceed 400 GB. The page has a fixed size of 512 KB with a maximum per blob capacity of 1 TB. The blocks and pages are replicated across different disks and racks, with a default replica count of 3. A strong consistency protocol is used for the local replicas. The consistency of concurrent updates is managed either explicitly through the use of timestamps or by applying a "first commit wins" strategy.

As its counterparts from other cloud providers (Amazon S3, etc.), Azure Blobs focus on data storage primarily and support other functionalities essentially as a side effect of their storage capability. The high-latency REST interfaces make them inadequate for data with high update rates. Typically, they are not concerned by achieving high throughput, nor by potential optimizations, let alone offer the ability to support different data services (e.g. geographically distributed transfers, placement etc.)

3.2   Storing NoSQL-Structured Data: Azure Tables

The Azure Tables store type-value pairs, through a no SQL interface. A Table contains entities (similar to rows in classical relational databases), which store multiple properties. While in many senses the Azure Table concept is similar to the tables found in relational databases, a key difference is that it does not enforce a fixed schema. Each entity can contain a different number of properties or different types of properties. This service mainly targets web-based applications, which require fast and flexible data schemas.

Each entity holds at least three properties: RowKey, PartitionKey and Timestamp. The PartitionKey is used by the Table service to balance the load across multiple storage nodes. The access to consecutive entities within a partition is optimized for performance. The distinction between entities of the same partition is made based on the RowKey, which in conjunction with the PartitionKey uniquely identify each row within a Table. An entity can hold at most 255 properties (including the 3 system properties), and the size of data stored by each entity cannot exceed 1 MB. The total data size per table is limited to 100 TB (the storage limit per account).

3.3   Synchronizing Processes for Concurrent Data Processing: Azure Queues

The Azure Queues provide short term storage for small messages. The service is designed as a communication mechanism for passing job descriptions between the compute nodes. The Queues are optimized to support a high number of concurrent operations from many clients and allow thousands of message transactions per second. Both cloud nodes and on-premises applications can access the Queue service via a REST API. A typical usage scenario consists of cloud web roles enqueueing jobs for the workers roles, as in a master–workers model.

A Queue message contains data, with a maximum size of 64 KB, and meta-data (e.g. timestamp, time to live, visibility etc.). As the service is designed for small transient data, the time to live field marks the time to deletion, with a maximum value of 1 week. Although this value seems fair, it can represent a limitation for some Big Data experiments which usually have a larger timespan. There is no guarantee about the order in which messages become visible in the queue. A message that is dequeued is not deleted from the system, but becomes hidden for a certain time period (i.e. the visibility field becomes false). The message is either explicitly deleted after it was processed or becomes visible again after the hide time period expires. This hiding period is limited to hours, which creates a management overhead for long running tasks, as users need to provide mechanisms that would allow longer compute intervals.

3.4 Others

Azure SQL. The Azure SQL service provides applications a classical relational data base management system. The service is built by porting the Microsoft SQL engine in the Azure cloud and offers a maximum storage space of 150 GBs. Cloud applications can access the database through the same API used by desktop or on-premises applications. Such an option, along with indexes, stored procedures or views ease the porting of native applications to the cloud. Azure SQL offers all the ACID guarantees of a traditional database, but additionally provides users the possibility to specify policies on how conflicts or updates should be handled.

Azure Drive. User can mount regular blobs from the Azure Blob service as virtual local disks within their VMs. The Azure Drives represent just a middleware to access the persistent storage. It offers the native applications the possibility to run in the cloud and use the cloud storage without any modifications (relying on the same NTFS API as for the local storage). A blob can be mounted as a virtual drive only to a single compute instance (i.e. worker or web role) at a certain moment. However, a VM can have multiple drives mounted at the same time.

Azure Disks. Similarly to Drives, the Disks use the cloud storage within the virtual machines. The difference is that doing I/O on the Disks does not use the bandwidth capacity of the virtual machine, only that of the physical node. A typical usage scenario is for web services that manage large datasets as local files with persistence guarantees.

Azure Caching. The Azure Caching service offers fast, in-memory storage for key-value pairs (with a maximum size of 4 MB for each such record), useful for memory intensive applications. There are two options for using it: dedicating full web/worker roles or dedicating part of the VM resources. With the first option, at least one node will be entirely dedicated to the Azure Caching service; this is more appropriate when one deploys a large number of nodes. The second option deploys the Azure Caching service across all the leased compute nodes. This is achieved by dedicating parts of the resources from each VM (mainly, its memory) to the service. Besides this low-latency storage facility, the service performs the caching between the node memories and the Azure Blob persistent storage. Each Azure Caching service is associated with a user storage blob account, where data is backed-up. This allows storing data with sizes superior to the capacity of the aggregated nodes memory. While performance is high due to data locality, the cache misses can be quite frequent, especially when the memory capacity is reached. This impacts on the response times, as it requires swapping data between the caching service and the Azure Blobs.

4   Getting Further: Dealing with Storage Latency under Heavy Concurrency

In order to address the previous limitations at the level of the cloud storage we introduce in this section a set of contributions. We present a concurrency-optimized data storage system which federates the virtual disks associated to VMs. Next, we propose an extension that provides a higher degree of reliability while remaining non-intrusive through the use of dedicated compute nodes. We demonstrate the performance of these solutions for efficient data-intensive processing on commercial clouds by building an optimized prototype MapReduce framework for Azure that leverages the benefits of our storage solutions. We further extend the MapReduce programming model to better support reduce-intensive applications and substantially improve their efficiency by eliminating the implicit barrier between the Map and the Reduce phase.

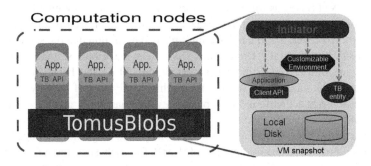

Fig. 2 The TomusBlobs architectural overview

4.1   Aggregating the Virtual Disks for Communication-Efficient Storage

In many cloud deployments, the disks locally attached to the VMs (with storage capacities of hundreds of GBs available at no extra cost) are not exploited at their full potential. Therefore, we propose to aggregate parts of the storage space from the virtual disks in a shared common pool that is managed in a distributed fashion. This pool is used to store the application level data. For scalability reasons, they are stored in a striped fashion, i.e. split into small chunks that are evenly distributed among the local disks of the storage. Each chunk is replicated on multiple local disks in order to survive failures. With this approach, read and write access performance under concurrency is greatly enhanced, as the global I/O workload is evenly distributed among the local disks. Furthermore, this scheme reduces latencies and has a potential for high scalability, as a growing number of VMs automatically leads to a larger storage system, which is not the case with the default cloud storage service.

Building on these design principles that exploit data locality, we introduce TomusBlobs [12], a system for concurrency-optimized PaaS-level cloud storage. We rely on the local disk of the VM instance directly in order to share input files and save the output files or intermediate data. This approach requires no changes to the application nor to the cloud middleware. Furthermore, it does not use any additional resources from the cloud, as the virtual disk is implicitly available to the user for storage, without any additional costs. We implemented this approach in the Microsoft Azure cloud platform.

The architecture of TomusBlobs consists of three loosely-coupled components presented in Fig. 2:

- The *Initiator* component is particular for each cloud. It has the role to deploy, setup and launch the data management system and to customize the scientific environment. It exposes a generic stub that can be easily implemented and customized for any cloud. The Initiator supports the system's elasticity, being able to scale up and down the computing platform at runtime, by integrating the new added nodes in the system or by seamlessly discarding the deleted ones.
- The *Distributed Storage* has the role of aggregating the virtual disks into a uniform shared storage, which is exposed to applications. It is generic as it does not depend on a specific storage solution. Any distributed file system capable to be deployed and executed in a cloud environment (and not changing the cloud middleware) can be used as a Distributed Storage.
- The *Client* consists of the API layer through which the storage is accessed by the applications. Data manipulation is supported transparently through a set of primitives. The interface is similar to the ones of commercial public clouds (Azure Blobs, Amazon S3).

The local storage of VMs on which we rely consists of virtual block-based storage devices that provide access to the physical storage. The virtual disks appear as devices to the virtual machine and can be formatted and accessed as if they were physical devices. However, they can hold data only for the lifetime of the VM. After the VM is terminated they are cleared. Hence, it is not possible to use them for long-term storage since this would mean leasing the computation nodes for long periods. Instead, we have designed a simple checkpoint mechanism that backups all the data from the TomusBlobs ephemeral storage to the persistent Azure Blobs, at configurable time intervals (the default being 1 h). This backup is done as a background job, privileging the periods with little/no network transfers of the application and remaining non-intrusive (it adds a 4 % computational overhead). Data is restored manually from Azure Blobs in case of failures at the beginning of new experiments.

Data striping and replication is performed transparently on blobs, therefore eliminating the need to explicitly manage chunks in the Distributed Storage. The default data management system which we integrated within the Storage uses an efficient version-oriented design that enables lock-free access to data, and thereby favors scalability under heavy concurrency (multiple readers and writers or multiple writers concurrently) [9]. Rather than updating the current pages, each write generates a new set of pages corresponding to a new version. Metadata is then generated and "weaved" together with the old metadata in such way as to create the illusion of a new incremental snapshot; this actually shares the unmodified pages of the blob with the older versions. Thanks to the decentralized data and metadata management, this provides high throughput and deals transparently with node failures.

4.2   Using Dedicated Compute Nodes for Scalable Data Management

Despite its evident advantages for some applications (especially the ones leveraging the data locality, e.g. MapReduce), the collocated storage schema introduced in the previous section has some important issues. First, it relies on commodity hardware that is prone to failures. An outage of the local storage system would make its host compute node inaccessible, effectively leading to loss of data and application failure. Second, the software stack that enables the aggregation of the local storage can become rather intrusive and impact on the application's perceived performance. Indeed, there is a direct correlation between the CPU usage and the data throughput [13], as over-tasked CPUs may introduce bottlenecks that slow down the computation. As a consequence, we need to deal with the reliability and the overhead of local storage in order to be able to leverage it for a larger set of data intensive applications. We propose to decouple storage and computation through the use of dedicated compute nodes for storage. This separation allows applications to efficiently access data without interfering with the underlying compute resources while the data locality is preserved as the storage nodes are selected within the same cloud deployment.

Our proposal in this context, DataSteward [11], harnesses the storage space of a set of dedicated VMs into a globally-shared data store in a scalable and efficient fashion. The dedicated nodes are chosen using a clustering-based algorithm that enables a topology-aware selection. With DataSteward, applications can sustain a high I/O data access throughput, as with collocated storage, but with less overhead and higher reliability through isolation. This approach allows to extensively use in-memory storage, as opposed to collocated solutions which only rely on virtual disks. To capitalize on this separation, we provide a set of higher-level data-centric services, that can overlap with the computation and reduce the application runtime. Compression, encryption, anonymization, geographical replication or broadcast are examples of *data processing-as-a-service* features that could exploit a dedicated infrastructure and serve cloud applications as a "data steward".

Fig. 3 DataSteward
architecture with dedicated
compute nodes for data
storage and a set of additional
data processing functions

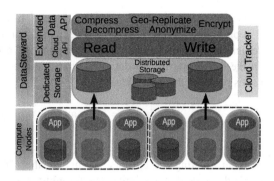

Our proposal relies on a layered architecture, built around three components, presented in Fig. 3.

- The *Cloud Tracker* has the role of selecting the dedicated nodes through a four steps process executed at the VM's booting time. First, a leader election algorithm is run, using the VM IDs. Second, each VM makes an evaluation of the network links and reports the results back to the leader, using a queue based communication system. Third, the leader runs a clustering algorithm to select the most fitted nodes for storage (throughput wise). Finally, these nodes are broadcasted within the deployment.

- The *Distributed Storage* is the data management system deployed in the dedicated nodes, that federates the local disks of the VMs. Users can select the distributed storage system of their choice. Additionally, the local memory is aggregated into an *in-memory storage*, used for storing, caching and buffering data. The Distributed Storage can dynamically scale up/down, dedicating new nodes when faced with data usage bursts or releasing some of them.

- The *Data Processing Services* are a set of data handling operations on top of the storage layer, that can overlap with the executing applications that they support. Examples include: compression, geographical replication, anonymization, etc.

As the selection of the storage VMs can significantly impact application performance, we believe that the topology and utilization of the cloud need to be carefully considered to come up with an optimized allocation policy. Since cloud users do not have fine-grained visibility into or control over the underlying infrastructure, they can only rely on some application-level optimization. In our case, the storage nodes are selected based on the (discovered) topology, such that the aggregated throughput from the application nodes to the dedicated storage nodes is maximized. To get an intuition of the cloud topology, we opted for a clustering algorithm, observing that the cloud providers tend to distribute the compute nodes in different fault domains (i.e. behind multiple switches). Hence, we aim to discover these clusters based on the proximity that exists between the nodes in a fault domain. To this end, we fitted the clustering algorithm with adequate hypotheses for centroid selection and nodes assignment to clusters, in order to maximize the data throughput. Finally, the selection of the dedicated nodes is done based on the discovered clusters.

In our scenario, the clusters are formed from compute nodes, and a cluster is represented by the node to be dedicated for storage (the centroid), with one dedicated node per cluster. The assignment of a node to a cluster is done based on the throughput to the data node that represents a cluster and by balancing the nodes between the data nodes:

$$cluster = \underset{i \in Servers}{\arg\max} \operatorname{Max} throughput[\ \underbrace{i, j}_{|Client[i]| < clients\_per\_server}\ ] \qquad (1)$$

After creating the clusters, we update the centroids. With our hypothesis, we select the node that maximizes the throughput to all VMs in the cluster:

$$maxserver = \underset{j \in Client[i]}{\arg\max} \sum_{k \in Client[i]} throughput[j, k] \qquad (2)$$

The motivation to use a dedicated infrastructure inside the deployment was to enable a set of data services that deliver the power and versatility of the cloud to users. The idea is to exploit the compute capabilities of the storage nodes to deploy data specific services, that otherwise couldn't be run on the application nodes. These services are loaded dynamically, from the default modules or from libraries provided by the users. We list bellow a set of data processing services that could leverage such a dedicated storage infrastructure:

- *Geographically-Distributed Data Management.* Being able to effectively harness multiple geographically distributed data centers and the high speed networks interconnecting them has become critical for wide-area data replication as well as for federated clouds ("sky computing" [8]). It is inefficient for applications to stall their execution in order to perform data movements across these data centers. DataSteward provides an alternative, as the applications can simply check-out their results to the dedicated nodes (through a low latency data transfer, within the deployment). Then, DataSteward performs the time consuming geographical data movement, while the application continues uninterrupted.
- *Scientific Big Data Processing Toolkit.* Scientific applications typically require additional processing of their input/output data, in order to make the results exploitable. Examples include: compression, filtering, aggregation, parallel transfers, etc. For large datasets, these manipulations are time and resource consuming; using dedicated nodes, such processing can overlap with the main computation and significantly decrease the time to solution. Let's take the example of data compression. Typically, the parallelization of scientific applications in multiple tasks leads to the output of multiple results. Before storing them persistently, one can decrease the incurred costs through compression. Grouping together these results on the dedicated nodes, we are able to achieve higher compression rates, than with results compressed independently on source nodes (by exploiting the data similarities and minimizing the compression overhead of multiple files/objects).

- *Cache for the Persistent Storage.* Its role would be to periodically backup into the cloud store service the data from the dedicated storage nodes. This approach complements DataSteward with persistency capabilities, following closely the structure of the physical storage hierarchy: machine memory, local and network disks, persistent storage.
- *Cloud Introspection as a Service.* Building on the previous clustering scheme and the measurements done in Sect. 5.1, we can design an introspection service that could reveal information about the cloud internals to the interested applications. The ability to collect large numbers of latency, bandwidth and throughput estimates without actively transferring data provides applications an inexpensive way to infer the cloud's internal details. These hints could be further used for topology-aware scheduling or for optimizing large data transfers.

Clearly this list is not exhaustive: the goal is rather to provide a software stack on top of the storage nodes, following a *data processing-as-a-service* paradigm. This "data steward" will be able, on one hand, to optimize the storage management and the end-to-end performance for a diverse set of data-intensive applications, and on the other hand, to prepare raw data issued/needed by experiments into a science-ready form used by scientists.

4.3 Leveraging Low Latency Storage for Reduction-Intensive Data Processing on Azure Clouds

Besides the efficient storage, data-intensive applications also need appropriate distributed computing frameworks to harness the power of clouds easily and effectively. In this respect, we devised a prototype MapReduce framework—TomusMapReduce—which specifically leverages the benefits of the TomusBlobs storage system to store input, intermediate and final results, by collocating data with computation (mappers and reducers). The framework uses a simple scheduling mechanism based on the Azure Queues to ensure coordination between its entities. With the storage and computation in the same virtualized environment, high throughout, protection and confidentiality are enhanced, as opposed to the remote Azure Blobs.

While this default MapReduce model can be used in numerous scenarios, when it comes to data processing flows that require a unique result, the model reaches its limitations. Many data intensive applications require *reduction* operations for aggregation, filtering, numerical integration, Monte Carlo simulations, etc. These algorithms have a common pattern: data are processed *iteratively* and aggregated into a *single final result*. While in the initial MapReduce proposal the reduce phase was a simple aggregation function, recently an increasing number of applications relying on MapReduce exhibit a reduce-intensive pattern, that is, an important part of the computations are done during the reduce phase. The existing distributed processing runtime engines lack explicit support for reduction or implement it in an inadequate way for clouds: they typically do not directly support full reduction into a single file. One can either use a single reducer and so the reduce step will loose its parallelism or can create an additional aggregator that will collect all the results from the reducers and combine them into a single result. For reduce-intensive workloads this final operation can become a bottleneck.

We propose MapIterativeReduce [10], a new execution model for reduce-intensive workloads that extends TomusMapReduce and exploits the inherent parallelism of the reduce tasks. In MapIterativeReduce, no barriers are needed between the map and the reduce phases: the reducers start the computation as soon as some data is available, reducing the total execution time. Our approach builds on the observation that a large class of scientific applications require the same operator to be applied to combine data from all nodes. In order to exploit any inherent parallelism in reduction, this operator has to be at least associative and/or commutative. Most operators that are used in scientific computing (e.g. max, min, sum, select) are both associative and commutative. Reduction may be also used with non-associative and non-commutative operations but offers less potential parallelism.

With the proposed execution model, the typical data flow is presented in Fig. 4. This consists of a classical *map* phase followed by an *iterative reduce* phase. The reducers apply the associative operator to a subset of intermediate data, issued either by the mappers or by other reducers from previous iterations. After the computation, the (partial) resultis fed back as input to other reducers. These iterations continue

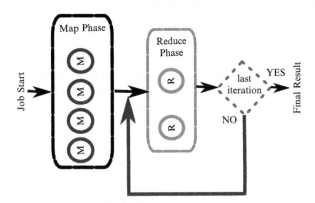

Fig. 4 The MapIterativeReduce conceptual model

until a reducer combines all the intermediate data into a unique result. All reducers check in a distributed fashion whether their output is the final result, using several parameters attached to the reduce tasks and thus avoiding the single point of failure represented by a centralised control entity.

We can now define the reduction as a scheduling problem: mapping the tasks to the reducers using a reduction tree. The iterative reduce phase can be viewed as a reduction tree, each iteration corresponding to a tree level. A clarifying example of an unfolding of the iterative process is given in Fig. 5. Each reducer processes three

Fig. 5 An example of a
reduction tree for five
mappers and a reduction ratio
of 3

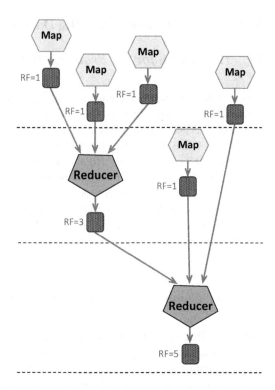

sets of data at a time and the initial number of mappers is 5. During the first iteration,
only one reducer has all the input available, while in the second iteration the bottom
reducer can process the two remaining data sets and the data issued from the first
iteration to produce the final result. With the associative operator, it is possible to
interleave the computation from different iterations to better exploit parallelism.

One of the key reasons for MapReduce framework's success is its runtime
support for fault tolerance. Our approach for dependability is two folded: on one
hand, we rely on the implicit fault tolerance support of the underlying platforms
(Azure, TomusBlobs), on the other hand, we implemented specific techniques for
dealing with failures in MapIterativeReduce. We use the visibility timeout of the
Azure Queues to guarantee that a submitted message will not be lost and will be
eventually executed by a Worker, as in TomusMapReduce. For the iterative reduce
phase, however, this mechanism is not enough. Since a Reducer has to process
several messages from different queues, a more complex technique for recovering
the jobs in case of failures is needed. We developed a distributed watchdog that
monitors the progress of the Reducers. It implements a light checkpointing scheme
by saving the state of the jobs to the file system, in parallel with the reduce
processing. In case of a failure of some Reducer, the system will rollback the
descriptions of the intermediate data and the reduce job, which will be assigned to
another Reducer from the pool. This allows MapIterativeReduce to restart a failed
task from the previous iteration, instead of starting the reduction from the beginning.

5   Executing a Large Scale Big Data Experiment on the Cloud

5.1   The Search for the Brain–Gene Correlations

Joint genetic and neuro-imaging data analysis may help identifying risk factors in target populations. Performing such studies on a large number of subjects is challenging as genotyping DNA chips can record several hundred thousands values per subject, while the fMRI images may contain 100 k to 1 M volumetric picture elements. Determining statistically the significant links between the two sets of data entails a massive amount of computation as one needs not only to compare all pairwise relations but also to correct for family-wise multiple comparisons. These false positives are controlled by generating permutations of the input data set. A-Brain [1, 6] is such a data analysis application involving large cohorts of subjects and used to study and understand the variability that exists between individuals.

5.2   The Computation and Storage Problems

Supposing that such an application could be executed on single machine, the computation would take years. Cloud infrastructures have the potential to decrease this computation time to days, by parallelizing and scaling out the application. After a preliminary analysis of the whole spectrum of genes and brain positions, a subset was chosen in which the potential correlations would have biological meaning. This subset consists of $\approx 21 * 10^{10}$ associations that need to be evaluated. In order to execute this computation in parallel at a large scale, we noticed that the A-Brain application can be easily described as a MapReduce processing. The problem was further divided into 28,000 computation tasks, which were executed as map jobs.

5.3   Experimental Setup

The MapReduce-based processing was performed using 1,000 CPUs in three deployments running in two US Azure data centers—North and West. In addition, a fourth deployment was used both for the initial data partition (i.e. using a *Splitter*) and for the global result computation using the MapIterativeReduce technique; the latter consisted of 563 reduce jobs, each having a reduction ratio of 50. For the computation, the Large Size VM Worker Roles were used, each having four CPUs, 7 GB of memory and 400 Mbps bandwidth and a local storage of 1 TB.

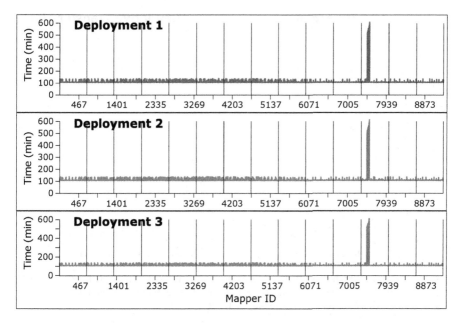

Fig. 6 The execution of the compute tasks in the three deployments: 28,000 tasks are executed as map jobs, ≈9,000 in each data center. The spike in the last part of each chart corresponds to the cloud services becoming temporary unavailable

5.4   Results

In Fig. 6 we present the execution time of the map jobs for each of the three deployments. The values are similar for all deployments, even though the computation is performed across two different data centers. This is due to the initial partitioning and the local buffering of the data that prevent mappers from remote accesses. The outage times shown towards the end of the experiment are due to a temporary failure in the cloud which made the cloud services inaccessible. During this period, the mappers became idle until the cloud became available again and the computation could be resumed. In addition to the map times, we present in Fig. 7 an analysis of the reduction times with respect to the number of reducers and the corresponding reduction ratio (i.e. the workload of a reducer–number of inputs to process). A parallel reduction process brings significant improvements up to the point where the communication overhead becomes important and the number of reducers is too big compared to the available resources. Hence, they will be executed in waves, increasing the timespan of the reduction process. Making such an analysis before the experiment allows the selection of a proper reduction ratio (i.e. 50 for our experiment) in order to reduce the overall execution time.

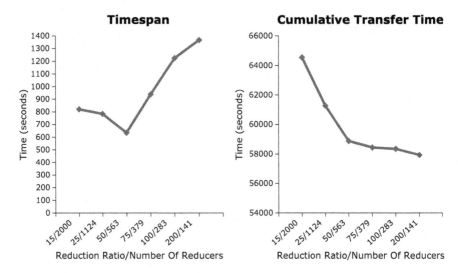

Fig. 7 Overview of the IterativeReduce processing times with respect to the reduction ratio and the number of reducers. On the *left chart*, the timespan of the overall reduction process with 250 nodes; on the *right chart*, the cumulative transfer times

A data analysis of the experiment is presented in Fig. 8, aiming to quantify the gains brought in terms of data transfers by our proposals. We start with a naive estimation of the overall data size per job by considering the amount of data that is needed to execute a job; this considers the input data size, the results size, the environment setup, the log file sizes, etc.—all multiplied with the total number of jobs. Considering the big number of jobs, this value easily reaches tens of terabytes, but such a situation is not realistic as it would imply that all jobs are executed in parallel on different nodes. The cost of transferring such amounts of data would be enormous, both in time and money, which shows that a tradeoff should be set for the parallelism of the system. In addition to restricting the number of independent processing nodes, different techniques can be used to avoid transferring data to and from them. Buffering data, both at compute node level and at deployment level is straightforward and brings important benefits as many transfers can be avoided. Additional techniques range from compression, which can be provided by the data management system, to application specific solutions like reordering the tasks. The parallelization order of the computation is also a key factor when analyzing the data, as a higher number of nodes require higher amounts of data to be transferred and generate more data within the deployment (e.g. the size difference between task based and compute node based estimation).

Big Data experiments generate and deal with a large number of files, holding input, output, intermediate, log or monitoring data. Dealing with many files, either directly by the user or autonomously by the system can be complex and takes time if the proper tools are missing. Figure 9 presents the performance analysis for different operations on the 28,000 monitoring files of the map jobs that result after running

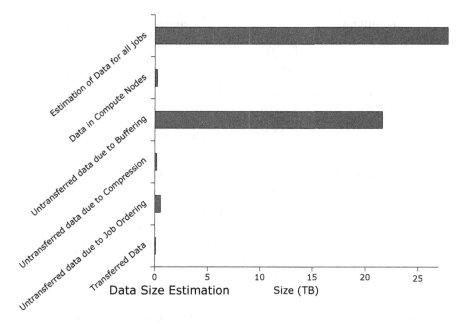

Fig. 8 Estimation of the managed data sizes

the A-Brain experiment. On the one hand, the cloud storage system provides a basic API, which leads to all basic functions like selection; filtering, aggregation, zipping etc., being implemented and executed at the client side (i.e. in the worker role). On the other hand, a storage system like DataSteward, which extends the cloud data API and provides data functions at server side (i.e. in the cloud nodes that hold the data) is able to reduce the time to manage the files and ease the job of the scientists who needs to prepare, deploy and manage their experimental environment in the cloud.

As discussed previously, the location of the data is critical for the read and write storage access performance. Figure 10 shows the cumulative throughput that multiple clients achieve when accessing data from different storage solutions. On the one hand, the performance of the remote cloud storage (within the same data center or from another geographically remote data center) is subject to high latency but has availability and durability guarantees. The local solutions (i.e. within the deployment) provide superior throughput at the expense of ephemerality. It is interesting to observe that when the overall amount of data accessed within the deployment increases, dedicating compute nodes to manage it brings the highest benefits. This is due to the fact that the throughput depends both on the bandwidth, which is no longer shared by the storage and the application, as well as on the CPU, which, in the case of the compute nodes used by DataSteward, is entirely dedicated to data handling.

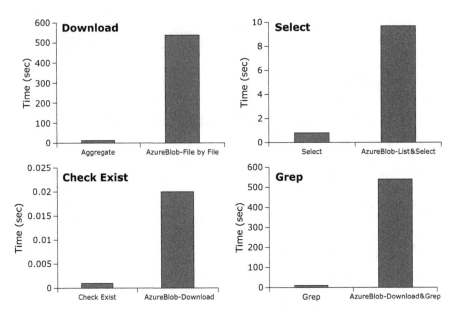

Fig. 9 The timespan of executing basic operations on 28,000 monitor files, when the operation is supported and executed on server side compared to client side

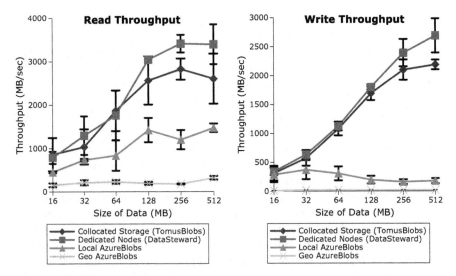

Fig. 10 The cumulative read and write throughput reached by 50 nodes for different locations of the storage system

5.5   Big Data Processing on Clouds: Lessons Learned

In the process of designing, implementing, supporting and validating our cloud storage solutions through large scale experiments, we had the opportunity to gain useful experience and learn several interesting lessons. This section details these issues and suggests our solutions to provide a roadmap for readers interested in leveraging public clouds storage for their applications. We believe that this discussion will help readers make informed design choices for their respective cloud-based data-intensive applications. While some of these lessons specifically relate to the Azure cloud platform, other could be considered from a more general perspective and could be relevant for any cloud storage platform.

5.5.1   Lessons Learned on How to Best Benefit from the Azure Cloud

Message Visibility Timeouts Within Azure Queues   We have experimented Azure Queues as a mechanism for scheduling and for communication between the running processes. They differ from the traditional queue data structures as they lack the ability to guarantee a FIFO operation, due to their inner support for fault tolerance: messages read from the queues are not deleted, but instead hidden until an explicit delete is received after a successful processing. If no such confirmation arrives, the message will become visible again in the queue, after a predefined visibility timeout. We rely on the visibility timeout of the queues to guarantee that a submitted message will not be lost and will be eventually executed by a worker. Initially set to 2 h, the visibility timeout was increased to a week at the latest Azure API update. The reason why the visibility timeout matters is that for larger workloads, it might take roles longer than the timeout period to process the jobs, making the synchronization messages disappear from the queue and hence leading to incorrect results. We faced this issue during long running executions (about 2 weeks) of our A-Brain application with large input data or fewer nodes. A solution to this problem can be an application level tracking mechanism for the submitted jobs, that automatically resubmits the failed jobs. We have implemented this in our design of TomusMapReduce for geographically distributed datacenters, but obviously this generated an additional overhead and requires deep knowledge of Azure's internals, which is generally not possessed by the average scientific user.

Application Deployment Times   While working with the Azure cloud storage platform we have observed that the resource allocation process plays a crucial role in the overall application performance. For each new or updated deployment on Azure, the fabric controller prepares the role instances requested by the application. This process is time-consuming and varies with the number of instances requested by the application as well as with the deployment size (application executables, related libraries, data dependencies etc.). The deployment time has reduced after the latest API release known at the time of writing this chapter, but can still be a major bottleneck. To minimize this time, we suggest building the environment setup at runtime, when possible.

Handling VM Failures An interesting observation relates to the Azure fault tolerance support. Built on top of clusters of commodity services and disk drives, the cloud hosts an abundance of failure sources that include hardware, software, network connectivity and power issues. To achieve high performance in such conditions, in our initial estimations and designs we had the provision for failures at the application level. However, we discovered that only a very small fraction of the machines failed even during the course of very long running executions: during the 2 weeks experiments on several hundred nodes, only three machines failed (fail-stop-restart). This high availability is due to the complex, multi-tiered distributed systems that transparently implement in Azure sophisticated data management, load balancing and recovery techniques. We note from our experience that though disk failures can result in permanent data loss, the multitude of transitory node failures account for most unavailability. To enhance robustness, one can further use the Azure Queues: their visibility timeout can be exploited to make an application both failsafe and efficient, as explained in the previous paragraph.

5.5.2 Beyond Azure: Lessons Learned on Big Data Processing on Clouds

Wave- Versus Pipelined-MapReduce Processing One lesson we learned while running complex MapReduce workloads is that starting all the jobs (e.g. maps) at once is inefficient as it leads to massively-concurrent accesses to data. For example, this happens in the following cases: concurrent access to the initial data or high pressure on the cloud storage system when the processing reaches its end. The network bandwidth is then basically in two states: either saturated or idle. As we have gained more experience with these problems, we have addressed them by improving the MapReduce model. For example, starting jobs in a pipeline manner proves to be a better approach. Map tasks are created along the pipeline, as soon as their input data becomes available, in order to speed up the execution. This approach allows successive jobs in the pipeline to overlap the execution of reduce tasks with that of map tasks. In this manner, by dynamically creating and scheduling tasks, the framework is able to complete the execution of the pipeline faster.

Data Buffering and Caching Another lesson we learned is that, during long running experiments, many data blocks are likely to be reused. It then becomes useful to buffer them locally and to avoid further costly transfers. The idea is to receive hints on the potential reuse of a file, before taking the decision of deleting it. These hints could be given by the components which deploy the workload into the system. To take the example of TomusMapReduce, this would be the responsibility of the Data Splitter, in charge of data sharding across the nodes.

Scheduling Mechanisms for Efficient Data Access In a cross-datacenter deployment, a high number of geographical distributed concurrent access are likely to lead to operation failures. For instance, if 100 nodes try to download the same file from a different geographical region, 70 % of the read attempts will fail. This situation typically occurs when some libraries or data sets are needed to setup the environment within the VMs. A naive solution in order to avoid re-scheduling is to retry the operation in a loop. Besides being inefficient and generating additional failures this approach might lead to starvation for some nodes. Adding random sleeps between retries (as in the network decongestion algorithms) works in some cases, but in general converges very slowly if there are many concurrent clients. Moreover, if the download operation is long, other ongoing downloads can fail due to the attempts made by the other nodes which will lead to deadlocks as in the previous point. We opted for a token-based scheduling approach, by allowing a predefined maximum number of nodes to concurrently access a shared resource. The use of dedicated data nodes can further improve the data access: by acting as proxies, they are used to disseminate data locally, close to the interested computation nodes.

Monitoring Services to Track the Real-Time Status of the Application A practical lesson that we learned is the importance of proper system-level monitoring and further estimating the I/O and storage performance accurately and robustly in a dynamic environment. It is essential to be able to predict the behavior of the underlying network and endsystems, in order to judiciouslycommit to decisions

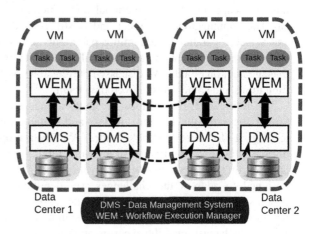

Fig. 11 A typical cloud deployment containing a workflow engine and a data management system

related to storage and transfer optimizations over federated datacenters. Estimates must be updated to reflect changing workloads, varying network-device conditions and configurations due to multi-tenancy. Building on this monitoring phase we were able to design performance models of cloud resources automatically. They are further leveraged to predict the best combination of protocol and transfer parameters (e.g. flow count, multicast enhancement, replication degree) in order to maximize throughput or minimize costs, according to users needs.

Going Beyond MapReduce: Cloud-Based Scientific Workflows The most important lesson we learned is that although MapReduce is the "de-facto" standard for cloud data processing, most scientific applications don't fit this model and require a more general data orchestration, independent of any programming model.

Executing a scientific workflow in the cloud involves moving its tasks and files to the execution nodes. This data movement is critical for performance and costs since when a task is assigned to an execution node, some of its required files may not be available locally. Currently, on public clouds, this is achieved by using the cloud storage services (e.g. Azure Blobs), which are unable to exploit the workflow semantics and are subject to low throughput and high latencies. Thus, properly scheduling the tasks according to the data layout within the compute VMs or placing the data according to the computation pattern becomes a necessity. In order to achieve this, we are advocating a two-way communication between the workflow engine deployed on the cloud and the data management system, as illustrated in Fig. 11. They should collaborate in order to optimize the data processing by migrating and scheduling the data or the tasks. We are currently investigating and experimenting this approach.

Conclusions

Porting data intensive applications to the clouds brings forward many issues in exploiting the benefits of current and upcoming cloud infrastructures. In this landscape, building a functional infrastructure for the requirements of Big Data applications is critical and is still a challenge. Efficient storage and scalable parallel programming paradigms are some critical examples. In this chapter, we investigated several hot challenges related to Big Data management on clouds. We discussed current state-of-the-art solutions, their limitations and some ways to overcome them.

We introduced TomusBlobs, a cloud storage solution aggregating the virtual disks on the compute nodes, and DataSteward, a storage system leveraging dedicated compute nodes. We then proposed TomusMapReduce, a prototype MapReduce framework relying on our storage solutions and MapIterativeReduce—its iterative reduction counterpart, specifically designed to address the challenges we identified. We demonstrated the benefits of our approach through multi-sites experiments on a thousand cores across three Azure data centres and consuming more than 200.000 compute hours—the largest scientific experimental setup on Azure up to date—using a real-life application.

The evaluation shows that it is clearly possible to sustain a high data throughput in the Azure cloud thanks to our low-latency storage. Nevertheless, several problems like task and data scheduling, application monitoring and workflow execution raise important challenges and open the avenue for future research.

References

1. A-Brain. http://www.irisa.fr/kerdata/doku.php?id=abrain.
2. Azure. http://www.windowsazure.com/.
3. Extracting Value from Chaos. EMC Corporation, June 2011. http://www.emc.com/collateral/analyst-reports/idc-extracting-value-from-chaos-ar.pdf.
4. B. Calder, J. Wang, A. Ogus, N. Nilakantan, A. Skjolsvold, S. McKelvie, Y. Xu, S. Srivastav, J. Wu, H. Simitci, J. Haridas, C. Uddaraju, H. Khatri, A. Edwards, V. Bedekar, S. Mainali, R. Abbasi, A. Agarwal, M. F. u. Haq, M. I. u. Haq, D. Bhardwaj, S. Dayanand, A. Adusumilli, M. McNett, S. Sankaran, K. Manivannan, and L. Rigas. Windows azure storage: a highly available cloud storage service with strong consistency. In *Proceedings of the Twenty-Third ACM Symposium on Operating Systems Principles*, SOSP '11, pages 143–157, New York, NY, USA, 2011. ACM.
5. D. Chappell. Introducing the Windows Azure Platform. Technical report, Microsoft. http://www.microsoft.com/windowsazure/whitepapers/.
6. A. Costan, R. Tudoran, G. Antoniu, and G. Brasche. TomusBlobs: Scalable Data-intensive Processing on Azure Clouds. *Journal of Concurrency and computation: practice and experience*, 2013.
7. A. Greenberg, J. Hamilton, D. A. Maltz, and P. Patel. The cost of a cloud: research problems in data center networks. *SIGCOMM Comput. Commun. Rev.*, 39(1):68–73, Dec. 2008.
8. K. Keahey, M. Tsugawa, A. Matsunaga, and J. Fortes. Sky computing. *IEEE Internet Computing*, 13(5):43–51, Sept. 2009.
9. B. Nicolae, G. Antoniu, L. Bougé, D. Moise, and A. Carpen-Amarie. BlobSeer: Next Generation Data Management for Large Scale Infrastructures. *Journal of Parallel and Distributed Computing*, 71(2):168–184, Feb. 2011.
10. R. Tudoran, A. Costan, and G. Antoniu. Mapiterativereduce: a framework for reduction-intensive data processing on azure clouds. In *Proceedings of third international workshop on MapReduce and its Applications Date*, MapReduce '12, pages 9–16, New York, NY, USA, 2012. ACM.
11. R. Tudoran, A. Costan, and G. Antoniu. Datasteward: Using dedicated compute nodes for scalable data management on public clouds. In *Proceedings of the 11th IEEE International Symposium on Parallel and Distributed Processing with Applications*, ISPA '13, Washington, DC, USA, 2013. IEEE Computer Society.
12. R. Tudoran, A. Costan, G. Antoniu, and H. Soncu. Tomusblobs: Towards communication-efficient storage for mapreduce applications in azure. In *Proceedings of the 2012 12th IEEE/ACM International Symposium on Cluster, Cloud and Grid Computing (ccgrid 2012)*, CCGRID '12, pages 427–434, Washington, DC, USA, 2012. IEEE Computer Society.
13. E. Yildirim and T. Kosar. Network-aware end-to-end data throughput optimization. In *Proceedings of the first international workshop on Network-aware data management*, NDM '11, pages 21–30, New York, NY, USA, 2011. ACM.

Storage and Data Life Cycle Management in Cloud Environments with FRIEDA

Lavanya Ramakrishnan, Devarshi Ghoshal, Valerie Hendrix, Eugen Feller, Pradeep Mantha, and Christine Morin

Abstract Infrastructure as a Service (IaaS) clouds provide a composable environment that is attractive for mid-range, high-throughput and data-intensive scientific workloads. However, the flexibility of IaaS clouds presents unique challenges for storage and data management in these environments. Users use manual and/or ad-hoc methods to manage storage selection, storage configuration and data management in these environments. We address these challenges via a novel storage and data life cycle management through FRIEDA (Flexible Robust Intelligent Elastic Data Management), an application specific storage and data management framework for composable infrastructure environments.

1 Introduction

In the last few years there has been a rapid growth in data-intensive scientific workloads. Data growth challenges have been considered to be multi-dimensional, i.e. increasing volume (size of data), velocity (data arrival rates), variety (multiple data types and sources), veracity (trust in the data source) and value (perceived value by the user). The data growth challenges have resulted in the increased use of cloud computing environments to serve the needs of data-intensive workloads.

The Infrastructure-as-a-Service (IaaS) cloud model provides a flexible environment where users get on-demand access to compute and storage hardware. In public clouds, the client typically pays on a per-use basis for use of the equipment. IaaS provides a "building block" approach to infrastructure where users can compose their infrastructure as it is best suited for their applications. However, the flexibility

---

L. Ramakrishnan (✉) • V. Hendrix • E. Feller • P. Mantha
Lawrence Berkeley National Lab, Berkeley, CA, USA
e-mail: LRamakrishnan@lbl.gov; vchendrix@lbl.gov; EFeller@lbl.gov; pkmantha@lbl.gov

D. Ghoshal
Indiana University, Bloomington, IN, USA
e-mail: dghoshal@cs.indiana.edu

C. Morin
Inria, Rennes, France
e-mail: Christine.Morin@inria.fr

© Springer Science+Business Media New York 2014
X. Li, J. Qiu (eds.), *Cloud Computing for Data-Intensive Applications*,
DOI 10.1007/978-1-4939-1905-5_15

of the IaaS model adds management complexity for the end user. For instance, the user needs to manage the operating system, system software, and the storage. Previous work has investigated various aspects of managing the compute resources and associated software stack for scientific applications in IaaS environments [15, 22]. However, the work in storage and data management has been largely focused on storage services that provides an interface to storage resources [9,18,25], which is by itself insufficient to manage complex data-intensive workloads.

Traditional supercomputing centers have served the needs of scientists that have large simulation codes with high communication needs and have limited support for other workloads. Supercomputing centers also provide access to high performance file systems and archival storage. Scientific applications and their users are used to the pre-configured storage models in clusters and HPC systems (e.g., shared file system, archive systems). The storage and data management challenges introduced by the IaaS model arise from the inherent transient model of resources. First, such an environment provides a myriad of temporary and permanent storage resources. Each virtual machine has transient local disks and can access more permanent storage such as block store volumes and object stores. Each of these resources has various performance, price and size trade-offs [17, 21]. Second, applications need to explicitly manage the data on the servers and/or virtual machines (VMs). It is the application's responsibility to move the input data and store the output data for archival either in the cloud or outside the cloud. Thus, users need to pick and compose their storage choices, layer it with appropriate system software and coordinate the management of data on these resources. Much of this work is time consuming and is currently performed manually or through ad-hoc scripts.

In this chapter, we describe a framework, FRIEDA (Flexible Robust Intelligent Elastic Data Management), for storage and data life cycle management in cloud. FRIEDA is a framework that provides application-specific customized storage planning, data placement and execution for scientific applications. We discuss related work, scientific applications and cloud and HPC resource models in Sects. 2 and 3. We describe the storage and data management life cycle as managed by FRIEDA in Sect. 4. We describe storage planning in Sect. 5, storage provisioning in Sect. 6 and data placement in Sect. 7. We describe FRIEDA's execution framework in Sect. 8. Finally, we summarize in Sect. 9.

2   Related Work

In this section, we summarize related work.

Data Management in Programming Models   The requirement for data-intensive applications to distribute and process data in parallel has given rise to many frameworks and programming models. MapReduce and its open source implementation Hadoop have been used for distributed data processing [13]. MapReduce and Hadoop use a specialized file system (i.e., Google File System [16] and

Hadoop Distributed File System [8]) that provides data locality and replication. MPI [2] is used for writing portable and scalable large-scale parallel applications. Hadoop provides minimal control over data distribution among the nodes. MPI, on the other hand requires the user to completely control data management and communication across different compute nodes. But, none of these techniques provide a generic solution to distribute data and execute applications without instrumentation or rewriting them. Hadoop streaming provides solutions to execute any existing script or program. There have been proposals to improve the existing MapReduce framework for adaptive data placement on heterogeneous Hadoop clusters [31]. Dryad [20] is a general-purpose distributed execution engine for coarse-grain data-parallel applications. However, these frameworks do not provide a generic framework that allows users to control data movement, data management and execution in cloud environments. FRIEDA is a generic framework to execute any script or program by combining data parallelization, data grouping, and data distribution without any instrumentation at the application-level.

Distributed Data Management Various aspects of distributed data management have been considered in the context of distributed and grid environments including tools for optimized wide area data transfer [4, 26], replica management [10], metadata catalog and data discovery systems [24, 27]. However, the characteristics of cloud environment (e.g., elasticity, transient nature of storage) present unique challenges which necessitate the need to revisit the data management framework design. Data parallelization and task farming approaches have been shown to significantly reduce execution times for embarrassingly parallel applications like BLAST [7, 23]. FRIEDA provides similar benefits to scientific applications but its approach is applicable to a large number of applications.

Workflow Tools Scientific workflow management systems [28] manage data-intensive workflows and associated volumes of data. Deelman et al. [14] highlight several challenges in data management for data-intensive scientific workflows. But, none of the workflow tools provide flexible mechanisms to partition the data. Moreover, workflow tools rely on existing locations of data and/or move data where there are dependencies. FRIEDA supports only data-parallel tasks. However, FRIEDA provides a flexible interface that can be used by workflow tools to control parts or all of its workflow execution.

Storage Planning Pesto [18] automates storage performance management for virtualized data centers using black-box performance models, providing IO load balancing, per-device congestion management and initial placement of workloads. Minerva [6] uses declarative specifications of application requirements and device capabilities along with constraint-based formulations for designing storage systems. FRIEDA's storage planner also has specifications for storage resources and application descriptions. However, they target storage management during execution and not the design of storage systems. Walker et al. [30] propose a modeling tool developed from empirical data to evaluate the benefits of using storage clouds versus purchasing disk drives. Thereska et al. [29] provides support for self-prediction in a storage system designed for clusters. FRIEDA provides a generic framework which has the ability to plug-in various models for automated storage models.

Elasticizer [19] allows users to express cluster sizing problems as queries and uses job profiling, estimation and simulation to answer the queries. However, its focus is on elastic compute planning and it does not support storage planning based on data characteristics.

Distributed storage systems (e.g., MosaStore [11, 12]) provide automated configuration for application needs. Currently, FRIEDA framework is designed to operate in cloud systems where the storage services cannot be configured dynamically at this time.

3 Background

Scientific applications have heterogeneous storage and data requirements based on their application characteristics. For example, BLAST, a bioinformatics application, compares sequences with a reference database. In contrast a tomography image comparison and normalization application operates on a set of images. Thus, the choice of storage components and data management strategies depends on the data source location, volume of data, scale of analysis and the access patterns (and cost, in the case of public clouds). In this section, we provide a brief overview of storage models and application characteristics that affect FRIEDA design.

3.1 Storage Models

Scientific users are accustomed to the storage model on local clusters and HPC systems that provides scratch, project workspaces and/or archival systems. Users typically have access to shared and high-performance file systems. The file systems maybe transient but might have lifetime of weeks or months associated with them (e.g., scratch) or more permanent (e.g., project or user home directories). Additionally, most HPC systems provide long-term archival storage. Users typically run their application codes on the system using scratch space and then move their data to either project space and/or archival storage as appropriate.

Cloud providers such as Amazon and other private cloud software solutions such as Eucalyptus provide multiple storage options. Users have access to non-persistent local disk on the instance. In addition, a user can mount a block level storage volume that persists independently from the life of an instance. These block stores are expected to be highly available, highly reliable storage volumes suitable for applications requiring a database, file system, or access to raw block level storage. Additionally, Amazon S3 is an object storage service that offers a highly-scalable, reliable, and low-latency data storage infrastructure through a web service interface. Each of the instances provided also have different advertised I/O performance. For example, the small instances provide moderate I/O performance while the high I/O instances provide high, low latency disk I/O performance using SSD-based local instance storage.

Different application use cases can also impact how cloud storage is utilized. For example, if data is going to be reused multiple times, using block store volumes can save data movement and placement costs. This makes it important to carefully select storage in cloud environments. Thus, we need a framework that provides a more systematic and coordinated, yet flexible, approach to storage and data management in IaaS environments.

3.2 I/O Performance in Cloud Environments

In previous work [17], we performed an extensive I/O benchmarking study comparing various cloud platforms and service offerings. The I/O performance on virtual hosts tends to show a fair amount of overhead and variability due to the contention and sharing of underlying resources. However, as hypervisor and storage technologies improve, we are seeing better I/O performance available in virtualized environments.

The performance of the local disk tends to be slightly higher than the block store volumes. This is especially true in the Amazon small instances that are bandwidth limited. The advertised I/O performance on the instance type is expected to get better with larger instances. In some cases better I/O performance has been reported on the small instance local disk than the large instance. However, small instances do tend to show a fair amount of variability. The EBS performance is definitely known to improve with the instance types possibly due to the better network bandwidth available to the larger instances.

Thus, an application will need to consider various factors—size, reliability, performance, cost, persistence needs, I/O access patterns while picking the appropriate storage options.

3.3 Resource Model

The storage devices most commonly used by scientific applications today are (a) local disks on virtual machines which are pre-mounted at boot-up time, (b) block store devices exposed as a physical device that end-user has to prepare (i.e., create partitions and format) and, (c) object stores. The first two classes might have size limits associated with them as configured by a site administrator.

The user can use the storage devices with different distributed and parallel file systems (e.g., NFS, GlusterFS, HDFS). Figure 1 shows the various configurations that are possible with the different storage options, file systems and provisioning models. We use the term "virtual cluster" to refer to a provisioned cluster (either

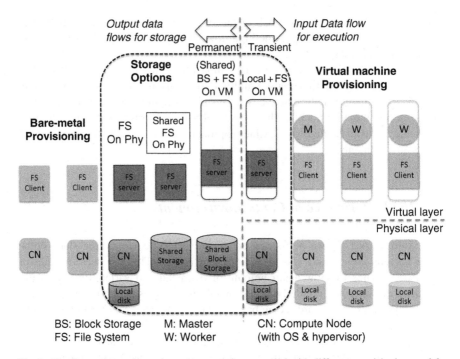

Fig. 1 The figure shows the various storage options coupled with different provisioning models. Compute provisioning models allow bare-metal and virtual machine provisioning where the nodes might be configured with different CPU, memory and disk options. The storage and file system can result in a variety of different configurations of virtual clusters

bare-metal or virtual machines) that is configured for a particular user or instance of application execution. Compute provisioning models allow bare-metal and virtual machine provisioning. Each node allocated is configured with different CPU, memory and disk options. In bare-metal provisioning, storage might be available through shared storage pools or through local disks available on each compute node. Similarly, in virtual machines, applications can use local disk accessible within each instance. Virtual machines might also act as clients to a file server running on a virtual server. In addition, it is possible to run hybrid modes where the physical file servers might be used in virtual machines. It is important to note here that input data flows from physical servers into virtual space for execution and output data when generated moves out from the virtual space to physical space for permanent storage.

3.4 Application Execution modes

Our focus is on data-intensive and high-throughput applications with negligible communication and hence FRIEDA is based on the master-worker (also known as task-farmer) programming paradigm. The master decomposes the problem into small tasks and distributes these tasks for execution on the workers. The communication is between the master and the workers and the master is responsible for aggregating the partial results to produce the final result.

We assume that there is no specific task affinity to a certain machine i.e., task placement considers all available virtual machines as viable for task scheduling. Each task might execute for different lengths of time depending on the task at hand but we have no pre-existing knowledge of the execution time of individual tasks.

Our framework is designed to work with both physical machines, virtual machines, or both.

3.5   Scientific Application Data Classes

Scientific applications have a variety of application data that needs to be available in the execution environments. We use the term "data" loosely to capture all execution variables including application sources and libraries. FRIEDA considers the following data classes for applications:

Application Executables Scientific application executable and dependent libraries need to be available on all execution nodes. Users have the option to include this in the image that they create. However, any version changes to the application or dependent libraries would require users to recreate the image. Thus, users often prefer to manage placement of these executables on the resource at run-time.

Input Data We consider input data to be the total non-shared data required by the tasks in the execution. In real-time mode, this data would be managed by the master and the data moved during execution to the workers. We assume that input data is either available on an existing device in the cloud or can be obtained from an external source over the internet.

Shared Data Scientific applications often rely on shared databases and/or data that needs to be accessed by all the workers. We consider shared data to be read-only for our applications.

Intermediate Data The intermediate data is generated by the tasks but does not need to be persisted beyond the lifetime of the execution. In this case, storage resources need to be allocated during the lifetime of the execution but need not be managed beyond that.

Output Data The output data is generated by the application during execution. We consider output data to be data that the user would like to persist beyond the lifetime of the execution. If there is intermediate data that needs to be persisted, we classify that as output data. Since output data needs to be persisted we consider only two storage options for the same, i.e., block-device type stores and/or object stores.

Log Data We need to provision storage space on all workers for log files.

4   FRIEDA Life Cycle

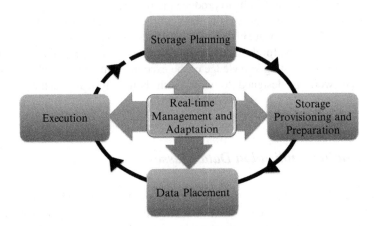

Fig. 2 The figure shows the life cycle of storage and data management in cloud environments. The storage planning component plans for the storage requirements for the particular application that triggers provisioning, preparation and data placement

FRIEDA (Flexible Robust Intelligent Elastic Data Management) manages the life cycle of storage and data management in IaaS environments. Figure 2 shows the life cycle of storage and data management as managed by FRIEDA. The first step in the life cycle is *storage planning*. The storage planning determines the best storage option as well as the appropriate data placement on the machines.

The storage planning drives the *provisioning and preparation* phase where the resources are procured from the site. The planning phase provides a recipe of the storage resources that need to be procured and setup (e.g., appropriate filesystem). Once the storage is setup, *data placement* occurs where data is placed on the resources as per the pre-determined plan.

In the next phase, the workload is *executed* on the resources using the guidelines from the storage planning and data placement phase. The execution framework uses the storage model setup by the previous phases and provides elastic data management of the intermediate and output data as appropriate.

Our architecture is designed such that the monitoring and state management can be used to drive the life cycle with changes (e.g., more data, resources failing) during the life cycle. FRIEDA gives users the control over the data partitioning and distribution across the nodes within a virtual cluster. Next, we describe the strategies currently supported in FRIEDA for data partitioning and data management.

4.1 Data Partitioning

Cloud computing has various resource options with different performance, reliability, scalability and cost trade-offs [17, 21]. Data management strategy needs to account for the storage options that might be available to an application at a given resource provider site and the application characteristics.

Every virtual machine has a local disk that provides the fastest I/O. However local disk space is very limited typically in the order of a few gigabytes. Thus, typically local disks are best used for application codes, checkpoint data and intermediate stage data. Additionally, various cloud providers provide a way to use block store volumes and/or external storage volumes within the virtual machines. Applications that need to operate on shared data might mount shared file systems. External storage, like iSCSI disks or any other network storage, provides a means to handle and store large amounts of data which can be shared across the network as well. FRIEDA's storage planning takes these characteristics into account when planning for storage and data placement.

There are trade-offs between locally placing the data versus dynamically fetching the data from remote sources. It is important to consider eliminating the network bottleneck and making best use of computation resources available. Thus, the resource configuration and the execution behavior of the analysis workflow can result in various data partitioning strategies:

No Partitioning The naive approach to data management would be to make the complete dataset available on every compute node. In this mode, we do not partition the data. The entire data is moved to each node and/or made available through a shared file system. This model is well suited for applications where every computation relies on a common data set (e.g., a database).

Pre-determined In pre-determined and homogeneous workloads, optimal solutions can be found by pre-partitioning the data before the computation starts. Thus, every node only has the data it needs for its computation thus saving on data movement costs and possible synchronization overheads. This method works best if every computation is more or less identical.

Real-Time The real-time partitioning of data is designed to suit experiments where each computation is not identical or the compute resources are heterogeneous or in elastic environments where additional resources might become available during the execution. This partitioning strategy inherently load-balances since overloaded nodes get less data to process.

4.2   Data Management

Figure 8 shows the data management strategies in FRIEDA. FRIEDA supports pre-partitioning of data where data is available locally and/or on a networked storage. Additionally, FRIEDA supports real-time data partitioning and distribution.

Pre-partitioned Task and Common Data   In this mode, tasks are pre-partitioned but the entire data-set is pre-distributed to all the nodes. Although processing the data locally is more efficient compared to over the network, transferring all the data to every node is expensive and not a practical solution for most applications.

Pre-partitioned Task and Data   In this strategy, partitioning happens before computation begins. Each computation unit processes the data-set assigned to it. This strategy helps applications where processing the data at the source is impossible due to resource constraints. Every partition is transferred to the respective compute node before the computation begins. In this case, the total execution cost is the transfer time of the data to the nodes plus the execution time of each computation.

Real-Time Task and Data Partitioning   A real-time task and data partitioning handles data partitioning and distribution dynamically when the computation unit asks for it. It is inherently load-balanced, specifically if every computation task does not consume same amount of resources or if computation happens in a heterogeneous environment. This type of partitioning is also capable of utilizing the network in an efficient manner since data transfer can be overlapped with computation over a shared network.

5   Storage Planning

Figure 3 shows our storage planning process. The storage planning takes as input information about the resources and the application data classes. The resource information includes an ordered storage list that includes size and scalability features of the storage option. It also takes compute description (e.g., virtual machine type, count, etc). The storage planning applies it to the application data classes in sequence. It generates three outputs (a) master storage description, (b) worker storage description and (c) data placement semantics. The master storage description and worker storage descriptions are used by FRIEDA's storage provisioning and preparation component. The data placement semantics are used to define the location where the application input data should be moved to on the virtual cluster.

The current implementation of FRIEDA planning assumes that the compute planning (i.e., determining the number of VMs) has either occurred previously through a compute provisioning system and/or the estimate is provided by the user. Thus, the storage planning comes up with the best storage plan for a given compute plan. Eventually, we envision that the compute and storage provisioning will be able to negotiate to come up with the best plan.

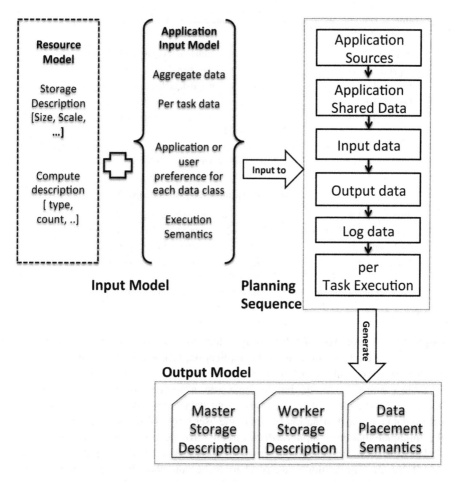

Fig. 3 The storage planning iterates over the different data classes for the application trying to determine the best storage fit given the ordered storage description and application or user preference for each data class

Planning Sequence Figure 3 shows the planning sequence that we currently implement. The planner first allocates storage for application sources on the first storage option on the storage description list. If the application sources will not fit on the storage device then the planner moves down the list of storage choices provided. Second, it allocates storage for application shared data on the next available item on the storage. We first allocate storage for these two data classes since they are applicable for all tasks in the workflow. Next, we allocate resources for input, output and log data. In the final step we verify that there is enough space available for execution time data per task.

Table 1 Description of aggregate data required for application execution (Application Input Model)

Application source	Size of the application binary and libraries
Input data	Size of the non-shared input data
Shared data	Size of the shared data that is required on all tasks
Output data	Expected total output data that will be generated
Intermediate data	Expected total intermediate data that will be generated
Output data destination	User specified destination for output data for persistence. Options are object or block store

Table 2 Per task data for application execution (Application Input Model)

Task input data	Input data required by a single task
Task intermediate data	Intermediate data generated by a single task
Task output data	Output data generated by a single task
Number of tasks	The total number of tasks that need to execute for this application
Number of concurrent tasks	The number of tasks that can run concurrently

Application Input Model The storage planning takes five classes of inputs. It takes aggregate information about the application, task-level information about the application, execution semantics, resource information and system-level parameters.

Table 1 shows the inputs that are aggregate information of the application data. It consists of the sizes of the binaries, input data, output data, intermediate data, shared data and the destination of where the user might like to save the final output. We anticipate that these inputs will be directly provided by the application user.

The next set of inputs gets information at the task level (i.e., a single execution) (see Table 2). These inputs are used to make sure that there are enough local resources available during execution. Task level data includes the data required by a single task (input, intermediate and output) and the number of tasks (total and concurrent). The concurrent tasks are used to understand the difference in the concurrency possible with given VMs to (e.g., given five VMs with a single core each, ten total tasks will get scheduled as five tasks followed by five more tasks). We anticipate that these user inputs might be provided by the user in the beginning but long term compute provisioning and application profiling tools might be used to come up with accurate estimates.

In the execution semantics, the user or an application component acting on behalf of the user specifies the FRIEDA data management mode (i.e., pre-determined or real-time) and the execution setup (currently master-worker applications are supported).

Resource Model We expect that either the user or the compute provisioning component will specify the number of provisioned resources and type and any existing storage components that need to be used (see Table 3). In addition, the

Table 3 Resource information (Resource Input Model)

Resource count	Count of virtual machines expected to be provisioned for the computation
Resource type	Corresponds to the instance type allocated by the compute provisioning
Existing stores	Ids of existing stores that might already contain the data
Instance description	Description of local storage available by instance type
Preferred ordered storage available on site	A list of storage options available to the application ordered by preference

algorithm takes a description of the instance types and the storage tiers available to the application. The system also accounts for storage for logs that might be generated during execution.

Storage Description Our storage planning component takes a storage description as input. The storage description is ordered (based on either performance and/or preference). The storage description might be provided either by a user or be configured to be site-wide. The storage description has storage size limits associated with each level. Currently, we consider the storage size limit and the scalability i.e., the maximum number of virtual machines the storage and filesystem are capable of scaling to (when applicable). These storage descriptions might include a combination of site-specific information combined with application information.

Output Model The output from the storage planning system is a recipe that can be then used for provisioning. The output describes the storage type for each class of data for each machine role (i.e., master and worker).

Additionally, for each data class storage choice is annotated with the appropriate information required for data placement. For example, existing volumes might be the source of data and the storage volume id will be included in the planner output. Similarly, the data source can be mentioned, which might be the local desktop or a remote url and/or also specific protocols to use for data transfer.

Additionally the storage planning component also outputs details of FRIEDA's execution mode and compute provisioning details (e.g., type of resource, count of resources, tasks per resource) that will be used during provisioning. The syntax of our output is shown in Fig. 4.

The plan has description of the *storage type* and *data placement* for each of the roles (i.e., master and workers). The storage type declares the type of storage and the size. The data placement specifies the storage choice where a particular data class must be placed. The *vm* and *frieda* roles specify provisioning and execution level semantics that will be used by frieda.

```
{
'master': {
    storage_type:
        '<storage type>' : {'size': <storage size>},
        ...
    data_placement:
        '<data class>': {'storage_choice': '<storage type>',
                        ... },
        ...
    }
'worker': {
    ...
    }

'vm': {
    'vm_type':  ...
    'tasks_per_vm':  ...
    'image_id':   ...
    'ssh_user':   ...
    'proposed_vm_count':  ...
    },

'frieda': {
    'mode':  ...
    }
}
```

Fig. 4 An example showing the output generated from a FRIEDA storage planner

6 Storage Provisioning and Preparation

Figure 5 shows the architecture of FRIEDA Monkey[1] that takes care of storage provisioning and preparation and, data placement. FRIEDA Monkey uses the recipe from the storage planning.

The storage planning component drives the storage provisioning. The appropriate storage resources are provisioned as specified by the recipe *storage type* in the output. For each role, the list of storage definitions is processed and appropriate storage procured from the site.

The current implementation provides device/block store provisioning. It is possible to create a new block store or using an existing one. During storage provisioning the storage resource (block storage) is created (if new) or found (if it exists) and then attached to the provisioned compute resource.

---

[1]Monkey is a play on words. It plays on FRIEDA by referencing Frieda Kahlo's use of Monkeys in her paintings. Additionally, the flexible nature of Monkey is highlighted which allows the user to "monkey-around" with different infrastructure deployments.

Fig. 5 The diagram shows the architecture of FRIEDA's Monkey that manages the storage provisioning, preparation and data placement phases. Monkey uses the output from the storage planning to drive the stages. FRIEDA's execution framework operates within the virtual cluster

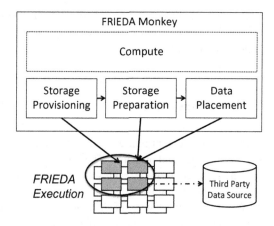

Monkey's focus is on storage provisioning but as a proof-of-concept it does basic compute provisioning, i.e., procures the compute resources that are part of the output from the planning phase. Monkey's compute provisioning allows the user to specify a single VM image which is used to provision each node irregardless of it's role.

Once the storage is provisioned, it needs to be prepared for use. Preparation can include mounting existing devices, creating the file system, creating directories, etc. Storage preparation in Monkey is handled through pre-defined *actions*. Our current implementation supports the preparation of the local or block device with a parallel or distributed file system (e.g., NFS, HDFS, etc).

Monkey is implemented as a flexible Python module based on Apache Libcloud [1]. Apache Libcloud provides a way to realize our storage planning with both compute and storage resource provisioning and preparation in the cloud environment. Monkey uses Apache Libcloud to support OpenStack and Amazon EC2 compatible APIs. Monkey is capable of supporting other stacks that Apache Libcloud expands to support in the future. Monkey's flexibility is inherent in its ability to support the many stages of the cluster development cycle and to define compute clusters with a complex set of services and data needs.

Monkey enables custom cluster deployment with a single YAML file. YAML is a serialization format that easily maps data types common to most high-level languages. The output from the storage planner is used to generate this YAML file. The Monkey YAML configuration contains cloud information (authentication values, image ids), node roles (master, worker) and orchestration required for the node preparation (software configuration and/or data placement). The YAML file has *roles* that define the type of resources to be procured and the quantity. Currently, we have two roles—master (unique) and workers. The compute and storage resource characteristics are specified in the YAML file. The YAML file also contains a list of *actions* that are used for resource preparation and data placement. These *actions* are executed on the resources after they are provisioned. Monkey allows applications to apply an existing Puppet manifest [3], deploy credentials, run shell commands and/or upload files. In summary, the YAML file defines a cluster with semantics for resource provisioning, resource preparation, data placement and semantics for application run-time.

7   Data Placement

In the data placement phase, the input data is moved to the appropriate storage that was provisioned and prepared. The semantics for data placement changes depending on where the input data resides and the data partitioning strategy (pre-determined and real-time) being used.

We support two types of data placement, from outside the virtual cluster and within the virtual cluster. Data placement can be defined as an 'action' in Cloud Monkey, which supports several file transfer protocols and data sources (launch node, third-party URL, etc.). This results in data placement right after the storage preparation phase. Placement can also be initiated by the execution system before or during the execution phase.

Specifically, we support use of *scp* and Globus Online [5] to transfer data from and to third-party sources.

8   FRIEDA Execution

Figure 6 shows the system architecture of FRIEDA execution. FRIEDA execution has a two plane architecture: a) control plane and b) execution plane. The control plane separates out the flexible data management strategies required for different applications from actual execution. The separation of the controller from the execution allows implementation of many of the cloud specific policies and decision processes (e.g., storage selection, elasticity) in the control plane.

The data management and application execution in FRIEDA is handled by three components—controller, master and workers. The controller and the partition generation algorithm, in the control plane, are responsible for setting up the environment for data management and program execution. The master and the workers operate in the execution plane and manage the execution of the program.

The control plane sets up the configurations for data transfer and process execution. The configuration setup generates the partitioned data-set for the workers. The 'controller' is the primary actor in the control phase and manages the master and the workers. The controller encapsulates the policies in our system. It communicates with the data partitioning algorithm and sets up the partition and distribution logic between the master and the workers.

FRIEDA supports two modes of partitioning and distribution. In case of pre-determined mode, the groups of files that will be processed by every worker is determined by the master at the beginning. Based on the partitioning algorithm,

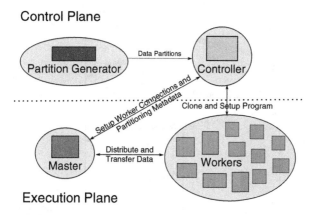

Fig. 6 FRIEDA System Architecture: the figure shows the two plane architecture of FRIEDA. The control plane is responsible for the setup of the system components and the execution plane handles the mechanics of data-management in real-time. The partition generator partitions the list of input files to be distributed to the tasks. The controller is responsible for controlling the setup for data transfer and program execution. The master is responsible for distributing and transferring data to respective workers. The workers, upon receiving the required data, do the computation and return the results

the files are transferred to the workers. In real-time mode, the transfer is 'lazy'—the master does not transfer a file until a worker asks for work units. The real-time mode inherently handles load balancing and process skew. Worker nodes that are heavily loaded, process less compared to the nodes which are lightly loaded. The controller can set up the workers to create as many instances of the program as there are cores.

8.1 Communication Protocol

Figure 7 captures the sequence of communication between the three system components—controller, master and worker. First, the controller starts the master. The master is initialized with the partition strategy to be used for execution. The controller and master retain an open channel that allows the controller to change the execution configuration of the master at run-time without requiring a master restart. Additionally, dynamic decisions such as elasticity can be relayed to the master through this channel.

The controller forks the remote workers on the nodes. The 'master' uses the controller's directive and partitions and transfers the data to the target nodes. The master process might also fetch data from an external resource if that was specified in the data placement plan.

The workers are initialized with the execution syntax of the program. For example, if *'app'* is the program that needs to be executed and takes *arg1* and *arg2* as

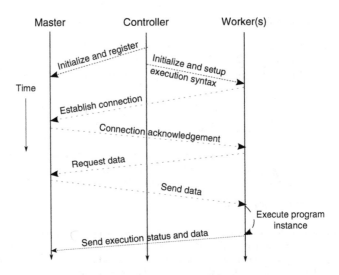

Fig. 7 Component Interaction and Event Sequence: the diagram shows the sequence of events and the interactions between the controller, master and workers in the FRIEDA system

parameters and *inp1* as input, then the execution command is sent to the workers as *app arg1 arg2 $inp1*, where $inp1 is replaced by the location of the file at run-time.

In the next step, the workers connect to the master and receive the assigned data to be processed. Once the workers complete the execution of the application, both the execution results and the status can be transferred to the master or left behind on the workers as the application might desire. Every worker continues to receive data and execute programs until all the inputs are processed. The workers are all symmetrical i.e., all workers perform identical work on different data.

Information on any failed worker gets reported to the controller allowing the controller to initiate remediation measures.

8.2 Execution Stages

FRIEDA's execution framework has two stages (a) data transfer, and (b) process execution to manage the interaction with the workers. For pre-partitioned data, the phases are sequential, i.e., process execution starts only when the transfer of data is completed. For real-time data partitioning strategies, the phases are interleaved.

The master sends the data and asks the workers to execute the tasks. The number of workers running on each node depends on the multi-core setting specified in the control phase. If multi-core computation is enabled, then every node will have as many workers as there are cores. FRIEDA's current implementation assumes that the worker nodes are homogeneous.

It is important to note that the 'process execution' phase is similar to a task-farmer. The process execution phase is responsible for executing a sequential program in parallel by distributing the data and parallelizing the program execution. FRIEDA does not modify any program code nor does it mandate a specific programming model for the applications. FRIEDA provides more flexible control on data partitioning, distribution, and computation while executing in a distributed cloud environment.

8.3 Data Grouping

Scientific applications have different input specifications and execution parameters. Data grouping divides the set of files within the directories into groups and sends the information to the controller (Fig. 8).

The 'partition generator' module at the control level generates file groupings based on the syntax of the program execution. The partitioning scheme determines the number of input files that will be used for every program instance. The module creates a list of files for each instance of the program. If a specific partitioning and grouping mechanism is not selected, every instance of the program execution takes one input as a file. We support three basic schemes (described below) but the design allows other schemes to be easily added.

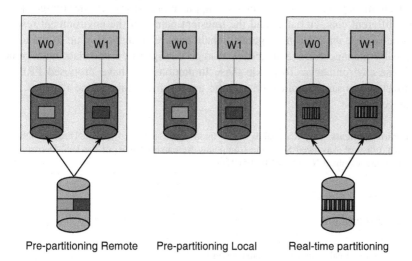

Pre-partitioning Remote   Pre-partitioning Local   Real-time partitioning

Fig. 8 Data Management Classes in FRIEDA. There are three major classes of how data is partitioned and managed (a) data is read from remote disks based on some pre-defined partitioning, (b) data is local to computation, and, (c) real time partitioning and distribution strategy where every worker receives the data as it requests for it

The three basic pairwise groupings that can be generated using the partition generator are listed below.

- One to all: one file in the input directory is paired with the rest of the files to be passed as arguments to the program. An example of such an application is an image comparison application where each image is compared with a control image.
- Pairwise adjacent: two adjacent files from the list are paired together and passed as arguments to the program. An example of such an application is when one studies the change between two adjacent experiment setups.
- All to all: every file is paired with all other files to be used as arguments to the program. An example of such an application is an image comparison application where each image is compared with other images in the set.

The partition file is used by the master to process the files from the input directories and build the actual run-time execution command for the program to be executed. The actual execution command is built by filling in the variables with appropriate file names in real-time the workers receive the data from the master

9 Summary

Infrastructure-as-a-Service (IaaS) cloud model provides a flexible and composable model to manage resources for scientific applications. However, the storage options with different characteristics and the transient nature of the environment result in unique storage and data management challenges. Currently, it is up to the user to manually manage storage selection, storage configuration and data management in these environments. To tackle these limitations, we have proposed FRIEDA, a novel composable application-specific approach to storage and data life cycle management.

Acknowledgements This material is based upon work supported by the Director, Office of Science, office of Advanced Scientific Computing Research (ASCR) of the U.S. Department of Energy under Contract No. DE-AC02-05CH11231.

References

1. Apache Libcloud. http://libcloud.apache.org/, 2013.
2. Open mpi. http://www.open-mpi.org/, 2013.
3. Puppet Labs Puppet Open Source. http://puppetlabs.com/puppet/puppet-open-source/, 2013.
4. W. Allcock, J. Bresnahan, R. Kettimuthu, M. Link, C. Dumitrescu, I. Raicu, and I. Foster. The globus striped gridftp framework and server. In *Proceedings of the 2005 ACM/IEEE conference on Supercomputing*, SC '05, pages 54–, Washington, DC, USA, 2005. IEEE Computer Society.

5. B. Allen, J. Bresnahan, L. Childers, I. Foster, G. Kandaswamy, R. Kettimuthu, J. Kordas, M. Link, S. Martin, K. Pickett, et al. Globus online: Radical simplification of data movement via saas. *Preprint CI-PP-5-0611, Computation Institute, The University of Chicago*, 2011.
6. G. A. Alvarez, E. Borowsky, S. Go, T. H. Romer, R. Becker-Szendy, R. Golding, A. Merchant, M. Spasojevic, A. Veitch, and J. Wilkes. Minerva: An automated resource provisioning tool for large-scale storage systems. *ACM Trans. Comput. Syst.*, 19(4):483–518, Nov. 2001.
7. R. D. Bjornson, A. H. Sherman, S. B. Weston, N. Willard, and J. Wing. Turboblast(r): A parallel implementation of blast built on the turbohub. In *Proceedings of the 16th International Parallel and Distributed Processing Symposium*, IPDPS '02, pages 325–, Washington, DC, USA, 2002. IEEE Computer Society.
8. D. Borthakur. *The Hadoop Distributed File System: Architecture and Design*. The Apache Software Foundation, 2007.
9. J. Bresnahan, K. Keahey, D. LaBissoniere, and T. Freeman. Cumulus: an open source storage cloud for science. In *Proceedings of the 2nd international workshop on Scientific cloud computing*, ScienceCloud '11, pages 25–32, New York, NY, USA, 2011. ACM.
10. A. Chervenak, R. Schuler, M. Ripeanu, M. Ali Amer, S. Bharathi, I. Foster, A. Iamnitchi, and C. Kesselman. The globus replica location service: Design and experience. *Parallel and Distributed Systems, IEEE Transactions on*, 20(9):1260 –1272, sept. 2009.
11. L. Costa and M. Ripeanu. Towards automating the configuration of a distributed storage system. In *Grid Computing (GRID), 2010 11th IEEE/ACM International Conference on*, pages 201–208, 2010.
12. L.B. Costa, S. Al-Kiswany, A. Barros, H. Yang, M. Ripeanu, Predicting intermediate storage performance for workflow applications. CoRR, abs/1302.4760, 2013.
13. J. Dean and S. Ghemawat. Mapreduce: simplified data processing on large clusters. *Commun. ACM*, 51(1):107–113, Jan. 2008.
14. E. Deelman and A. Chervenak. Data management challenges of data-intensive scientific workflows. In *Cluster Computing and the Grid, 2008. CCGRID'08. 8th IEEE International Symposium on*, pages 687–692. IEEE, 2008.
15. E. Deelman, G. Singh, M. Livny, B. Berriman, and J. Good. The cost of doing science on the cloud: the montage example. In *Proceedings of the 2008 ACM/IEEE conference on Supercomputing*, SC '08, pages 50:1–50:12, 2008.
16. S. Ghemawat, H. Gobioff, and S.-T. Leung. The google file system. In *Proceedings of the nineteenth ACM symposium on Operating systems principles*, SOSP '03, pages 29–43, New York, NY, USA, 2003. ACM.
17. D. Ghoshal, R. S. Canon, and L. Ramakrishnan. I/o performance of virtualized cloud environments. In *Proceedings of the second international workshop on Data intensive computing in the clouds*, DataCloud-SC '11, pages 71–80, 2011.
18. A. Gulati, G. Shanmuganathan, I. Ahmad, C. Waldspurger, and M. Uysal. Pesto: online storage performance management in virtualized datacenters. In *Proceedings of the 2nd ACM Symposium on Cloud Computing*, SOCC '11, pages 19:1–19:14, New York, NY, USA, 2011. ACM.
19. H. Herodotou, F. Dong, and S. Babu. No one (cluster) size fits all: automatic cluster sizing for data-intensive analytics. In *Proceedings of the 2nd ACM Symposium on Cloud Computing*, SOCC '11, pages 18:1–18:14, New York, NY, USA, 2011. ACM.
20. M. Isard, M. Budiu, Y. Yu, A. Birrell, and D. Fetterly. Dryad: distributed data-parallel programs from sequential building blocks. In *Proceedings of the 2nd ACM SIGOPS/EuroSys European Conference on Computer Systems 2007*, EuroSys '07, pages 59–72, New York, NY, USA, 2007. ACM.
21. K. R. Jackson, L. Ramakrishnan, K. J. Runge, and R. C. Thomas. Seeking supernovae in the clouds: a performance study. In *Proceedings of the 19th ACM International Symposium on High Performance Distributed Computing*, HPDC '10, 2010.

22. K. Keahey, P. Armstrong, J. Bresnahan, D. LaBissoniere, and P. Riteau. Infrastructure outsourcing in multi-cloud environment. In *Proceedings of the 2012 workshop on Cloud services, federation, and the 8th open cirrus summit*, FederatedClouds '12, pages 33–38, New York, NY, USA, 2012. ACM.

23. A. Krishnan. Gridblast: a globus-based high-throughput implementation of blast in a grid computing framework. *Concurrency Computat.: Pract. Exper.*, 43(2):1607ÂŬ1623, Apr. 2005.

24. A. Rajasekar, R. Moore, C.-Y. Hou, C. A. Lee, R. Marciano, A. de Torcy, M. Wan, W. Schroeder, S.-Y. Chen, L. Gilbert, P. Tooby, and B. Zhu. irods primer: Integrated rule-oriented data system. *Synthesis Lectures on Information Concepts, Retrieval, and Services*, 2(1):1–143, 2010.

25. S. Sakr, A. Liu, D. Batista, and M. Alomari. A survey of large scale data management approaches in cloud environments. *Communications Surveys Tutorials, IEEE*, 13(3):311–336, 2011.

26. A. Shoshani, A. Sim, and J. Gu. Storage resource managers: Middleware components for grid storage. NASA Conference Publication. NASA, 2002.

27. G. Singh, S. Bharathi, A. Chervenak, E. Deelman, C. Kesselman, M. Manohar, S. Patil, and L. Pearlman. A metadata catalog service for data intensive applications. In *Proceedings of the 2003 ACM/IEEE conference on Supercomputing*, SC '03, pages 33–, New York, NY, USA, 2003. ACM.

28. I. J. Taylor, E. Deelman, and D. B. Gannon. *Workflows for e-Science: Scientific Workflows for Grids*. Springer, Dec. 2006.

29. E. Thereska, M. Abd-El-Malek, J. J. Wylie, D. Narayanan, and G. R. Ganger. Informed data distribution selection in a self-predicting storage system. In *Proceedings of the 2006 IEEE International Conference on Autonomic Computing*, ICAC '06, pages 187–198, Washington, DC, USA, 2006. IEEE Computer Society.

30. E. Walker, W. Brisken, and J. Romney. To lease or not to lease from storage clouds. *Computer*, 43(4):44–50, 2010.

31. J. Xie, S. Yin, X. Ruan, Z. Ding, Y. Tian, J. Majors, A. Manzanares, and X. Qin. Improving mapreduce performance through data placement in heterogeneous hadoop clusters. In *Parallel and Distributed Processing, Workshops and Phd Forum (IPDPSW)*, pages 1–9, Atlanta, Georgia, April 2010.

Managed File Transfer as a Cloud Service

Brandon Ross, Engin Arslan, Bing Zhang, and Tevfik Kosar

Abstract Applications in science and industry have become increasingly complex and more demanding in terms of their computational and data requirements. Sharing and disseminating large datasets has become a big challenge despite the deployment of petascale computing systems and optical networking speeds reaching into the hundreds of gigabits per second. Having high-speed networks in place is necessary but not sufficient for achieving high data transfer rates. Being able to effectively use high-speed networks is becoming increasingly important for cloud computing. Cloud-hosted managed file transfer (MFT) applications simplify high-performance data transfer in the cloud by efficiently utilizing underlying networks and effectively coscheduling concurrent data transfer tasks. This chapter explores the concept of MFT in the cloud and looks at the design and implementation of one such MFT system—StorkCloud—as a case study.

1 Introduction

Data analysis is now more important to industrial and scientific research than ever before. As its importance has grown, so too has the need to share and analyze the very large datasets that are now commonplace in research. Large scientific experiments, including environmental and coastal hazard prediction [15], climate modeling [13], high-energy physics simulations, and genome mapping [7] generate petascale data volumes on a yearly basis [11]. Data collected from remote sensors and satellites, dynamic data-driven applications, and digital libraries and preservations also produce large datasets [9, 20].

Today, a large portion of big-data processing and analysis is performed with the help of cloud services. Economies of scale have made outsourcing the processing of this data to distributed cloud services a popular alternative to deploying and maintaining similar services on-site. However, this change in system architecture from local to distributed has not come without its complications. The importance

B. Ross • E. Arslan • B. Zhang • T. Kosar (✉)
Department of Computer Science & Engineering, University at Buffalo,
The State University of New York, 338J Davis Hall, Buffalo, NY 14260, USA
e-mail: bwross@buffalo.edu; earslan@buffalo.edu; bingzhan@buffalo.edu; tkosar@buffalo.edu

© Springer Science+Business Media New York 2014   379
X. Li, J. Qiu (eds.), *Cloud Computing for Data-Intensive Applications*,
DOI 10.1007/978-1-4939-1905-5__16

of data analysis to modern research and industry necessitates global collaboration and sharing among many organizations, which results in frequent large-scale data movements across widely distributed sites.

Several national and regional optical networking initiatives such as Internet2 [4], ESnet [3], XSEDE/TeraGrid [21], and LONI [18] provide high-speed network infrastructure for sharing this data, and recent developments in networking technology make high-speed optical links reaching up to and beyond 100 Gbps in capacity available [1] for members of the scientific community. Yet despite the availability of these high-speed wide-area networks and the use of modern data transfer protocols designed for high performance, data transfers in practice often only attain fractions of their theoretical maximum throughput. Indeed, many organizations even resort to sending their data through shipment services such as UPS or FedEx rather than moving data through the Internet [10]. This inability to fully utilize network infrastructure and easily move data is a contributing factor to the "data deluge" we are now in the midst of.

From this, it is apparent that having high-speed networking infrastructure in place is a necessary but not sufficient condition for performing high-speed data transfers. Being able to effectively use these high-speed networks is increasingly important for wide-area data replication and federated cloud computing in a distributed setting. Doing so requires effectively coscheduling and dynamically optimizing data replication tasks in a way that maximizes transfer efficiency and minimizes resource contention.

A number of cloud services have been established that aim to do just this. These cloud-based **managed file transfer** (MFT) applications offer a solution to the problem of making effective use of networking infrastructure for cloud data transfer by providing a service-based approach to the planning, scheduling, monitoring, and management of data placement tasks. Their position as a centralized and dedicated data transfer coordination system allows these services to offer increased data transfer reliability and security, effectively coschedule concurrent data transfer operations, and deliver performance improvements through capabilities such as connection caching, scheduled storage management, and end-to-end throughput optimization for broad ranges of data-intensive cloud computing applications and storage systems. This chapter will introduce the concept of MFT and describe its role in today's widely distributed cloud computing ecosystem.

StorkCloud, developed by the Data Intensive Distributed Computing Lab at the University at Buffalo, is one example of an MFT system, and will be used as a case study of such systems in this chapter.

This chapter will also discuss various data transfer optimization techniques that can be employed by MFT applications. Techniques such as command pipelining, data channel parallelism, concurrent file transfers, and other techniques which can mitigate the factors which lead to poor network utilization will be discussed, along with algorithms and heuristics which can be used in centralized scheduling to increase long-term transfer throughput.

2 The Problem of Data Insolubility

The complementary roles of processing and storage have a long history in the field of computing. The flow of data from storage medium to locus of processing and back again could be said to be computation's defining feature. Given the importance of computation to all modern technology, it's no surprise that bigger data storage and faster processing systems are always in demand.

With the advent of cloud computing and the benefits it brings, outsourcing data storage and processing to the cloud is a very compelling option for many organizations versus providing such services on-site. However, the transition to the cloud has not been without its difficulties, particularly where data needs to be moved to, from, and especially within the cloud—activities that are becoming more common as both storage media and loci of processing disappear into the cloud.

Most storage services focus on data storage primarily and offer simple—usually proprietary—data transfer schemes solely for the purpose of allowing clients to store and retrieve data directly. As their primary focus is on storage, they typically do not concern themselves heavily with transfer performance, optimization, scheduling, or the details of the underlying transfer protocols. Migrating or copying data between cloud storage services also poses a challenge due to the proprietary data access solutions employed by many cloud storage providers. Indeed, storage services may even have incentive to keep it that way if it makes it more difficult for a client to switch to a competitor.

Staging data into cloud data processing centers from an external storage system poses similar challenges. These processing services often either provide their own proprietary data staging schemes, or otherwise require users to manage data placement themselves. In most cases, unless the cloud storage service and computation service are both managed by the same provider, the exercise of moving data from one site to the other is a detail left to the client. Cloud computation services, like storage services, likewise do not usually concern themselves much with transfer performance. The data staging process is frequently treated like an afterthought, or at least something outside of the provider's domain of concern.

This insularity has unfortunately led to an ecosystem in which users must make sacrifices in order to reap the cloud's benefits. Either they forsake flexibility and constrain their applications to services explicitly designed to exchange data— usually limited to a single provider or a small handful of cooperating ones—or else they take on the burden of custom rigging their own data transfer solution, as well as guaranteeing its reliability, security, compliance to regulation, availability, performance, and future maintainability. Is this choice between inconvenience and inflexibility not antithetical to the nature of the cloud, whose very benediction is supposed to be the flexibility and convenience it offers over traditional solutions?

2.1   Solutions

There are two immediately apparent solutions to the problem of data insolubility in the cloud:

1. widespread agreement on and subsequent deployment of an open standard for data placement, or
2. the institution of services which manage data transfer on clients' behalf.

The first solution has a number of issues. Whose standard do we use? Many competing standards, open and otherwise, already exist and have not seen widespread adoption. History tells us that new "universal" standards intended to replace competing standards often turn out to be just another competing standard, exacerbating the problem. Furthermore, as was mentioned, cloud storage providers have economic incentive to continue using proprietary standards. The inertia required to change the ecosystem at the provider level likely makes this approach infeasible, at least in the short term.

The second solution is perhaps a more feasible approach, and the one that seems to be gaining the most traction. Cloud-hosted MFT applications which aim to provide large-scale data placement between remote sites have begun to appear as recently as 2010. These services provide a "software as a service" (SaaS) approach to data management, and purport to offer a solution to the problems of vendor lock-in and incompatible APIs (application programming interfaces) that are responsible for the data insolubility problem we face today.

At the very least, MFT in the cloud provides a stopgap measure to mitigate these problems. However, these services also confer a wide range of potential benefits and new possibilities, as we shall soon see. Indeed, the future may very well find MFT a valuable and permanent resident in the cloud ecosystem.

3   Managed File Transfer

Before going any further, a clarification must be made regarding the meaning of the "MFT" as used in this chapter. MFT has been used in the past to describe any kind of solution which facilitates large-scale secure data transfer over wide areas and allows organizations to centrally control and monitor data transfers as they take place. This includes hardware and software installed on local sites to manage the movement of data into and out of the physical premises in which the data is stored or processed.

This chapter uses the term MFT to describe such a solution *provided as a cloud service*—that is, entirely off-site and without special provisions at the endpoints. Each instance of "MFT" in this text could very well be replaced with "MFT as a service" or "MFT in the cloud", however this would be considerably more onerous to read, and should be obvious given the subject of this book. It should be assumed that when "MFT" is used in this chapter it is referring to MFT as a cloud service unless otherwise noted.

A distinction must also be made between MFT applications and other types of services which are commonly identified as data or file transfer services. Many so-called data transfer services are temporary data storage systems used as an intermediary for exchanging files between individuals. In these systems, file data is uploaded to the hosting system by the sender and stored there for a limited amount of time or until it has been retrieved by the recipient. Such services are mostly indistinguishable from cloud storage services, with the difference being that files are hosted temporarily with the intention of being downloaded only by a small number of recipients.

An MFT application, in contrast, is used to schedule and coordinate data transfers between distributed endpoints, in a sense acting as "glue" for data storage and processing systems in the cloud. MFT applications do not necessarily act as a physical intermediary for data, though they are of course not excluded from doing so. They may instead communicate with remote storage systems using protocols understood by the end systems, and negotiate direct system-to-system transfers without data flowing through the MFT system. Such transfers are called **third-party transfers**. An MFT system might offer temporary data hosting (sometimes called "data parking" in this context) in order to offer improved transfer reliability, though this is not necessarily the case.

MFT introduces a number of benefits over *ad hoc* data transfer implementations. For one, MFT services can offer asynchronous "fire-and-forget" functionality, where a client can specify an immediate or future data transfer and delegate reliability and performance concerns to the MFT system. The system will monitor transfer progress and deal with issues as they arise. Clients can check on transfer progress through the system, cancel or reschedule transfers if they so desire, and be notified by the system when the transfer completes or if it cannot be completed.

MFT applications can also provide support for numerous transfer protocols, and even perform translations between otherwise incompatible protocols by acting as an intermediary. This allows existing storage infrastructure to be used without needing to reconfigure end systems to "speak" the same protocols.

MFT applications may also offer suites of transfer performance optimizers to algorithmically tweak transfer settings and schedule transfers in order to minimize conflicts and avoid network congestion. Such optimizers can take into account transfer priority and user-specified deadlines. An MFT system can also maintain a historical transfer performance database for different systems to better estimate transfer completion time and schedule transfers to meet deadlines.

An MFT system should also be able to access remote system directory listings and file metadata for the systems and protocols it supports and present it in a unified format. In most cases, the capability of accessing remote metadata is a prerequisite for performing remote data transfers in first place, making the provision of directory listing information by an MFT system straightforward. In this chapter, a service offering such functionality is referred to as a **directory listing service** (DLS). Such services can be used for the development of interactive interfaces for browsing file system hierarchies on remote endpoints. With user interactivity in mind, a DLS may also take measures to improve the responsiveness of metadata and listing access operations by, for example, caching and prefetching directory listings.

As is typical of cloud services, an MFT system should offer both a graphical (typically web-based) front end for users to interact with the system, as well as an API for allowing programmatic access to the system's services and the development of third-party client applications. The availability of a machine-accessible API is important for an MFT system to serve its role as an in-cloud connectivity layer between distributed cloud-based data storage and processing services.

Lastly, MFT applications can relieve users of the burden of having to manage transfer security themselves. Such applications can securely manage remote system credentials on a per-user or per-organization basis, allowing clients to schedule regular secure transfers and reduce the frequency of credential exchanges with the system. MFT applications may also take the steps necessary to comply with regulations regarding secure and private transfer of sensitive data, such as those put forth in HIPAA.[1]

An MFT application has the advantage of not needing to invest heavily in either storage or computation resources. Instead, the only critical resource in an MFT system is network connectivity, allowing for inexpensive, geographically distributed deployment of the system.

3.1 Examples of MFT

A number of MFT services exhibiting some or all of these features already exist and are well-established in the cloud ecosystem. Even at the time of writing this list is not complete; these are only a few examples.

Globus[2] is a service offered by The Globus Alliance at the University of Chicago [6]. It is aimed at the scientific community and, introduced in November 2010, is one of the earliest examples of an MFT service in the cloud. Globus offers fire-and-forget GridFTP file transfers as a service, and provides a web-based front end to their transfer scheduler, as well as a unified interface for requesting authentication credentials for various well-known Grid computing resources. In addition, the interface offers the ability to graphically list and browse directory contents on remote GridFTP servers in real time. Globus also applies a number of heuristic optimizations to its transfers [12] which will be detailed later in the chapter.

Ipswitch's MOVEit Cloud[3] is an MFT service aimed at enterprise organizations with large-scale data requirements [5]. MOVEit Cloud is built on top of Ipswitch's MOVEit File Transfer application. MOVEit Cloud supports a number of protocols and authentication mechanisms, secure person-to-person file transfers, and is HIPAA and PCI compliant.

---

[1]The Health Insurance Portability and Accountability Act of 1996—a United States legislative act regarding the privacy of medical records.

[2]http://globus.org/.

[3]http://www.moveitmanagedfiletransfer.com/.

Mover[4] is another MFT application designed for use with popular cloud-hosted data storage systems such as Dropbox and SkyDrive, though it also supports transfers via FTP and WebDAV [2]. Mover provides an interface for browsing cloud storage systems and a web-based REST API for interacting with the service programmatically. It can be used to schedule future and recurring data transfers, and offers a simplified method for reusing transfer parameters using transfer templates.

StorkCloud[5] is an MFT application created by the Data Intensive Distributed Computing Lab at the University at Buffalo (Fig. 1). It provides support for a number of data transfer protocols and storage systems, including FTP, GridFTP, HTTP, SMTP, BitTorrent, SCP/SFTP, and iRODS, as well as a collection of protocol-agnostic transfer optimization algorithms. The architecture of StorkCloud will be discussed in detail as a case study of an MFT system in the next section.

4   StorkCloud

StorkCloud is an MFT application based on open source software and is available to the public free of charge. This chapter will take an in depth look at StorkCloud as a case study on the design and implementation of MFT systems.

The major components of the StorkCloud system include:

- an extensible multi-protocol transfer job scheduler for queuing, scheduling, monitoring, and optimizing data transfer jobs;
- a directory listing service (DLS) for prefetching and caching remote directory metadata in the cloud to minimize response time to users;
- a web API adhering to representational state transfer (REST) design principles;
- pluggable transfer modules which can be used to communicate and negotiate with different data transfer protocols and storage systems; and
- pluggable protocol-agnostic optimization modules which can be used to dynamically optimize various transfer settings to improve performance.

StorkCloud schedules, optimizes, and monitors data transfer requests from users through its lightweight thin client utilities (including an Android application, a web browser interface, and command line tools). The API it exposes through its client interface layer can be used by third-party clients and libraries, allowing for StorkCloud to be used as a data connectivity layer in federated cloud systems. The StorkCloud core is written in Java and is open source. The source code can be downloaded from the Stork GitHub repository.[6]

---

[4]https://mover.io/.

[5]https://storkcloud.org/.

[6]https://github.com/didclab/stork.

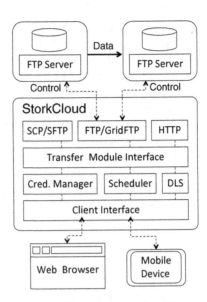

Fig. 1 This illustration depicts the interactions between StorkCloud system components

4.1   StorkCloud Scheduler

StorkCloud's scheduler is a modular, multi-protocol task scheduler which handles the queuing and execution of data transfer jobs and ensures that they complete successfully and in a timely manner. The scheduler's external module interface allows arbitrary protocol support to be implemented as standalone modules and introduced to the system with minimal hassle. As the core component of the StorkCloud system, the scheduler's job is to take in transfer jobs and provide clients with information about the progress of jobs upon request.

Jobs submitted to the scheduler are assigned a numerical identifier—the job ID—which can be used to reference jobs in subsequent requests. The scheduler can be queried to obtain a job status report, which includes information such as the source and destination endpoint URLs, the job state (e.g., scheduled, in progress, failed, complete), the size of the transfer in bytes, the progress of the transfer, instantaneous and average transfer speeds, job submission and start times, and estimated transfer completion time.

StorkCloud provides additional reliability to cloud data transfers via data transfer checkpointing and checksumming for protocols that support them, as well as alternative protocol fallback mechanisms. These are especially useful in large file transfers where the likelihood of errors over the lifetime of a transfer is increased.

StorkCloud also provides mechanisms to monitor end-to-end data transfer tasks to provide clients with real-time progress information as well as to detect failures and performance problems as early as possible. StorkCloud's error reporting framework can distinguish the locus of failure (e.g, network, server, client, software, hardware) in the event of problems, classify problems as transient or permanent, and provide possible recovery options. These error detection, classification, and recovery mechanisms provide greater reliability and agility to transfers performed by the system.

The StorkCloud scheduler is based heavily on the Stork Data Scheduler [16]. The Stork Data Scheduler is considered to be one of the first examples of data scheduling and optimization tools and has been actively used in many data-intensive application areas including coastal hazard prediction and storm surge modeling, oil flow and reservoir uncertainty analysis, numerical relativity and black hole collisions, digital sky imaging educational video processing and behavioral assessment, and multiscale computational fluid dynamics.

4.2   Directory Listing Service (DLS)

StorkCloud's Directory Listing Service (DLS) provides a metadata retrieval service to clients to enable efficient remote file system browsing before issuing a data transfer request. Conceptually, DLS is an intermediate layer between StorkCloud thin clients and arbitrary remote data storage systems that provides access to directory listings as well as other metadata information in a unified format. In that sense, DLS acts as a centralized metadata server hosted in the cloud. When a thin client wants to list a directory or access file metadata on a remote server, it sends a request containing necessary information (i.e., URL of the top directory to perform listing on, along with required credentials) to DLS, and DLS responds back to the client with the requested metadata.

During this process, DLS first checks if the requested metadata is available in its cache. If it is available in the cache (and the provided credentials match the associated cached credentials, and the cache entry has not expired, etc.), DLS directly sends the cached information to the client without connecting to the remote server. Otherwise, it connects to the remote server, retrieves the requested metadata, and sends it to the client. Meanwhile, several levels of subdirectories will be prefetched in the background and cached under the assumption that the user will visit one of the subdirectories in the near future [24].

Any metadata information handled by DLS will be cached and periodically checked with the remote server to ensure freshness of the information. Clients also have the option to refresh/update the DLS cache on demand to bypass the cached metadata and make sure they are receiving the most up-to-date directory listings and metadata.

4.3   Web API and Thin Client GUIs

StorkCloud exposes a RESTful web API that allows thin clients—or even other cloud services and applications—to log in to the system, schedule and control transfer jobs, perform remote directory listings, manage user credentials, and more. Responses to REST requests are represented in JSON, allowing for easy development of browser-based thin client applications. The web API can also be used to develop hybrid web applications which may use StorkCloud's data transfer or metadata retrieval services in conjunction with other cloud-based services.

StorkCloud provides two thin client user interfaces: a web browser interface accessible through the StorkCloud website and a native Android client. Through these interfaces, users can visually observe transfer progress in real time and stop, pause, and cancel transfer jobs using a point-and-click interface. Users can also browse two remote servers simultaneously through a graphical interface which communicates with StorkCloud's DLS to access remote directory contents. Users can traverse remote file systems, select files and directories for transfer, and initiate a transfer between them.

The thin clients provided by StorkCloud cache and prefetch remote directory data provided by StorkCloud's DLS—much in the same way as DLS itself—to provide a much more responsive and interactive user experience.

In addition to these client interfaces which communicate with StorkCloud using the web API, the open source scheduler component comes bundled with a command line utility for communicating with the scheduler directly using either HTTP or a raw TCP connection.

4.4   Transfer Module Interface

StorkCloud acts as a negotiating system between different data storage systems and protocols. In order to do this, StorkCloud must be able to "speak" the protocols of the remote systems it aims to coordinate between. This is done using pluggable, independent "transfer modules" that provide StorkCloud with a uniform interface to a given protocol or storage system.

The transfer module interface allows StorkCloud users to develop modules to support their favorite storage systems, protocols, or middleware easily. Modules can be written in any language recognized by the operating system, as all communication between the transfer modules and scheduler is done in JSON. Users who want to have tighter integration with the system as well as better communication performance may implement transfer modules in Java to communicate directly with the StorkCloud scheduler in memory.

StorkCloud supports a mechanism for protocol translation for cross-protocol data movement using the StorkCloud system as a rendezvous point. It also offers direct access to file data through its HTTP interface, allowing other StorkCloud thin clients and third-party applications to access data though any supported protocol or storage system, with StorkCloud operating as a proxy.

4.5   Optimization Modules

StorkCloud can perform protocol-agnostic optimization of data transfers using pluggable optimization algorithms. Optimization modules (also called optimizers), similar to transfer modules, can be plugged into the server, and incoming jobs can then request an optimization algorithm to be used for the transfer. Optimizers advertise which parameters they are designed to optimize, and transfer modules can likewise advertise which parameters they allow to be adjusted.

If a transfer module allows an optimization algorithm to be used, it queries the optimizer for sample parameters, runs a sample, and reports the throughput back to the optimizer. The optimizer uses the reported information to determine parameters for the next sampling, and continues until either the transfer is complete or the sampling phase is over. This design allows optimizers to be protocol-agnostic— as long as the transfer module supports the features the optimizer exposes, neither needs to know the other's implementation details.

StorkCloud implements a number of dynamic optimization techniques as optimization modules to provide a method for determining which combination of parameters is "just right" for a given transfer. The optimization techniques Stork-Cloud implements try to maximize transfer throughput by choosing optimal parallelism, concurrency, and pipelining levels through combinations of sampling, file set analysis, heuristic clustering, and learning algorithms applied to historical transfer statistics.

The optimization algorithms StorkCloud supports will be discussed in the following sections.

5   Transfer Level Throughput Optimization

Oftentimes during the course of a data transfer, one may experience periods of poor transfer performance where transfer throughput drops to mere fractions of maximum possible network capacity. Sometimes such effects are intermittent and/or out of the control of the user, such as during times of heavy network utilization on shared networks. However, poor transfer performance can be due to a number of other confounding factors, e.g., underutilization of end system CPU cores, low disk I/O speeds, traffic at inter-system routing nodes, unsuitable system-level tuning of networking protocols, servers not taking advantage of parallel I/O opportunities. Many of these effects can be remedied by properly configuring application-level transfer settings at either the source or destination endpoints and dynamically applying combinations of optimization techniques.

This section will cover algorithms and methodologies for optimizing data placement operations from the perspective of an MFT application.

5.1 Optimization Techniques

Per-transfer optimizations can be used to increase the goodput[7] of an individual data transfer. Adjusting transfer parameters and applying different techniques can play a significant role in increasing transfer throughput. However, determining the appropriate transfer settings and the degree to which techniques should be applied can be difficult, and poor application of the techniques can either cause underutilization of the network or overburden the network and degrade the performance due to factors such as increased packet loss. Inappropriate application of certain techniques can also violate network policies or cause service disruption in environments with shared resources. It is therefore important that care is taken when applying optimization techniques so as to avoid potential issues (Fig. 2).

A number of transfer options and techniques can be applied to many different file transfer protocols, and the appropriateness of their application differer depending on the nature of the end-system subnets, storage systems, and network interconnects. This section will talk about some of these techniques and parameters from the perspective of an MFT system using the following definitions:

- **Pipelining**—This involves queuing up multiple sending or receiving commands at the end-systems in control channel-based transfer applications, as opposed to waiting for transfer to complete before issuing subsequent commands. This helps mitigate the effect of latency in a multi-file transfer.
- **TCP tuning**—A large majority of data transfer protocols are based on TCP, making TCP tuning techniques a valuable tool for optimizing data transfers. In particular, TCP tuning refers to reconfiguring end system TCP buffer sizes to increase performance on networks with high Bandwidth–Delay Products. However, the effectiveness of this technique only goes so far, as oftentimes end systems enforce a maximum buffer size that is less than optimal, requiring the use of other techniques.
- **Data channel parallelism** (or just **parallelism**)—This refers to the use of multiple aggregated data streams (e.g., TCP connections) to a single endpoint, and can be used to overcome the effect of system level limitations on buffer size. The throughput of the aggregate channel approximates that of a single connection with buffer sizes equal to the sum of the individual stream buffer sizes.
- **Concurrency**—This technique involves transferring different files simultaneously, which can take advantage of concurrent I/O in parallel and distributed storage systems. In some application protocols (e.g., FTP and HTTP), this is achieved using parallel control channel or session connections, and in those cases can be used to almost identical effect as parallelism, even when the underlying storage system does not allow parallel I/O.

---

[7]**Goodput** is the number of useful bits of information transmitted per unit time in a data transfer, in distinction to the amount of bandwidth actually consumed. The ratio of goodput to throughput is the **transfer efficiency**.

- **Striping**—This is the use of multiple source and/or destination endpoints to transfer file data to or from a shared (usually networked) storage subsystem. Like concurrency, this takes advantage of parallel I/O in the storage system, but the use of multiple endpoint hosts also allows it to take advantage of parallel CPUs and sometimes network routes. In the context of network data transfers, the concept of striping is different from, though analogous to, the concept of striping in a disk storage array.[8]
- **Compression**—This can increase the efficiency of a transfer by increasing the number of useful bits of information transferred per transmission unit. However, the use of compression comes at increased computational overhead at both endpoints, and might not be worth it in cases where file data is highly random and thus of poor compressibility.[9]

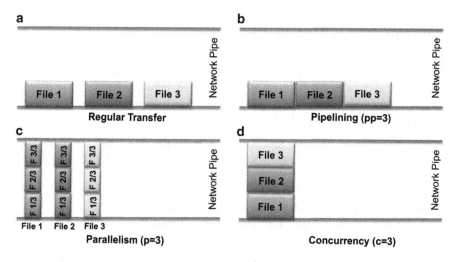

Fig. 2 Effects of pipelining, parallelism, and concurrency on network load

---

[8]In the context of storage systems, striping refers to dividing file contents across several disks in a RAID to improve read throughput.

[9]Specifically this refers to *lossless* compression, as the file data must be totally reconstructible at the destination endpoint. This chapter does not consider *lossy* compression for purposes of data transfer, though it might be useful depending on the application. Imagining examples of such applications is left as an exercise for the reader.

5.2 Dynamic Optimization

These optimization techniques can be used in combination to different degrees to improve the efficiency of the transfer, insofar as the underlying transfer protocol supports them. However, the degree to which each technique should be used—and when—depends highly on the configuration of the network and end systems, and temporal network conditions. Oftentimes these factors are not explicitly known by users initiating transfers, and so automatic optimization subroutines are an enticing feature for an MFT application to have. Such optimization subroutines can range from simple heuristics that optimize according to file size or historical performance to advanced algorithms that discover network conditions on the fly and tune transfer parameters accordingly.

5.3 Examples in MFT Systems

Globus applies a heuristic optimization for GridFTP transfers based on the average file size of a dataset. At the time of writing, their optimization heuristic always transfers two files concurrently, and chooses parallelism and pipelining levels according to the following rules [12].

- If there are more than 100 files with an average file size smaller than 50 MB, it uses two parallel data channels per file and pipelines up to 20 outstanding commands a time.[10]
- If the average file size is larger than 250 MB, it uses eight parallel data channels per file and pipelines up to five outstanding commands.
- In the default case, it uses four parallel data channels and pipelines up to 10 outstanding commands.

StorkCloud employs a number of dynamic throughput optimization algorithms designed for optimizing different sets of transfer parameters, which users may select when they submit a transfer job. Some of these algorithms "sense" the network between the remote endpoints by performing sample transfers and measuring transfer performance. Others refer to performance information from past transfers between the same endpoints, or use additional information about end-system and configuration to choose theoretically optimal transfer settings. The algorithms provided by StorkCloud include:

---

[10]In the case of Globus, a pipelined command does not necessarily correspond to one data transfer, meaning pipelining in this sense does not precisely fit the definition given earlier in the chapter. Nevertheless, the relationship between pipelined commands and pipelined data transfers is effectively linear.

- a number of parallel stream modeling and prediction algorithms [14, 22, 23],
- the Parallelism–Concurrency–Pipelining optimizer which uses historical database information and clustering, and
- the Single Chunk Concurrency and Multi Chunk Concurrency algorithms which optimize parallelism, concurrency, and pipelining using clustering and heuristics [8].

Some transfer options can also be used to limit the maximum speed of a data transfer. For example, limiting the TCP buffer size will constrain the number of bits that may be transferred in a given window of time, thus imposing an upper limit on the speed of the transfer. Though this may seem counterproductive, it can be useful in cases where a data transfer is low priority or has a far-off deadline, and minimizing the strain a transfer puts on the network might be desirable. This technique is especially useful when scheduling simultaneous transfers with known start times and deadlines.

6 Scheduling Optimization and Reservation

Aside from optimizing individual data transfers for maximum performance, MFT systems also have the responsibility of coscheduling data transfer jobs of widely variable scale with arbitrary earliest start times and deadlines specified by clients.

As was mentioned in the beginning of the previous section, drops in transfer throughput can sometimes be time-dependent, as is often the case with slowdowns during hours of peak usage. These predictable periods of poor performance can sometimes be mitigated through effective use of timing strategies, especially in cases of very large transfers. Strategies which take transfer priority and desired transfer completion time into account can also increase overall throughput and the number of transfers which complete successfully before their due time.

In practice, an MFT system will be presented with a variety of data transfer tasks with different requirements. This can include small jobs that should complete as quickly as possible, to large, long-running jobs that might have a much broader window of time for completion. Much of the time these transfer jobs are independent and can be coscheduled without the risk of competing for resources (e.g., bandwidth at inter-system routing nodes or end system storage devices). However, there will inevitably be jobs scheduled with destinations that have overlapping routes or are transferring from the same source endpoint, as well as jobs that have a deadline in the far future and need not begin immediately. In these cases, MFT applications are in an advantageous position to make scheduling decisions that reduce resource contention and network load, and maximize the number of deadlines met.

This section will discuss algorithms and practical considerations for performing coscheduling from the perspective of an MFT system.

6.1 Coscheduling Algorithms

In the context of data transfer, **coscheduling** is the process of scheduling multiple concurrent transfer tasks of varying degrees of dependence on shared resources while taking into account time constraints and minimizing the **lateness**—time spent incomplete after the deadline—of a job. In this sense, the coscheduling problem is "merely" a problem of mathematical optimization.

A number of algorithms exist for coscheduling transfer tasks to minimize resource contention, maximize long-term throughput, and reduce the probability of missing transfer deadlines. Depending on the algorithm used, different sets of information regarding the underlying network characteristics and the nature and constraints of the data transfers in question may be necessary.

One intuitive approach to coscheduling involves framing it as a variant of the bin packing problem with two-dimensional "objects" representing transfer jobs being packed into "bins" which represent available bandwidth between a given source and destination. The "volume" of the objects being packed corresponds to the size of the data that must be transferred for a particular job, and the "dimensions" of the objects are the throughput of the job at particular times.

The dimensions of the objects can vary subject to the time constraints of the job, so long as the volume remains the same. This allows for some great variability—some "squishiness"—in the shape of the object (job) being packed into the bin. It is even permissible to "split" the objects into unconnected parts by having periods of time in which the throughput dimension is zero.

By varying the dimensions of object—making them "thinner" or "fatter"—or splitting them, it may be possible to fit more objects in the bin while satisfying all the constraints. This packing corresponds to a schedule which satisfies the constraints of all the jobs being coscheduled. The manipulation of the dimensions of the objects being packed manifests in actual systems as taking measures which might at first seem to be counterproductive, such as throttling the rate of a transfer or intermittently pausing transfers. Despite its counterintuitive nature, the concept of throttling jobs to achieve overall greater across multiple jobs throughput is an established and well-explored technique [19].

One difficulty with the bin packing approach, however, is introduced by the fact that the volume of the bins cannot be so simply defined as "available bandwidth". Indeed, faithfully representing the nature of the Internet in the reduced problem would involve overlapping and interdependent bins corresponding to the convoluted nature of data paths through the Internet. This detail is likely too fine to capture in the metaphor of bin packing. Nevertheless, the bin packing reduction of the coscheduling problem can still be applied with useful results [17].

6.2   Estimation with Historical Performance Data

In addition to having knowledge about transfers in advance, MFT applications can also take advantage of historical transfer performance to make better decisions about future data transfers. This information can be fed into learning algorithms to discover patterns in network usage and make better predictions about optimal transfer settings. This historical data can also be exchanged with third-party scheduling applications or even other MFT services to allow for an even richer transfer history database to be built collaboratively.

Combining information about historical and future transfer jobs can also be used to develop better methods for estimating transfer completion time. This information can be used by MFT schedulers for the sake of making smarter scheduling decisions and for providing users with better estimations of data transfer duration.

Using its historical transfer database and information about ongoing and scheduled transfer jobs, StorkCloud is able to provide information to its clients regarding available end-to-end throughput for the user, the estimated total time it would take to transfer a particular dataset, and the parameters that need to be used in order to achieve the highest end-to-end throughput. If the information necessary to make this predication cannot be found in the historical database, StorkCloud can perform dummy transfers on the fly and use the results to make predictions.

This estimation service allows users to test network resources and conditions, and lets data transfer operations be scheduled in advance with preferred time constraints given by the user—i.e., the requested earliest start time and desired latest completion time. It also lets users and higher level meta-schedulers plan ahead and reserve a time period for their data movement operations. This service can potentially be used to eliminate long delays in transfer completion and increase utilization by giving opportunities to provision required network and storage resources in advance, and also enables third-party data schedulers to make more informed scheduling decisions by organizing requests and focusing on a specific time frame to maximize performance and resource utilization.

6.3   Practical Considerations

Although in some cases information regarding underlying networks may be provided by users, ideally such information would be discovered by the MFT system itself. However, it may not always be possible to do so, especially when conducting third-party transfers as many transfer protocols and applications do not offer ways to collect diagnostics information that may be necessary to determine certain network characteristics.

For example, because of its decentralized nature, data transfers between Internet hosts may not always take the same route. Furthermore, the routes a given transfer may take might not be even discoverable by the MFT system (or sometimes even the remote hosts themselves), because diagnostic protocols for discovering routing information are not universally implemented and much of the time are blocked by intermediate routing nodes for purposes of security. This means it might not always be possible to determine with certainty which data transfers might have overlapping routes, and thus potentially interfere during data transfers.

Even if the route a given data transfer will take is knowable, because of the heterogeneous nature of the Internet and the lack of diagnostic protocols for doing so, it is generally difficult to determine the capacity and transient load of the links in a route. This makes doing beforehand estimations of the maximum data rate of a transfer, even knowing the routes it will take, a difficult task.

Another difficulty arises in actually controlling transfer rate and guaranteeing a transfer will be able to maintain a given rate for the entirety of its scheduled time. The extent to which an MFT application can utilize these techniques varies depending on the capabilities of the underlying network, the system's ability to control and sense the network between two end systems remotely, and the nature of the transfer protocol underlying the transfer. The use of reservations on networks that support them can give an MFT application much more control over and predictive power regarding a transfer.

One other difficulty is that, given that the bin packing approach is NP-hard, it is infeasible to expect that an exactly optimal coscheduling can be found in every case. It is more likely then that a heuristic approach will be necessary in real applications. Combining a heuristic bin packing approach with machine learning techniques applied to historical transfer data can likely produce near-optimal schedulings without succumbing to the potential pitfalls of non-polynomial algorithms.

7   Potential Applications of MFT

Many practical applications exist for MFT in the cloud ecosystem. This section will list a few possible applications in a cloud-connected environment.

7.1   Cloud Data Placement Middleware

One application that was mentioned earlier in the chapter was using MFT as a sort of "glue" to bridge the gap between cloud storage and cloud computation services. Centralized data transfer managers have been used successfully to manage dataset staging in locally distributed computation systems, e.g. HTCondor [16]. MFT would fulfill an analogous role and confer the same benefits for cloud-based computation systems.

An MFT system can be used to stage data between cloud storage systems and cloud computation systems, freeing users from needing to manage staging themselves and also taking advantage of transfer and scheduling optimizations provided by the MFT system.

7.2   Backup Management and Replication

MFT systems can also perform automatic backup of data in cloud storage or replicate and synchronize data across multiple cloud services. Individuals and organizations who make regular backups of data can outsource this task to cloud-hosted MFT systems and take advantage of reliability guarantees and optimized data transfers.

7.3   Data Transfer for Thin Applications

One of the useful properties of cloud service systems is that they give client applications the opportunity to offload expensive or difficult tasks to remote systems. The client then only has to worry about communicating with the remote system and presenting responses from the server to the user.

MFT systems that offers a programmatic interface for transferring data and navigating remote file systems could be integrated into a thin client application to allow it to support multiple protocols and optimization algorithms without increasing the size of the application or burdening the developer to worry about application details. These applications could even be very lightweight web applications that run in the browser, allowing web applications to perform file transfers and access file metadata for multiple protocols and storage systems—something that has until now been difficult to do in web applications.

7.4   Going Further with MFT

The uses of MFT systems can also reach beyond simply managing data transfers and fetching directory listings. Indeed, some creative cases may elicit the need for categorization as something other than "managed file transfer". Advanced MFT systems are essentially protocol polyglots, and may be extended to take advantage of this.

Consider that MFT systems are necessarily capable of listing and crawling storage systems. Add an indexing mechanism, and it can become something else entirely. Imagine providing a service that allows organizations to index and search their own data stores, and easily locate, collate, and compare organizational documents no matter where or how they are stored. Typically such services are provided only for particular storage systems, but with MFT-as-abstraction layer, the underlying system can be anything. Imagine applying this to build a search engine on an index of publicly accessible storage systems—Google, but for more than just common web protocols.

Consider now that an MFT system that performs protocol translation is essentially a "Swiss Army knife" of storage system clients. Imagine going an extra step and making it a "Swiss Army knife" of server facades as well. Such systems could act as gateway to any supported protocol or storage system, accessible by anything that speaks the "language" of any other supported protocol or storage system. For example, a system that speaks FTP would be able to interface with a system that speaks HTTP—the MFT system acting as a translator—and meanwhile both systems would think they're speaking to a "native speaker" of the protocol they are configured to use.

Imagine a world where data transfer is routinely handled by cloud services. Users would not need to install special software in order to transfer files to or from other users or services in the cloud. The specifics of the underlying protocol or storage system would no longer matter. All of the details of the transfer will be offloaded to the cloud, and when the details change the cloud will adapt and users will never need to know.

It is left up to the reader to imagine other such creative use cases. Certainly the possibilities are great when data can flow so readily in the cloud.

Conclusion

This chapter has taken a look at the challenges faced in moving data into, out of, and around in the cloud. We've seen the issues surrounding data solubility that have arisen as data storage and processing have moved into the cloud, and how these issues can be addressed by MFT services.

We've examined the features of an ideal MFT system, and seen how MFT services in the cloud can take advantage of their centralized nature in order to offer benefits over other transfer management solutions. We've seen a number of established examples of research and commercial MFT systems, and we've taken a close look at the architecture of one such system—StorkCloud.

Hopefully this chapter has made a convincing case for MFT. Perhaps in the future MFT will be as commonplace in the cloud as storage and processing are today.

References

1. ARRA/ANI testbed. https://sites.google.com/a/lbl.gov/ani-100g-network.
2. Backup, copy, and migrate files between cloud storage services | Mover. https://mover.io/.
3. Energy Sciences Network (ESnet). http://www.es.net/.
4. Internet2. http://www.internet2.edu/.
5. Ipswitch MOVEit Managed File Transfer. http://www.moveitmanagedfiletransfer.com/.
6. ALLEN, B., BRESNAHAN, J., CHILDERS, L., FOSTER, I., KANDASWAMY, G., KETTIMUTHU, R., KORDAS, J., LINK, M., MARTIN, S., PICKETT, K., AND TUECKE, S. Software as a service for data scientists. *Communications of the ACM 55:2* (2012), 81–88.
7. ALTSCHUL, S. F., GISH, W., MILLER, W., MYERS, E. W., AND LIPMAN, D. J. Basic Local Alignment Search Tool. *Journal of Molecular Biology 3*, 215 (October 1990), 403–410.
8. ARSLAN, E., ROSS, B., AND KOSAR, T. Dynamic protocol tuning algorithms for high performance data transfers. In *Euro-Par* (2013), F. Wolf, B. Mohr, and D. an Mey, Eds., Lecture Notes in Computer Science, Springer, pp. 725–736.
9. CEYHAN, E., AND KOSAR, T. Large scale data management in sensor networking applications. In *In Proceedings of Secure Cyberspace Workshop* (Shreveport, LA, November 2007).
10. CHO, B., AND GUPTA, I. Budget-constrained bulk data transfer via internet and shipping networks. In *The 8th International Conference on Autonomic Computing (ICAC)* (2011).
11. HEY, T., AND TREFETHEN, A. The data deluge: An e-Science perspective. In *In Grid Computing - Making the Global Infrastructure a Reality*, pp. chapter 36, pp. 809–824. Wiley and Sons, 2003.
12. JUNG, E.-S., KETTIMUTHU, R., AND VISHWANATH, V. Toward optimizing disk-to-disk transfer on 100G networks.
13. KIEHL, J., HACK, J. J., BONAN, G. B., BOVILLE, B. A., WILLIAMSON, D. L., AND RASCH, P. J. The national center for atmospheric research community climate model: Ccm3. *Journal of Climate 11:6* (1998), 1131–1149.
14. KIM, J., YILDIRIM, E., AND KOSAR, T. A highly-accurate and low-overhead prediction model for transfer throughput optimization. In *Proceedings of ACM SC'12 DISCS Workshop* (2012).
15. KLEIN, R. J. T., NICHOLLS, R. J., AND THOMALLA, F. Resilience to natural hazards: How useful is this concept? *Global Environmental Change Part B: Environmental Hazards 5*, 1–2 (2003), 35–45.
16. KOSAR, T., BALMAN, M., YILDIRIM, E., KULASEKARAN, S., AND ROSS, B. Stork data scheduler: Mitigating the data bottleneck in e-science. *The Phil. Transactions of the Royal Society A 369(3254–3267)* (2011).
17. LEINBERGER, W., KARYPIS, G., AND KUMAR, V. Multi-capacity bin packing algorithms with applications to job scheduling under multiple constraints. In *Parallel Processing, 1999. Proceedings. 1999 International Conference on* (1999), IEEE, pp. 404–412.
18. LONI. Louisiana Optical Network Initiative (LONI). http://www.loni.org/.
19. SOUDAN, S., CHEN, B. B., AND VICAT-BLANC PRIMET, P. Flow scheduling and endpoint rate control in gridnetworks. *Future Generation Computer Systems 25*, 8 (2009), 904–911.
20. TUMMALA, S., AND KOSAR, T. Data management challenges in coastal applications. *Journal of Coastal Research special Issue No.50* (2007), 1188–1193.
21. XSEDE. Extreme Science and Engineering Discovery Environment. http://www.xsede.org/.
22. YILDIRIM, E., YIN, D., AND KOSAR, T. Prediction of optimal parallelism level in wide area data transfers. *IEEE TPDS 22(12)* (2011).
23. YIN, D., YILDIRIM, E., AND KOSAR, T. A data throughput prediction and optimization service for widely distributed many-task computing. *IEEE TPDS 22(6)* (2011).
24. ZHANG, B., ROSS, B., TRIPATHI, S., BATRA, S., AND KOSAR, T. Network-aware data caching and prefetching for cloud-hosted metadata retrieval. In *Proceedings of the Third International Workshop on Network-Aware Data Management* (2013), ACM, p. 4.

Supporting a Social Media Observatory with Customizable Index Structures: Architecture and Performance

Xiaoming Gao, Evan Roth, Karissa McKelvey, Clayton Davis,
Andrew Younge, Emilio Ferrara, Filippo Menczer, and Judy Qiu

Abstract The intensive research activity in analysis of social media and micro-blogging data in recent years suggests the necessity and great potential of platforms that can efficiently store, query, analyze, and visualize social media data. To support these "social media observatories" effectively, a storage platform must satisfy special requirements for loading and storage of multi-terabyte datasets, as well as efficient evaluation of queries involving analysis of the text of millions of social updates. Traditional inverted indexing techniques do not meet such requirements. As a solution, we propose a general indexing framework, IndexedHBase, to build specially customized index structures for facilitating efficient queries on an HBase distributed data storage system. IndexedHBase is used to support a social media observatory that collects and analyzes data obtained through the Twitter streaming API. We develop a parallel query evaluation strategy that can explore the customized index structures efficiently, and test it on a set of typical social media data queries. We evaluate the performance of IndexedHBase on FutureGrid and compare it with Riak, a widely adopted commercial NoSQL database system. The results show that IndexedHBase provides a data loading speed that is six times faster than Riak and is significantly more efficient in evaluating queries involving large result sets.

X. Gao (✉) • A. Younge • J. Qiu
School of Informatics and Computing, Indiana University, Lindley Hall, Room 215 150 S.
Woodlawn Avenue Bloomington, IN 47405
e-mail: gao4@indiana.edu; xqiu@indiana.edu; ajyounge@indiana.edu

E. Roth
Department of Computer Science & Information Technology, University of the District
of Columbia, Washington, DC, USA
e-mail: evanroth@me.com; eroth@indiana.edu

K. McKelvey • C. Davis • E. Ferrara • F. Menczer
School of Informatics and Computing, Indiana University, Informatics West, Room 233, 901 E.
10th Street, Bloomington, IN 47408
e-mail: karissa.mckelvey@gmail.com; krmckelv@indiana.edu; claydavi@indiana.edu;
ferrarae@indiana.edu; fil@indiana.edu

© Springer Science+Business Media New York 2014   401
X. Li, J. Qiu (eds.), *Cloud Computing for Data-Intensive Applications*,
DOI 10.1007/978-1-4939-1905-5__17

1 Introduction

Data-intensive computing brings challenges in both large-scale batch analysis and real-time streaming data processing. To meet these challenges, improvements to various levels of cloud storage systems are necessary. Specifically, regarding the problem of search in Big Data, the usage of indices to facilitate query evaluation has been a well-researched topic in the area of databases [16], and inverted indices [37] are specially designed for full-text search. A basic idea is to first build index data structures through a full scan of data and documents and then facilitate fast access to the data via indices to achieve highly optimized search performance.

Beyond these system features, it is a challenge to enable real-time search and efficient analysis over a broader spectrum of social media data scenarios. For example, Derczynski et al. [14] discussed the temporal and spatial challenges in context-aware search and analysis on social media data. Padmanabhan et al. presented FluMapper [20], an interactive map-based interface for flu-risk analysis using near real-time processing of social updates collected from the Twitter streaming API [30]. As an additional scenario within this line of research, we utilize Truthy (http://truthy.indiana.edu) [18], a public social media observatory that analyzes and visualizes information diffusion on Twitter. Research performed on the data collected by this system covers a broad spectrum of social activities, including political polarization [7, 8], congressional elections [9, 15], protest events [10, 11], and the spread of misinformation [23, 24]. Truthy has also been instrumental in shedding light on communication dynamics such as user attention allocation [34] and social link creation [35]. This platform processes and analyzes some general entities and relationship, contained in its large-scale social dataset, such as tweets, users, hashtags, retweets, and user-mentions during specific time windows of social events. Truthy consumes a stream that includes a sample of public tweets. Currently, the total size of historical data collected continuously by the system since August 2010 is approximately 10 Terabytes (stored in compressed JSON format). At the time of this writing, the data rate of the Twitter streaming API is in the range of 45–50 million tweets per day, leading to a growth of approximately 20 GB per day in the total data size.

This chapter describes our research towards building an efficient and scalable storage platform for this large set of social microblogging data collected by the Truthy system. Many existing NoSQL databases, such as Solandra (now known as DataStax) [13] and Riak [25], support distributed inverted indices [37] to facilitate searching text data. However, traditional distributed inverted indices are designed for text retrieval applications; they may incur unnecessary storage and computation overhead during indexing and query evaluation, and thus they are not suitable for handling social media data queries. For example, the issue of how to efficiently evaluate temporal queries involving text search on hundreds of millions of social updates remains a challenge. As a possible solution, we propose IndexedHBase, a general, customizable indexing framework. It uses HBase [3] as the underlying storage platform, and provides users with the added flexibility to define the most suitable index structures to facilitate their queries. Using Hadoop MapReduce [2] we implement a parallel query evaluation strategy that can make the best use of the customized index structures to achieve efficient evaluation of social media data queries typical for an application such as Truthy. We develop efficient data loading strategies that can accommodate fast loading of historical files as well as fast processing of streaming data from real-time tweets. We evaluate the performance of IndexedHBase on FutureGrid [32]. Our preliminary results show that, compared with Riak, IndexedHBase is significantly more efficient. It is six times faster for data loading, while requiring much less storage. Furthermore, it is clearly more efficient in evaluating queries derived from large result sets.

The rest of this chapter is organized as follows. Section 2 analyzes the characteristics of data and queries. Section 3 gives a brief introduction of HBase. Section 4 describes the architecture of IndexedHBase and explains the design and implementation of its data loading, indexing, and query evaluation strategies. Section 5 evaluates the performance of IndexedHBase and compares it with Riak. Section 6 discusses related work. "Conclusions and Future Work" section concludes and describes our future work.

2 Data and Query Patterns

The entire dataset consists of two parts: historical data in .json.gz files, and real-time data collected from the Twitter streaming API. Figure 1 illustrates a sample data item, which is a structured JSON string containing information about a tweet and the user who posted it. Furthermore, if the tweet is a retweet, the original tweet content is also included in a "retweeted_status" field. For hashtags, user-mentions, and URLs contained in the text of the tweet, an "entities" field is included to give detailed information, such as the ID of the mentioned user and the expanded URLs.

In social network analysis, the concept of "meme" is often used to represent a set of related posts corresponding to a specific discussion topic, communication channel, or information source shared by users on platforms such as Twitter. Memes can be identified through elements contained in the text of tweets, such as keywords, hashtags (e.g., #euro2012), user-mentions (e.g., youtube), and URLs. Our social media observatory, Truthy, supports a set of temporal queries for extracting and generating various information about tweets, users, and memes. These queries can be categorized into two subsets. The first contains basic queries for getting the ID or content of tweets created during a given time window from their text or user information, including:

get-tweets-with-meme *(memes, time_window)*
get-tweets-with-text *(keywords, time_window)*
get-tweets-with-user *(user_id, time_window)*
get-retweets *(tweet_id, time_window)*

```
{
    "text":"RT @sengineland: My Single Best... ",
    "created_at":"Fri Apr 15 23:37:26 +0000 2011",
    "retweet_count":0,
    "id_str":"59037647649259521",
    "entities":{
        "user_mentions":[{
                    "screen_name":"sengineland",
                    "id_str":"1059801",
                    "name":"Search Engine Land",
            }],
        "hashtags":[],
        "urls":[{
                    "url":"http:\/\/selnd.com\/e2QPS1",
                    "expanded_url":null
            }]
    },
    "user":{
        "created_at":"Sat Jan 22 18:39:46 +0000 2011",
        "friends_count":63,
        "id_str":"241622902",
        ...
    },
    "retweeted_status":{
        "text":"My Single Best... ",
        "created_at":"Fri Apr 15 21:40:10 +0000 2011",
        "id_str":"59008136320786432",
                    ...
    },
    ...
}
```

Fig. 1 An example tweet in JSON format

For the parameters, *time_window* is given in the form of a pair of strings marking the start and end points of a time window, e.g., [2012-06-08T00:00:00, 2012-06-23T23:59:59]. The memes parameter is given as a list of hashtags, user-mentions, or URLs; memes and keywords may contain wildcards, e.g., "#occupy*" will match all tweets containing hashtags starting with "#occupy".

The second subset of queries need information extracted from the tweets returned by queries in the first subset. These include *timestamp-count*, *user-post-count*, *meme-post-count*, *meme-cooccurrence-count*, *get-retweet-edges*, and *get-mention-edges*. Here for example, *user-post-count* returns the number of posts about a given meme by each user. Each "edge" has three components: a "from" user ID, a "to" user ID, and a "weight" indicating how many times the "from" user has retweeted the tweets from the "to" user or mentioned the "to" user in his/her tweets.

The most significant characteristic of these queries is that they all take a time window as a parameter. This originates from the temporal nature of social activities. An obvious brute-force solution is to scan the whole dataset, try to match the content and creation time of each tweet with the query parameters, and generate the results using information contained in the matched tweets. However, due to the drastic difference between the size of the entire dataset and the size of the query result, this strategy is prohibitively expensive. For example, in the time window [2012-06-01, 2012-06-20] there are over 600 million tweets, while the number of tweets containing the most popular meme "youtube" is less than two million, which is smaller by more than two orders of magnitude.

Traditional distributed inverted indices [37], supported by many existing distributed NoSQL database systems such as Solandra (DataStax) [13] and Riak [25], do not provide the most efficient solution to locate relevant tweets by their text content. One reason is that traditional inverted indices are mainly designed for text retrieval applications, where the main goal is to efficiently find the top K (with a typical value of 20 or 50 for K) most relevant text documents regarding a query comprising a set of keywords. To achieve this goal, information, such as frequency and position of keywords in the documents, is stored and used for computing relevance scores between documents and keywords during query evaluation. In contrast, social media data queries are designed for analysis purposes, meaning that they have to process all the related tweets, instead of the top K most relevant ones, to generate the results. Therefore, data regarding frequency and position are extra overhead for the storage of inverted indices, and relevance scoring is unnecessary in the query evaluation process. The query evaluation performance can be further improved by removing these items from traditional inverted indices.

Secondly, social media queries do not favor query execution plans using traditional inverted indices. Figure 2 illustrates a typical query execution plan for *get-tweets-with-meme*, using two separate indices on memes and tweet creation time. This plan uses the meme index to find the IDs of all tweets containing the given memes and utilizes the time index to find the set of tweet IDs within the given time window, finally computing the intersection of these two sets to get the results. Assuming the size of the posting lists for the given memes to be m, and the number of tweet IDs coming from the time index to be n, the complexity of the

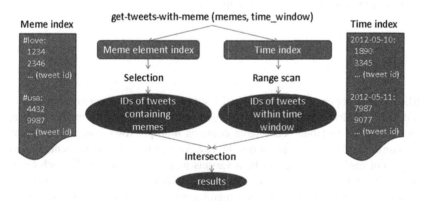

Fig. 2 A typical query execution plan using indices on meme and creation time

whole query evaluation process will be O(m + n) = O(max(m, n)), using a merge-based or hashing-based algorithm for the intersection operation. However, due to the characteristics of large social media and microblogging datasets, there is normally an orders-of-magnitude difference between m and n, as discussed above. As a result, although the size of the query result is bounded by min(m, n), a major part of query evaluation time is actually spent on scanning and checking irrelevant entries of the time index. In classic text search engines, techniques such as skipping or frequency-ordered inverted lists [37] may be utilized to quickly return the top K most relevant results without evaluating all the related documents. However, such optimizations are not applicable to our social media observatory. Furthermore, in case of a high cost estimation for accessing the time index, the search engine may choose to only use the meme index and generate the results by checking the content of relevant tweets. However, valuable time is still wasted in checking irrelevant tweets falling out of the given time window. The query evaluation performance can be further improved if the unnecessary scanning cost can be avoided.

We propose using a customized index structure in IndexedHBase, as illustrated in Fig. 3. It merges the meme index and time index, and replaces the frequency and position information in the posting lists of the meme index with creation time of corresponding tweets. Facilitated by this customized index structure, the query evaluation process for *get-tweets-with-meme* can be easily implemented by going through the index entries related to the given memes and selecting the tweet IDs associated with a creation time within the given time window. The complexity of the new query evaluation process is O(m), which is significantly lower than O(max(m, n)). To support such index structures, IndexedHBase provides a general customizable indexing framework, which will be explained in Sect. 4.

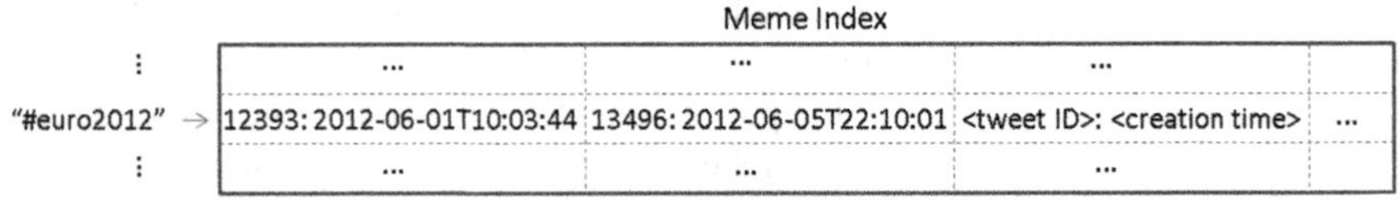

Meme Index

	...	...	...	
"#euro2012" →	12393: 2012-06-01T10:03:44	13496: 2012-06-05T22:10:01	<tweet ID>: <creation time>	...
	...	...	...	

Fig. 3 A customized meme element index structure

3 HBase

HBase [3] is an open-source, distributed, column-oriented, and sorted-map datastore modeled after Google's BigTable [6]. Figure 4 illustrates the data model of HBase. Data are stored in tables; each table contains multiple rows, and a fixed number of column families. Rows are sorted by row keys, which are implemented as byte arrays. For each row, there can be a various number of qualifiers in each column family, and at the intersections of rows and qualifiers are table cells. Cell contents are uninterpreted byte arrays. Cells contents are versioned based on timestamps, and a table can be configured to maintain a certain number of versions.

	BasicInfo			ClassGrades		
	Name	Office	···	Database	Independent study	···
aaa@indiana.edu →	t0 →aaa	t1 → LH201 t2 → IE339	···	t4 → A+	t5 → I t6 → A	···
bbb@indiana.edu →	t3 →bbb	...	...		...	
	⋮	⋮	⋮		⋮	

Column families: **BasicInfo, ClassGrades**
Qualifiers: **Name, Office, Database, Independent Study**
Row keys: **aaa@indiana.edu, bbb@indian.edu**
Version timestamps: **t0, t1, t2, t3, t4, t5, t6**

Fig. 4 An example of the HBase data model

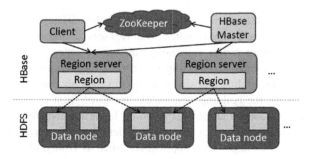

Fig. 5 HBase architecture

Figure 5 shows the architecture of HBase. At any time, there can be one working HBase master and multiple region servers running in the system. One or more backup HBase masters can be set up to prevent single point of failure. The Apache ZooKeeper [5] is used to coordinate the activities of the master and region servers. Tables are horizontally split into regions, and regions are assigned to different region servers by the HBase master. Each region is further divided vertically into stores by column families, and stores are saved as store files in Hadoop Distributed File System (HDFS) [27]. Data replication in HDFS and region server failover ensure high availability of table data. Load balance is done through dynamic region splitting, and scalability can be achieved by adding more data nodes and region servers. HBase is inherently integrated with Hadoop MapReduce. It supports MapReduce jobs using HBase tables as both input and output.

Based on this distributed architecture, HBase can store and serve huge amounts of data. HBase is designed for efficient processing of large volumes of small data operations. Inside store files, cell values are sorted in the hierarchical order of <row key, column family, qualifier, timestamp>. Therefore, HBase is efficient at scanning operations of consecutive rows or columns. HBase supports three types of compression to the data blocks of store files: LZO, Gzip, and Snappy. The compression details are transparent to user applications.

All these features of HBase make it a good option for hosting and processing the Truthy data set. The only problem is that it does not provide an inherent mechanism for searching cell values within tables efficiently. IndexedHBase, as will be described in Sect. 4, is exactly designed to bridge this gap.

4   Design and Implementation of IndexedHBase

4.1   System Architecture

Figure 6 shows our system architecture based on IndexedHBase. HBase is used to host the entire dataset and related indices with two sets of tables: data tables for the original data, and index tables containing customized index structures for query evaluation. The customizable indexing framework supports two mechanisms for building index tables: online indexing that indexes data upon upload to the tables, and batch indexing for building new index structures from existing data tables. Two data loading strategies are implemented for historical and streaming data. The parallel query evaluation strategy provides efficient evaluation mechanisms for all queries, and is used by upper-level applications, such as Truthy, to generate various statistics and visualizations.

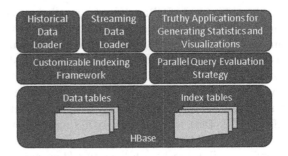

Fig. 6 System architecture of IndexedHBase

4.2   Customizable Indexing Framework

4.2.1   Table Schemas on HBase

Working off the HBase data model, we design the table schemas in Fig. 7. Tables are managed in units of months. This has two benefits. First, the loading of streaming

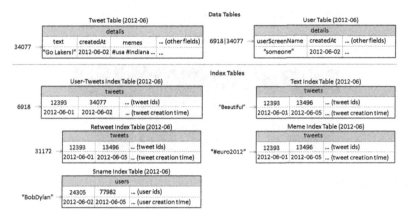

Fig. 7 Table schemas used in IndexedHBase for Twitter data

data only changes the tables relative to the current month. Secondly, during query evaluations, the amount of index data and original data scanned is limited by the time window parameter.

Some details need to be clarified before proceeding further. Each table contains only one column family, e.g. "details" or "tweets". The user table uses a concatenation of user ID and tweet ID as the row key, because analysis benefits from tracking changes in a tweet's user metadata. For example, a user can change profile information, which can give insights into her behavior. Another meme index table is created for the included hashtags, user-mentions, and URLs. This is because some special cases, such as expandable URLs, cannot be handled properly by the text index. The memes are used as row keys, each followed by a different number of columns, named after the IDs of tweets containing the corresponding meme. The timestamp of the cell value marks the tweet creation time (Fig. 7).

Using HBase tables for customized index has several advantages. The data model of HBase can scale out horizontally for distributed index structure and embed additional information within the columns. Since the data access pattern in social media analysis is "write-once-read-many", IndexedHBase builds a separate table for each index structure for easy update and access. Rows in the tables are sorted by row keys, facilitating prefix queries through range scans over index tables. Using Hadoop MapReduce, the framework can generate efficient parallel analysis on the index data, such as meme popularity distribution [34].

4.2.2 Customizable Indexer Implementation

IndexedHBase implements a customizable indexer library, shown in Fig. 8, to generate index table records automatically according to the configuration file and insert them upon the client application's request.

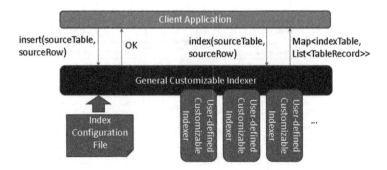

Fig. 8 Components of customizable indexer

```
<?xml version="1.0" encoding="UTF-8"?>
<configurations>
    <index-config>
        <source-table>tweetTable-[month]</source-table>
        <source-column-family>details</source-column-family>
        <source-qualifier>text</source-qualifier>
        <source-timestamp></source-timestamp>
        <source-value-type>full-text</source-value-type>
        <index-table>textIndexTable-[month]</index-table>
        <index-column-family>tweets</index-column-family>
        <index-qualifier>{source}.{rowkey}</index-qualifier>
        <index-timestamp>{source}.details.createdAt</index-timestamp>
        <index-value>{null}</index-value>
    </index-config>
    <index-config>
        <source-table>userTable-[month]</source-table>
        <index-table>snameIndexTable-[month]</index-table>
        <indexer-class>iu.pti.hbaseapp.truthy.UserSnameIndexer</indexer-class>
    </index-config>
</configurations>
```

Fig. 9 An example customized index configuration file

Figure 9 gives an example of the index configuration file in XML format containing multiple "index-config" elements that hold the mapping information between one source table and one index table. This element can flexibly define how to generate records for the index table off a given row from the source table. For more complicated index structures, users can implement a customizable indexer and use it by setting the "indexer-class" element.

Both general and user-defined indexers must implement a common interface which declares one *index()* method, as presented in Fig. 10. This method takes the name and row data of a source table as parameters and returns a map as a result. The key of each map entry is the name of one index table, and the value is a list of that table's records.

```
public interface CustomizableIndexer {
    public Map<String, List<TableRecord>> index(sourceTableName, sourceTableRow);
}
```

Fig. 10 Pseudocode for the "CustomizableIndexer" interface

Upon initialization, the general customizable indexer reads the index configuration file from the user. If a user-defined indexer class is specified, a corresponding indexer instance will be created. When *index()* is invoked during runtime, all related "index-config" elements are used to generate records for each index table, either by following the rules defined in "index-config" or by invoking a user-defined indexer. Finally, all index table names and records are added to the result map and returned to the client application.

4.2.3 Online Indexing Mechanism and Batch Indexing Mechanism

IndexedHBase provides two means of indexing data: online and batch. The online mechanism is implemented through the *insert()* method of the general customizable indexer, displayed in Fig. 8. The client application invokes the *insert()* method of the general customizable indexer to insert one row into a source table. The indexer will first insert the given row into the source table and then generate index table records for this row by invoking *index()* and insert them into the corresponding index tables. Therefore, from the client application's perspective, data in the source table are indexed "online" when first inserted into the table.

The batch indexing mechanism is designed for generating new customized index tables after all the data have been loaded into the source table. This mechanism is implemented as a "map-only" MapReduce job using the source table as input. The job accepts a source table and index table name as parameters and starts multiple mappers to index data in the source table in parallel, each processing one region of the table. Each mapper works as a client application to the general customizable indexer and creates one indexer instance at its initialization time. The indexer is initialized using the given index table name so that when *index()* is invoked, it will only generate index records for that single table. The *map()* function takes a <key, value> pair as input, where "key" is a row key in the source table and "value" is the corresponding row data. For each row of the source table, the mapper uses the general customizable indexer to generate index table records and write these records as output. All output records are handled by the table output format, which will automatically insert them into the index table.

4.3   Data Loading Strategies

IndexedHBase supports distributed loading strategies for both streaming data and historical data. Figure 11 shows the architecture of the streaming data loading strategy, where one or more distributed loaders are running concurrently and are connected to the same stream using the Twitter streaming API. Each loader is assigned a unique ID and works as a client application to the general customizable indexer. Upon receiving a tweet JSON string, the loader will first take the tweet ID and do a modulus operation over the total number of loaders in the system. If the result equals its loader ID, it will load the tweet to IndexedHBase. Otherwise the tweet is skipped. To load a tweet, the loader first generates records for the tweet table and user table based on the JSON string, then loads them into the tables by invoking the *insert()* method of the general customizable indexer, which will complete online indexing and update all the data tables as well as the relevant index tables.

Fig. 11   Streaming data
loading strategy

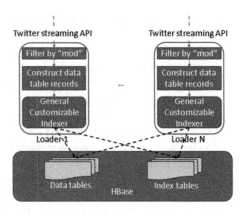

The historical data loading strategy is implemented as a MapReduce program. One separate job is launched to load the historical files for each month, and multiple jobs can be running simultaneously. Each job starts multiple mappers in parallel, each responsible for loading one file. At running time, each line in the .json.gz file is given to the mapper as one input, which contains the string of one tweet. The mapper first creates records for the tweet table and user table and then invokes the general customizable indexer to get all the related index table records. All table records are handled by the multi-table output format, which automatically inserts them into the related tables. Finally, if the JSON string contains a "retweeted_status", the corresponding substring will be extracted and processed in the same way.

4.4 Parallel Query Evaluation Strategy

We develop a two-phase parallel query evaluation strategy viewable in Fig. 12. For any given query, the first phase uses multiple threads to find the IDs of all related tweets from the index tables, and saves them in a series of files containing a fixed number (e.g., 30,000) of tweet IDs. The second phase launches a MapReduce job to process the tweets in parallel and extract the necessary information to complete the query. For example, to evaluate *user-post-count*, each mapper in the job will access the tweet table to figure out the user ID corresponding to a particular tweet ID, count the number of tweets by each user, and output all counts when it finishes. The output of all the mappers will be processed to finally generate the total tweet count of each user ID.

Two aspects of the query evaluation strategy deserve further discussion. First, as described in Sect. 2, prefix queries can be constructed by using parameters such as "#occupy*". IndexedHBase provides two options for getting the related tweet IDs in the first phase. One is simply to complete a sequential range scan of rows in the corresponding index tables. The other is to use a MapReduce program to complete parallel scans over the range of rows. The latter option is only faster for parameters covering a large range spanning multiple regions of the index table.

Second, the number of tweet IDs in each file implies a tradeoff between parallelism and scheduling overhead. When this number is set lower, more mappers will be launched in the parallel evaluation phase, which means the amount of work done by a mapper decreases while the total task scheduling overhead increases. The optimal number depends on the total number of related tweets and the amount of resources available in the infrastructure. We set the default value of this number to 30,000 and leave it configurable by the user. Future work will explore automatic optimization.

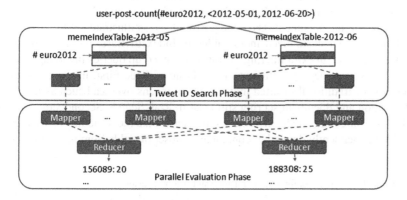

Fig. 12 Two-phase parallel evaluation process for an example *user-post-count* query

5 Performance Evaluation Results and Comparison with Riak

5.1 Testing Environment Configuration

We use eight nodes on the Bravo cluster of FutureGrid to complete tests for both IndexedHBase and Riak. The hardware configuration for all eight nodes is listed in Table 1. Each node runs CentOS 6.4 and Java 1.7.0_21. For IndexedHBase, Hadoop 1.0.4 and HBase 0.94.2 are used. One node is used to host the HDFS headnode, Hadoop jobtracker, Zookeeper, and HBase master. The other seven nodes are used to host HDFS datanodes, Hadoop tasktrackers, and HBase region servers. The data replication level is set to two on HDFS. The configuration details of Riak will be given in Sect. 5.2. In addition to Bravo, we also use the Alamo HPC cluster of FutureGrid to test the scalability of the historical data loading strategy of IndexedHBase, since Alamo can provide a larger number of nodes through dynamic HPC jobs. Software configuration of Alamo is mostly the same as Bravo.

5.2 Configuration and Implementation on Riak

Riak is a distributed NoSQL database for storing data in the form of <key, value> objects. It uses a P2P architecture to organize the distributed nodes and distributes data objects among them using consistent hashing. Data are replicated to achieve high availability, and failures are handled by a handoff mechanism among neighboring nodes. A "Riak Search" module can build distributed inverted indices on data objects for full-text search purposes. Users can use buckets to organize their data objects and configure indexed fields on the bucket level. Riak supports a special feature called "inline fields." If a field is specified as an "inline" field, its value will be attached to the document IDs in the posting lists, as illustrated in Fig. 13.

Similar to our customized index tables in IndexedHBase, inline fields can be used to carry out an extra filtering operation to speed up queries involving multiple fields. However, they are different in two basic aspects. First, inline fields are an extension of traditional inverted indices, which means overhead such as frequency information and document scoring still exist in Riak Search. Second, customizable index structures are totally flexible in the sense that the structure of each index can be independently defined to contain any subset of fields from the original data.

Table 1 Per-node configuration on Bravo and Alamo Clusters

Cluster	CPU	RAM	Hard disk	Network
Bravo	8 * 2.40 GHz (Intel Xeon E5620)	192 G	2 T	40 Gb InfiniBand
Alamo	8 * 2.66 GHz (Intel Xeon X5550)	12 G	500 G	40 Gb InfiniBand

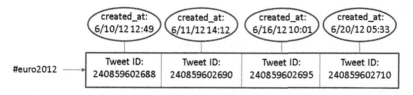

Fig. 13 An example of inline field (created_at) in Riak

```
("inputs":(
            "bucket":"truthyTest201206",
            "query":"memes:'#euro2012'",
            "filter":"created_at:['2012-06-08' TO '2012-06-20']"
        ),
    "query":[
            ("map":( /* JavaScript function */ )
            ),
            ("reduce":( /* JavaScript function */ )
            )
        ]
    )
```

Fig. 14 An example query implementation on Riak

In contrast, if one field is defined as an inline field on Riak, its value will be attached to the posting lists of the indices of all indexed fields, regardless of whether it is useful. As an example, the "sname index table" in Fig. 17 uses the creation time of user accounts as timestamps, while the "meme index table" uses creation time of tweets. Such flexibility is not achievable on Riak.

In our tests, all eight nodes of Bravo are used to construct a Riak ring. Each node runs Riak 1.2.1, using LevelDB as the storage backend. We create two different buckets to index data with different search schemas. The data replication level is set to two on both buckets. The tweet ID and JSON string of each tweet are directly stored into <key, value> pairs. The original JSON string is extended with an extra "memes" field, which contains all the hashtags, user-mentions, and URLs in the tweet, separated by tab characters. Riak Search is enabled on both buckets, and the user_id, memes, text, retweeted_status_id, user_screen_name, and created_at fields are indexed. Specifically, created_at is defined as a separate indexed field on one bucket, and as an "inline only" field on the other bucket, meaning that it does not have a separate index but is stored together with the indices of other fields.

Riak provides a lightweight MapReduce framework for users to query the data by defining MapReduce functions in JavaScript. Furthermore, Riak supports MapReduce over the results of Riak Search. We use this feature to implement queries, and Fig. 14 shows an example query implementation. When this query is submitted, Riak will first use the index on "memes" to find related tweet objects (as specified in the "input" field), then apply the map and reduce functions to these tweets (as defined in the "query" field) to get the final result.

5.3   Data Loading Performance

5.3.1   Historical Data Loading Performance

We use all the .json.gz files from June 2012 to test the historical data loading performance of IndexedHBase and Riak. The total data size is 352 GB. With IndexedHBase, a MapReduce job is launched for historical data loading, with each mapper processing one file. With Riak, all 30 files are distributed among eight nodes of the cluster, so each node ends up with three or four files. Then an equal number of threads per node were created to load all the files concurrently to the bucket where "created_at" is configured as an inline field. Threads continue reading the next tweet, apply preprocessing with the "created_at" and "memes" field, and then send the tweet to the Riak server for indexing and insertion.

Table 2 summarizes the data loading time and loaded data size on both platforms. We can see that IndexedHBase is over six times faster than Riak in loading historical data and uses significantly less disk space for storage. Considering the original file size of 352 GB and a replication level of two, the storage space overhead for index data on IndexedHBase is moderate.

We analyze these performance measurements below. By storing data with tables, IndexedHBase applies a certain degree of data model normalization, and thus avoids storing some redundant data. For example, many tweets in the original .json.gz files contain retweeted status, and many of them are retweeted multiple times. With IndexedHBase, even if a tweet is retweeted repeatedly, only one record is kept for it in the tweet table. With Riak, such a "popular" tweet will be stored within the JSON string of every corresponding retweet. The difference in loaded index data size clearly demonstrates the advantage of a fully customizable indexing framework. By avoiding frequency and position information and only incorporating useful fields in the index tables, IndexedHBase saves 455 GB of disk space in storing index data, which is more than 1/3 the total loaded data size of 1,167 GB. Also note that IndexedHBase compresses table data using Gzip, which generally provides a better compression ratio than Snappy used on Riak.

Table 2 Historical data loading performance comparison

	Loading time (h)	Loaded total data size (GB)	Loaded original data size (GB)	Loaded index data size (GB)
Riak	294.11	3258	2591	667
IndexedHBase	45.47	1167	955	212
Riak/IndexedHBase	6.47	2.79	2.71	3.15

The difference in loaded data size only explains a part of the difference in total loading time. Two other reasons are:

1. The loaders of IndexedHBase are responsible for generating both data tables and index tables. Therefore, the JSON string of each tweet is parsed only once when it is read from the .json.gz files and converted to table records. On the other hand, Riak uses servers for its indexing and so each JSON string is actually parsed twice: first by the loaders for preprocessing, and again by the server for indexing.
2. When building inverted indices, Riak not only uses more space to store the frequency and position information, but also spends more time collecting them.

5.3.2 Scalable Historical Data Loading on IndexedHBase

We test the scalability of historical data loading on IndexedHBase with the Alamo cluster of FutureGrid. In this test we take a dataset for two months, May and June 2012, and measure the total loading time with different cluster sizes. The results are illustrated in Fig. 15. When the cluster size is doubled from 16 to 32 data nodes, the total loading time drops from 142.72 to 93.22 h, which implies a sub-linear scalability coming from the concurrent access from mappers of the loading jobs to HBase region servers. Nonetheless, these results clearly demonstrate that we get more system throughput and faster data loading speed by adding more nodes to the cluster.

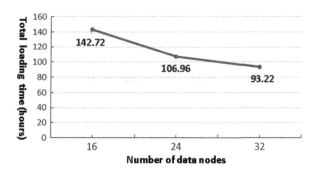

Fig. 15 Historical data loading scalability

5.3.3 Streaming Data Loading Performance on IndexedHBase

The purpose of streaming data loading tests is to verify that IndexedHBase can provide enough throughput to accommodate the growing data speed of the Twitter streaming API. To test the performance of IndexedHBase for handling potential data rates even faster than the current streams, we design a simulation test using a recent

.json.gz file from July 3, 2013. We vary the number of distributed streaming loaders and test the corresponding system data loading speed. For each case, the whole file is evenly split into the same number of fragments as the loaders and then distributed across all the nodes. One loader is started to process each fragment. The loader reads data from the stream of the local file fragment rather than from the Twitter streaming API. So this test measures how the system performs when each loader gets an extremely high data rate that is equal to local disk I/O speed.

Figure 16 shows the total loading time when the number of distributed loaders increases by powers of two from one to 16. Once again, concurrent access to HBase region servers results in a decrease in speed-up as the number of loaders is doubled each time. The system throughput is almost saturated when we have eight distributed loaders. For the case of eight loaders, it takes 3.85 h to load all 45,753,194 tweets, indicating the number of tweets that can be processed per day on eight nodes is about six times the current daily data rate. Therefore, IndexedHBase can easily handle a high-volume stream of social media data. In the case of vastly accelerated data rates, as would be the case for the Twitter firehose (a stream of all public tweets), one could increase the system throughput by adding more nodes.

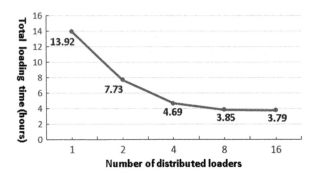

Fig. 16 Results for streaming data loading test

5.4 Query Evaluation Performance

5.4.1 Separate Index Structures vs. Customized Index Structures

As discussed in Sect. 2, one major purpose of using customized index structures is to achieve lower query evaluation complexity compared to traditional inverted indices on separate data fields. To verify this, we use a simple *get-tweets-with-meme* query to compare the performance of IndexedHBase with a solution using separate indices on the fields of memes and tweet creation time, which is implemented through the Riak bucket where "created_at" is defined as a separately indexed field.

In this test we load 4 days of data to both IndexedHBase and the Riak bucket and measure the query evaluation time with different memes and time windows. For memes, we choose "#usa", "#ff", and "@youtube", each contained in a different subset of tweets. The "#ff" hashtag is a popular meme for "Follow Friday." For each meme, we use three different time windows with a length between 1 and 3 h. Queries in this test only return tweet IDs they don't launch an extra MapReduce phase to get the content. Figures 17 and 18 present the query execution time for each indexing strategy. As shown in the plots, IndexedHBase not only achieves a query evaluation speed that is tens to hundreds of times faster, but also demonstrates a different pattern in query evaluation time. When separate meme index and time index are used, the query evaluation time mainly depends on the length of time window; the meme parameter has little impact. In contrast, using a customized

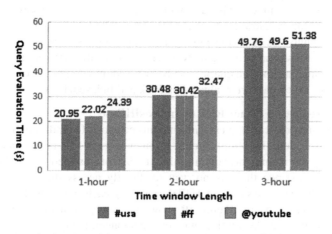

Fig. 17 Query evaluation time with separate meme and time indices (Riak)

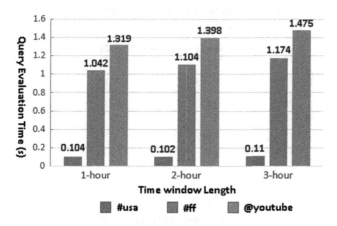

Fig. 18 Query evaluation time with customized meme index (IndexedHBase)

meme index, the query evaluation time mainly depends on the meme parameter. For the same meme, the evaluation time only increases marginally as the time window gets longer. These observations confirm our theoretical analysis in Sect. 2.

5.4.2 Query Evaluation Performance Comparison

This set of tests is designed to compare the performance of Riak and IndexedHBase for evaluating queries involving different numbers of tweets and different result sizes. Since using separate indices has proven inefficient on Riak, we choose to test the query implementation using "created_at" as an inline field. Queries are executed on both platforms against the data loaded in the historical data loading tests. For query parameters, we choose the popular meme "#euro2012," along with a time window with a length varied from 3 h to 16 days. The start point of the time window is fixed at 2012-06-08T00:00:00, and the end point is correspondingly varied exponentially from 2012-06-08T02:59:59 to 2012-06-23T23:59:59. This time period covers a major part of the 2012 UEFA European Football Championship. The queries can be grouped into three categories based on the manner in which they are evaluated on Riak and IndexedHBase.

1. No MapReduce on Either Riak or IndexedHBase

The *meme-post-count* query falls into this category. On IndexedHBase, query evaluation is done by simply going through the rows in meme index tables for each given meme and counting the number of qualified tweet IDs. In the case of Riak, since there is no way to directly access the index data, this is accomplished by issuing an HTTP query for each meme to fetch the "id" field of matched tweets. Figure 19 shows the query evaluation time on Riak and IndexedHBase. As the time window gets longer, the query evaluation time increases for both. However, the absolute evaluation time is much shorter for IndexedHBase, because Riak has to spend extra time to retrieve the "id" field.

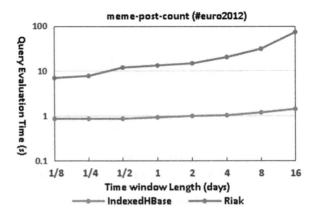

Fig. 19 Query evaluation time for *meme-post-count*

2. No MapReduce on IndexedHBase; MapReduce on Riak

The *timestamp-count* query belongs to this category. Inferring from the schema of the meme index table, this query can also be evaluated by only accessing the index data on IndexedHBase. On Riak it is implemented with MapReduce over Riak search results, where the MapReduce phase completes the timestamp counting based on the content of the related tweets. Figure 20 shows the query evaluation time on both platforms. Since IndexedHBase does not need to analyze the content of the tweets at all, its query evaluation speed is orders of magnitude faster than Riak.

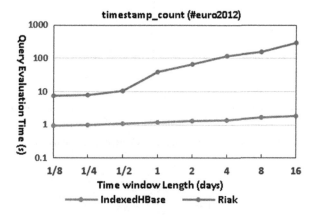

Fig. 20 Query evaluation time for *timestamp-count*

3. MapReduce on Both Riak and IndexedHBase

Most queries require a MapReduce phase on both Riak and IndexedHBase. Figure 21 shows the evaluation time for several of them. An obvious trend is that Riak is faster on queries involving a smaller number of related tweets, but IndexedHBase is significantly faster on queries involving a larger number of related tweets and results. Figure 22 lists the results sizes for two of the queries. The other queries have a similar pattern.

The main reason for the observed performance difference is the different characteristics of the MapReduce framework on these two platforms. IndexedHBase relies on Hadoop MapReduce, which is designed for fault tolerant parallel processing of large batches of data. It implements the full semantics of the MapReduce computing model and applies a comprehensive initialization process for setting up the runtime environment on the worker nodes. Hadoop MapReduce uses disks on worker nodes to save intermediate data and does grouping and sorting before passing them to reducers. A job can be configured to use zero or multiple reducers. Since most social media queries use time windows at the level of weeks or months, IndexedHBase can handle these long time period queries well.

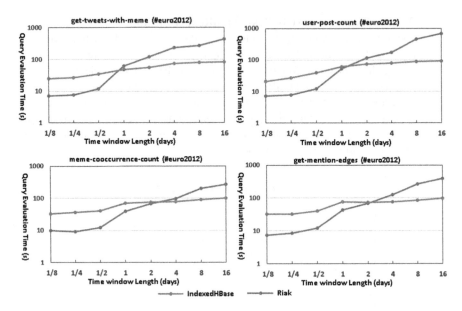

Fig. 21 Query evaluation time for queries requiring MapReduce on both platforms

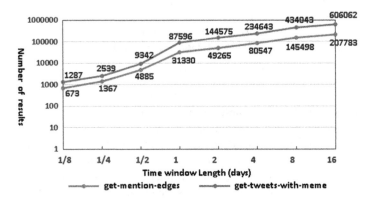

Fig. 22 Result sizes for *get-tweets-with-meme* and *get-mention-edges*

The MapReduce framework on Riak, on the other hand, is designed for lightweight use cases where users can write simple query logic with JavaScript and get them running on the data nodes quickly without a complicated initialization process. There is always only one reducer running for each MapReduce job. Intermediate data are transmitted directly from mappers to the reducer without being sorted or grouped. The reducer relies on its memory stack to store the whole list of intermediate data, and has a default timeout of only 5 s. Therefore, Riak MapReduce is not suitable for processing the large datasets produced by queries corresponding to long time periods.

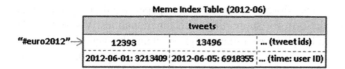

Meme Index Table (2012-06)

	tweets		
"#euro2012"→	12393	13496	... (tweet ids)
	2012-06-01: 3213409	2012-06-05: 6918355	... (time: user ID)

Fig. 23 Extended meme index table schema

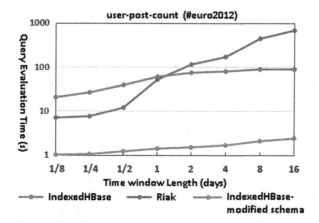

Fig. 24 Query evaluation time with modified meme index table schema

5.4.3 Improving Query Evaluation Performance with Modified Index Structures

IndexedHBase accepts dynamic changes to the index structures for efficient query evaluation. To verify this, we extend the meme index table to also include user IDs of tweets in the cell values, as illustrated in Fig. 23. Using this new index structure, IndexedHBase is able to evaluate the *user-post-count* query by only accessing index data.

We use the batch indexing mechanism of IndexedHBase to rebuild the meme index table, which takes 3.89 h. The table size increases from 14.23 to 18.13 GB, which is 27.4 % larger. Figure 24 illustrates the query evaluation time comparison. The query with the new index structure is faster by more than an order of magnitude. In cases where *user-post-count* is frequently used, the query speed improvement is clearly worth the additional storage required.

6 Related Work

To the best of our knowledge, Truthy [18] is the first complete social media observatory that provides not only analysis tools and visualization of their results, but also ways to retrieve derived data such as social network information and statistics about users and memes. Moreover, this is the first paper that describes the underlying data processing platform for supporting such functionalities. VisPolitics [31], TwitInfo [29], and Ripples [26] are similar analysis systems that generate visualizations about different aspects of social media network, but do not provide a rich set of statistics and derived data as Truthy does. Meanwhile, the techniques and indices presented in this paper could be useful for certain functions in these systems, such as generating the 'repost network' in Ripples, and supporting search of topic keywords and URL counting in TwitInfo. Commercial entities such as PeopleBrowsr [22], Datasift [12], and SocialFlow [28] provide consulting services to their customers through analytics over social media data, but they don't expose their raw data or results to the public for research purposes.

IndexedHBase aims to address the temporal challenge in social media analytics scenarios. Derczynski et al. [14] provide a more complete list of related work about temporal and spatial queries involving social data. In particular, Alonso et al. [1] give a detailed discussion about the challenges in extracting temporal information from online data and applying such information in queries. Notably, they mention the use case of text queries with temporal constraints in information retrieval scenarios, where ranking is still important. Weikum et al. [33] further elaborate on the open research problems for this specific use case in the context of longitudinal analytics on web archive data. Although the Truthy queries are not designed for information retrieval purposes, our experience in this project may still shed light on possible solutions for these problems in multiple aspects, including customizable index structures, scalable storage platforms, and efficient index building strategies. The customizable index structures we use share similar inspiration to multiple-column indices used in relational databases, but index a combination of full-text and primitive-type fields. Compared with traditional inverted indices [37], IndexedHBase provides more flexibility about what fields to use as keys and entries, so as to achieve more efficient query evaluation with less storage and computation overhead.

Solandra (DataStax) [13] and Riak [25] are two typical NoSQL database systems that support distributed inverted indices for full-text search. Specifically, Solandra is an offshoot of Cassandra, which uses a similar data model to HBase. Comparable to Riak, Cassandra also employs P2P architecture to support scalable data storage and relies on data replication to achieve fault-tolerance. As discussed in Sect. 2, inverted indices on Solandra and Riak are designed for text retrieval applications, making them unsuitable for social media analytics.

Google's Dremel [19] achieves efficient evaluation of aggregation queries on large-scale nested datasets by using distributed columnar storage and multi-level serving trees. Power Drill [17] explores special caching and data skipping mechanisms to provide even faster interactive query performance for certain selected datasets. Percolator [21] replaces batch indexing system with incremental processing for Google search. Inspired by Dremel and Power Drill, we will consider splitting the tweet table into more column families for even better query evaluation performance. On the other hand, our customizable indexing strategies could also potentially help Dremel for handling aggregation queries with highly selective operations.

Zaharia et al. [36] propose a fault-tolerant distributed processing model for streaming data by breaking continuous data streams into small batches and then applying existing fault-tolerance mechanisms used in batch processing frameworks. This idea of discretized streams will be useful for our next step of developing a fault-tolerant streaming data processing framework. Since streaming data are mainly involved in the loading and indexing phase, simpler failure recovery mechanisms may be more suitable.

Conclusions and Future Work

This chapter studies an efficient and scalable storage platform supporting a large Twitter dataset that powers the Truthy system, a public social media observatory. Our experimentation with IndexedHBase led to interesting conclusions of general significance. Parallelization and indexing are key factors in addressing the sheer data size and temporal queries of social data observatories. Parallelism in particular requires attention to every stage of data processing. Furthermore, a general customizable indexing framework is necessary. Index structures should be flexible, rather than static, to facilitate special characteristics of the dataset and queries, where optimal query evaluation performance is achieved at lower cost in storage and computation overhead. Reliable parallel processing frameworks such as Hadoop MapReduce can handle large intermediate data and results involved in the query evaluation process.

To the best of our knowledge, IndexedHBase is the first effort in developing a totally customizable indexing framework on a distributed NoSQL database. In the future we will add failure recovery to the distributed streaming data loading strategy. The efficiency of parallel query evaluation can be further improved with data locality considerations. Spatial queries will be supported by inferring and indexing spatial information contained in tweets. Thanks to the batch index building mechanism in IndexedHBase, adding spatial indices can be done efficiently without completely reloading the original dataset. Finally, we will integrate IndexedHBase with Hive [4] to provide a SQL-like data operation interface for easy implementation in social media observatories such as Truthy.

Acknowledgements We would like to thank Onur Varol, Mohsen JafariAsbagh, Alessandro Flammini, Geoffrey Fox, and other colleagues and members of the Center for Complex Networks and Systems Research (cnets.indiana.edu) at Indiana University for helpful discussions and contributions to the Truthy project and the present work. We would also like to personally thank Koji Tanaka and the rest of the FutureGrid team for their continued help. We gratefully acknowledge support from the National Science Foundation (grant CCF-1101743), DARPA (grant W911NF-12-1-0037), and the J. S. McDonnell Foundation. FutureGrid is supported by the National Science Foundation under Grant 0910812 to Indiana University for "An Experimental, High-Performance Grid Test-bed." IndexedHBased is in part supported by National Science Foundation CAREER Award OCI-1149432.

References

1. Alonso, O., Strötgen, J., Baeza-Yates, R. A., Gertz. M. Temporal Information Retrieval: Challenges and Opportunities. In: Proc. 1st Temporal Web Analytics Workshop (TWAW 2011)
2. Apache Hadoop. http://hadoop.apache.org/
3. Apache HBase. http://hbase.apache.org/
4. Apache Hive. http://hive.apache.org/
5. Apache Zookeeper. http://zookeeper.apache.org/
6. Chang, F., Dean, J., Ghemawat, S., Hsieh, W., Wallach, D., Burrows, M., Chandra, T., Fikes, A., Gruber, R. Bigtable: A Distributed Storage System for Structured Data. In: Proc. 7th Symp. Operating System Design and Implementation (OSDI 2006)
7. Conover, M., Ratkiewicz, J., Francisco, M., Goncalves, B., Flammini, A., Menczer, F. Political Polarization on Twitter. In: Proc. 5th Intl. AAAI Conf. Weblogs and Social Media (ICWSM 2011)
8. Conover, M., Gonçalves, B., Ratkiewicz, J., Flammini, A., Menczer, Filippo. Predicting the Political Alignment of Twitter Users. In: Proc. IEEE 3rd Intl. Conf. Social Computing (SocialCom 2011)
9. Conover, M., Gonçalves, B., Flammini, A., Menczer, F. Partisan Asymmetries in Online Political Activity. EPJ Data Science, 1:6 (2012)
10. Conover, M., Davis, C., Ferrara, E., McKelvey, K., Menczer, F., Flammini, A. The Geospatial Characteristics of a Social Movement Communication Network. PLoS ONE, 8(3): e55957 (2013)
11. Conover, M., Ferrara, E., Menczer, F., Flammini, A. The Digital Evolution of Occupy Wall Street. PloS ONE, 8(5), e64679 (2013)
12. Datasift. http://datasift.com
13. DataStax. http://www.datastax.com/
14. Derczynski, L., Yang, B., Jensen, C. Towards Context-Aware Search and Analysis on Social Media Data. In: Proc. 16th Intl. Conf. Extending Database Technology (EDBT 2013)
15. DiGrazia, J., McKelvey, K., Bollen, J., Rojas, F. More Tweets, More Votes: Social Media as a Quantitative Indicator of Political Behavior. Available at SSRN: http://dx.doi.org/10.2139/ssrn.2235423 (2013)
16. Graefe, G. Query Evaluation Techniques for Large Databases. ACM Computing Surveys (CSUR), 25(2): 73–169 (1993)
17. Hall, A., Bachmann, O., Büssow, R., Gănceanu, S., Nunkesser, M. Processing a Trillion Cells per Mouse Click. In: Proc. 38th Intl. Conf. Very Large Data Bases (VLDB 2012)
18. McKelvey, K., Menczer, F. Design and Prototyping of a Social Media Observatory. In: Proc. 22nd Intl. Conf. World Wide Web Companion (WWW 2013)
19. Melnik, S., Gubarev, A., Long, J., Romer, G., Shivakumar, S., Tolton, M., Vassilakis, T. Dremel: Interactive Analysis of Web-Scale Datasets. In: Proc. 36th Intl. Conf. Very Large Data Bases (VLDB 2010)
20. Padmanabhan, A., Wang, S., Cao, G., Hwang, M., Zhao, Y., Zhang, Z., Gao, Y. FluMapper: An Interactive CyberGIS Environment for Massive Location-based Social Media Data Analysis. In: Proc. Extreme Science and Engineering Discovery Environment: Gateway to Discovery (XSEDE 2013)
21. Peng, D., Dabek, F. Large-scale Incremental Processing Using Distributed Transactions and Notifications. In: Proc. 9th USENIX Symp. Operating Systems Design and Implementation (USENIX 2010)
22. PeopleBrowsr. http://peoplebrowsr.com
23. Ratkiewicz, J., Conover, M., Meiss, M., Gonçalves, B., Flammini, A., Menczer, F. Detecting and Tracking Political Abuse in Social Media. In: Proc. 5th Intl. AAAI Conf. Weblogs and Social Media (ICWSM 2011)

24. Ratkiewicz, J. Conover, M., Meiss, M., Goncalves, B., Patil, S., Flammini, A., Menczer, F. Truthy: Mapping the Spread of Astroturf in Microblog Streams. In: Proc. 20th Intl. Conf. World Wide Web Companion (WWW 2011)
25. Riak. http://basho.com/riak/
26. Ripples. https://plus.google.com/ripple/details?url=google.com
27. Shvachko, K., Kuang, H., Radia, S. and Chansler, R. The Hadoop Distributed File System. In: Proc. 26th IEEE Symp. Mass Storage Systems and Technologies (MSST 2010)
28. SocialFlow. http://socialflow.com
29. TwitInfo. http://twitinfo.csail.mit.edu
30. Twitter Streaming API. https://dev.twitter.com/docs/streaming-apis
31. VisPolitics. http://vispolitics.com
32. Von Laszewski, G., Fox, G., Wang, F., Younge, A., Kulshrestha, A., Pike, G. Design of the FutureGrid Experiment Management Framework. In: Proc. Gateway Computing Environments Workshop (GCE 2010)
33. Weikum, G., Ntarmos, N., Spaniol, M., Triantafillou, P., Benczúr, A., Kirkpatrick, S., Rigaux, P., Williamson, M. Longitudinal Analytics on Web Archive Data: It's About Time! In: Proc. 5th Biennial Conf. Innovative Data Systems Research (CIDR 2011)
34. Weng, L., Flammini, A., Vespignani, A., Menczer, F. Competition among Memes in a World with Limited Attention. Nature Sci. Rep., (2) 335 (2012).
35. Weng, L., Ratkiewicz, J., Perra, N., Gonçalves, B., Castillo, C., Bonchi, F., Schifanella, S., Menczer, F., Flammini, F. The Role of Information Diffusion in the Evolution of Social Networks. In: Proc. 19th ACM Conf. Knowledge Discovery and Data Mining (SIGKDD 2013)
36. Zaharia, M., Das, T., Li, H., Shenker, S., Stoica, I. Discretized Streams: an Efficient and Fault-Tolerant Model for Stream Processing on Large Clusters. In: Proc. 4th USENIX Conf. Hot Topics in Cloud Computing (HotCloud 2012)
37. Zobel, J. Moffat, A. Inverted files for text search engines. ACM Computing Surveys, 38(2) - 6 (2006)

Printed in the United States
By Bookmasters